*Middle Tennessee Society
Transformed, 1860–1870*

Middle Tennessee
Society Transformed
1860 – 1870

War and Peace in the Upper South

STEPHEN V. ASH

Louisiana State University Press

Baton Rouge and London

Typeface: Linotron Janson
Typesetter: G & S Typesetters, Inc.
Printer: Thomson-Shore, Inc.
Binder: John H. Dekker & Sons, Inc.

10 9 8 7 6 5 4 3 2 1

Tables III, VI, VIII, and IX previously appeared in "Middle Tennessee Society in
Transition, 1860–1870," *Maryland Historian*, XIII (1982), 18–38.

Library of Congress Cataloging-in-Publication Data

Ash, Stephen V.
   Middle Tennessee society transformed, 1860–1870.

   Bibliography: p.
   Includes index.
   1. Tennessee, Middle—History.   2. Tennessee—History—
Civil War, 1861–1865.   3. Tennessee, Middle—Social—
conditions.   4. Reconstruction—Tennessee, Middle.
I. Title.
E531.9.A84   1987   976.8   87-3337
ISBN 0-8071-1400-6

To Jeanie

Contents

Maps and Tables

Preface and Acknowledgments

This book recounts the story of the people in one part of the South during the central moment of their history: the years of secession, war, emancipation, and reconstruction between 1860 and 1870. Middle Tennessee was one of the most important subdomains of the Old South. Its inhabitants saw the transforming fury of war and occupation at first hand, for the region was one of the Civil War's most fought-over battlegrounds and one of the North's first conquests. In the years after 1865 this land remained a conspicuous and turbulent arena of conflict and change.

Social historians in recent years have immensely enriched our understanding of the people of the nineteenth-century South. Typically, however, they focus on a single class—slaves, for example, or planters, or yeomen—and more often than not they end the story in 1860 or begin it in 1865. Even studies that contrast antebellum and postbellum society often give short shrift to the war years. Those that deal with the war generally say little about events before Fort Sumter or after Appomattox. It is my purpose to provide a comprehensive portrait of the people of Middle Tennessee—blacks and whites, aristocrats and plain folk, townspeople and villagers and farmers—and to explain not only the social and economic distinctions that set them apart but also the collective experiences and shared convictions that bound them together. I shall also fully explore the ordeal of that society during the Civil War, as well as before and after it, for I believe that the war years in Middle Tennessee, though both an epilogue and a prologue to other eras, were also an epoch in their own right.

Two themes undergird this study. The first is Middle Tennessee's role as a "third South." Broad prosperity, a large slave population, and widespread slaveholding sharply distinguished Middle Tennessee from the Southern highlands; yet the absence of King Cotton and of the economic hegemony of planters set it equally apart from the Deep South. This exceptional region nurtured a distinctive society whose economic, communal, hierarchical, and ideological foundations I explore in the first three chapters.

The second theme is the evolution of a dual society divided by race. Although I acknowledge the existence of a separate black culture in antebellum Middle Tennessee, I take issue with those who assert that such a culture was capable of full independence under slavery. I believe instead that black culture reached fruition only after emancipation, when the region's biracial families, churches, and communities were sundered by black self-assertion, a process of mitosis which ultimately divided society in two. Furthermore, I believe that this phenomenon had consequences as important for whites as for blacks.

My account touches upon some of the major questions about the South which have piqued historians' curiosity and challenged their interpretive and forensic skills. The evidence and conclusions I offer will certainly not lay any debates to rest; but I trust that they will broaden our understanding of such controversial matters as the character of antebellum society, the process of emancipation, the nature of wartime social change, and the evolution of postbellum society. Rather than interrupt the narrative or overburden the footnotes, I have explicitly addressed these historiographical issues in the separate bibliographical essay.

Middle Tennessee is not the entire South, of course. I have tried to show in this study just how the experience of its people compares with that of Southerners elsewhere, but I admit—indeed, insist—that Middle Tennessee's story is distinctive and in certain crucial respects it diverges sharply from the Southern experience as a whole. I hope, however, that what I have sacrificed in geographical breadth I have made up in analytical depth. So many of the outstanding recent contributions to social history have focused on single regions (or even counties) that it is surely no longer necessary to apologize for a regional study. The nineteenth-century South was in many ways a transcendent whole; but it was also an aggregation of diverse parts, of which Middle Tennessee was one—and one certainly as worthy of attention as any other.

A separate chapter, at least, would be required to express fully my appreciation to all those who have assisted me through the years of research and writing. Unfortunately, a few lines must suffice. John Dobson and the staff of the Special Collections Department of the University of Tennessee Library provided not only comfortable research accommodations but wonderful company. The entire staff of the Tennessee State Library and Archives in Nashville was unfailingly helpful and gracious; in particular,

Sara Harwell and Marylin Bell helped make my weeks there productive and pleasant. The University of Tennessee awarded me a Hilton A. Smith Graduate Fellowship for the 1978–1979 year, and the Department of History provided research grants from its Bernadotte Schmitt Fund.

At various stages in its evolution this book benefited from the comments of Catherine Clinton, Jonathan M. Wiener, Lawrence N. Powell, Eric Foner, Peter Maslowski, and a host of scholars at the 1984 conference of the Milan Group in Early United States History. Members of the University of Tennessee History Department held a colloquium in 1984 at which I tested some of my ideas. Ralph W. Haskins subjected the entire manuscript to a thorough and judicious evaluation of the kind for which he has long been esteemed.

Over the years I have relied on the expertise and enjoyed the friendship of a number of scholars who, like myself, have found an intellectual home in nineteenth-century Tennessee. My thanks especially to Susanna Delfino, Charles F. Bryan, Jr., Fred A. Bailey, John Cimprich, and Arthur Howington. Although their fields of interest lie elsewhere, Jim Kelly, Jim Burran, Carl Vines, Pete Daniel, and Jonathan Utley have provided intellectual stimulation and valued companionship. The Friday afternoon gang at Sam & Andy's has long offered a convivial haven from the rigors of research and writing. This does not exhaust the list of those who have meant much to me through the years; I cannot mention them all, but they know who they are.

My debt to my mentor, Paul H. Bergeron, is greater than he could know and more than I can ever repay. Good friend and patient adviser as well as keen and learned critic, he has guided not only my academic work in the narrow sense but my professional and intellectual development in the broadest sense. My mother, Juanita, has been a fount of encouragement and a tower of strength. My greatest debt, however, is to my wife, Jeanie, without whose love and support all this would have come to naught.

Abbreviations

DUL	Duke University Library, Durham, North Carolina
ETHS*P*	East Tennessee Historical Society's *Publications*
FB	Freedmen's Bureau (Bureau of Refugees, Freedmen, and Abandoned Land)
JSH	*Journal of Southern History*
LC	Library of Congress, Washington, D.C.
MVHR	*Mississippi Valley Historical Review*
NA	National Archives, Washington, D.C.
OR	*The War of the Rebellion: A Compilation of the Official Records of the Union and Confederate Armies*
RCC	Records of the U.S. Army Continental Commands, 1821–1920
SHC	Southern Historical Collection, University of North Carolina, Chapel Hill
THM	*Tennessee Historical Magazine*
THQ	*Tennessee Historical Quarterly*
TSLA	Tennessee State Library and Archives, Nashville

*Middle Tennessee Society
Transformed, 1860–1870*

Chapter I

A Fair and Fruitful Country

The Middle Tennessee Heartland in 1860

I N THE early weeks of 1863, long columns of General Braxton Bragg's
ragged Confederate troops tramped along the muddy country roads
and turnpikes of Middle Tennessee. Hungry and cold, and unhindered by their sympathetic officers, the soldiers greedily pilfered food
and fence rails wherever they passed, leaving trails of wasted fields, empty
barns, and destitute farm families already despoiled by Yankee plunder-
ers. A conscientious commander, Bragg deplored such misconduct as de-
moralizing to the army, and he resolved to halt the pillaging and discipline
the ranks. But the soldierly formality of his subsequent edict failed to conceal his profound personal sorrow at this scourging of an innocent land.
"The general commanding has perceived with surprise and pain," the
published orders began, "that some of the troops of this army have been
engaged in the indiscriminate destruction of fences and houses, devastating a fair and fruitful country."[1]

Bragg's anguish was shared by many who had known this land at peace,
for all who lived or traveled in Middle Tennessee in the mid-nineteenth
century agreed that nature had bestowed its benediction thereon most lav-
ishly. Few who sojourned in the region and described it for contemporaries
failed to extol its fertile limestone soil and luxuriant fields of corn, wheat,
tobacco, cotton, and a host of other crops. Like the ancient Israelites who
came unto the valley of Eshcol, "they took of the fruit of the land in their
hands . . . and said, It is a good land." To a generation that gauged worldly

---

1 General Orders, No. 2, Army of Tennessee, January 9, 1863, in *OR*, Ser. I, Vol. XX,
Pt. 2, p. 492. Unless otherwise indicated, all citations are to Series I.

worth by an agrarian measure, such riches bespoke a realm of wonderful opulence.[2]

When those witnesses thus testified, however, they did not envisage the Middle Tennessee of geographers and politicians, a vast area of some thirty-five counties and nineteen thousand square miles, stretching from the Cumberland Mountain plateau on the east to the Tennessee River on the west and constituting one of the three grand divisions of the state. They described instead what may be called the heartland of Middle Tennessee—the most prosperous central counties bordered on the north by Kentucky and on the south by Alabama. This subregion coincided roughly with the Nashville Basin, the "garden of Tennessee," a lush oval of lowland at the core of the region, bracketed by generally barren highlands on either side. Yet the heartland did encompass two highland counties to the northwest, Montgomery and Robertson, whose fecund farmlands and abundant harvests rivaled those of the basin (see Map 1).

Man's exploitation of the natural bounty of the heartland had begun with the migrations unleashed by the American Revolution. Settlers penetrated the new land by way of Kentucky in 1779 and 1780, trekking overland along the Wilderness Road and by water up the Cumberland River, which flows southwestward from the Kentucky mountains, dips into the northern part of Middle Tennessee, and then turns northwestward toward the Ohio River. These pioneers rapidly overran the heartland, and before the 1780s ended the new town of Nashville on the Cumberland had become the center of a flourishing frontier agricultural region and the river its lifeline of trade.

Statehood was achieved in 1796, embracing both "states" of Tennessee that the citizens had by then come to recognize: East, spreading along the Tennessee River, and Middle (at first called West), the two separated by the Cumberland Mountains and evolving almost independently. With the settlement of far West Tennessee after 1818, three-way interregional rivalries became the dominant theme of state politics. Steamboat navigation on the Cumberland River beginning in 1819, a wave of turnpike construction in the 1830s, and the railroad boom of the 1850s all swelled Nashville's population and economic importance and bound the rest of Middle Tennessee more closely to the city. Prosperity and the accomplishments of some illustrious native and adopted sons (among them Andrew Jackson, James K. Polk, and John Bell) brought the heartland in particular to national prominence in the antebellum decades.

By 1860 the thirteen counties of the heartland counted nearly 308,000

2 Deut. 1: 24–25.

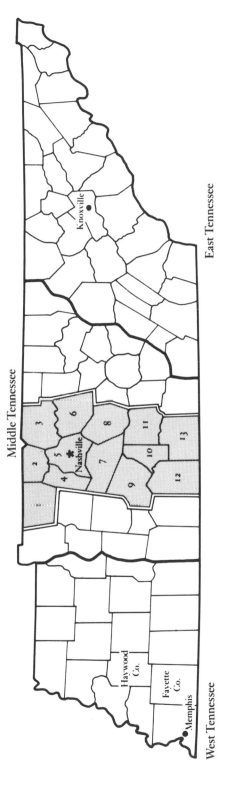

Map I. Tennessee in 1860

Middle Tennessee

East Tennessee

West Tennessee

Knoxville

Nashville

Memphis

Haywood Co.

Fayette Co.

Counties of the Middle Tennessee Heartland

1. Montgomery
2. Robertson
3. Sumner
4. Cheatham
5. Davidson
6. Wilson
7. Williamson
8. Rutherford
9. Maury
10. Marshall
11. Bedford
12. Giles
13. Lincoln

Map by William Fontanez

inhabitants, or 28 percent of the state's total. (This was twice the population of the entire state of Florida in this period, half that of Texas.) About
four of every ten heartlanders were Negro slaves. Black or white, these
were overwhelmingly a people of farm and village rather than town and
city. Even by the broadest definition (nonfarmers living in civil districts
with 1,500 inhabitants or more), less than one-fifth were townspeople; and
of these only Nashvillians could fairly be called city folk. The "Queen
City of the Cumberland" numbered 17,000 residents; its nearest com-
petitor, Columbia (in Maury County), about 5,400. No other towns in the
heartland exceeded 3,300.[3]

Ruralism and slavery were two distinctive features of the antebellum
South. But to say merely that the South had slaves and was rural and agricultural rather than urban and industrial is to slight its wide regional disparities. Within the South as demarcated by these broad criteria, there
were many Souths. The heartland of Middle Tennessee was a singular
Southern domain whose peculiarity merits consideration.

By conferring the blessing of rich soil, nature had decreed a special destiny for the heartland within the broad expanse of Middle Tennessee. That
edict was ratified by subsequent acts of man. The railroads that stretched
across the land from Nashville in several directions visited every county in
the heartland save three; yet they skirted the eastern and western highlands except at a couple of points where it was necessary to cross. Of the
twenty-two Middle Tennessee counties outside the heartland, only four
were tied to Nashville and the outside world by the iron tracks.[4]

Thus insulated in an age when rail links might spell the difference between progress and stagnation, the highland counties stood in ever starker
contrast to the luster of the heartland. In 1860 the counties of the heartland, making up perhaps 40 percent of the area of Middle Tennessee, supported more than 60 percent of the region's population and enjoyed almost
80 percent of its wealth (see Map II). Of the farms on which most Middle
Tennesseans earned their livelihood, those in the hard-scrabble highlands
were on the whole substantially smaller and poorer than those in the
idyllic heartland (see Maps III and IV). State tax records for 1860 show

3   *Population of the United States in 1860* . . . (Washington, D.C., 1864), 466–67; *The Statistics of the Population of the United States (June 1, 1870)* (Washington, D.C., 1872), 261–69. My
computations from the raw data given in these published sources and in the manuscript census returns are the basis of the statistics in this chapter. Appendix A discusses the problem of
defining towns and townspeople in 1860.

4   Of the three heartland counties unconnected by rail, one (Marshall) was surrounded
by counties with railroads and the others (Wilson and Cheatham) lay directly east and west,
respectively, of Nashville along the Cumberland River. Thus all three were intimately linked
to the city.

Map II. Average Wealth of Free Inhabitants, by County, 1860

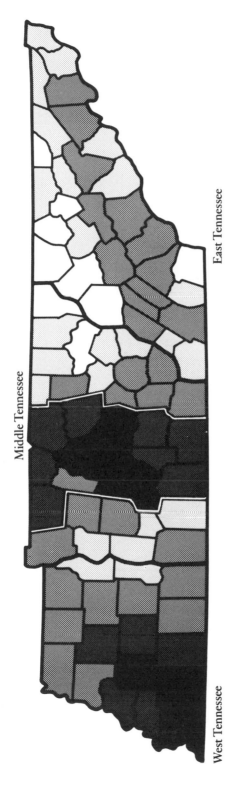

Middle Tennessee

West Tennessee

East Tennessee

Average Wealth of Free Inhabitants

☐ $0 to $299

☐ $300 to $499

▨ $500 to $999

■ $1,000 to $1,999

■ $2,000 to $3,500

Source: 1860 Census Aggregates.   Map by William Fontanez

Map III. Average Improved Acreage of Farms, by County, 1860

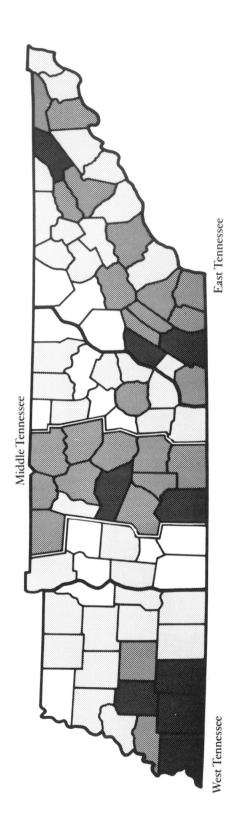

West Tennessee

Middle Tennessee

East Tennessee

Average Improved Acreage of Farms

0 to 59 acres

60 to 89 acres

90 to 119 acres

120 to 196 acres

Source: 1860 Census Aggregates.   Map by William Fontanez

Map IV. Average Cash Value of Farms, by County, 1860

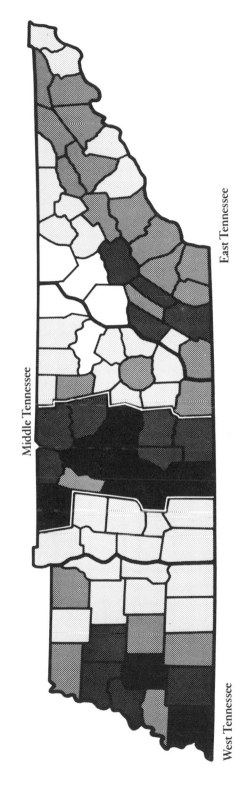

Middle Tennessee

West Tennessee

East Tennessee

Average Cash Value of Farms

☐ $0 to $1,249

▨ $1,250 to $2,499

▨ $2,500 to $3,749

■ $3,750 to $4,999

■ $5,000 to $12,220

Source: 1860 Census Aggregates.

Map by William Fontanez

Map V. Proportion of Slaves in Population, by County, 1860

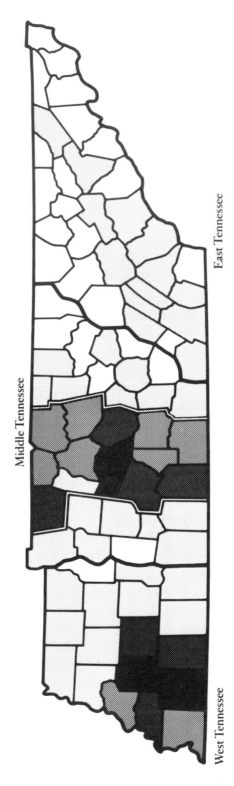

Middle Tennessee

West Tennessee

East Tennessee

Proportion of Slaves in Population

▢ 0 to 9 percent slave ▢ 10 to 29 percent slave ▨ 30 to 39 percent slave ▨ 40 to 49 percent slave ■ 50 to 64 percent slave

Source: 1860 Census Aggregates.   Map by William Fontanez

that an acre of land in the heartland was worth, on an average, more than four times the value of an acre in the highlands. The distribution of slaves—next to land, the most meaningful index of wealth to an antebellum Southerner—was similarly skewed. Thirty-eight of every one hundred heartlanders were chattels; in the highlands, only sixteen of one hundred (see Map V). Altogether, white heartlanders held nearly 80 percent of Middle Tennessee's slaves.[5]

These figures suggest the distinctiveness of the heartland within its wider region, but what of its place in the state and the South? Tennessee's geographical diversity is proverbial. East Tennessee, drained by the south-westward-flowing Tennessee River and bounded by the Appalachian range to the east and the Cumberlands to the west, is a land of hills, mountains, and (except for the narrow ribbon of the river valley) generally poor soil. No Southern region further from the grand plantation image of the South could be imagined. Farms there were mostly isolated, small, and self-sufficient, slaves few. Andrew Johnson, antipatrician and former illiterate tailor, was one of the region's leading spokesmen. His constituents likewise rejected aristocratic pretensions and proslavery extremism, and they would for the most part remain loyal to the Union in the Civil War and be faithful to the Republican party thereafter.

West Tennessee, a broad, fairly flat alluvial plain, which gradually slopes westward down to the Mississippi River, conformed more closely to the plantation stereotype and resembled (at least in its southwestern subregion around Memphis) the Deep South. Here were great plantations, gangs of slaves, and immense fields of cotton. Isham G. Harris, unyielding champion of slavery and Southern rights, and secessionist governor, was West Tennessee's most representative political leader.

Between these two extremes—physically and culturally—stood the Middle Tennessee heartland, representing a "third South," whose uniqueness has not been fully recognized by interpreters of Southern history. Deeply committed to Dixie's peculiar institution and way of life, yet conservative withal (as exemplified by their favorite son, John Bell, a moderate compromise candidate in the 1860 presidential election), the free people of the heartland gazed Janus-like toward the egalitarian, nonslaveholding South of the yeoman farmer and toward the plutocratic, plantation South

5 *Population, 1860*, 466–67; *Statistics of the United States . . . in 1860 . . .* (Washington, D.C., 1866), 312, 348; *Agriculture of the United States in 1860 . . .* (Washington, D.C., 1864), 132–39, 215, 238–39; Tennessee, *Report of James T. Dunlap, Comptroller of the Treasury . . . 1861* (Nashville, 1861), 4–5. Map II is based on per capita rather than family averages, but the pattern would be identical if the latter were used. "Wealth" is combined real and personal property value as listed in the census returns.

of the cotton nabobs. To ask which of these, if any of the three, was the "real" South misses the fundamental importance of Southern regionalism. Each was a South, and the South was all of them, and each must be understood in its own right.

The heartland (roughly 7,000 square miles in area) exceeded in total population, though just barely, both East Tennessee with its thirty-one counties and 14,500 square miles and West Tennessee with its eighteen counties and 9,000 square miles. (But if white population alone is considered, heartlanders were outnumbered by both East and West Tennesseans.) In East Tennessee only one person out of ten was a slave, in the heartland four of ten, in West Tennessee as a whole one of three, and in the richest West Tennessee plantation domains (specifically, Fayette and Haywood counties) six of ten (see Maps I and V). For every one hundred free families, in East Tennessee there were eleven slaveholders, in the heartland forty-one, and in West Tennessee's Fayette and Haywood counties sixty-seven. Among slaveholders, those who held at least twenty bondsmen (the minimum needed to work a true "plantation") amounted to only three out of one hundred in East Tennessee, less than one out of ten in the heartland, but one out of five in Fayette and Haywood. These last-named counties alone accounted for thirteen of the state's forty-seven owners of one hundred or more slaves (there were but nineteen of these great patriarchs in the heartland and one in East Tennessee).[6]

Large plantations were few outside the West Tennessee cotton lands. In East Tennessee, less than one farm out of one hundred exceeded five hundred acres (improved and unimproved). The average improved acreage per farm in that region was ninety, and the average cash value per farm was $2,876 (see Maps III and IV). The husbandmen of the heartland worked on the average 104 improved acres on a farm worth $5,723. Only two farmers out of every one hundred in the heartland could boast holdings of five hundred or more total acres, improved and unimproved. In Fayette and Haywood counties eight of every one hundred met that criterion. Improved acreage there averaged 166; yet it is a measure of the peculiar richness of the heartland's soil that the average cash value of these larger West Tennessee cotton farms ($5,799), hardly exceeded that of the heartland's smaller holdings.[7]

Land and slaves meant wealth in the antebellum South, and wealth

---

6 *Population, 1860*, 466–67; *Statistics of the United States, 1860*, 348; *Agriculture, 1860*, 238–39. For reasons explained in Appendix A, the proportion of slaveowning families in the heartland given here varies from that given in Chapters II and III and is used here for comparative purposes only.

7 *Agriculture, 1860*, 132–39, 215. Improved acreage is the best gauge of farm size, and I

meant land and slaves. It is therefore no surprise that the typical East Tennessean in 1860 was impecunious by the standards of the heartland and West Tennessee. East Tennessee's free families averaged real and personal property totals of $2,812, those in the heartland $9,791, and those in Fayette and Haywood $17,090 (see Map II). Slaves accounted for 36 percent of the value of East Tennessee's personal property. In the heartland the figure was 55 percent, and in slave-rich Fayette and Haywood, 78 percent.[8]

The heartland of Middle Tennessee stood prominently among the subregions of the South, its lands and people celebrated and its influence farreaching. It is justifiably seen (and was so viewed by contemporaries) as a coherent whole, manifesting certain broad qualities that marked it off from the rest of the state and the South. But statistical averages are not people and places. Within the embracing unity of the heartland there was much diversity, and anyone who peers closely enough can discover there a little bit of each South.

Whether by calculation, or chance, or merely whimsicality, nature had declined to grant its gifts of procreant soil and level land uniformly throughout the heartland. Long fingers of highlands poke into the Nashville Basin from every direction. Rocky wasteland patches of cedar mottle the landscape. A wide band of "barrens"—infertile, scrub oak terrain—runs through Cheatham County and severs the northwestern highland counties of the heartland from the basin. More barrens sully the edges of the heartland at other points.

In the farther reaches of the heartland, on the poorer lands distant from towns and railroads, existed enclaves of yeomanry akin to East Tennessee society. Two districts in Cheatham County had slave populations of only 11 percent of the whole; two in Bedford less than 9 percent; one in Lincoln had no slaves at all. Every county had at least one or two districts where the slave population was less than 20 percent. Farms there were small and relatively unproductive, and their seclusion discouraged cultivation beyond that needed for self-sustenance. In these places farmland might be worth only a few dollars per acre: one district in Lincoln averaged $1.81.[9]

By contrast, a few of the very richest parts of the heartland, especially those close to the towns and rail or river transportation, were almost indistinguishable from the Deep South plantation regions. An impressionable

---

have used that statistic for comparisons when possible. But the published census reports combine improved and unimproved acreage in reporting the number of large farms.

8 *Statistics of the United States, 1860*, 312, 348; Tennessee, *Report of Comptroller, 1861*, 2–5.

9 *Statistics of Population, 1870*, 261–69; Tennessee Comptroller of the Treasury, 1857 Tax Aggregates, in TSLA.

Yankee who in 1858 journeyed from the outskirts of the heartland to Shelbyville, in Bedford County, marveled that "it was like getting into a new world." Here were imposing manors, aristocratic refinements, and extensive landholdings worked by throngs of slaves. Staple crops were plentiful in these areas (tobacco in the northern heartland, cotton to the south), and surpluses of corn, wheat, and livestock were raised for export. Seven districts (one each in Davidson, Giles, Maury, and Williamson counties and three in Rutherford) were over 65 percent black; a number of others exceeded 50 percent. Land values in these favored precincts were high, generally over $20 per acre, but (for example, in the ninth district of Davidson, near Nashville, and around Franklin, in Williamson County) could surpass $100.[10]

Wide variations among the free folk of the heartland's farms and villages should not, however, obscure their fundamental kinship. Most were neither rich nor poor, neither august patrician-planters nor indigent dirt farmers. Most owned no slaves, or few. Most lived close to the soil, shared a common cultural heritage and like economic interests, and were tied closely enough to Nashville and the rest of the heartland by rail, river, turnpike, and history that they felt a genuine regional identity and community of interest. Their basic affinity is further highlighted by considering a small but important minority of heartlanders who lived in very different circumstances. Though still diminutive by today's standards, Nashville had evolved by 1860 into a true city. Within the traditional agrarian culture of the rural heartland sat an islet of modern urban society, an antithesis to be explored more fully in the next chapter.

One and yet many, a realm *sui generis* but one that mirrored the manifold faces of the Old South, the heartland of Middle Tennessee seems peculiarly worthy of exploration for what it may reveal about itself and the entire South. To this end, the people of the heartland must be scrutinized more closely, along with the customs and institutions that marked their world.

10   A. T. Hamilton to John Hamilton, September 9, 1858, in Hamilton Letters, TSLA; *Statistics of Population, 1870*, 261–69; Tennessee Comptroller, 1857 Tax Aggregates.

Chapter II

Works and Days

The People and Institutions of the Heartland

T HE PEOPLE of the Middle Tennessee heartland were tillers of
the soil. Six of every ten heads of free families in 1860 called
themselves farmers, farm laborers, or overseers, accounting for
about twenty-two thousand of the region's thirty-five thousand
families. Another twenty-two hundred or so operated farms though they
did not claim agriculture as their principal occupation. Thus, two-thirds
of all free families in the heartland drew at least part of their livelihood
directly from the soil.[1]

The majority (63 percent) of these farm families—those whose head
listed an agricultural occupation or listed a nonagricultural occupation but
ran a farm—called themselves farmers and owned their own farms (see
Table I). About three of every ten, however (29 percent), were headed by
landless agricultural workers. Some of these were hired hands who worked
other men's fields for fifty cents or a dollar a day. But most were tenant
farmers who rented plots of land and operated them as independent farms.
The small proportion of farm families (8 percent) whose head listed a non-

1   The tables presented in this study, and all other statistics not otherwise attributed, are
derived from computer-analyzed samples of Middle Tennessee families in the 1860 and 1870
manuscript census returns. (See Appendix A for a full explanation of the sampling procedure, terminology, and analytical methodology employed.) From this point on, the terms
"heartland" and "Middle Tennessee" will be used interchangeably to refer to the thirteen-
county region of study. As explained in Chapter I, however, this region is but a part of the
broader region properly called Middle Tennessee, and the two terms are thus technically not
synonymous.

Table I. Residence by Occupation of Family Head, 1860 (free population only)

Occupation	Percentage of families, categorized by residence			N	Percentage of total families
	Town	Village	Farm		
Professional	19	8	4	57	7
Landed farmer	0	0	63	323	42
Minor professional	4	4	1	14	2
Skilled worker	35	31	3	104	14
Overseer	0	0	2	8	1
Unskilled laborer	25	25	0	64	8
Landless agricultural worker	0	0	29	148	19
None	16	30	0	54	7
	Town	Village	Farm		
N	161	96	517		
Percentage of total families	21	12	67		

$\chi^2 = 670.7$ with 14 d.f., signif. $= .0$ $N = 772$
$C = .68184$

agricultural occupation included some who owned the farms they operated as well as some who rented.[2]

Few men hired out as wage laborers in the Middle Tennessee countryside not only because land was available to rent but because farmers had a plentiful supply of black labor. Almost half (43 percent) of farm families owned slaves (see Table II), but the great majority of these held but a few slaves. Only one farm family out of twenty (5 percent) owned twenty or more slaves and thereby attained the status of planter.

Since not every "farm" family (as defined here) actually operated a farm, there were fewer farms than farm families in the heartland. Altogether the region encompassed in 1860 about 18,600 farms, the homesteads of fifty-three of every one hundred free families. That these farms were mostly of middling size, neither great nor small, has already been pointed out in contrasting the heartland with East and West Tennessee; yet further examination is in order. Only one farm out of ten had fewer than twenty improved acres; a like proportion exceeded two hundred improved acres. Half of all farms were under sixty-five improved acres. Only one

2   Categories of residence and occupation employed in the tables are defined in Appendix A. See Appendix B for a complete list of occupations by category. Average wages paid to farmhands by county are given in Eighth Census, 1860, Manuscript Returns of Social Statistics, Tennessee, in NA.

Table II. Residence by Slaveholding, 1860 (free population only)

Slaveholdings	Percentage of families, categorized by residence			N	Percentage of total families
	Town	Village	Farm		
20+	0	0	5	26	3
10–19	2	0	9	49	6
5–9	8	3	10	64	8
1–4	14	6	19	129	17
0	76	91	57	506	65
	Town	Village	Farm		
N	161	96	517		
Percentage of total families	21	12	67		
Mean number of slaves	1	0.3	4		
Percentage of total slaves	7	1	91		

$\chi^2 = 60.2$ with 8 d.f., signif. = .0   N = 774
C = .26856

farm out of ten was worth less than $500; a similar proportion exceeded
$12,520 in value. Half of all farms fell below $2,400 in value. Great plantations existed in the heartland—G. A. Washington's 5,100 improved acres in
Robertson County, for example, worth a quarter of a million dollars and
worked by 274 slaves, could compare with anything in the Black Belt—
but their conspicuousness obscures their rarity.[3]

That the large plantations were few did not, however, mean that they
were economically insignificant. Indeed, their role in Middle Tennessee
agriculture was well out of proportion to their numbers. Farms with twenty
or more slaves (just 7 percent of all farms) accounted for 25 percent of all
improved acreage in the region, 31 percent of all farm value, 50 percent of
all farm slaves, 18 percent of all corn production, and 24 percent of all
livestock value. Nevertheless, plantations did not dominate Middle Tennessee's agricultural economy as they did the Deep South's. By far the
greater part of the antebellum heartland's agricultural wealth was in the
hands of middle-class farmers with a few slaves or none.

More than one-fifth (22 percent) of the heartland's farms were occupied
by tenants. These rented farms were generally small, however (averaging
just 52 improved acres worth $1,936, as opposed to 113 improved acres

3 On G. A. Washington see Chase C. Mooney, *Slavery in Tennessee* (Bloomington, 1957),
198–99.

worth $5,829 for owner-operated farms), and they accounted for only 11 percent of all improved acreage, 7 percent of all farm value, 2 percent of all farm slaves, 15 percent of all corn production, and 11 percent of all livestock value. Farm tenancy, though not uncommon, was thus clearly not a significant element of the region's agriculture, which was dominated by medium-sized owner-operated family farms.

The last killing frost of spring in Middle Tennessee usually comes no later than mid-April. It returns in mid-October, or sometimes later, and so the farmers of the heartland enjoyed a liberal growing season. Rainfall is plentiful, and winter and spring are generally the wettest seasons. But climatic amenities are a notoriously capricious boon: Middle Tennessee farmers understood how nature's vagaries could play havoc with their expectations and their crops, and a late spring frost or a rainy harvest were ever-threatening hazards.[4]

In the good years, though, and most years were good, farming in the heartland was for the majority of husbandmen not just a subsistence but a lucrative enterprise. The generous soil yielded far more than was needed to fill the tables of the farmers, their families, and their slaves, and each harvest provided a surplus for which Southerners elsewhere were hungry. To the south and west, in the Black Belt and the expanding cotton frontier, planters found it profitable to concentrate on cotton and import much of their foodstuffs. These the heartland farmers were glad to provide from their surplus, on the hoof or in the barrel. Within Middle Tennessee, too, villages and towns offered a ready market for the superabundance of the farms. The heartland was thus one of the very few prosperous Southern regions (the Kentucky Bluegrass and the Shenandoah Valley of Virginia being two others) that were not reliant on a staple crop but practiced instead a general agriculture that rendered good profits and kept land and slave prices rising. "Our country is in a flourishing condition," wrote an exuberant Bedford countian early in 1857; "lands have got Remarkably high so that it is not uncommon to bring 50 or 60 dollars per acre and some as high evin as $100.00 dollars per acre Negroes also sell high likely men from 14 to 17 hundred dollars without any trade and produce of all kinds demand the cash at fair prices."[5]

It had not always been so. In the early years, as frontier farming evolved into a more settled stage and steamboats furnished access to outside markets, cotton, tobacco, and hemp culture boomed in the heartland and it

4   *Report on Cotton Production in the United States . . .* (Washington, D.C., 1884), 384–85; James M. Safford, *Geology of Tennessee* (Nashville, 1869), 529–32.

5   Joel Shoffner to Michael Shoffner, January 11, 1857, in Michael Shoffner Papers, SHC.

seemed that the region was destined to be an adjunct of the plantation South. But wasteful agricultural practices, a legacy of frontier farming, sapped the vitality of even the heartland's prolific soil in the antebellum decades (as had already happened in the eastern states) and eroded the profitability of the staple crops, particularly after the national cotton and tobacco busts of the 1830s and 1840s. Aggravating the situation was the skyrocketing price of slaves in the Lower South because of high demand there, which threatened to siphon off many of the heartland's black hands. Casting about for a system of agriculture that would make money yet not squander precious soil and labor, farmers in Middle Tennessee settled increasingly on a corn and livestock economy.[6]

On broad pastures of bluegrass, amid lush fields of corn, timothy, red clover, and rye waiting to be cut for winter feed, the husbandmen of the heartland reared great hosts of horses, mules, cattle, sheep, and hogs, breeding them assiduously over generations to win a national reputation for excellence. (L. J. Polk of Maury County was one of the most famous horse breeders in the country; on a vast, five-thousand-acre farm in Davidson, Mark Cockrill raised thousands of sheep whose fine wool won him international attention.) Professional drovers, or sometimes ambitious local men, gathered surplus animals in the fall (especially swine and cattle, but even turkeys) and drove them to Nashville to be slaughtered, packed, and shipped south by rail or river; or, more commonly, they herded the stock directly south to the cotton region of Alabama. Whether a great planter-breeder with hundreds of blooded animals browsing in ample pastures or a lowly yeoman with a few hogs fattening in the pen, virtually all Middle Tennessee farmers shared to some extent in this agriculture of grain and grazing: 98 percent of all farms in 1860 reported growing some corn, and 99 percent reported livestock, pigs and cows being universal and horses, mules, sheep, and other cattle nearly so.[7]

This is not to say that the heartland scorned completely the great staples that distinguished the South. In some parts the green expanses of grass and corn were interrupted by the fleecy white of cotton fields. Despite its promising start, however, cotton had fared poorly in Middle Tennessee. It grew satisfactorily there but did not bloom in quantity or quality as it did in the prime areas of the Lower South. Besides, cotton and corn competed

6   Lewis C. Gray, *History of Agriculture in the Southern United States to 1860* (1933; rpr. New York, 1949), II, 644–45, 691, 753–55, 812, 821–22, 870, 878, 887, 892; Blanche Henry Clark, *The Tennessee Yeomen, 1840–1860* (Nashville, 1942), 108–12, 146.

7   Sam B. Hilliard, *Hog Meat and Hoecake: Food Supply in the Old South, 1840–1860* (Carbondale, Ill., 1972), 193–95; Gray, *History of Agriculture*, II, 837–41, 854, 878; Clark, *Tennessee Yeomen*, 121–28.

directly for labor because their cycles of planting, maturing, and harvesting coincided. Consequently, cotton production in the region dwindled in the antebellum decades. By 1860 only 12 percent of farms grew any of the fiber, and most of these raised just a bale or two as a small money crop or for home use. Only a few mimicked the great cotton plantations of the Deep South, gleaning their dozens or hundreds of bales. Moreover, cotton in 1860 was confined pretty much to the southern half of the region, whereas in earlier years it had been omnipresent.[8]

Of greater significance in the heartland was tobacco, its other big money crop. Concentrated preponderantly in the northern counties, and especially in the red clay lands above the Nashville Basin, tobacco was a staple for a small but influential portion of farmers. Though overall only 14 percent grew the weed, those who did so tended to do it on a large scale, unlike cotton growers. Thus in the principal tobacco districts, although corn and livestock were plentiful, land- and labor-intensive tobacco culture excluded the general agriculture that reigned in the balance of the heartland. This tobacco was of the dark variety, bound for the ports of Europe, and to help send it on its way there grew up a sizable marketing and processing industry centered in Nashville and in Clarksville, in Montgomery County.[9]

Other crops were plenteous—indeed, visitors to the heartland marveled at the omnifarious offerings of its fields—though none could emulate the primacy of corn, tobacco, and cotton. In the early antebellum years, apprehension about soil depletion and general agricultural decline had sparked an agrarian "awakening" in the state, pioneered by Middle Tennessee, which encouraged crop diversification and rotation, manuring, and conservational plowing and drainage. Through the media of journals, societies, fairs, and exhibitions, progressive agriculturalists struggled to reform farming practices against the inveterate prejudices and traditions of generations. The results were mixed, but there was an appreciable movement in the region toward diversification. Wheat, which had theretofore been sown in negligible amounts, was by 1860 being raised in surplus by Middle Tennesseans. Oats and rye were less abundant but still common. Timothy and clover simultaneously fed cattle and replenished worn soil. A variety of fruits and vegetables was tried, and a short-lived fad for silkworms in the 1840s indicated perhaps that the spirit of diversification had for some become a mania. Yet old and profligate habits lingered on to plague the more backward farms: a Northerner observing the fringes of the heartland

8   Gray, *History of Agriculture*, II, 707, 878, 892.
9   *Ibid.*, 753–58, 836, 878, 885–86; Clark, *Tennessee Yeomen*, 147, 149–50.

in 1858 concluded that "the people are very far behind the age but are looking ahead. The land is hardly ever manured. The fields are run out then left to rest, until they become capable of producing."[10]

A further consequence of the agricultural awakening was a slow but steady improvement in tools, equipment, and stock. Cradles supplanted sickles and scythes for cutting wheat and hay and by the 1850s were themselves being replaced with mechanical reapers by the more enterprising farmers. A Shelbyville businessman excitedly reported in 1858 doing "a heavey business" selling reapers and threshing machines, the latter superseding the traditional ritual of trampling the grain and winnowing it with a fan mill. Crude hoes gave way to horse-drawn harrows and wooden plows to iron. The last antebellum decade also witnessed a considerable expansion of cleared land, improved fencing, and redoubled importation and systematic breeding of livestock. The reported value of farm animals in Middle Tennessee swelled impressively in these years while their numbers leveled off, bespeaking the stock raiser's predilection for diligent improvement over mere expansion of his herd. Nevertheless, these refinements were not achieved universally in the region. The well-to-do, educated farmer conversant with the latest scientific literature and with money to invest in improvements possessed vast advantages over his humbler neighbors. In some communities in 1860 yeomen could yet be observed trudging stoically behind rude, homemade plows, their scrawny hogs rooting freely and happily through the woods.[11]

Among the agrarian folk of the heartland a common goal prevailed. Whether high or low, exalted planters or tenant farmers, all tried in their separate ways to achieve a good measure of self-sufficiency, and most did. On the biggest farms this self-sufficiency was very nearly complete. Westview, the twelve-hundred-acre plantation of Samuel Perkins in Williamson County, for example, was a self-contained world, boasting its own blacksmith shop, cotton gin, tobacco shed, gristmill, slaughterhouse, wagon scales, waterworks, icehouse, and fish pond. Slave artisans on the plantations fashioned everything from shoes for man and horse, to shuck-bottom chairs, to coffins.[12]

Among the yeomen community self-sufficiency obtained. For example, a farmer would bring his cowhide to the village tanner, who would finish it in return for a half share. In exchange for another portion, a shoemaker

10   Clark, *Tennessee Yeomen*, 69–101, 111–19, 134, 140, 147–50; A. T. Hamilton to John Hamilton, June 17, 1858, in Hamilton Letters.

11   Clark, *Tennessee Yeomen*, 121, 125–32, 147–48; Thomas B. Wilson Reminiscences, 15 (MS in SHC); Joel Shoffner to Michael Shoffner, January 17, 1858, in Shoffner Papers.

12   John Jordan, "My Recollections" (Typescript in John Leland Jordan Papers, TSLA).

would turn the leather into rough shoes. Felled trees would be hauled from the farm to the local sawmill, and threshed grain to the gristmill, and cut or ground under a similar share arrangement. The farmer who raised no cotton or wool might swap for a little with his neighbor who did and carry it home for his wife to assail with spinning wheel and loom. (A Bedford County entrepreneur, contemplating opening a store in 1858, lamented that these machines were busily at work in every farmhouse, thus robbing him of a market for finished cloth.) Jeans and shirts, soap and dyes, horse collars and saddles, horseshoes and buckets, all were improvised on the farm or in the village, save for a few exotic items purchased in town, such as intricate hardware and tools, fancy clothes, and hard, scented soap for special house guests.[13]

Those living in the countryside who dubbed themselves other than farmers or farm workers were nevertheless bound closely to the soil, sharing its bounty in a symbiosis of village and farm. So many of them had pigs and cows and fields of their own that in any community the line between farm and village was blurred. (Dual occupations are commonly found in the 1860 census; memoirs of antebellum heartlanders are likewise replete with examples, such as the father of David Bodenhamer in Giles County, whom his son proudly remembered as a farmer, justice of the peace, and jack-of-all-trades; and Benjamin Batey's father in Rutherford, a "Mechanic Farmer and Stock raiser.")[14]

Among villagers (rural folk who did not operate or work on farms), one of twelve families (8 percent) was headed by a professional man—doctor or merchant or minister, for example—who dealt daily with the farmers and received payment from them in produce, the common medium of exchange (see Table I). A smaller proportion of village family heads (4 percent) likewise refrained from manual labor but held less exalted status as clerks, constables, schoolteachers, and the like. The backbone of the village community was the nearly one-third of family heads (31 percent) learned in trades—the coopers, shoemakers, blacksmiths, millers, wagon makers, carpenters, furniture makers, and other artisans whose skills the farmers relied on, and who in turn needed the fruits of the farmer's toil. Common laborers, shop hands, teamsters, and other unskilled workers accounted for one-fourth (25 percent) of village families (a figure kept low, as with farmhands, by the prevalence of slaves available for such work). An-

13   A. T. Hamilton to John Hamilton, November 28, 1858, in Hamilton Letters; Richard M. Winn and David Bodenhamer files, Civil War Veterans Questionnaires (Confederate) (MSS in TSLA); James Washington Matthews Journal, 1858–60, *passim* (MS in TSLA).

14   David Bodenhamer and Benjamin Batey files, Civil War Questionnaires (Confederate).

other three-tenths (30 percent) of village family heads—mostly women—listed no occupation or a nonremunerative domestic one. Village families were very unlikely to own slaves (nine out of ten—91 percent—had none; see Table II), although the professionals sometimes had a house servant or two.

The husbandmen of the heartland and their village neighbors lived and labored in the midst of an agricultural cornucopia. Reverently they offered thanks for the abundance it proffered, and sumptuously they provisioned themselves from it. Corn was planted in the early spring in quantity ample to feed family, slaves, and animals and still leave a surplus to sell or trade when ripe in the fall. Many favored a small wheat crop, enough for a little white bread to break the monotony of pone. Straw, hay, and corn leaves stripped from the stalk furnished fodder to keep the cattle through the winter. Hogs cleaned up after the other animals and then fattened on corn. At slaughtering time farmers first set aside plenty of pork and beef for themselves and then sold or traded the rest. Every farmer and most villagers planted a garden (on the plantations slaves had their own), growing Irish and sweet potatoes, peas, and beans enough to victual the family through the year. The ubiquitous cow provided milk and more; for those with a different thirst, whiskey flowed copiously from local stills. About all that the prudent family need buy for the table were salt, coffee, and sugar.

This rustic condition of plenty abounded among the generality of the rural free folk, but not all partook. At the basest level subsisted a wretched few, such as the family a census taker discovered in the summer of 1860 only a few miles out in the country from Nashville. There, living literally in a hole dug out of a wooded hillside and sheltered with boards, wearing rags, and sleeping on the ground, were a middle-aged white man and his two maiden sisters. To eke out an existence, the head of this sylvan household hunted in the woods as the spirit moved him; the women took in a little knitting. More than two miles from their nearest neighbor, thoroughly and contentedly ignorant of the outside world, they declined all offers of assistance. Such squalor, by contrast with which even the slave quarters seemed elegant, was uncommon but not unknown throughout the rural heartland and represented yet another form of self-sufficiency, which some found congenial.[15]

For most of the country people, however, self-sufficiency did not mean independence and isolation. Except on the great plantations and in the meanest hovels (and both were scarce in Middle Tennessee), self-suffi-

15   Nashville *Patriot*, August 15, 1860.

ciency was in great part the reward of communal efforts impelled by the awareness of mutual dependence. The rhythms of rural life dictated a routine of tasks—barn raisings, log rollings, corn shuckings, hog killings—that brought neighbors together in toil, and a cycle of respites—after the laying-by of the crops in the summer, for example, and after harvest in the fall—that united them in leisure and diversion. A cult of neighborliness and hospitality among these people, which invariably impressed outsiders, was one manifestation of this interdependence, betokening a common recognition and affirmation of their abiding reliance; and networks of kinship among the rural folk further bound them. A Northerner wrote of his visit to Bedford County in 1858 that "the people are so hospitable kind and obliging that I enjoyed myself beyond measure. Myself and horse received the kindest attention." The country people he had met "like to go to church and spend a meal hour with those who invite them. . . . It is one of the greatest pleasures to the Tennessee farmer to entertain strangers or friends—the latch string is always out." "People didn't look on money like they do now," recalled an elderly former slave about her youth in Rutherford County in the 1850s. "They was free with one another about eating and visiting and work too when a man got behind with the work." The loan of a mule or wagon to a needy neighbor, or a visit to a sick friend on the next farm, were essential elements of the fabric of rural life, symbol and substance of a tenacious social bond.[16]

The towns of the heartland, defined as districts with fifteen hundred or more inhabitants, were few and far between in 1860. Two counties (Cheatham and Robertson) had none—even their county seats were nothing more than villages huddled around the courthouse. Lincoln, Marshall, Rutherford, and Wilson had but one apiece, in each case the county seat. (In Giles, Montgomery, and Williamson census takers failed to itemize district populations in 1860, but the county seats of all three were substantial towns.) Bedford and Sumner boasted three towns each. Maury and Davidson encompassed the heartland's two largest towns (Columbia and Nashville, the latter more properly a city) and each contained five others besides; three of Davidson's, however, were really but suburbs of the capital.[17]

Perhaps, then, twenty-five towns embraced what may be called the urban population of Middle Tennessee. Among whites, that population grew

16 John Duling Memoir (Typescript in TSLA); Matthews Journal, 1858–60; A. T. Hamilton to John Hamilton, July 30, September 9, 1858, in Hamilton Letters; George P. Rawick (ed.), *The American Slave: A Composite Autobiography* (Westport, Conn., 1972–), Ser. Two, Vol. XI (Ark.), Pt. 7, p. 149.

17 *Statistics of Population, 1870*, 261–69.

rapidly during the 1850s and by 1860 included about one of every five families in the region. Slaves were far less likely than whites to live in towns: only about seven out of one hundred did so. Free blacks were far more likely, but their numbers were comparatively few. Thus the proportion of the urban population which was black (free and slave) was substantially smaller than the proportion of blacks in the heartland's population as a whole. Even in Nashville, which had probably a greater proportion of blacks than most other towns, slaves and free blacks made up only 23 percent of the populace.[18]

Divorced from the soil, townspeople traded the security of self-sufficiency for the conveniences of town life: rail and telegraph service, paved streets, running water, gas for home and street lighting, and even chemically manufactured ice all year-round (not every town enjoyed all of these advantages, however). Newspapers (every county seat but Cheatham's published at least one), colleges and academies, large mercantile establishments, banks, and the courthouses made the towns the foci of local news, culture, business, and politics.[19]

The occupational structure of the free urbanites resembled that of the villagers (see Table I): a professional class included about one family head out of five (19 percent, a larger proportion than that among the village folk because it included virtually all the region's judges, lawyers, newspaper publishers, professors, bankers, and other professionals who were not to be found outside the towns); a small segment (four of every one hundred family heads) of lesser professionals such as clerks; substantial groups of skilled workers (35 percent of family heads) and unskilled laborers (25 percent); and a portion (16 percent), again mostly female, without a listed occupation. One-fourth (24 percent) of all town families owned slaves; thus slaveholding among urbanites was more widespread than among villagers, but less so than among farm families (see Table II). The majority of urban bondsmen were the house servants of the professionals or were rented out by them as laborers.

Though necessary for comparative purposes, any fixed population limit defining "town" versus "country" is of course artificial. Urbanization in Middle Tennessee is properly viewed as a continuum, ranging from the tiniest towns (arguably nothing more than villages writ large), through bigger towns with increasingly "urban" characteristics, to the region's one

18 *Ibid.* In 1850 10 percent of whites lived in towns. In the succeeding decade that proportion more than doubled to 21 percent. See Stephen V. Ash, "Town, Village, and Countryside in Middle Tennessee, 1850–1870" (paper presented at the meeting of the Milan Group in Early American History, Milan, Italy, June, 1984).

19 Eighth Census, Social Statistics.

true city, which most thoroughly embodied the distinctive features of urban life. Nashville can be viewed as the paradigm of the heartland town, but it must be recognized that the smaller towns emulated it only in proportion to their size.

The milieu in which Nashvillians lived and worked can be contrasted in every feature with the surrounding rural heartland. Extremes of wealth and poverty were conspicuous in the city, and class segregation of neighborhoods separated plutocrat from pauper. Teeming, ramshackle tenements crowded the poor districts on the fringes of the warehouse and commercial blocks; these housed a mostly Irish proletariat that did the city's dirty work. The riverfront "Jungle" offered bars, brothels, and violence for urbanites who craved those diversions, and a bustling underworld of thieves, pickpockets, confidence men, and whores provided vocational opportunities unknown in the villages. The mansions of the rich adorned the heart of the city, each with its complement of black servants. To the consternation of whites, these slaves mingled promiscuously with free blacks, who numbered hundreds in Nashville though few in the countryside. German immigrants, among them Lutherans, Catholics, and Jews, enriched the city's ethnic and religious hodgepodge. Trade, some rudimentary industry, and state government formed the foundation of the capital's economy, removing Nashvillians from immediate dependence on the land and loosening their personal ties. A host of formal institutions—city government, a police force, an advanced school system—ordered the lives of the heterogeneous city folk in place of the informalities and rural ethic that bound together the country people of Middle Tennessee.

Whether big-city merchant, village carpenter, or yeoman farmer, most free heartlanders enjoyed a share of the vast riches the region yielded. But not all of this wealth grew directly out of the soil; a portion of it was generated by manufacturing establishments. To be sure, these were mostly small affairs, the one- or two- or three-man shops of the village artisans, scattered across the countryside, fashioning simple equipment for local farmers or transforming raw farm products into usable goods. (The Census Bureau's liberal definition made a manufacturer of almost any smithy who shoed a few mules.) Though most of these undertakings could therefore hardly be dignified as "industries," the most important by far in the grain-rich heartland were flour and meal mills, which produced more than $1 million worth of goods annually at eighty-four sites with 198 workers. The rocky plots of cedar and oak that dotted the region apologized for their barrenness by furnishing wood for a thriving lumber industry, behind flour and meal in value of products though of first rank in number of hands employed (595); 134 sawmills turned out lumber worth $800,000.

Beyond these were leather curing and tanning, blacksmithing, and a dozen other small rural industries.[20]

The towns had their share of local shops and mills but boasted as well the only real industries to be found in Middle Tennessee, that is, those that produced goods on a large scale and for more than just the local market. Most notable was tobacco processing, centered in Clarksville. All told, fifteen factories employed 420 hands to prepare nearly $1 million worth of exportable weed each year. Machinery manufacturing, the next largest enterprise, was concentrated in four Nashville factories engaging 442 men. At other towns, women in factories wove much of the cotton not woven by women in homes. Five fair-sized textile plants, all but one in the southern counties, employed 244 hands, two-thirds of them female. Nearly 300 workers sweated in the region's nine iron furnaces and mills, the most important of which were in Clarksville. Though the census ignored it, pork packing was a prominent industry in several heartland towns, including Nashville, Clarksville, and Shelbyville.[21]

Yet in reckoning with antebellum industry a proper perspective is essential, and that perspective lays bare one cardinal fact: agriculture dwarfed all other endeavors in Middle Tennessee. The total capital invested in manufacturing in the region, even using the Census Bureau's generous definitions, equaled only about 4 percent of the total cash value of farms, not to mention the value of slaves and equipment used in agriculture. Members of fewer than four free families out of one hundred were employed in the true industries (tobacco, machinery, cotton, and iron). In just two counties did manufacturing have a significant economic role: Montgomery, with its tobacco and iron plants, and Davidson, embracing Nashville's machinery factories and a few other industries, especially printing. These two counties generated 55 percent of the heartland's industrial output, 87 percent of the output of the four true industries. The millions of dollars worth of goods issuing from the mills and shops and factories of most of the important industries—flour and meal, cotton, tobacco, lumber, leather, and pork—evinced fundamentally the richness of the heartland's farms, not the marshaling of its industrial resources.[22]

"Judges and officers shalt thou make thee in all thy gates . . . and they shall judge the people with just judgment": like the children of Israel, the people of Middle Tennessee hearkened faithfully to the biblical injunction to raise up institutions of law and government. English and colonial law

---

20   *Manufactures of the United States in 1860* . . . (Washington, D.C., 1865), 560–78.
21   *Ibid.*
22   *Ibid.; Agriculture, 1860*, 132, 136; *Statistics of the United States, 1860*, 348.

had bequeathed forms and usages common to all the Southern states, and antebellum reforming enthusiasm had tempered these ancient ways with a full measure of Jacksonian democracy. Local government in the heartland was for the most part unobtrusive, however, its apparatus simple, as befitted a rural and self-reliant folk. The day-to-day dealings of neighbor with neighbor in the countryside were customarily regulated by informal, personal arrangements (whether consummated with a friendly handshake or a threatening fist) and by community consensus. Grave indeed was the neighborhood squabble that provoked the intervention of constable, sheriff, or judge. The prevailing narrow definition of government prerogatives likewise circumscribed the legislative and administrative powers of local authorities.[23]

At the heart of local government was the county court, composed of the elected justices of the peace of each civil district. Rarely learned in the law and devoting only part time to official duties, these magistrates were not professional administrators but merely respected men of the community, farmers and doctors and merchants like their neighbors. Sitting each January, April, July, and October as a quarterly court—the county's legislative and executive body—the justices levied county taxes, passed major appropriations, appointed and bonded various court and county officers, and supervised elections.

From among their number the justices designated three to serve as a quorum court—the county's judicial body—which met monthly for as many days as necessary to handle the routine matters of county business: probating wills, administering estates, supervising slave patrols and the maintenance of roads and public buildings, overseeing guardianships for orphans with property and apprenticing those with none, adjudicating adoption and bastardy cases, regulating free blacks, and provisioning paupers. Within their home districts, justices served individually as the bedrock of the state's judiciary, setting apart one day a month to resolve small debt haggles among their neighbors and to fine and scold the drunkards and brawlers who dared disturb the peace of the community.

Of the other county officials, the most prominent was the sheriff. Although the days of the notorious, autocratic colonial sheriff were long past, this elected officer was still a redoubtable force within his little demesne. Legally the representative of the state in his county, he was responsible for enforcing the law, making arrests, managing the jail, holding elections, collecting taxes, and seizing the property of tax delinquents. These

23   Deut. 16: 18.

powers endowed the sheriff with considerable influence in local politics, and the commissions he was allowed made his office lucrative.

Other elected county functionaries included a trustee, a register, constables (one for each district), public school commissioners, a county court clerk, and a circuit court clerk (assistant to the circuit judge, who presided over criminal and some civil cases beyond the jurisdiction of the magistrates). The county court appointed revenue commissioners in each district, a ranger to round up stray animals, a surveyor, and a coroner. Every courthouse accommodated also a chancery clerk, commissioned by the chancery court (which had jurisdiction over most civil matters). Like the circuit court, the chancery court met periodically in each county to hear cases beyond the purview of the justices.[24]

These few officials carried on all the business of county government in antebellum Middle Tennessee, and with diminutive budgets. Most counties levied a property tax of less than fifteen cents per hundred dollars and a poll tax of twenty-five or fifty cents (state taxes were roughly equivalent); thus, the citizenry was hardly overburdened. Even responsibilities that might be expected to impose considerable expense—upkeep of the jail and its inmates, for instance, and care of the poor—did not in actuality unduly tax the county's resources. When the census takers made their rounds in the summer of 1860, they found, for example, only six prisoners in the Montgomery County jail and one each in Williamson's and Wilson's; Robertson's cells were empty. Furthermore, they counted but forty-six paupers on the dole in all of Davidson County outside Nashville, thirty in Sumner, twenty in Giles, and even fewer elsewhere; Rutherford County supported just one pauper and Marshall none. Where rural habits of self-sufficiency, neighborliness, and personal retribution prevailed, a man could depend upon his neighbor equally for the loan of a little cornmeal to see him through a hard spell and a swift, summary pummeling if he should steal that corn rather than ask for it.[25]

Moreover, because kinfolk and neighbors were commonly nearby to care for orphaned children, few had to be bound out as apprentices, though the courts were empowered to do so when unavoidable. Even when government did act, it often merely gave legal imprimatur to accomplished fact. Thus, for example, the Davidson County court in 1860 consented to the

24 In three counties (Williamson, Davidson, and Montgomery) a single elected county judge replaced the quorum court. These last two counties, along with Rutherford, also had special criminal courts.

25 Eighth Census, Social Statistics; Tennessee, *Report of Comptroller 1861*, 1. A few counties also assessed special-purpose taxes for schools, railroads, and the like.

formal adoption of three-year-old Ida Wilcox by George Stubbs and his wife, who sometime earlier had on their own initiative taken in the girl after her abusive father and stepmother abandoned her. In the country-side, therefore, wards of the county (whether lawbreaker, orphan, or hap-less indigent) were few and the official agencies of justice and welfare minimal.[26]

The situation was different in the towns (and especially in Nashville), where the complexities of urban life demanded more formal institutions. The larger towns in Middle Tennessee—Columbia, Clarksville, and a few others, including of course the capital city—had incorporated under state law and were privileged to elect their own guardians of the public weal (a mayor, aldermen, and so on) distinct from the county officeholders. Thus the towns endeavored to cope with characteristically urban problems—the need for streets, police, fire departments, water, and gas—with which the county governments were unequipped or unwilling to deal.[27]

Of necessity, Nashville advanced far beyond the other towns in elaborat-ing its bureaucracy. The city's Board of Aldermen appointed standing committees to regulate such matters as finance, improvements and expen-ditures, public property, market house, springs, wharf, streets, schools, waterworks, gas, fire department, police, and slaves. Under the aegis of other committees, the city maintained several institutions to succor the helpless and coerce the fractious: for the sick, a hospital; for the con-tagious, a pesthouse; for the unruly, a police court; for the incorrigible, a workhouse; and, for those beyond earthly affliction and corruption, a cemetery. Paupers in Nashville numbered 145 in 1860, nearly as many as the counties supported in all the rest of the heartland.[28]

Although far from a cradle-to-grave authoritarianism, government in the towns was a more palpable and pervasive entity than in the country, a faceless authority confronting the townsman at every turn and accustom-ing him to day-to-day regulation and obedience, even in such matters as how fast he might ride his horse down Main Street and how far out his doorway he might throw the kitchen slops. To the country folk, civil au-thority was the sheriff calling once a year to collect taxes, and obedience was giving up a few days to work on county roads or serve on the circuit

26   Joseph Buckner Killebrew Autobiography (Typescript in SHC), I, 35–48; Davidson County, Tennessee, County Court Clerk's Office, County Court Minutes, July 5, 1860, Bk. H, 466–67 (Microfilm copy in TSLA).

27   Tennessee General Assembly, *The Code of Tennessee, Enacted by the General Assembly of 1857–'8* (Nashville, 1858), 301–304.

28   Nashville *Patriot*, October 2, 1860; Nashville *Daily Gazette*, April 25, 1860; Eighth Census, Social Statistics.

court jury. Of far greater social consequence in the rural areas than the tension between government and citizen was the interplay of community consensus and individual volition.

As government touched only lightly the country folk of the antebellum heartland, so did another institution—education. In this rural culture, children customarily followed the livelihoods of their parents, and a boy learned from his father the necessary arts of butchering a hog, shoeing a horse, and cajoling a team of otherwise-minded mules to pull a plow in a straight line. A young girl similarly mastered the mysteries of spinning wheel and loom at her mother's knee. Book learning was a luxury to the common people, and the village schoolmaster did well to inculcate enough of the three R's to enable his pupils to add up a few simple figures, read their Bibles, and scribble their names. Many, like John W. Carpenter of Lincoln County, "never went to school but very little. Didn't want to go—could have gone but cared nothing about it." Even those youngsters with bookish inclinations were lucky to attend school a few weeks or months out of the year; "those in deep poverty," recalled a Giles countian, "could go to school only when not needed at home." The onerous demands of farm work and house chores left little time for the blue-back speller and *McGuffey's Eclectic Reader.*[29]

Though basic literacy was widespread in Middle Tennessee (only about one free family head out of eight could not read and write), thorough, formal schooling was not. Public education was still in its infancy in the antebellum years. Prominent among Jacksonian precepts was a commitment to free education for the masses, but that worthy mission remained more a faith than a practice in the heartland before the Civil War. The state had created, in name at least, a public school system, and provided for its support a permanent common school fund and (thanks to the exertions of Governor Andrew Johnson) a modicum of tax revenues. But the system was altogether disorganized, badly administered, and underfunded. There was never enough money, never enough enthusiasm at the state or local level to fashion a true system of education.[30]

Many districts declined to set up public schools, and their citizens fell back on the tradition of subscription schools, in which neighbors pooled their efforts to hire a teacher—generally one of indifferent merit—and to

29 Duling Memoir; John W. Carpenter and David Bodenhamer files, Civil War Questionnaires (Confederate).

30 Robert H. White, *The Development of the Tennessee State Education Organization, 1796–1929* (Kingsport, Tenn., 1929), 39–77; A. P. Whitaker, "The Public School System in Tennessee, 1834–1860," *THM*, II (1916), 5–30.

erect a community schoolhouse or beg the use of a church or other building. (One Rutherford countian told of attending classes in an "old log cabbin with cracks that you could [have] thown a dog thou." W. R. H. Matthews of Maury County remembered his first teacher as a woman who "couldent spell tobakker" but who did teach young Matthews "to take my daley whippings.") Good or bad, public or subscription, these schools were few and generally uncrowded. In 1860 census takers counted fewer than five hundred of them and no more than eighteen thousand pupils in a region whose free, school-age population could not have numbered fewer than forty thousand.[31]

In the towns, urban mores fostered a social climate more amenable to public education. Significantly, the only heartlanders to petition the state legislature in the late antebellum period for permission to levy a local school tax were the townspeople of Edgefield, in Davidson County, who declared it "the earnest & almost unanimous wish of the residents." Not surprisingly, of all the region's towns Nashville had progressed the farthest. The city operated its own school system, stiffly taxed property and polls to sustain it, and staffed it with trained teachers. Alfred Hume, "father of the Nashville public schools," had conceived the system in the early 1850s after touring the most advanced schools of the North. Noteworthy in this era of the one-room schoolhouse was the three-tiered hierarchy of the city system, offering a succession of primary, grammar, and high schools to the ripening young scholar. The Nashville Board of Education supervised altogether in 1860 five schools with thirty-five teachers and more than eighteen hundred students, a very large proportion indeed of the city's school-age free children.[32]

For those with money and with elite status or pretensions to it, the preferred agent of education was the private academy. Scattered among the towns and villages of the heartland were at least fifty-five academies, almost all of them managed under religious or fraternal auspices. There some thirty-four hundred young ladies and gentlemen imbibed classical literature and aristocratic refinements along with their spelling and ciphering. Some of these institutions were rather rustic, only a little more elegant than the log schoolhouse down the road, but a few were outstanding—the Clarksville Female Academy, for one, and Reverend C. D. Elliott's Nashville Female Academy—boasting some of the South's most prominent educators and enjoying a renown that extended far beyond the boundaries of

31   George D. Fleming and W. R. H. Matthews files, Civil War Questionnaires (Confederate); Eighth Census, Social Statistics.

32   Tennessee Legislative Petitions, 1861, No. 32, in TSLA; F. Garvin Davenport, *Cultural Life in Nashville on the Eve of the Civil War, 1825–1860* (Chapel Hill, 1941), 52–54.

Middle Tennessee. On the whole, the academies provided a good education as defined by antebellum Americans, probably the equal of the best
Northern schools. In contrast to the wretched state of education for the
many, education for the few was flourishing on the eve of the Civil War.[33]

Very few, even of the elite, sent sons or daughters to college, for in the
antebellum era few callings demanded such training. Lawyers for the most
part still prepared by reading law in the office of a practicing attorney, and
most doctors acquired their healing skills by making house calls with an
established physician. Would-be ministers likewise learned in the pulpit
rather than the classroom, and normal schools for prospective teachers
were still in the future. Nevertheless, some initiates in these and other professions did earn degrees of higher learning, and Middle Tennessee was
home to several notable institutions. The University of Nashville with its
celebrated medical department enrolled more than six hundred students;
Cumberland University in Lebanon (Wilson County), under the patronage of the Cumberland Presbyterian Church, enrolled five hundred, most
of them studying law, theology, or civil engineering; Stewart College in
Clarksville, a Presbyterian school, adhered to a classical curriculum. At
least eight other smaller colleges, with perhaps nine hundred budding
bachelors, adorned other of the heartland's towns.[34]

It is tempting to conclude that the pitiful education doled out to the
common folk of the heartland was no worse than their due, given their
seeming lack of interest in formal schooling and the natural hindrances to
it that their rural culture presented. Yet the few memoirs of these people
often betray a whisper of wistfulness, even bitterness, as they recall school
days, a hint of regret for their inadequate education and of envy of those
with better. In perhaps no other aspects of life in antebellum Middle Tennessee save courtship, marriage, and slavery were class distinctions so
glaring, and so telling, as in education. The well-to-do farmer or merchant
resisted the proliferation of public schools in his community because he
sent his own sons and daughters to the local academy, and he perceived no
benefit in subsidizing the education of the lower ranks. The plain folk, for
their part, felt keenly the stigma of attending a free school and thus partook only grudgingly of the minimal education offered them. "Some poor
families would not send their children to school," one upper-class heartlander recalled disdainfully; "these children of course were never ambitious or fitted to rise in the world."[35]

33   Eighth Census, Social Statistics.
34   Robert E. Corlew, *Tennessee: A Short History* (2nd ed.; Knoxville, 1981), 238, 240;
Eighth Census, Social Statistics.
35   Whitaker, "Public School System," 28–30; Fred A. Bailey, "Caste and Classroom in

The pernicious consequences of relegating members of a free society to ignorance or semi-ignorance were not fully grasped in the South in that era. The notion that education (in its narrow sense) could transform the most impecunious plowman into a prosperous, scientific planter was widely held. But few understood how education in the broad sense could expand the common man's world—a world otherwise limited by the distance he could drive his wagon—and render him as self-reliant in his intellect as he was in his livelihood, better prepared to judge critically and independently the momentous social and political questions of the 1850s and 1860s.

In contrast to courthouse and schoolhouse, the ubiquitous meetinghouse reached out vigorously to embrace the people of the heartland. More than five hundred churches, from the steepled edifices of the towns to the log chapels of the country, dotted the landscape of the thirteen counties of the region. No institution save the family loomed larger in the eyes of the rural folk, whose churches served not only as houses of worship but as emotional vent, moral arbiter, and social adhesive.

The early nineteenth-century wave of evangelicalism that swept the South had engulfed the heartland. With their frenetic revivals, their zealous and unpolished clergy, and their exaltation of emotional experience, personal conversion, and devout commitment to the Christian life, the evangelicals touched the souls of the rough-hewn frontier folk and lured them from the solemn, intellectual Presbyterianism of their fathers. No sooner were the people conquered, however, than they were divided, as the evangelical movement fractured into competing denominations, each with its own keys of the Kingdom. By 1860 the crudities of evangelicalism had been considerably refined and its countercultural flavor much diluted, but its precepts of conversion, devotion, and salvation endured as the vital impulse of religion in Middle Tennessee and the South.

The Southern Methodists (severed from their Northern brethren in 1845) won the largest following of any denomination in the heartland, as throughout the South, thanks to the thoroughness of their ecclesiastical organization, the labors of their hard-riding circuit preachers, and the appeal of their free-will Arminianism. In 1860 Methodists worshiped at 191 churches in Middle Tennessee; nearly four churches of every ten in the region were theirs.[36]

Not far behind were the Southern Baptists (similarly split from their

Antebellum Tennessee," *Maryland Historian*, XIII (1982), 39–54; John A. Pickard file, Civil War Questionnaires (Confederate).

36 *Statistics of the United States, 1860*, 465–70.

Northern coreligionists over slavery), who had 115 churches, or more than two of every ten. Though rent by dissension (exemplified in the secession of the "Missionary" Baptists), aggravated by its lack of a cohesive ecclesiastical authority, this church of modified Calvinists enthralled many of the commonalty, including slaves. The plain people liked the Baptists' emotional affirmation of human equality and future rewards and their doctrinal practicality: a visitor in the heartland in 1858 noted wryly that the Baptists "believe that God does every thing right but when they get sick He has not done that right—consequently they send for a physician to controvert or annul afflictions." [37]

Unlike the Methodists and Baptists, who antedated the Great Revival in Tennessee and used it to multiply their flocks, the Cumberland Presbyterians were the progeny of the revival. Their church was born in 1810 in Middle Tennessee, when evangelical revivalists in the Cumberland Presbytery abandoned the Presbyterian church and its dogmas of predestination, election, and an educated ministry. The Cumberland Presbyterians thereafter spread rapidly throughout the South, but their main strength remained in Tennessee, especially the heartland. In 1860 their congregations in the region outnumbered those of their parent church (by now mildly infected by evangelicalism itself, especially among its rural churches) by eighty-three to forty-seven. [38]

A somewhat later addition to the ranks of the evangelicals were the Disciples of Christ (or Campbellites, or Christians), a coalescence of groups led by disaffected Upper South Presbyterian ministers who espoused biblical fundamentalism and urged a great ecumenical union of all Christians. These men energetically diffused their persuasion through North, South, and West. Some of their successors, in the radical Protestant tradition of civil noninvolvement, stubbornly preached pacifism during the Mexican War and afterward. Like the Baptists, the Disciples were riven by doctrinal bickering and congregational autonomy, but like the Cumberland Presbyterians they regarded Middle Tennessee as a fortress of their strength. They had thirty-seven churches in the region in 1860, and Nashville was the home of two of their outstanding national spokesmen, Philip Fall and Tolbert Fanning. [39]

These four faiths—Methodist, Baptist, Cumberland Presbyterian, and Christian—along with the Presbyterians, accounted for more than nine of every ten churches in Middle Tennessee. The Episcopalians had failed to

37   *Ibid.*; A. T. Hamilton to John Hamilton, September 9, 1858, in Hamilton Letters.
38   Corlew, *Tennessee,* 243–44; *Statistics of the United States, 1860,* 465–70.
39   David E. Harrell, Jr., "Disciples of Christ Pacifism in Nineteenth Century Tennessee," *THQ,* XXI (1962), 263–70; *Statistics of the United States, 1860,* 465–70.

capture many souls in the region, for their sedate liturgy could compete but feebly with the fervent suasion pouring forth from the evangelical pulpits. In 1860 there were only eight Episcopal churches in the heartland, all in or near towns. Six Catholic churches, also in the towns, served the growing population of poor Irish and more prosperous German immigrants. Lutherans were very few in the region: Nashville had one Lutheran church (a German congregation) and Lincoln County two. The capital was also the home of a small Jewish synagogue.[40]

Religion in Middle Tennessee's towns exemplified the diversity and extensive institutionalization of urban life. The faithful taken as a whole—the exotic Episcopalians, Catholics, Lutherans, and Jews, sprinkled among the more familiar denominations—presented a variegated aspect. Yet each urban congregation was very homogeneous—in its creed, of course, but in its social constitution as well. Only in the towns were to be found the stately cathedrals patronized by the (generally nonevangelical) affluent: Christ Church, Episcopal, in Nashville, for example, a Gothic edifice where many of the city's prominent citizens worshiped; the magnificent First Presbyterian Church in the same city, with its ornate, neo-Egyptian decor; and Trinity Episcopal in Clarksville, a church that owned slaves.[41]

Many blacks, free and slave, in the towns belonged to white churches, but they very often met separately for services. Such was the case, for instance, at the Cumberland Presbyterian Church of Lebanon, whose elders purchased an old church building nearby for the use of their black brethren. There were as well several all-black urban congregations, such as the semi-autonomous Negro mission of Nashville's First Baptist Church and the fully independent black Christian Church in the city. With the rich, the poor, the black, and the foreign-born thus assembling for the most part separately to worship their God, the remaining urban congregations were distinctly white and middle class and generally evangelical.[42]

Whether high church or low, the town church was likely to be large and highly structured. The Cumberland Presbyterian Church of Lebanon, for

40   *Statistics of the United States, 1860,* 465–70; Davenport, *Cultural Life in Nashville,* 84–116.

41   Davenport, *Cultural Life in Nashville,* 84–116; Trinity Episcopal Church, Clarksville, Records, Session Minutes, December 21, 1858 (Microfilm copy in TSLA).

42   Historical Records Survey, Tennessee, *Cumberland Presbyterian Church Records* (Nashville, 1938–41), II, 28, 31; Mechal Sobel, "'They Can Never Both Prosper Together': Black and White Baptists in Antebellum Nashville, Tennessee," *THQ,* XXXVIII (1979), 296; Herman A. Norton, *Tennessee Christians: A History of the Christian Church in Tennessee* (Nashville, 1971), 129–30. Segregation of urban churches by class and race was a general rule, not an inflexible law; some aristocratic churches had poor members, and many white churches had black members.

example, elaborately organized its congregation by residential districts and assigned its elders to formal committees on education, finances, discipline, public worship, benevolent enterprises, relief, and pastoral relations; in 1858 the church applied for incorporation under state law.[43]

The urban churches, like the segregated urban neighborhoods, illustrate the nature of institutions in Middle Tennessee's towns. Each had a rigidly defined constituency and sphere of activity, and all were circumfused by a pervasive civil authority. The urbanite found refuge from this impersonal authority and bewildering complexity in the comforting homogeneity of his neighborhood and his church.

In the countryside, by contrast, just as there were no segregated neighborhoods in any community, so there were no rich or poor, no white or black churches. A permeating rural culture subsumed all classes and races, and each church, like each community, was a motley assemblage of planter, yeoman, artisan, and slave families, all joined in an informal, eclectic fellowship. (The rural churches as a body, though, lacked the variety of the town churches, for virtually all were of one or the other major evangelical faiths, and their preachers, as one contemporary remarked, "of the old fogy stamp mostly—rough and unpolished.") This unifying culture, a product of the shared interests and mutual dependence of the country folk, generated an informal ethic of consensus that governed the rural communities in place of the political authority necessary to control the clashing interests in the towns. The country church served as a key agent of, indeed was inseparable from, that communal consensus, and the boundary between God's dominion and man's was thus blurred in the rural areas as it was not in the towns. By demanding from every member an absolute commitment to the Christian life, the evangelical rural churches sought to harmonize the relations of the country folk with each other as well as with their Creator. Surviving records reveal the churches' scrupulous concern for the earthly propriety as well as the future salvation of their flocks.[44]

To avoid offense to the commandments of God and man, the churches enjoined a strict morality on their members and urged them to report breaches of it by their brethren. Sister E. A. Dandrige of Maury County learned this to her dismay when McCains Cumberland Presbyterian Church accused her in 1859 of winning "public fame of immoral conduct. . . . That she has for a number of years lived in such connecton and

43 Historical Records Survey, *Cumberland Presbyterian Records*, II, 23–24, 44, 54–58.

44 A. T. Hamilton to John Hamilton, June 17, 1858, in Hamilton Letters. The mingling of classes and races is exemplified by Wilson Creek Primitive Baptist Church of Williamson County, described in Jordan, "My Recollections."

intimacy with James Kannon, as to bring a reproch upon her self and the church of *Christ*." Found guilty in a full-scale church trial of allowing "said Kannon to visite her house at untimely hours . . . [which] caused the publick to question her chastity," Sister Dandrige was suspended indefinitely from membership "for the Glory of *God*, and the good of the *Church*." Witnesses at her trial reported that some neighborhood women had stopped calling on her because of the rumors. Sister Dandrige's ordeal illustrates the frequent confluence of social and religious sanctions in disciplining the wayward of the rural communities.[45]

To keep peace in the congregation, each church claimed exclusive jurisdiction in settling disputes among its brethren. The fathers of Mt. Olivet Primitive Baptist Church in Lincoln County were grieved to hear in March, 1860, that a certain Brother Crofford had brought suit in civil court against Brother Troop for some property. Although Crofford admitted before the session "that he was rong in bringing sute before going to the church," he declined to withdraw the action, and the churchmen reluctantly concluded that in light of his transgression "thay can not feloship him."[46]

The rural church sought to fuse its diverse constituency into a self-contained community, at once temporal and spiritual, with the church its touchstone and arbiter. This ideal community would exclude competing institutions such as government but assimilate complementary institutions such as the family; and it would be self-consciously distinct from and opposed to the "world"—the undisciplined, freethinking, sinful world identified with the towns, the Babylons of drinking, dancing, gambling, and plays, the haunts of Catholics, free blacks, and foreigners. The fate of the unrepentant sinner was spiritual banishment to that world to purge the righteous community of all that was evil in the sight of God or disruptive to social concord. To the believer, no punishment could be worse than that meted out to the slave Sam, a "cullard Brother" of the Wilson Creek Primitive Baptist Church of Williamson County. Accused of theft in 1860, Sam failed to explain himself to the satisfaction of his fellow church members, who ordered that "he ise thire fore excommunicated from fellow ship with this church Sam ise no more of us."[47]

Zion Church in Maury County illustrates almost paradigmatically the rural antebellum religious community. The Zion brethren—originally

45 McCains Cumberland Presbyterian Church, McCains, Maury County, Records, Session Minutes, July 23, August 6, 10, 1859 (Microfilm copy in TSLA).

46 Mt. Olivet Primitive Baptist Church, Lincoln County, Records, Session Minutes, March, 1860 (Microfilm copy in TSLA).

47 Wilson Creek Primitive Baptist Church, Williamson County, Records, Session Minutes, November, 1860, January, 1861 (Microfilm copy in TSLA).

a band of South Carolina Presbyterians who migrated to the heartland early in the century as a group and were thus a preexistent community with ancient traditions—consciously maintained, through generations of church guardianship and endogamous marriage, their distinctive customs and "oneness of belief." They were noted for their strict Sabbath observance, for example, which forbade even shaving or cooking on Sunday, and for their uncompromising moral standards. Sin the "Zionists" did, as their church trial records show, but so impermeable was their communalism that few of their indiscretions ever claimed the attention of the civil courts. Quarrel among themselves they did, too, but records for the period from the founding of the church in 1807 to the Civil War reveal only five lawsuits between church members. The church session, Zionists held, was "practically the Supreme Court of the community and settled all differences without appeal to Civil Courts." Slaves (who made up more than half the population of this affluent agricultural community) worshiped, learned liturgy and Bible, took communion, and on occasion endured sessional castigation along with their masters. Membership in the church by no means debarred men of Zion from worldly affairs—many served as local magistrates or other officials—but it did engender that "oneness" which made the church their first point of reference and set the Zionists apart, regarded by the world and defined by themselves as a social and spiritual entity.[48]

To nurture their communities the churches applied not only the negative sanction of church discipline but the positive inducement of appeals to the spirit. Besides the weekly or monthly preaching that every congregation attended, all the evangelical denominations continued the traditions of camp meetings and revivals. All across the heartland, a series of stirring revivals in the late antebellum years compelled thousands into the churches as worshipers, up to the front bench as penitent "mourners," and finally forward to the altar as proselytes to begin a new life. The Nashville *Daily Gazette* in 1860 reported revivals in progress at dozens of sites in or near Nashville, Clarksville, Columbia, Shelbyville, Murfreesboro (Rutherford County), Gallatin (Sumner County), and Lebanon, at which many of the faithful were seeking, and the fortunate ones had found, the "pearl of great price."[49]

Obviously, the power of the rural churches to impose order and virtue

48   Mary W. Highsaw, "A History of Zion Community in Maury County, 1806–1860," *THQ*, V (1946), 3–34, 111–40, 222–33.

49   Nashville *Daily Gazette*, February 24, March 10, 25, July 31, August 18, September 14, October 5, December 15, 1860. An excellent description of an antebellum camp meeting is in Killebrew Autobiography, I, 75–77.

on the country folk was not absolute. It was checked by denominational rivalries, the geographical mobility of the people, the numbers of un-churched, and the proximity of the towns; thus the occasional recourse in every community to justice of the peace, sheriff, courts, or personal vio-lence. Nevertheless, the country churches and the folk communities they embodied gave rural life much of the unity and stability it possessed.

Examining the role of the churches and other institutions of Middle Tennessee and understanding how the region's people earned their live-lihoods together reveal much about the structure of life in the antebellum heartland but little about its content. To flesh out the portrait of Middle Tennessee society it is essential to delineate how that society's constituents viewed themselves and their world and how they conducted their relation-ships with one another. These crucial matters are the subject of the next chapter.

Chapter III

Their Father's House

Class, Race, and Slavery in the Heartland

O N SUNDAY, the first day of January, 1860, the faithful of the Wilson Creek Primitive Baptist Church of Williamson County gathered to hear their preacher inaugurate the new decade. "Bro Watson delivered a very interesting discourse," the congregation's scribe recorded with satisfaction, "on the relative duties of Parents to their Children; children to their Parents; Husbands to their wives, wives to their husbands; masters to their servants, servants to their masters,—and the duty of all classes to the authorities and powers that be;—and of all mankind to God as supreme—all of which we believe to be in strict harmony with the letter and true Spirit of the Gospel, and with which we were truly delighted." [1]

That same day, horrified Nashvillians read the sensational newspaper account of a "Fiendish Rape by a Negro" in that city. Jo, a slave, had accosted a white woman on the street, grabbed her from behind, overpowered her as she struggled, and, ignoring her "begging and imploring for mercy," choked her until she submitted. The "infuriated brute" was quickly caught and jailed by the city marshal. [2]

The coincidence of these two episodes underscores their essential affinity, for both illuminate elements of the ideology which at the zenith of the antebellum era permeated and cemented white society like a social mucilage binding disparate parts. Common assumptions, habits, and

1 Wilson Creek Primitive Baptist Church, Williamson County, Minutes of Sermons, January, 1860.
2 Nashville *Daily Gazette*, January 1, 1860.

modes of perceiving the world constituted in a sense another of the heart-land's institutions, this one not confined to town, village, or farm, nor to courthouse, schoolhouse, or meetinghouse, but immanent in nearly every white mind.

As Brother Watson affirmed, white Middle Tennesseans interpreted their society as a happy congruence of distinct components, congealed by the faithful fulfillment of mutual obligations. But as Watson insinuated, this was not a mutuality of equals but a hierarchical mutuality of superior and inferior. Middle Tennesseans, like Southerners elsewhere, often en-visaged their society metaphorically as a household, that familiar, subtle synthesis of unity and inequality. The household of society, like the literal household, ideally subordinated all members to a benevolent patriarchy, mitigating potential conflicts of race, sex, age, or class. Other institu-tions—the churches or local government—might act to buttress the societal and familial patriarchies, or in extraordinary circumstances intervene to influence or correct them, but they did not challenge fundamentally the authority of those patriarchies over their respective households.

In the hierarchies of family and society (as defined by whites), slaves occupied the lowermost rank. Indeed, white heartlanders agreed that their society's admirable harmony rested on this foundation. "Society is a pyra-mid," explained the editor of the Nashville *Daily Gazette* late in 1860. "Slavery is the only base on which a stable republican government ever was or ever will be built. We may sympathise with the stones at the bottom of the pyramid of Cheops, but we know that some stones have to be at the bottom, and that they must be permanent in their place." Another Nash-villian reminded his fellows early in 1861 that the existence of a slave class elevated all whites, slaveholders and nonslaveholders alike: "It seems to me that we are all bound up in the institution of slavery," he wrote, concluding that it was "morally, socially, politically, and religiously right, and a great blessing to the master and the slave—to the rich man as well as to the poor man—to the farmer as well as to the mechanic." [3]

Yet the slave's subjection, though unequivocal, was defined always within the context of his membership in the households of family and so-ciety. "The bible recognises servants as a part of the household of their masters," reported a committee of the First Presbyterian Church of Clarks-ville in 1860, "and it is clearly the duty of all & especially of every Chris-tian Master to endeavour to meet the solemn obligation arising out of the very intimate responsible relation which he bears with his servants." Thus the shock with which Nashvillians received the lurid news of the "Fiend-

3   *Ibid.*, November 25, 1860; Nashville *Patriot*, January 24, 1861.

ish Rape by a Negro" on the first day of 1860 stemmed perhaps not only from the overt transgression of the boundary lines of race and sexual propriety which the act signified but from its darkly veiled suggestion of filial betrayal, and worse.[4]

In the household of the family, higher but still subordinate niches were occupied by wife, sons, daughters, other relatives, boarders, and apprentices, each with his or her assigned role, obligations, and tasks. Over all, free and slave, in the ideal family presided the benign patriarch, whose prestige swelled with the size of his household. The patriarch exercised dominion over his lieges and expected from them deference, obedience, fealty, and service. In return he owed them protection, physical sustenance, and moral guidance. Such were the duties which Brother Watson was moved to recount on New Year's Day.[5]

In the household of society, with its many mansions, the patriarchy was made up of wealthy planters and professionals and their families—most of them slaveholders, many of them large slaveholders—who monopolized important political offices and social prestige. They included men such as William G. Harding, Davidson County planter and fabled host, whose thirty-five-hundred-acre Belle Meade plantation, with its deer and buffalo park, was a showpiece of the South and the embodiment of gracious society.[6]

Harding and his lofty coterie were among the "authorities and powers that be" to whom Brother Watson urged obedience. They reigned over a loose but definable hierarchy of families of small slaveholders, yeomen, artisans, and poor white laborers—and, of course, slaves. Much ink has flowed in the historiographical battle over the nature of antebellum Southern society, but perhaps the fairest verdict is that Jacksonian reform had ushered in the forms of democracy (as it was understood in that era) to Middle Tennessee and the South while leaving intact much of the essence of aristocracy: conspicuous class distinctions as well as habits of deference on one hand and noblesse oblige on the other.

These traits unfailingly impressed travelers in the South accustomed to

---

4   First Presbyterian Church, Clarksville, Montgomery County, Records, Session Minutes, Vol. II, June 1, 1860 (Microfilm copy in TSLA).

5   The division of labor by age and sex on the farm is illustrated in the Duling Memoir. Men headed 86 percent of all free Middle Tennessee households in 1860. A third—32 percent—of all families were extended by nonnuclear relatives or unrelated free persons. If slaves are counted, the figure is 53 percent.

6   William M. Moss and M. B. Toney files, Civil War Questionnaires (Confederate); Herschel Gower, "Belle Meade: Queen of Tennessee Plantations," *THQ*, XXII (1963), 203–22.

the relatively vibrant bourgeois democracy of the North. One who accompanied the invading Union army into Nashville early in the Civil War marveled at how the "leading families had had things all their own way" there. Another entering Murfreesboro at about that time pronounced it "an aristocratic town," declaring with considerable if pardonable exaggeration that "the poor whites are as poor as rot, and the rich are very rich. There is no substantial well-to-do middle class here." Yet even one native, looking back over many decades on the time of his youth in antebellum Middle Tennessee, characterized it discerningly as the "medieval period of American history [which] presented the bright side and the dark side of medieval civilization."[7]

Social distinctions among whites protruded starkly in the antebellum heartland. Though smooth gradations rather than sharp cleavages marked the hierarchy, on the whole patrician and plebeian did not mix socially. Aristocrats were "clannish," one upper-class Middle Tennessean recalled, and they "did not make the black-smith, the carpenter, the ordinary day laborer . . . a part of [their] social life." Another wealthy heartlander insisted that people of his rank "always recognized & spoke courteously" to those of lower station, but he acknowledged that they "did not invite them to their social functions." Friendship and courtship similarly followed class lines. A Davidson County man observed that the blue-blooded young ladies "seemed at times to shun poor girls," and another heartlander noted that "the laboring white man did not visit the aristocratic girls." Even the all-inclusive rural churches and kinship networks sometimes failed to smother class divisions altogether. John S. Luna, of yeoman stock, wrote that in his locality planter families sought the "high seat" in church and "did not mingle much" with their poor relatives.[8]

Table III documents one important aspect of aristocratic social hegemony—its economic basis—by illustrating the unequal distribution of wealth and the close relationship between occupation and economic rank. The richest tenth of Middle Tennessee families owned 65 percent of the region's wealth in 1860; the poorer half of families owned only 2 percent. Rich families (those in the top decile) were almost all headed by professionals (23 percent) or landed farmers (69 percent). In fact, these two occupational groups together, though accounting for only 49 percent of all

7   Sir Christopher Chancellor (ed.), *An Englishman in the American Civil War: The Diaries of Henry Yates Thompson, 1863* (New York, 1971), 141; John Beatty, *Memoirs of a Volunteer, 1861–1863*, ed. Harvey S. Ford (New York, 1946), 96; John W. Burgess, *Reminiscences of an American Scholar: The Beginnings of Columbia University* (New York, 1934), 3.

8   Robert L. Morris, J. F. Osborne, James B. Thompson, William G. Lillard, and J. S. Luna files, Civil War Questionnaires (Confederate).

Table III. Wealth by Occupation of Family Head, 1860 (free population only)

Occupation	Percentage of families, ranked by wealth (deciles)									N	Percentage of total families	Percentage of total wealth	Mean wealth ($)
	1	2	3	4	5	6	7	8	9+ 10				
Professional	23	14	12	7	8	1	1	1	1	69	7	19	24,977
Landed farmer	69	75	72	71	63	44	15	5	1	417	42	71	15,145
Minor professional	1	2	0	2	3	2	1	3	2	18	2	1	4,122
Skilled worker	4	3	10	10	13	22	17	23	21	144	15	4	2,364
Overseer	0	0	1	0	0	2	4	3	3	15	2	0	952
Unskilled laborer	1	0	0	0	1	2	7	7	29	75	8	0	453
Landless agricultural worker	0	1	3	10	8	23	47	48	24	187	19	2	783
None	2	5	2	1	4	4	6	11	18	70	7	3	4,278
	1	2	3	4	5	6	7	8	9+ 10				
Percentage of total wealth	65	17	9	5	2	1	1	0	0				

Sample mean = $8,957
Sample median = $1,500
Proportion of families with zero wealth = 13 percent

χ^2 = 722.2 with 56 d.f., signif. = .0
C = .64851
N = 995

families, owned 90 percent of the region's wealth and enjoyed average wealth per family far exceeding that of other occupational groups. The poor (families in deciles nine and ten) were made up mostly of skilled workers (21 percent), unskilled laborers (29 percent), and landless agricultural workers (24 percent). Overseers and family heads without occupation were also overrepresented among the poor. Families in these last five occupational categories, constituting half of all families, owned less than one-tenth of the region's wealth.[9]

Slaveholding provided the most obvious contrast between classes. Slaves were both symbol and substance of wealth, and their possession afforded that leisure which was one of the often-noted hallmarks of the upper crust. A Union officer stationed in Fayetteville (Lincoln County) during the war wrote in his memoirs, "It was curious to see what a difference slavery had made in the social life of these people. Everywhere work was considered disgraceful for a white man, and as only the occupation of the 'nigger.' In order to succeed socially, it was necessary to own slaves. The idea of hiring labor, or of being rich without negroes, was apparently incomprehensible. . . . All of the people who had obtained any sort of success . . . had owned slaves."[10]

This prim Yankee may have magnified the slaveowners' slothfulness, but his testimony is corroborated by the accounts of a number of natives. Samuel B. Clemmons of Wilson County, who worked in the fields alongside his family's two slaves, noted that "in familys with [a] large amount of slaves the whites as a rule did very little work." Louis Bledsoe of Lincoln affirmed that his father, owner of twenty slaves and four hundred acres, devoted his time to pursuits more congenial than farming: "He followed deer and fox hunting. . . . Dad didnt do anything but hunt in the barns [barrens]." Slaveholders' offspring, too, luxuriated in the blessings of leisure. One poor heartlander recollected that "slave holder boys did not work any. They would even make a negro slave hand them a drink of water." A middle-class Montgomery County man scornfully described rich families in his neighborhood who "raised their children up in idleness [to] ride fine horses & smoke fine cigars."[11]

9 Wealth, as calculated here, is the combined value of real and personal property held by all family members. The lower limit of each wealth decile is as follows: first decile, $23,537; second, $10,013; third, $5,690; fourth, $3,000; fifth, $1,500; sixth, $800; seventh, $400; eighth, $150; ninth and tenth, zero. In this table and others, rounding sometimes brings column totals slightly above or below 100 percent.

10 Julian Wisner Hinkley, *A Narrative of Service with the Third Wisconsin Infantry* (Madison, 1912), 112.

11 Samuel B. Clemmons, Louis J. Bledsoe, William D. Beard, and Richard M. Winn files, Civil War Questionnaires (Confederate).

Table IV shows quantitatively the close connection between wealth and slaveholding in the antebellum heartland. Virtually all rich families (95 percent) were slaveholders and virtually all the poor (98 percent) were non-slaveholders. Moreover, the majority of the rich were large slaveholders (67 percent owned ten slaves or more), and the majority of slaves (64 percent) were owned by the rich. Slaveholding was monopolized by families in the top three wealth deciles, who held 95 percent of all slaves. Nonslave-holding families—two-thirds of all families—owned only 12 percent of the region's wealth, and their average wealth was but a small fraction of that of even the small slaveholders. Families with ten or more slaves, by contrast, constituting but 10 percent of all families, owned nearly half of all wealth and boasted enormous average wealth.

Table V depicts the occupational structure of each slaveholding rank. Not surprisingly, the owners of twenty or more slaves were nearly all landed farmers (92 percent). No other occupations were represented in that rank except professionals. Landed farmers constituted, moreover, a majority of every rank of slaveholders, though they were a minority in the population as a whole; and they owned 80 percent of the region's slaves. Professionals, too, were overrepresented in each rank of slaveholders, es-pecially those with between five and nineteen slaves. Skilled workers and landless agricultural laborers could be found in every slaveholding rank save the highest, but their representation in each of those ranks was far below their representation in the population as a whole. Unskilled laborers were completely unrepresented among slaveholders, except those with four slaves or fewer. The combined proportion of slaves held by all occupa-tional groups below the rank of landed farmer (half the population) was a mere 8 percent.

Among the darker consequences of such class distinctions were un-doubtedly arrogance from above and resentment, even bitterness, from be-low. John W. Burgess, who grew up in a wealthy Giles County family, re-called unfondly the "ignorant, slovenly, poor white trash in the country," who "were jealous of the riches and the social standing of the slave lords. They were ignorant, suspicious, superstitious, and vindictive." A North-erner in Murfreesboro commented on the local aristocrats' contempt for their social inferiors: "The slaves are, in fact, the middle class here. They are not considered so good, of course, as their masters, but a great deal better than the white trash."[12]

Heartlanders of the poor and yeoman classes agreed. "The slaveholders thought more of their slaves," one wrote, "than they did a poor hones

12 Burgess, *Reminiscences*, 3, 5; Beatty, *Memoirs of a Volunteer*, 96.

Table IV. Wealth by Slaveholding, 1860 (free population only)

Slaveholdings	Percentage of families, ranked by wealth (deciles)									N	Percent- age of total families	Percent- age of total wealth	Mean wealth ($)
	1	2	3	4	5	6	7	8	9+ 10				
20+	35	1	0	0	0	0	0	0	0	36	4	25	61,533
10–19	32	26	2	0	0	0	0	0	0	60	6	22	32,204
5–9	18	37	21	5	1	1	0	0	0	83	8	18	19,600
1–4	10	31	48	39	13	4	2	2	2	154	15	23	13,507
0	5	5	29	57	86	95	98	98	98	666	67	12	1,642

	1	2	3	4	5	6	7	8	9+ 10
Mean number of slaves	19	7	3	1	0	0	0	0	0
Percentage of total slaves	64	22	9	3	1	0	0	0	0

χ^2 = 1,094.8 with 32 d.f., signif. = .0   N = 999
C = .72311

Table V. Slaveholding by Occupation of Family Head, 1860 (free population only)

Occupation	Percentage of families, ranked by number of slaves held					N	Percentage of total families	Percentage of total slaves
	20+	10–19	5–9	1–4	0			
Professional	8	17	17	8	4	70	7	11
Landed farmer	92	70	70	62	28	417	42	80
Minor professional	0	0	1	3	2	18	2	0
Skilled worker	0	5	7	8	18	144	15	3
Overseer	0	0	1	0	2	15	2	0
Unskilled laborer	0	0	0	3	11	75	8	0
Landless agricultural worker	0	2	1	10	26	187	19	2
None	0	7	2	5	8	70	7	3
	20+	10–19	5–9	1–4	0			
N	~36	60	83	154	663	N = 996		
Percentage of total families	4	6	8	15	67			
Percentage of total slaves	44	26	18	11	0			

$\chi^2 = 241.5$ with 28 d.f., signif. = .0
C = .44173

young white man." A Sumner County man recalled acridly that slave-owners "did not want [a poor man] to stop on the high way and talk to [their] slaves. . . . The slave holder kept a cold shulder to him unless he [was worth] as mutch as a thousand dollars." Another in Williamson wrote that manual labor "was looked on as a low caling by most of the welthy peple . . . [working people] wer calde clod hopers."[13]

Such aristocratic disdain was repaid in kind. The poor keenly felt slights from the rich, and many sullenly harbored grudges all their lives. Further-more, some complained, at least in retrospect, that patrician hegemony and exploitation constricted the poor man's opportunities. In political con-tests, slaveholders, with their money and leisure time, were thought by some to hold a decisive advantage over workingmen, one of whom charged that slaveholders "could buy votes, with liquor and cigars." The economic ladder was similarly obstructed for some. "A renter had no chance to save anything," wrote William Beard of Bedford County; "slave holders were the only men that could make enough money to do any thing." "Slavehold-ers wanted to hire [the poor man] at a low rate and trafick out of his labor," declared a Sumner countian; "I no this by self experience." Upward mo-bility for the poor was stifled, another heartlander believed, because "the sons of rich men always got in first."[14]

A few were deeply embittered by poverty and ruling-class oppression. "There was a class of 'poor whites,'" one aristocratic Maury countian re-called, "who hated those who owned any kind of property." One was William Eskew of Sumner, who described himself as a "hirlan on the farms of Rich Men" and resentfully contrasted the comfortable lives of the elite with those of the poor, who "had to work or starve." Another was Robert Lackey of Lincoln, who worked in the fields, lived in a two-room log cabin "dobed with dirt," and attended school for only three months in his life. "The poor class of peopl was al moust slaves them selves," Lackey wrote, "had to work hard and live hard. . . . It took al we could do to make a living and then a hard living."[15]

Nevertheless, social distinctions—even social antagonisms—are en-demic to mature societies and do not always represent fundamental social divisions or conflicts. This was the case in antebellum Middle Tennessee, where ultimately the centripetal forces in white society overwhelmed the centrifugal. To that end the quintessential elements of life in the region—biracialism, slavery, ruralism, prosperity, and patriarchy—all contributed.

13   J. P. Dillehay and Robert H. Mosely files, Civil War Questionnaires (Confederate); Marcus Wiks file, *ibid.* (Federal).
14   Napoleon B. Abbott, William D. Beard, and John L. Young files, *ibid.* (Confederate); Marcus Wiks file, *ibid.* (Federal).
15   Isaac N. Rainey, William T. Eskew, and Robert P. Lackey files, *ibid.* (Confederate).

Whatever snobbery and resentment slaveholding aggravated, the existence of a black slave caste did in fact unify all whites, as many recognized. This was most dramatically confirmed during the slave revolt panics that sporadically swept Middle Tennessee and the rest of the South. But even in quiet times, nonslaveholders acknowledged their stake in, and professed their loyalty to, their slaveholding society. White skin was a badge of superiority for even the most miserable laborer or farmhand, a symbol of identity with the high-born and a source of self-esteem—perhaps the only source for those without great wealth, exalted station, cultured manners, classical education, or illustrious pedigree in a society that venerated those attributes. This sense of racial identity tended to deflect the hostility of lower-class whites away from the rich slaveholders and toward the slaves. As a well-to-do Montgomery County man remarked, "The poorer class of people hated the slaves much more than their owners." The patrician John W. Burgess wrote reprovingly, "The chief amount of slave whipping of which I had any cognizance was inflicted by gatherings of nonslaveholding whites. . . . It was the vast mass of the whites owning no slaves, who were the greatest enemy of the slaves." Of course, however much some slaveholders wagged their heads and clucked their tongues over the poor whites' abuse of slaves, it was ultimately a source of profound satisfaction to them that their society cleaved fundamentally along the line of color, not class.[16]

The prevailing ruralism of the heartland also muted social dissonance. The vivid disparities of class that impressed many witnesses were most characteristic of the towns, where institutional segregation exaggerated social differences. In the countryside, kinship ties, the communal demands of agriculture, the ethic of neighborliness, and the broad embrace of the churches made white society in the eyes of its constituents (with a few exceptions) more a partnership of blood, work, and faith than a dichotomy of wealth and want. "Every man was a neighbor," wrote E. K. Cook of Wilson County, "whether he owned slaves or not."[17]

Slavery and ruralism and their social consequences were of course pandemic in the antebellum South. But prosperity was not, and the heartland's peculiar prosperity branded the region's society and marked it off from the South's other subsocieties. As suggested in Chapters I and II, the heartland represented a third South, with agricultural riches rivaling those of the Black Belt but with fewer of the grand plantations characteristic of that region, and with pockets of slaveless yeomanry not unlike the highland South but withal a much greater incidence of slaveholding and

16   Charles Mison file, *ibid.;* Burgess, *Reminiscences*, 4–5.
17   E. K. Cook file, Civil War Questionnaires (Confederate).

good-sized farms than that poorer region could boast. Whatever inequalities white Middle Tennesseans perceived among themselves, they could also perceive that in their land both the very rich and the very poor were few and that the large majority in between lived affluently by the standards of most Southerners. (Even if it were true, as asserted by the aforementioned poor heartlander, that slaveholders scorned anyone worth less than a thousand dollars, in 1860 well over half of all free families in the region held at least that much property—surely a much higher proportion than in most other parts of the South.) This common awareness of shared abundance (however unequally shared) drew the vast majority of the white folk of the heartland together in a bountiful feast of celebration, a kind of worldly agape.

Furthermore, whatever obstacles to their upward progress some of the poor discerned, most Middle Tennesseans were persuaded by the prosperity evident all around them (and by Jacksonian rhetoric) that by sweat and perseverance any white man could scale society's ladder. A Nashvillian affirmed this article of faith in 1861 when he declared that, unlike his Yankee counterpart, the Southern white laborer was comfortable and well paid and confident that he could save money to buy slaves and eventually "relieve his wife from the necessities of the kitchen and the laundry, and his children from the labors of the field," or at least was certain that his sons could so succeed. Many leading men, he asserted (affirming a second tenet of popular faith), had risen from humble origins.[18]

Above all, however, though some Middle Tennesseans chafed at aristocratic condescension and grumbled at aristocratic slights, the typical common man benefited in small ways and large from the paternalism of the patriarchy and agreed tacitly that a hierarchical society was natural, inevitable, and right (as long as slavery and biracialism assured a place for him above society's bottom rung). A Wilson County man wrote that among the big slaveholders in his community "it was the custom to assist all poor boys making an honest effort by loaning them money and giving them advice." Another in Rutherford affirmed that local aristocrats "encouraged and advised [the lower class] both by precept and Example." Many heartlanders recounted instances of wealthy men sending provisions to their poorer neighbors free of charge or providing funds to send a poor boy to school or start his own farm or business. "My father bought a piece of land," recalled John Pickard, who grew up on a Maury County plantation, "and mother moved three or four poor families on it and they lived there for years without rent. How could [class relations] be unfriendly. Father called it 'Mary's poor farm.'" Theodore Harris of Lincoln undoubtedly

18 Nashville *Patriot*, January 24, 1861.

conveyed the sentiments of most white Middle Tennesseans when he declared that "the poore was not neglected [or] over looked in this part of the country. In fact the slave holder was good to the poore man."[19]

The white common folk of the heartland repaid aristocratic paternalism with deference, loyalty, and a more or less uncomplaining acceptance of economic and social inequality. A wealthy Robertson County plantation mistress recounted a conversation she had with a poor white man during the secession crisis of 1861: "He said there were many men in the country like himself they could read a little but not well enough to understand much of what they did read and so all they could do in politics was to follow what some other man who had more education said was right." "If any of the slave owners felt better than those that didn't own slaves," wrote George Wray, the son of a Sumner County yeoman-blacksmith, "We alowed them that privalage and did not push our selves on them." Most would have agreed with John D. Bryant, a nonslaveholder whose family farmed a fifty-acre plot in Lincoln County, that relations with aristocrats were "peecible": "We never did have any trouble with them . . . they was all ways good to the poor white people as far as I can say." The aristocracy that ruled Middle Tennessee white society did so on the whole by consent of the governed.[20]

In antebellum Middle Tennessee the tributaries of slavery, race, ruralism, prosperity, and patriarchy flowed together to form a broad river of ideology that ran undammed through all parts of white society, bringing justification to the rich and powerful along with comfort to the poor and powerless, hope to the ambitious along with contentment to the complacent, and to all a sense of quiet satisfaction with the present and assured optimism about the future.

"We hold it here that African Slavry is an ordinance of God": thus a Robertson County farmer in 1860 succinctly affirmed the salience of slavery in the lives of Middle Tennesseans. Slavery invaded every aspect of life in the heartland, acting reciprocally with other institutions, altering them, and in turn being altered—even transformed—by them. Wherever one turned in the antebellum heartland, the relationship of black bondsman to white master thrust itself into the line of vision.[21]

19 Jacob Young, Joseph P. J. Hoover, Robert E. B. Floyd, William G. Lillard, W. R. H. Matthews, John A. Pickard, and Theodore F. Harris files, Civil War Questionnaires (Confederate).

20 Jane S. Washington to George A. Washington, April 17, 1861, in Washington Family Papers, TSLA; George F. Wray and John D. Bryant files, Civil War Questionnaires (Confederate).

21 Daniel P. Braden to Andrew Johnson, January 10, 1860, in LeRoy P. Graf and Ralph W. Haskins (eds.), *The Papers of Andrew Johnson* (Knoxville, 1967–), III, 374.

The history of slavery in the heartland is inextricably entwined with the region's history as a whole, for slaves were among the first settlers there. Arduously they broke the virgin soil alongside their pioneer masters, and fruitfully they multiplied themselves over generations. But the early Middle Tennessee free folk shared the doubts and guilt about slavery that pervaded postrevolutionary America. Some worked to ameliorate or abolish it through societies for gradual emancipation and colonization, in which the Methodists—whose church officially opposed slavery—were especially active. Maury County in 1824 even spawned a radical antislavery association, the Moral Religious Manumission Society of West Tennessee, composed of nonslaveholders inspired by Christian piety. But the 1831 Nat Turner slave uprising in Virginia and wild rumors of armed and murderous slaves in the heartland in 1832 chilled the hearts of Middle Tennesseans; and alarm at the subsequent rise of radical abolitionism in the North conspired with awareness of slavery's economic importance to harden those hearts. Thereafter fear and practical necessity vanquished moral and religious principle. Antislavery advocates departed or were silenced, and no more was heard of emancipation in the heartland.[22]

The slave population of the region waxed steadily through the antebellum years, and the price of slaves rose as a revived agriculture demanded their toil. The proportion of slaves in the population grew as well, as the lure of the West drew away many white heartlanders. The triumph of slavery in thought and practice was consummated in Tennessee in 1855, when the state revoked its long-standing ban on the importation of slaves as merchandise. Nashville and other towns thereupon became nexuses of the interstate slave trade, and soon black chattels could be seen crowding the same wagons, steamboats, and railroad cars that bore southward the heartland's surplus corn and hogs.[23]

Even more so than the free people of the heartland, the unfree were an agrarian folk. Whether they worked the land, plied a craft, or waited on master and mistress in the big house, nearly all slaves lived on farms. (As Table II in the previous chapter indicated, only 7 percent lived in towns and 1 percent in villages; the rest were on farms.) Slavery in the heartland was thus closely bound to agriculture, and agriculture to slavery: half of all farms depended on black laborers—whether one, few, or many—and in general the bigger and more prolific the farm, the more dependent it was.

22   Asa Earl Martin, "The Anti-Slavery Societies of Tennessee," *THM*, I (1915), 261–81; James W. Patton, "The Progress of Emancipation in Tennessee, 1796–1860," *Journal of Negro History*, XVII (1932), 67–102.
23   Lewis C. Gray, *History of Agriculture in the Southern United States to 1860* (1933; rpr. New York, 1949), II, 648–67, 871–75.

Not all the richness of these farms was in their dark soil. Much of it was in their dark workers, whose skills with tools and crops and animals the farmers needed as they needed sun and rain. One may well understand, then, the plaintive lament of a Williamson County planter in 1857 after a series of deaths among his slaves: "It appears like I am under the frown of Providence for I am losing all my negroes and becoming poor. Lord help me to bear the misfortune without a murmur."[24]

The realities of farm life transfigured slavery just as slavery transfigured farm life. On the plantations, where implacable overseers rigorously and meticulously regimented the work force and great social distance separated master from slave, and, therefore, the strongest affirmation of the theoretically near-absolute power of the master might be expected, the slave's utter subjection was in practice tempered by circumstances. Ironically, the very dependence of the planter upon slave labor, which gave him wealth, power, and status, endowed his slaves with a measure, however small, of bargaining power. Most masters found it considerably more profitable in the long run to compromise with their laborers on such matters as working hours and food allotments than to try, by the unsparing use of the whip, to extract the maximum work at the minimum cost. (Bedford County former slave William Gant recalled his master, planter Jim Gant, as one who dealt reasonably with his "people" and "didn't whoop much. Give 'em three or four licks.") This practice was especially beneficial to the skilled slave artisan or driver or trusted house servant, who often used his position to win enviable privileges on the plantation. Too, the very possession of large numbers of slaves, strictly regulated and cloistered far from their aloof master—which distinguished the great, autocratic planter from the mere farmer—paradoxically removed those slaves in a sense from the planter's rule. It did so by fostering the evolution of a distinctive black culture in the slave quarters, a world within a world, into which the slaves stepped after sundown, sheltered for a time from the master's harsh command and the overseer's lash.[25]

On the smaller farms slaves lived singly or in small groups very close to their white families, working side by side with them in the fields, sharing chores, eating the same food, and often sleeping in the same room. Here the absolutism of slavery was checked by intimate, even familial, connection and affection. In his reminiscences of antebellum Davidson County farm life, Thomas B. Wilson spoke sincerely and unpatronizingly of his

---

24 Joseph B. Killebrew, *et al.*, *Introduction to the Resources of Tennessee* (Nashville, 1874), 841; Chase C. Mooney, *Slavery in Tennessee* (Bloomington, 1957), 177.
25 Rawick (ed.), *American Slave*, Ser. Two, Vol. IX (Ark.), Pt. 3, pp. 11–12.

few slaves as the "negro part of the family," one of whom, Uncle Wilkerson, "was a sort of foreman or boss as my father was rarely at home." Edwin Payne of Sumner County told of frequent visits to the home of a neighbor who "would read a [Bible] chaptr & have prear every night he would have the old negroes called in the Family Room while he held Family prear." And here, too, the slave was an integral constituent of that interdependence which underpinned the rural community: his master's lot, and that of his black and white neighbors, was the slave's lot, their bread his bread.[26]

This mutuality of interest between owner and owned was always qualified, however, and never fully reciprocal. Whether on a great plantation or small family farm, slavery rested fundamentally on compulsion. On the plantation this truth was naked and undisguised, and the whipping ceremony was a daily or weekly spectacle. On the farm it was obscured by the gloss of paternalism and intimacy, but it was nonetheless real. The near-limitless authority of master over slave (however moderated in practice), and the distinctions of race, kept blacks from full partnership in family or community. The white farmer helped his neighbor freely because he himself expected help freely given later on, and the mutual advantage was obvious. The slave did as he was told partly because the benefit to himself, his master, and his community was apparent and partly because he would be beaten or sold away if he refused. Thus the slave retained a curiously equivocal status: at once family member and work animal, community member and helot. The bonds of kinship and mutual reliance that tied together the rural free folk reached out around their slaves but were offset in a kind of Newtonian equipoise by the countervailing tension of the slave's physical subjugation—taut tethers ready to snap at the touch of an outside force.

Slaves inhabited the heartland's towns in lesser proportion than did the free people: only about one slave out of fourteen lived in town. Most who did were servants of the well-to-do, but some (perhaps as many as one-fourth in Nashville) were hired out to work in streets, shops, or factories. But for all, the towns offered a measure of independence that would have seemed to a country slave, bound closely to farm or plantation and under the watchful eye of master or overseer, like the next thing to freedom. Since a black walking the streets might be on any legitimate errand, white urbanites could not assume, as country folk did when spying a Negro off

26 Testimony of Edward H. East, Letters Received (Main Series), 1861–70, American Freedmen's Inquiry Commission, Preliminary and Final Reports, Records of the Office of the Adjutant General, Record Group 94, NA; Wilson Reminiscences, 15–16; Edwin S. Payne file, Civil War Questionnaires (Confederate).

the farm, that he was shirking work or running away. State law recognized this fact and softened restrictions on slaves traveling at large in towns. And since the size and bustle of the towns precluded minute surveillance of everyone's activities, slaves were able, despite state and local ordinances discouraging it, to fraternize regularly with free blacks and to taste a morsel of their freedom. This communion of Negroes free and slave, nurtured by the black church congregations in the towns, inspired a distinctive black urban subculture—yet another of those homogeneous entities within which self-conscious groups of urbanites sought sanctuary.[27]

The unseemly behavior of urban slaves was the most persistent complaint of whites in the towns. Clarksvillians, to judge from their frequent grumbling, were singularly vexed by black rascality. In March, 1860, the Clarksville *Chronicle* noted that frolicking Negroes were virtually taking over the town's omnibuses every Sunday afternoon and riding all over town. "Better stop the nigger line," was the editor's caustic advice to the omnibus officials, "if they want to establish a white-folks line." A few weeks later slaves buying liquor at the wharf raised the editor's hackles and evoked his condemnation of the "intolerable evil" of this "vile practice." Some months afterward he bewailed the prevalence of slaves living in town away from their masters and ruminated on the mischief provoked by such "darkey house-keeping." Those privileges so eagerly seized by urban blacks as tokens of their independence were to whites merely proofs of the degeneracy of inadequately controlled Negroes.[28]

Perturbed by the perceived breakdown of servile discipline, urban whites loudly demanded that slaves be policed. The only force capable of doing so (since urban slaveowners could not closely supervise their slaves) was civil authority, which thus by necessity assumed in the towns much of the master's responsibility for his servant, just as it replaced the rural community ethic, which found no footing among the factious urbanites. The Nashville Board of Aldermen formed a special committee to deal with the city's slave population. The Nashville police and the recorder's court (which disposed of misdemeanors) were kept busy by unruly slaves as well as unruly citizens. When, for example, the police apprehended Eli, Lin, and Willis throwing rocks at an Irishman one September night in 1860, the slaves were hauled directly before the recorder and sentenced to fifteen lashes apiece, promptly given them at the city's slave market. One may wonder whether their masters were even aware of the incident. In the countryside such a matter would have prompted the immediate interces-

27 Clement Eaton, "Slave-Hiring in the Upper South: A Step Toward Freedom," *MVHR*, XLVI (1960), 663–78; Tennessee General Assembly, *Code of Tennessee*, 505–506.
28 Clarksville *Chronicle*, March 9, 30, 1860, February 22, 1861.

sion of the slaves' owners to administer stripes to the slaves and apologies to the Irishman. Thus slavery helped transform the towns by stimulating the expansion of that civil power which characterized them, as surely as the towns transformed slavery by impairing the authority of the slave-owner and sustaining an insular black subculture.[29]

Law and formal authority visited the slave but rarely in the countryside, for his master stood always over him as lord and protector, interposed between government and chattel. Except in the most flagrant cases, the punishment of slave crimes and misdemeanors in the rural heartland was personal, informal, and summary—a matter of the master's prerogative, beyond the official ken of sheriff or judge. (The law permitted "moderate correction," though it professed to safeguard the slave's life and limb.) By the same token, aged or orphaned slaves never demanded the succor of the county court, for the master was charged with the care of his people, in sickness and in health, for as long as they lived.[30]

The law assumed that it was often unnecessary, barring unusual circumstances, to act directly on the slave. The slave code, long part of the corpus of law in every Southern state but strongly reinforced in Tennessee and elsewhere after 1831, did undertake to regulate in detail how the slave behaved, where he traveled, and whom he met—statutes that betrayed, of course, the nightmare vision of slave insurrection which lurked in the back of every white Southerner's mind. But the greater portion of these laws in fact coerced not slaves but whites, prohibiting any action by them that undermined control of the servile class: furnishing false passes to slaves, selling them liquor, harboring runaways, or any deed tending to "excite discontent" among the black masses. Even where the law compelled official supervision of slaves—every county was to maintain regular patrols, for example, to police slaves in the rural areas—it was very often ignored. Only two counties in the heartland (Davidson and Montgomery) had active patrols in 1860. The day-to-day regulation of slavery in the countryside, except in periods of emergency or panic, was a matter of master's whim and community custom.[31]

When law did intervene—most often in cases of serious slave crimes deemed a threat to the social order and in manumission proceedings—it regarded the slave not in light of civil law, which defined the bondsman as

29 Nashville *Daily Gazette*, September 1, 1860.

30 H. M. Henry, "The Slave Laws of Tennessee," *THM*, II (1916), 178; Tennessee General Assembly, *Code of Tennessee*, 502, 512.

31 Tennessee General Assembly, *Code of Tennessee*, 502–508, 510–11, 514–19; Henry, "Slave Laws," 180–181, 187–97, 202–203; Mooney, *Slavery in Tennessee*, 7–8, 10–18, 24, 27–28.

a chattel, but of common law, which endowed all persons with inalienable rights. In the courthouse, at least, the slave was elevated from a mere creature of his master's will to a "moral agent," made in God's image and knowing right from wrong, with rights as well as responsibilities; the slave stood before the law (in the words of the Tennessee Supreme Court) "not in the condition of a horse or an ox." Any slave charged with a serious offense was by law due a jury trial "in the same manner as that of a free person." In cases when slaves were manumitted by testament but procedural complications or the objections of heirs delayed execution of the will, the slave could sue for his freedom through a white "next friend." Thus the law complemented that social consensus which reckoned the slave something more than property, something less than citizen.[32]

Far from town and courthouse, however, the typical slave lived in a world shaped by the daily interplay of community, master, and slave. The social-religious community of the rural heartland embraced the slave as fellow Christian and fellow tiller of the soil. But as a rule it could do so only indirectly, through the agency (and with the consent) of the master, who stood between community and slave as he stood between slave and law. When, for example, the Wilson Creek Primitive Baptist Church cited Brother Sam to appear on charges of theft, it was with the stipulation that "his master ise willing." Thus the churches incorporated the master-slave relationship differently from the way they incorporated the white family. Church elders frequently stepped in to resolve quarrels between husband and wife (the session records are full of such incidents), but they hesitated when master and slave were at odds. The long history of the Zion Church of Maury County, for example, reveals but one case (in 1825) of a master accused of mistreating slaves.[33]

The rural church's social mission overshadowed even its godly tasks. Mundane actualities—the need to control slaves and compel them to work—prevailed over spiritual ideals of ecumenical Christian fellowship and the salvation of black souls. The words directed to the back pews on Sunday morning were more often injunctions to earthly docility than encouragements to spiritual fulfillment. As a Marshall County former slave remembered, the "preacher-man would git up dere en tell us 'Now you

32   Tennessee General Assembly, *Code of Tennessee*, 508–11, 520; Arthur F. Howington, "'Not in the Condition of a Horse or an Ox': Ford v. Ford, the Law of Testamentary Manumission, and the Tennessee Courts' Recognition of Slave Humanity," *THQ*, XXXIV (1975), 249–63.

33   Wilson Creek Primitive Baptist Church, Williamson County, Session Minutes, November, 1860; Mary W. Highsaw, "A History of Zion Community in Maury County, 1806–1860," *THQ*, V (1946), 135.

min' yo Marster en Missis en don' steal fum dem.'" The church was not so much a religious body held "captive" by a slaveholding culture, as some have described it, as it was an institutional expression, a precipitate, of the broad social realities of slavery, race, and ruralism.[34]

Nevertheless, the church community did affect slavery by frequently reminding the master of his spiritual kinship with the slave and by disciplining the slave—when the master permitted—to remind him of his responsibilities as a member of the communities of God and man. And in extraordinary circumstances the community at large asserted direct control over the slave, ignoring master, God, and law: a Sumner County slave who cut his owner's throat was hanged by a mob early in 1861, and the local newspaper applauded the "summary disposal" of the case. But slavery in return touched the community. By standing as a reminder that some matters lay above or below the purview of community consensus, slavery obliged free heartlanders to concede a place in their world for both personal volition and higher authority, for the will of the master as well as the constraints of law. When a Montgomery County overseer fatally shot a slave man in February, 1860, the Clarksville *Chronicle* insouciantly brushed the incident aside by announcing that it would "forbear giving particulars"; and when, at the opposite pole, the slave Alfred was ceremoniously executed in Fayetteville for the murder of his master, after taking his case to the state supreme court, the local newspaper crowed the citizens' self-congratulations for their "adherence to the forms of law in this case. The murder was of an aggravated kind, yet the people . . . allowed justice to take its tardy but certain course through the proper tribunals." Far more commonly, of course, the "proper tribunals" for slave misdeeds were defined not as the white man's courts but as the white man's conscience or consensus.[35]

The exclusion of slave men and women from full communion in any part of the culture of the heartland left a vacuum which they filled with a remarkable culture of their own. This eclectic black folk culture constituted a separate (though not wholly independent) world, which afforded its denizens some measure of the justice, the learning, the religious sodality, the family and communal bonds, and ultimately the sense of dignity and worth that were denied them or but meagerly offered in the various institutions of the white world.

The breeding ground of slave culture was in the limited autonomy, the

34   Rawick (ed.), *American Slave*, Ser. Two, Vol. XVI (Tenn.), 5–6.
35   Gallatin *Courier*, March 27, 1861; Clarksville *Chronicle*, February 3, 1860; Fayetteville *Observer*, March 7, 1861.

"breathing room" away from master, white community, and law, which the slaves carved out for themselves. The isolation of the plantation slave quarters and the quasi-independence of the urban black neighborhoods have already been cited. Slaves elsewhere—in villages and on small farms— had access to this culture through the church, which regularly brought together slaves from all over the community; and through camp meetings, where after whites ended services and retired to their tents, blacks emerged to celebrate with emotional song and prayer their spiritual and social affinity. Certain black secular gatherings, too, were sanctified by local custom and tolerated by paternalistic whites. The big "June Meeting," a day-long, outdoor festival, was an old tradition among Maury County slaves, and Negro soirees and suppers were familiar features of social life in the towns. And after sundown a clandestine black community stirred to life in every neighborhood (despite the best efforts of whites to stifle it), as slaves gathered furtively in woods or cabins to share their stories, their dreams, and their prayers.[36]

Within this subculture, which surrounded the slaves like a chrysalis and kept the constricting chains of slavery from suffocating them, the black family struggled to survive, black elders struggled to educate the young in the deep folk wisdom of the unlettered, the black faithful struggled to transmute the Christianity of obedience preached by their churches into a Christianity of liberation and fulfillment, and the black community as a whole struggled to raise up leaders. The triumphs and the limits of black culture are epitomized in Brother Jim, a slave owned by an officer of the Cumberland Presbyterian Church of Lebanon. Appointed pastor to the church's 150 blacks, Jim energetically ministered to them in their homes and in their chapel and made himself prominent and respected among them. Nevertheless, every Sunday he dutifully submitted the text of his sermon for the approval of the white minister, who also monitored the black service and was never disappointed at the "pure gospel" Jim preached. In 1859 Jim's ministry and membership were abruptly suspended when the church session found him guilty of fornication.[37]

Slaves recognized that they could manipulate their bondage within narrow bounds but could never assault it frontally with any hope of victory. Their acknowledgment of this blunt fact, conjoined with their success in fashioning an alternate world on earth, accounts—more than personal and

36 B. W. McDonnold, *History of the Cumberland Presbyterian Church* (Nashville, 1899), 433–34; Columbia *Herald*, June 10, 1870; Nashville *Daily Gazette*, September 12, 26, 1860; Rawick (ed.), *American Slave*, Ser. One, Vol. VI (Ind.), 53.

37 Historical Records Survey, *Cumberland Presbyterian Records*, II, 28, 31, 46–47, 49; McDonnold, *History of the Cumberland Presbyterian Church*, 432–33.

communal bonds between black and white, more than slavery's debasing effects on personality—for their overall accommodation to slavery. Resistance by slaves in the heartland (most often in the form of running away) was not unknown, but it was sporadic, short-lived, and generally reflected incidental, personal clashes between master and slave rather than any widespread revolutionary temperament among the enslaved masses. Rare was the master whose hands had not on occasion run off for an hour or a day after a whipping or an undeserved rebuke. But rare was the slave who dared go as far as one in Sumner County who, seeing an overseer beat the slave's mother, "picked up a chunk and that overseer stopped a'beating her." Not until the overwhelming physical power of master and community over the slave was stripped away by an intervening force could the potential rewards of radical, overt defiance outweigh, in the bondsman's mind, the threat of swift and savage retribution.[38]

The ambiguities and anomalies of slavery—its degraded victims who were yet to their masters rational beings, family and community members, legal and moral entities, and brothers in Christ; and its imperious masters who were yet to their slaves patriarchs, workmates, and fellow sinners before God—generated tensions that plagued antebellum heartlanders, white and black alike. The slave diffused his tension as far as possible in his black folk-world and in the day-to-day process of compromise with forces almost, but not quite, beyond his influence. Whites assuaged their stricken consciences by contriving a proslavery ethic and by bringing God into the slave quarters and assuaged their fears by whipping and hanging enough recalcitrant slaves to set an example for the rest. Some masters found paternalism a soothing balm, such as the Giles County lawyer, who, as he liberally doled out money for his slaves' provisions, joked that if his people "did not work more and get along better he would *stop practicing law for them.*" A few turned their paternalistic words into deeds, such as two maiden sisters in Sumner County, who in their 1858 wills freed their slaves and gave them all their property. Most slaveholders convinced themselves that their servants were, or should have been, grateful for the master's benevolence. "You know that we reared you as we reared our own children," wrote a hurt and uncomprehending Maury County woman to her runaway slave in the North, "you was never abused."[39]

38   Rawick (ed.), *American Slave*, Ser. One, Vol. VII (Okla.), 146.

39   Richard W. Johnson, *A Soldier's Reminiscences in Peace and War* (Philadelphia, 1886), 301–302; Charles C. Trabue, "The Voluntary Emancipation of Slaves in Tennessee as Reflected in the State's Legislation and Judicial Decisions," *THM*, IV (1918), 60; Herbert Aptheker (ed.), *A Documentary History of the Negro People in the United States* (1951; rpr. New York, 1969), I, 449–51.

To assess slavery dispassionately as an institution without illumining its tragic human dimension is to betray the ideal of historical understanding. Slavery in the heartland, however tempered by affection or conscience, was first and last a system of brutal exploitation of black people by white people, and the fruit it bore was ugly and bitter. That fruit was corrupted dignity: a Northerner in Pulaski (Giles County) wrote that he was "quite sure that in half the negro children I can see white blood. . . . This fact alone is enough to stamp slavery as an unholy & a scandalous thing—Licentiousness seems a natural result of slavery." That fruit was broken promises: "Ould John Kimbrow died some few months back," a Shelbyville man reported in 1860, "was blind and had lost nearly all his reason made his will and sat his negroes all free . . . but the Heirs broke the will and [the slaves] will be soled shortley." That fruit was mangled bodies: Annie Young, a slave on a Sumner County farm, watched as an overseer one day "staked a [slave] man down with two forked sticks 'cross his wrist nailed in de ground and beat him half to death with a hand saw 'til it drawed blisters. Den he mopped his back wid vinegar, salt and pepper. Sometimes dey'd drop dat hot rosin from pine knots on dose blisters." That fruit was sundered families: former slave Annie Griegg painfully retold in her old age how, not yet ten years old, she was sold away from her mother in Nashville for $100, sent to Arkansas, and never saw her family again.[40]

Ambiguity and tragedy also afflicted another of the heartland's human entities—the free black. Perhaps even more anomalous than the slave who was more than slave or the master who was more than master was this freeman who was less than free. In the heartland, free blacks numbered fewer than twenty-four hundred, most of them in Davidson County, most of those in Nashville, and most of those in one ward of the city. In the course of a typical day, most heartlanders never saw a free Negro. There were only twenty-three in all of Giles County, for example, and none at all in Cheatham, and even in the counties where they were more numerous they concentrated in the towns. But despite their rarity free blacks constantly troubled the minds of whites, who saw them as a moral denial of the beneficence of racial slavery and a provocative example to the slaves: in the words of some Wilson County citizens, "a pest to society generally, and a dangerous element in our midst."[41]

40 Elijah P. Burton, *Diary of E. P. Burton, Surgeon, 7th Reg. Ill.; 3rd Brig., 2nd Div., 16 A.C.* (Des Moines, 1939), 5; Joel Shoffner to Michael Shoffner, February 11, 1860, in Shoffner Papers; Rawick (ed.), *American Slave*, Ser. One, Vol. VII (Okla.), 359–60; *ibid.*, Ser. Two, Vol. IX (Ark.), Pt. 3, pp. 113–14.

41 *Statistics of Population, 1870,* 466–67; Legislative Petitions, 1860, No. 37.

If most whites were of one mind about free blacks, the law was of three. In some respects free blacks were equal before the law to any white. They could, for example, own property and bequeath it to their heirs. In other respects they were lumped with slaves: they were not citizens and could not vote or testify against whites in court, and they could receive lashes as legal punishment. But some laws set them apart as a distinct class, neither slave nor free. They were required, for example, to register annually with the county court and to carry their "freedom papers" at all times. The poor laws that provided aid for indigent whites stipulated that destitute free blacks could be hired out by the county. Increasingly through the antebellum period (and concurrently with the tightening of the slave code) public attitudes and official enactments discouraged free blacks from entering or remaining in the state. By the 1850s state law required that any slave thereafter manumitted be removed to Africa. Magnanimously, the legislature permitted any freed slave wishing to avoid removal to reenslave himself voluntarily, but apparently no black heartlander ever seized that opportunity.[42]

In their day-to-day existence, however, free blacks ameliorated the harshness of law and white animosity, as did their enslaved brothers, by accommodation and compromise; and they succeeded in finding a place—however cramped—in a world that sought to deny them a place. Some whites were sympathetic, and local custom more than law usually determined the extent to which annual registration, the carrying of papers, and deportation were actually enforced. Some free blacks were thus able, by manifesting the required deference, and perhaps by putting themselves under the patronage of friendly whites, to live unbothered in the countryside. Most, however, migrated to the towns, where—though generally poor, illiterate, and relegated to menial labor and domestic work—they found fulfillment mingling with slaves in the urban black subworld. Some mastered trades and achieved a measure of prosperity and independence, and a few rose to prominence in the professions. Peter Lowery, for one, purchaser of his own freedom, successful businessman, and minister of Nashville's independent black Christian congregation, was one of the antebellum South's outstanding black leaders. Given the paucity of their numbers, however, it was the symbolic role of free blacks which defined their true importance in the antebellum heartland. For white and slave alike, free blacks stood as a

---

42 James M. England, "The Free Negro in Ante-Bellum Tennessee," *JSH*, IX (1943), 37–58; Tennessee General Assembly, *Code of Tennessee*, 502, 517–18, 520–28; Henry, "Slave Laws," 193–201.

challenge—for the one a baneful, for the other a welcome, challenge—to the received wisdom of racial ideology.[43]

Race and class, freedom and bondage, wealth and power, land and institutions, faith and ideology, work and culture, family and community: the intricate interrelationship of all these defined the social world of Middle Tennesseans in the late antebellum era. It is time now to examine the events that destroyed that world and brought forth a new one to take its place.

43   England, "Free Negro," 55–57; Herman A. Norton, *Tennessee Christians: A History of the Christian Church in Tennessee* (Nashville, 1971), 129–30.

Chapter IV

Those Whom the Gods Destroy

Fear, Secession, and War, 1860–1862

I T IS one of the ironies of the Southern experience that in the very hour of the region's greatest public optimism and self-assurance, external and internal forces were conspiring to overturn the Southern world. White Middle Tennesseans had begun to sense the danger by 1860, even as they congratulated themselves on the sublimity and solidity of their society and the radiance of their future.

A generation of sectional political strife and mounting Southern alienation culminated dramatically, to many incredibly, during the seventeen months from October, 1859, to February, 1861, which witnessed John Brown's Harpers Ferry raid, the election of Abraham Lincoln, the secession of South Carolina and all the Lower South, and the establishment of the Confederate States of America. Increasingly through this period Middle Tennesseans were swept up in a torrent of political excitement unlike anything they had known, even in this land where the citizenry traditionally battened themselves on politics as zestfully as on their cornbread, meat, and whiskey. Politics was on every tongue, the latest news from Washington and Nashville eagerly awaited and ravenously devoured. A veteran Clarksville political observer at a public meeting in January, 1861, found the Montgomery County courthouse "jammed with one of the most excited crowds I ever saw." A Maury countian in early February invoked and misquoted the Bard in describing the turbulent state of affairs: "'Bubble, Bubble, Toil and Trouble,'" he wrote, "has been the order of the day for the last three months."[1]

1   Charles O. Faxon to Andrew Johnson, January 15, 1861, in Graf and Haskins (eds.),

Underlying all the ferment and the impassioned rhetoric of these months was profound anxiety. In the eyes of many white Middle Tennesseans, the nomination and election of a Republican president who opposed the spread of slavery, along with the verbal (and now physical) attacks of abolitionists who condemned the institution and its advocates, together constituted a dire threat to three of the underpinnings of the Southern way of life—slavery, white supremacy, and the patriarchal society. A letter to a Nashville newspaper in January, 1860, reaffirmed the credo of the white South and summarized with a familiar metaphor the interpretation read into recent events by uneasy Middle Tennesseans: "The position of the white and black races, as it exists among us, cannot be changed by fanaticism or by Black Republicanism. It exists, in obedience to the laws of nature. . . . No foreign power pretends to disturb our quiet on this subject; but a worthless crusade is waged by a portion of our own household, upon this 'domestic relation.'. . . This institution must and ought to be preserved; and the best mode of meeting this assault upon our rights is a question of moment."[2]

Such apprehensions, of course, blanketed the entire South in this period, but in Middle Tennessee they were exacerbated by peculiar economic problems that simultaneously imperiled society's other foundations—prosperity and the integrity of rural life. Drought struck the heartland in the summer of 1860. Crops withered in the fields, harvests fell short, barns earlier crammed with surpluses emptied; in a few areas there was actual want. Reverberations sounded throughout the economy, bound as it was so intimately to the soil. A Nashville merchant pronounced "all business and financial matters gloomy indeed in middle Tennessee." In Maury County a newspaper editor discussed the epidemic of debt default and predicted that "until another crop is made . . . the sheriff's hammer will resound more frequently than is desirable within the sound of our Court House."[3]

With the cornerstones of their society thus seemingly battered and undermined, Middle Tennesseans saw their optimism turn slowly to doubt. A Sumner County teacher floridly echoed this mood in his diary entry for January 1, 1861: "Another year is inaugurated today. . . . What will its panoramic views disclose, as they pass successively before us? What will be the history of my afflicted country for the next twelve months? Will it

---

Papers of Andrew Johnson, IV, 170–71; L. J. Polk to Emily, February 1, 1861, in Polk-Yeatman Papers, SHC.

2   Nashville *Daily Gazette,* January 8, 1860.

3   Nashville *Patriot,* September 11, 1860; Alexander J. D. Thurston to Andrew Johnson, March 11, 1861, in Graf and Haskins (eds.), *Papers of Andrew Johnson,* IV, 383–84, 384n.; Columbia *Mirror,* quoted in Fayetteville *Observer,* October 25, 1860.

be a record of disasters and revolutions? . . . What shall be the end of all this, we know not."[4]

As the national crisis deepened, doubt turned to trepidation, trepidation to fear, and fear to near-hysteria, which as it intensified also became more sharply focused. Even as they peremptorily proclaimed the loyalty and docility of their slaves, white Middle Tennesseans became convinced that the ultimate consequence of unchecked Republicanism, abolitionism, and sectional agitation would be a bloody slave uprising. A Maury County planter declared in February, 1861, that "a servile rebellion . . . is more to be feared now than [it] was in the days of the Revolution against the mother country. *Then* there were no religious fanatics to urge our slaves to deeds of rapine, murder, &c.—now the villainous blood hounds of Abolitionism will glory in gloating in the blood of the 'Slave Drivers' and turn loose upon us the very worse material in our midst." An anonymous correspondent of a Clarksville paper asserted that if civil war came, Southerners would face "two powerful and blood-thirsty foes, the one without and the other within"; he advocated a statewide patrol system, which by a show of force and "a few examples of shooting judiciously executed" would overawe the restless slaves and prevent "a fate to our wives and children equal to the sacking of a city by barbarians." This scheme, he blandly advised his readers, held both practical and humane advantages over that proposed by others to "massacre the slave population, at the first note of civil war, as a measure of self defence."[5]

Local incidents small and great also fed the burgeoning fears of white Middle Tennesseans in these months. A rash of fires broke out in Nashville, Clarksville, and elsewhere in 1860, and in almost every case "some devilish incendiary" was blamed, as often as not a "refractory" Negro. The entire region was aroused in March, 1861, when a Sumner County master was murdered by his slave, who died promptly at the hands of a lynch mob. On three occasions in 1860 public furor exploded when "suspicious" white men were overheard uttering antislavery sentiments or were caught associating too intimately with blacks. Two in Nashville were deemed outright abolitionists and ordered out of town with the threat of tar and feathers. One of these culprits had reportedly worked undetected for months in the guise of a minister and corresponded seditiously with the North. "Let the people of the South be diligent in watching him," the Nashville *Daily Gazette* urged, "and all others of his ilk."[6]

4   Francis M. Carmack Diary, January 1, 1861 (MS in SHC).

5   L. J. Polk to Emily, February 1, 1861, in Polk-Yeatman Papers; Clarksville *Jeffersonian*, January 18, 1860.

6   Clarksville *Chronicle*, April 6, July 27, 1860; Nashville *Patriot*, March 26, 1861; Nashville *Daily Gazette*, January 25, April 10, 17, November 18, December 1, 1860.

Many of the deeply brewing apprehensions of white Middle Tennesseans surfaced in the Nashville "Express Negro" episode, the local public
sensation of the spring of 1860. On April 17 the newspapers reported that
a large box shipped from the city two days earlier by Adams Express had
broken open in Indiana, revealing a smuggled slave, Alec, the property of
a Nashville man. City police quickly arrested the drayman (a slave) who
had delivered the box to the express company, and a free black whom the
drayman named as an accomplice. Authorities returned Alec and the black
driver of the express wagon to the city, whereupon Alec implicated another slave and (to the immense consternation of Nashvillians) a white
man, who was never found. Investigation revealed that the box had been
addressed to a Cincinnati mercantile firm that was "not at all sound on the
negro question." ("They are now spotted, at least so far as Southern
people are concerned," the *Daily Gazette* warned.) When the box was
hauled back to Nashville and displayed at the express company office,
large and excited crowds turned out to see the curiosity, "carefully scrutinizing its dimensions, marks, odor, &c." [7]

Fear of enemies without, fear of conspirators and traitors within, fear of
slave unrest and the unholy collusion of slaves and free blacks all were laid
bare by the Express Negro case. How much of this and other sensational
affairs was genuine and how much merely a phantom concoction of para-
noid minds can never be known. Whether grounded in fact or fantasy,
however, these incidents are revealing, for they illuminate starkly the
writhings of an ideology under siege.

The more firmly Middle Tennesseans persuaded themselves that the foe
was at their gates and within their walls, the more they turned to the task
of reinforcing their fortress battlements and assuring the security of the
keep and the safety of its beleaguered defenders. Volunteer military companies sprang up around the region: Davidson, Williamson, and Maury
counties boasted showy uniformed cohorts by the summer of 1860. These
were ostensibly political marching clubs, but some like the Bell Greys of
Davidson reorganized in the wake of Lincoln's election "on a neutral and
permanent basis." The election results spawned new companies in several
counties, their militancy now boldly declared. The Maury Guards, for example, organized in Columbia in late November "as an encouragement of
the military spirit among us, and . . . for the permanent defence of the
county." [8]

Controlling the black population became an even greater concern than
military preparedness by late 1860, as the racial anxieties of white heart-

7 Nashville *Daily Gazette*, April 17, 20, 26, 27, 1860; Nashville *Patriot*, April 19, 1860.
8 Nashville *Daily Gazette*, August 2, 11, November 10, 21, December 1, 1860.

landers continued to fester. Noting apprehensively the approach of Christmas—traditionally a time of relaxed discipline for slaves—the editor of the Fayetteville *Observer* urged the reactivation of the dormant patrol system in Lincoln County. "While we do not learn of any misgivings as to continued quiet hereabouts," he wrote, "yet the news that is frequently reaching us of attempted insurrectionary movements elsewhere, are a warning." The Maury County court revived the patrol in that county early in 1861 and levied a special tax on slave property to maintain it. The Davidson County patrol, active throughout 1860, redoubled its vigilance in the winter of 1861, invading the cabins of slaves and free blacks and seizing an occasional gun, knife, or powder flask.[9]

In other places citizens rode as informal patrols, endeavoring to spread terror among the supposedly mutinous slaves and their coconspirators. A Rutherford County woman described in 1863 the temper of the times three years earlier in her rural neighborhood: "If a negro was found away from home without a pass he was taken up and whipped or beat most cruelly with a paddle or a leather strap and stripped naked at that[.] patrollers were out all night watching. The martial law was in force and any one was punished who was seen conversing with a negro." But some whites put their trust in renewed moral suasion rather than increased physical force to keep blacks in line. Across the region, churches, for example, devoted more attention to the religious instruction of black members and debated more earnestly the nature of their mission to the slaves.[10]

Racial nightmares haunted townsfolk, for urban blacks exercised considerable independence and freedom of movement. The Clarksville city council moved toward restricting that independence in February, 1861, with an ordinance prohibiting slaves in the town from living apart from their masters. A Nashville newspaper editor, troubled by the growing number of quasi-independent slave artisans, went so far as to urge masters and lawmakers to ban slaves from skilled trades and restrict them to positions more readily supervised and less competitive with white labor. "The proper field for slave labor," he declared, "is agricultural pursuits and menial service."[11]

A more sinister threat than the slaves in the eyes of some white heart-

9   Fayetteville *Observer*, October 18, 1860; Maury County, Tennessee, County Court Clerk's Office, Minute Books, January 7, April 1, 1861, Vol. XIII, 328, 435 (Microfilm copy in TSLA); Davidson County Court Minutes, January 7, April 1, 1861, Bk. H, 580, 644.

10   Jane C. Warren to Electa Ames, August 27, 1863, in Electa Ames Papers, DUL; First Presbyterian Church, Clarksville, Session Minutes, Vol. II, May 8, June 1, 1860.

11   Clarksville *Chronicle*, February 22, 1861; Nashville *News*, quoted in Fayetteville *Observer*, March 1, 1860.

landers was the free blacks, long abominated but now sometimes viewed as the critical link between seditious abolitionists and disaffected slaves. "They are a source of discontent among slaves," wrote a correspondent to a Nashville paper, "they are the channel through which our household enemies may reach the slave with evil suggestions, and thus increase the dangers lately shown at Harper's Ferry." Free blacks fell increasingly under suspicion through 1860, especially in Nashville, where they numbered in the hundreds. By November the city council was sufficiently concerned to pass a resolution to "ascertain the number of free negroes in the city, their rights to remain here, &c." In December the city marshal and his deputies raided an eatery run by two free blacks, which had become a Sunday gambling hangout; the officers rounded up at least twenty Negroes whom they caught with whiskey and cards. The newspaper noted that the culprits had been suspect for several weeks, and "their movements have been closely watched." The following January, Wiley, a recently emancipated slave, petitioned the Davidson County court for permission to remain in Tennessee under a proviso of state law and offered to post the required bond. Though in the recent past such requests had been granted, now the court demurred and ordered Wiley out of the state.[12]

More slowly than their fellows in the Deep South, but nonetheless surely, some white Middle Tennesseans arrived at the certainty that the only real security against black enemies at home and white enemies at the gates lay in secession. Early in 1861 a Nashville proslavery advocate prophesied that emancipation would inevitably follow the Republican assumption of power and, being "unwilling to see [slavery's] speed retarded or its abolition worked out among us," he called for the immediate secession of Tennessee, with or without the rest of the Upper South. Some, having reluctantly accepted the necessity of secession, began to work actively for it and even welcomed further abolitionist outrages as a goad to conservative Southerners. "I think a few more Such developments as Browns Revelations, would do more good for the South," wrote a Robertson County farmer, "than a twelve month Seshion of debates would do in Congress. 'Old vanwincle' has awoke Out of his twenty years Sleep."[13]

Despite the radical persuasion of some white Middle Tennesseans, however, and the misgivings of nearly all, political conservatism reigned in the heartland through 1860 and the winter of 1861. Most remained convinced, even after Lincoln's election and the secession of the Lower South, that the

12 Nashville *Daily Gazette*, January 8, November 21, December 11, 1860; Davidson County Court Minutes, January 11, 1861, Bk. H, 586.

13 Nashville *Patriot*, January 24, 1861; Daniel P. Braden to Andrew Johnson, January 10, 1860, in Graf and Haskins (eds.), *Papers of Andrew Johnson*, III, 373–75.

drastic measures necessary to neutralize the undeniable threats to the Southern way of life were better taken within the Union than outside of it. Repeatedly heartlanders denounced fire-eating secessionism as stupidity or insanity engendered by the triumph of hot passion over cool reason. One drew on a martial simile to make his case: "To go out of the Union to fight for our rights would be like the commander of a fortress going outside of his walls to fight mutineers who were left within, with all the advantage of arms, and works, while the commander exposed himself in the open field. We might possibly admire the bravery of the man, but what would we think of his judgment?" A Williamson County state legislator castigated abolitionism and secessionism in the same breath; both, he sneered, "are the remedies of political quacks." Other heartlanders were yet more blunt. A Nashville lawyer declared that "the course pursued by South Carolina [is] one of madness, demented folly."[14]

Many conservatives espied in secessionism a plot by a clique of ambitious politicians to dupe the masses and seize power. A Williamson County planter condemned the secessionist ringleaders of the Deep South "with their madness for place and position." A few compromise amendments to the Constitution might, he believed, "deprive [such] Politicians of *food* to *feast* upon, to elevate themselves to office, such as the 'Negro' question, 'Territorial' question, &c., but they will in their corrupt and fruitful imagination, find out something else to Demagogue or mislead an unsuspecting People!"[15]

Some conservatives sought to allay the burgeoning racial phobias of their fellow whites. In November, 1860, the editor of the Nashville *Patriot* ridiculed a widely circulating "cock and bull story" about an imminent, abolitionist-led slave insurrection: "The thing is too absurd to deceive any one having an ounce of brains. . . . Let the people of Tennessee be on guard. No means will be left untried to alarm their fears, in a crisis like the present." Soon after the presidential election a Nashvillian published a plea for moderation and denounced the rising tide of antiabolitionist mob violence in the South. The specter of abolitionists massing to invade the South like a barbarian horde was a chimera, he pointed out: they would have to "sneak through the land with cautious tread" and could corrupt no

14 O. N. Chapin to Andrew Johnson, December 20, 1860, in Graf and Haskins (eds.), *Papers of Andrew Johnson*, IV, 58; Nashville *Patriot*, January 11, 1860; A. Waldo Putnam to Andrew Johnson, December 22, 1860, in Graf and Haskins (eds.), *Papers of Andrew Johnson*, IV, 73–74.

15 John S. Claybrooke to [?], February 25, 1861, in Claybrooke and Overton Papers, TSLA.

one. And besides, he added, "Our slaves are well cared for, and *they know it*: They also know that their *masters are their only and their best friends*." [16]

Despite reasoned disquisitions and calm reassurances, however, conservatives shared the fundamental convictions and fears that inspired every white heartlander. All recognized slavery and white supremacy as the groundsills of society, and all saw that foundation violently buffeted by recent events. But conservatives and secessionists were divided by their conflicting interpretations of the ultimate source of the danger. Secessionists believed that Northern abolitionists were working—through both law and revolution—to overthrow slavery and that the longer the South stayed in the Union the more certain was that outcome. Conservatives envisioned an identical phantasmagoria of bloody servile rebellion but saw it as the result of continued agitation by extremists of both North and South. The Clarksville *Chronicle* censured a fire-eating election speaker for his all-too-graphic portrayal of the horrors of a slave uprising, delivered before a local audience which included blacks: "It is no sufficient apology to say that he was only pointing out the effects of Republican policy. . . . [Such a speech] prompts negroes to fly to free States, stirs up insubordination, and suggests murder, and one such man . . . does more mischief than a thousand Black Republicans. Had a Northern man made such a speech here, he would have been lynched." [17]

Moderation and compromise were the true safeguards of slavery, conservatives insisted, and those could be achieved only by stifling hotheads and by staying in the Union. Secession would mean war, and the consequences of war were dreaded by secessionists and conservatives alike. A Nashville unionist summed it up pointedly and prophetically in December, 1860: "Secession is the short Cut to abolitionism." [18]

Through the hectic autumn of 1860 and winter of 1861, and even into early spring, Middle Tennessee unionists remained sanguine, for the people of the region and the state repeatedly reaffirmed their conservatism. A bill to expel free blacks from the state had gone down in defeat in the legislature in February, 1860. Voters in the heartland chose their favorite son, the moderate former Whig John Bell, by a slight margin over the Southern-rights candidate John C. Breckinridge in the November presidential election. A February, 1861, plebiscite on the subject of a state convention to consider secession sparked a great fulmination of unionism in the heart-

16   Nashville *Patriot*, November 1, 28, 1860.
17   Clarksville *Chronicle*, September 28, 1860.
18   William R. Hurley to Andrew Johnson, December 23, 1860, in Graf and Haskins (eds.), *Papers of Andrew Johnson*, IV, 74–75.

land and across the state; "Tennessee has indeed spoken in thunder tones," an exultant Shelbyville conservative proclaimed. When Marshall County unionists assembled on April 2, an old Whig among them rejoiced at the optimism that pervaded the meeting: "Struck with the harmony and zeal that seamed to beam from evry eye," he wrote, "I acosted some old weather beaten democrats that I had been fighting for nearly twenty years, and said to them we have at last met on a common platform *the Union* & herd the reply yes the Union fo[re]ver."[19]

Ten days later, with the bombardment of Fort Sumter, the unionists' tower of hope and faith came crashing down. War was now a reality, and Lincoln's subsequent call for troops to coerce the seceded states made neutrality impossible. Faced with two all but unthinkable choices—to make war on the Union or to make war on the South—Middle Tennesseans overwhelmingly resolved to join hands with the seceders to defend the South.

For most the change of heart came almost literally overnight, so forceful was the shock of Sumter. A Nashville woman wrote on April 19 that the city "is in a perfect uproar, nothing is thought of or talked of . . . but the coming struggle. . . . Every night speeches are made and the union men are fast disappearing by becoming secessionists." On the sixteenth a delirious public assembly in Clarksville—including a number of the town's leading men, who were without exception erstwhile conservatives—resolved for immediate secession; the next day the Confederate flag unfurled over the Montgomery County courthouse. A witness in Davidson County, who was later asked to give an account of what he saw, could only reply that he would "not pretend to undertake to describe the state of things when this rebellion first broke out in Tennessee, but no man who was not there will ever comprehend it. Never." The statewide referendum on June 8, in which heartlanders voted 37,262 to 1,927 for secession, was an anticlimax: Middle Tennessee had been effectively out of the Union for almost two months.[20]

The course of secession reaffirmed the primacy of race over class as a social force in the heartland. Despite the later asseverations of a few North-

19 Mary E. R. Campbell, *The Attitude of Tennesseans Toward the Union, 1847–1861* (New York, 1961), 130–33, 175–76, 285–86, 289–90; Joseph H. Thompson to Andrew Johnson, February 10, 1861, in Graf and Haskins (eds.), *Papers of Andrew Johnson*, IV, 269–70; J. D. Johnson to G. W. Gordon, April 3, 1861, in George W. Gordon and William T. Avery Papers, TSLA.

20 Annie R. Maney to Bettie Kimberly, April 19, 1861, in John Kimberly Papers, SHC; Clarksville *Chronicle*, April 19, 1861; testimony of Russell Huston (1863), in *OR*, Vol. XVI, Pt. 1, p. 501; Campbell, *Attitude of Tennesseans*, 205–206, 292–93.

erners and die-hard unionists, there is no good evidence that slaveholding aristocrats for their own selfish purposes tricked, cajoled, or browbeat the ignorant, ingenuous common folk into following them out of the Union. Middle Tennesseans high and low were on the whole conservative until Fort Sumter but turned radical in the main thereafter, executing a *volte-face* so instantaneous as to negate the possibility of aristocratic manipulation. Only a fierce jolt to a society's ideological nervous system could provoke such a reaction. The great majority of white heartlanders of every rank shared a common nervous system, were simultaneously galvanized by the events in Charleston harbor, perceived as with one pair of eyes a mortal threat to their racist, slaveholding society, and subsequently marched shoulder to shoulder into the ranks of the rebels. The Clarksville *Chronicle* described with some hyperbole the scene just after the news of Sumter burst upon Montgomery County: "Every class and condition, every age and sex, united in glorification of the event. . . . Whatever differences of opinion may have existed, heretofore, there were *none now*, and but one single heart seemed to animate the entire town, and that heart to throb under one single impulse of patriotic exultation!"[21]

In the hothouse atmosphere of the weeks following Fort Sumter the frenzy and paranoia that had sprouted in the preceding months proliferated like rank weeds. "Every body is and has been in a state of the most intense excitement," a Murfreesboro girl recorded in her diary in July. "The War is the all absorbing topic of conversation and of letters." "Farmers, look to your safety," cautioned the Fayetteville *Observer* in a May 2 editorial urging the arming of every household: "The times are uncertain. Black Republicanism is bent on war and insurrection. . . . You should organize patrols in every neighborhood, and see that all trampers give an account of themselves." A later column warned of "Northern spies scattered throughout the South. . . . Look out for them."[22]

Under the dual impetus of war and fear, Middle Tennessee became an armed camp. Young men flocked to the colors, and volunteer companies by the dozens mustered and marched off to training camps in the region to prepare to defend the South against Yankee invaders. Those left behind poured nearly as much spirit, energy, and treasure into the defense of the heartland against enemies at home, giving free rein now to their nightmarish anxieties about the menace within. Under mandate of a hurriedly

21   Clarksville *Chronicle*, April 19, 1861. Assertions of the class basis of secessionism are in Burgess, *Reminiscences*, 13, 16; testimony of Marc Mundy (1863), in *OR*, Vol. XVI, Pt. 1, p. 633; report of J. J. Reynolds, February 10, 1863, *ibid.*, Vol. XXIII, Pt. 2, pp. 54–55.

22   C. Alice Ready Diary, July 15, 1861 (Typescript in SHC); Fayetteville *Observer*, May 2, June 27, 1861.

enacted state law, every county began in May or June to organize, equip, and drill home guards—"minute men" they were called in these weeks of revolutionary fervor. The Cheatham County court concurrently appointed commissioners to "employ good Gun Smiths to repair all the guns in the County that need repairing," and the Robertson County court ordered its justices to enumerate all shotguns, rifles, and muskets in their respective districts. Towns across the region reinforced their police squads—Clarksville doubled its own before the end of April. Not content to wait for official measures, some Middle Tennesseans frantically organized extralegal vigilante groups almost as the smoke cleared from Fort Sumter: the Nashville Committee of Vigilance and Safety offered its services to the city as early as April 27.[23]

These guardians of domestic tranquillity, whether constituted legally or extralegally, formally or informally, moved immediately to secure the heartland against supposed enemies within the household. In the process, and with the support of an increasingly apprehensive and intolerant public temperament, they assumed vast powers in their neighborhoods and in some cases established a virtual tyranny. The Norris Creek Home Guards of Lincoln County declared themselves pledged to "the purpose of protecting our homes and firesides from the aggression and unholy crusade of Abe Lincoln and his army, and for the protection of our home from secret enemies, whether they be negro insurrectioners, abolition emissaries, or home traitors," and to those ends asserted their right and determination to arrest, try, and punish anyone suspected of treachery or insurrection. In Bedford County a man who ran afoul of home guards and vigilantes reported in June that "a perfect reign of terror has existed among us for some weeks."[24]

From the welter of private fears and public threats, haunting apparitions and dark prophecies, there emerged a common theme: the heartland could be preserved through this crisis, many concluded, only by the absolute, unremitting unity in thought and spirit of its people. "Let us stand together as a band of brothers," the editor of the Nashville *Patriot* pleaded, "and when the work is accomplished, and we are a free and independent

23   Clarksville *Chronicle*, April 19, 26, 1861; Gallatin *Courier*, April 17, 1861; Nashville *Patriot*, April 19, 21, 23, 28, 1861; Cheatham County, Tennessee, County Court Clerk's Office, Court Minute Books, June 3, July 1, August 7, 1861, Vol. B, 167–69, 181, 188–89 (Microfilm copy in TSLA); Robertson County, Tennessee, County Court Clerk's Office, County Court Minutes, May 13, 1861, Vol. XIV, 624–26 (Microfilm copy in TSLA). A good sense of the excitement and activity in this period is conveyed in the journal of Maury County farmer James W. Matthews, May 4, 8, 22, June 22, 29, August 10, 16, 31, 1861.

24   Fayetteville *Observer*, May 16, August 22, 1861.

people, then we can afford to differ . . . but for God's sake, have no quarrel sooner." Another heartlander cautioned, "No society or government can long remain where the people are divided and distracted by discordant sentiments. . . . Let party names be done away. . . . We should avoid the rock on which many thousands have made shipwreck. 'A prudent man foreseeth the evil, and hideth himself; but the simple pass on, and are punished.'" The citizens of Boone Hill, in Lincoln County, invoked a less elegant but pithier maxim when they met in May to organize their home guard: "He who is not for us," they warned, "is against us."[25]

Indeed, in those ebullient weeks the spark of patriotic unity kindled by the news of Sumter appeared to wax to a glorious blaze. On May 1 sixty-two-year-old James Matthews rode into Columbia, shouldered a musket, and marched alongside the young men in one of the volunteer companies drilling there. In June, Fayetteville boys under military age—some as young as twelve—formed their own company and paraded. Similarly inspiring scenes were cheered all across the region. "Our people are now united," the Fayetteville *Observer* announced; "political barriers are broken down, and but one spirit, a determination to protect Southern homes and defend Southern honor, animates all."[26]

Those who proclaimed such sentiments as the *Observer*'s, however, either were dissembling for patriotic purposes or were blinded by the dazzle of jingoistic effusions. Whether the consummate unanimity they celebrated was lie, myth, or mirage, their people were in truth divided, and most of them discerned the rift, acknowledged it, loathed it, and feared it. Despite the shock of Sumter and the overwhelming reversal of opinion, a small number of heartlanders remained resolutely opposed to secession. Some were prominent and influential leaders, such as Jordan Stokes of Lebanon and Robert S. Northcott, editor of the Murfreesboro *Telegraph*. These indomitable unionists, whose political principles held fast amid the ideological tidal wave of April, were few; but in the eyes of the majority, their meager numbers did not mitigate the threat they posed to the sacred unity of the people demanded in this parlous hour. As the unionists stubbornly persisted in the weeks after Sumter, the high-minded call for unity degenerated into a vicious crusade to crush the dissenters.

Across the heartland angry, fearful men and women turned the power of psychological and physical coercion against any hint of defiance. "Several persons have been sent off or promised a coat of tar & feathers with a lighted match a little closer than would be agreeable," a Nashville woman

25 Nashville *Patriot*, July 6, August 9, 1861; Fayetteville *Observer*, May 16, 1861.
26 Matthews Journal, May 1, 1861; Fayetteville *Observer*, April 25, June 6, 1861.

wrote on April 27. "Mrs McEwen has her union flag still waving. . . . She refuses to take it down, but that . . . will not be tolerated and her flag will soon be taken down for her." A Bedford County unionist wrote acridly after the war of his travail in 1861: "I with the few Union men were denounced by the Rebels as being traitors, Abolitionists and black republicans, and every vile epithet that a wicked heart could imagine & a bitter tongue express and some of those persons who call themselves Christians indulged freely in the abuse." "A Union man is looked upon as the verriest enemy on earth," a Bedford County minister wrote in June; "I have been threatened with the halter, and am now a marked subject for future operations." Bitterly he cursed his tormentors as he affirmed his own certainty of ultimate vindication: "One truth remains—God is judge and He has a purpose to fulfil. Those whom the Gods destroy, they first make mad."[27]

The repudiation of political dissent and the persecution of the otherwise-minded marked an ominous departure in the heartland. Though free debate on sensitive racial issues had, of course, been silenced for a generation, popular politics in Middle Tennessee had long remained vibrant, expansive, and exuberantly competitive because all participants implicitly professed the fundamental social creed. But democracy died in Middle Tennessee in April, 1861, at the hands of an ideology driven frantic by fear for its own life. Confronting a sword seemingly poised to eviscerate their society, and reckoning a political maneuver—secession—their only shield, heartlanders came to identify the political unity theretofore unattainable and unnecessary with the ideological unity now more than ever compulsory. Those few who declined to make that identification felt the hysterical wrath of the many who did make it, and the victims sensed what a profound transformation had been wrought in their land. A Bedford County unionist wrote that the furious abuse heaped on him by his secessionist neighbors "convinced me that they ware my personal enemies as well as my political enemies, and the horrid wishes too that was hurled against the Union people was shocking to humanity . . . all prooveing deepe personal animosity."[28]

The ideological implications of the defection of the unionists, especially of those who were among the heartland's leaders, most deeply disturbed

27   Annie R. Maney to Bettie Kimberly, April 27, 1861, in Kimberly Papers; William Taylor to Enon Primitive Baptist Church, August 18, 1867, in Enon Primitive Baptist Church, Unionville, Bedford County, Records, Church Letters (MS in TSLA); Fayetteville *Observer*, August 22, 1861. The Duling Memoir documents the banishment of unionists from a Marshall County church in 1861.

28   William Taylor to Enon Primitive Baptist Church, August 18, 1867, in Enon Primitive Baptist Church, Bedford County, Church Letters.

the mass of Middle Tennesseans and provoked their extreme reaction. Suddenly it appeared that this once harmonious, tightly woven society was discordant and unraveled—consensus fractured, mutual obligations repudiated, the revered patriarchy at odds with itself. No longer, it seemed, were unity and concord inherent qualities of this society which might be taken for granted; now they were elusive and vital prizes to be hunted down, seized, and jealously guarded. Those who jeopardized the success of the hunt or questioned its necessity found the hunters' weapons turned on themselves: "He who is not for us is against us."

The preservation of harmony demanded, besides enforced unity, the severing of "foreign" connections and the purging of incongruent elements that could not be coaxed or hounded into the fold. Northerners were of course a prime target. The Nashville *Patriot* recommended that each one in the region should, in the course of "the elimination [from] our population of dangerous elements," be scrutinized for signs of Black Republicanism or "over-zealous . . . sympathy for the poor slave." That newspaper also reported that many voters had written on their June referendum ballots "No more Yankee school teachers." On July 1 the Davidson County court resolved not to pay interest on its bonds held by citizens of any non-Confederate state. Four days later the First Presbyterian Church of Clarksville advised its presbytery to cut ties with the national church, and not long afterward all Middle Tennessee "Old School" Presbyterians ended their affiliation with their Northern coreligionists. Before the summer was out, Northern insurance agents in the towns packed up their papers and departed. On the same trains that bore the outcast Yankees northward rode many of the die-hard native unionists, pariahs now, too, who reasoned sadly like Robert S. Northcott that "I did all I could, to check the monster, but when I saw my State . . . completely under the influence of the 'reign of terror,' I concluded that my duty called me elsewhere." [29]

As they solidified and purged their society, white Middle Tennesseans in the first months of the war also intensified their efforts to suppress the black population, convinced now more than ever that, as a manifesto of leading Nashvillians declared, "The horrors of *servile* war are to be added to the merciless butchery and plunder to be carried on over the South by the vandal hordes of the Northern cities." Slave patrols revived and burgeoned across the region, assisted in their nocturnal vigils by home guards

29 Nashville *Patriot*, June 13, 21, 1861; Davidson County Court Minutes, July 1, 1861, Bk. H, 668; First Presbyterian Church, Clarksville, Session Minutes, Vol. II, July 5, 1861; D. Little, *History of the Presbytery of Columbia, Tennessee* (Columbia, Tenn., 1928), 24; Clarksville *Chronicle*, February 14, 1862; Robert S. Northcott to Andrew Johnson, February 17, 1862, in Graf and Haskins (eds.), *Papers of Andrew Johnson*, V, 145.

and vigilantes. Blacks free and slave were watched with renewed suspicion, their gatherings more closely regulated or altogether proscribed. The Cumberland Presbyterian Church of Lebanon, for example, appointed one of its congregation to take charge of the separate, theretofore casually overseen Sunday services held by black members, and to "see that some white man attend with them at every meeting."[30]

The primary instrument of the crusade for self-preservation, unification, purification, and subjugation was violence. Apprehending onslaughts from within and without, Middle Tennesseans determined to meet force with force, and as they did so a violent aura suffused their society as never before. The rabid imprecation of a normally staid Nashville woman in May, as she contemplated the coming "unholy war" contrived by the North, vividly illustrated the heartland's increasingly militant social consciousness: "If come it must . . . I only pray God may be with us to give us strength to conquer them, to exterminate *them*, to lay waste every Northern city, town and village, to destroy them utterly. It is nothing more than they deserve, nothing but what they wish to do for us."[31]

The same fury was turned against domestic enemies. Violence against blacks was an old acquaintance, of course; only its redoubled frequency and ferocity were new: "Negro hung for incendiaryism," a Maury County farmer noted almost insouciantly on May 28, 1861, among the minutiae in his journal of farm activities. But the purposeful violence by white against white—much of it collective violence—which stained the heartland in these months was a decidedly new phenomenon. The threat of physical abuse and even death which accompanied every new rumor of unionist perfidy or abolitionist subversion was real. A Lebanon unionist who spoke out at a public meeting in April was harassed at his home that night by a mob of twenty men, as his effigy burned nearby; he drove off the attackers only after an exchange of pistol fire. Such incidents (and there were many), along with frequent public and private muttering about "hemp cravats," were spawned by and in turn fed the new consensus of violence and persuaded even the most obstinate nonconformists that their only alternatives were silence or flight.[32]

The casual observer in Middle Tennessee in the latter half of 1861 might understandably have concluded, however, that the heartland at war dif-

30   Nashville *Patriot*, May 18, 1861; Historical Records Survey, *Cumberland Presbyterian Records*, II, 50.
31   Annie R. Maney to Bettie Kimberly, May 12, 1861, in Kimberly Papers.
32   Matthews Journal, May 28, 1861; Gallatin *Courier*, April 3, 1861.

fered but little from the heartland at peace. The Second Revolution to that point was predominantly a revolution of mind and spirit; the barricades Middle Tennesseans manned were ideological ones, the monarch they deposed an abstract principle. Tearful, romantic scenes at railway stations were plentiful, of course. Young men were already dying in filthy army hospitals and on faraway battlefields. And even the dullest onlooker could hardly pretermit the tension and ferment of these months, as he read the newspapers teeming with news of war and rumors of war, or eavesdropped on the excited conversations at every street corner, or watched eager, awkward volunteers drill on the courthouse square, or woke to the furious galloping of patrollers in the dark of night. But for most Middle Tennesseans the wonted routines of life abided, and the river of their existence flowed smoothly in its accustomed channel.

Continuity was evident in the heartland's institutions, which evinced a mostly seamless transition from old flag to new, from peace to war. Southern-born teachers took up chalk and pointers abandoned by departing Yankee schoolmarms and the education of the young proceeded. With the adoption of a prayer for the Confederate president and Congress, and with a more watchful eye on their black brethren, the churches of the heartland pursued their dual task of proclaiming the glory of God in heaven while battling the sins of man on earth. Labor shortages and inflated wages plagued the towns as men went off to war, but trade was lively, spirits high, and the busy pulse of urban life beat unabated, even quickened, in these feverish months. As the soldier's call for swords drowned out the farmer's call for plowshares the heartland's fledgling industry was spurred to greater efforts. In Clarksville alone, between July and October an iron foundry began casting cannons, shells, and grapeshot; a grocer began baking army crackers; the government rented a pork house and converted it to military use; and a wagon factory began producing army supply wagons.[33]

The rhythm of the seasons continued as always to rule the world of the farmers, who toiled on in their fields, inspired now to expand acreage and raise more corn and cattle to feed the hungry armies. In those fields, too, still labored black bondsmen, conscious of the enormity of the crisis at hand yet unsure of its outcome and, at the mercy of the new tyranny, unable yet to seek advantage from it.[34]

Political contests still evoked excited crowds and retained their raucous

33 J. F. Gilmer to W. W. Mackall, December 7, 1861, in *OR*, VII, 741; Clarksville *Chronicle*, July 5, August 16, 30, October 25, 1861.

34 Fayetteville *Observer*, May 2, 23, 1861. The Matthews Journal gives a good sense of the undisturbed routine of agriculture and daily business through 1861 and early 1862. That

prewar flavor, though contestants debated now within narrowly constricted bounds. In the courthouses, over which the Stars and Bars now flew, the proceedings of local government went on uninterrupted and the same men sat gravely in the same seats of power, the transition of polity imperceptible at this level. So unjarring was the bureaucratic experience in that summer of 1861 that well into August the Rutherford County court clerk still mechanically prefaced each meeting's minutes with the customary flourish "the year of American Independence the 86th." [35]

Disruptions and discontinuities there were, of course, sufficient to remind Middle Tennesseans that they were indeed at war. Railroad service and mail deliveries were frequently delayed all over the region, as northern connections were broken and military authorities monopolized tracks and rolling stock. Shortages of some goods and high prices for many others were chronic in these months. Coffee, liquor, and a dozen other commodities were in very short supply; in Clarksville an unusually quiet Christmas was ascribed to "the absence of Cincinnati tangle foot and chain lightning, cut off by the war." On top of these vexations, most counties imposed sharp tax increases to equip and pay patrollers and home guards and to provide for the growing number of indigents. [36]

Middle Tennesseans bore delays, shortages, inflation, and taxes with patriotic stoicism and humor. But conflicts with the army were a rankling irritant in this period. Farmers close to Nashville complained loudly about pilfering of hogs, chickens, and timber by poorly provisioned and worse disciplined Confederate soldiers camped nearby, who acted "with violence and utter contempt for *the rights of the sufferers*," as one victim protested. Even more exasperating were the constant appeals by the military for slave laborers from the already hard-pressed farmers. Army officials eventually threw up their hands at the slaveowners' grumbling and foot-dragging and resorted to impressment. In the winter of 1862 soldiers rounded up hundreds of slaves all over the region and marched them off with picks and shovels to dig fortifications around Nashville and Clarksville. [37]

The heartland's most intimate institution—the family—endured the

---

slaves were well aware of current events from hearing their masters discuss them is shown in Rawick (ed.), *American Slave*, Ser. Two, Vol. VIII (Ark.), Pt. 2, pp. 137–38.

35 Rutherford County, Tennessee, County Court Clerk's Office, Minute Books, August, 1861, Bk. DD, 545 (Microfilm copy in TSLA). All county court records in this period evince unbroken continuity of leadership and administration.

36 Clarksville *Chronicle*, July 12, 26, 1861, January 10, 17, 1862; Clarksville *Jeffersonian*, November 13, 20, 1861, January 3, 1862.

37 Nashville *Patriot*, December 28, 1861; Isham G. Harris to A. Sidney Johnston, December 31, 1861, in *OR*, VII, 811–12; Matthews Journal, February 13, 1862.

heaviest affliction in these early months of war. Every man and boy who donned a uniform, took up a musket, and trooped away left behind a family weakened, more vulnerable, an entity headless or limbless. This knowledge made the choice very painful for some. "I am pulled between two inclinations most unpleasantly," a Nashvillian sadly wrote his wife in August, 1861, just before his enlistment. "The first & strongest is to stay near you my precious wife & my little daughter. The other is to go & do my part as a soldier. . . . I cant make up my mind to leave [you] & yet I feel dissatisfied with myself."[38]

Other institutions—churches and especially local government—stepped in to sustain the family in its travail. Every county court in the heartland moved immediately upon the outbreak of war to succor needy families of volunteers. Most counties raised considerable revenues to be doled out in cash or kind by magistrates or home guards, who in some cases distributed to their charges food, clothing, soap, candles, wood, coal, and even subsidies for house rent and medical care. This was direct public assistance on a far greater scale than ever before in the region, and it evidenced the profound public solicitude for society's central institution in this crisis of unprecedented magnitude. By the winter of 1862, Maury County supported perhaps two hundred families, Davidson more than five hundred at a cost of $22,000.[39]

As the turbulent spring and summer of 1861 gave way to autumn, white Middle Tennesseans came gradually to believe that, despite the earlier prophecies of some, Armageddon was not yet at hand. Many grew hopeful that the months ahead would bring not the winter of their discontent but the springtime of their now secure and revitalized world. They saw their people at last wholly unified and strongly armed against the twin evils within and without; they saw their land purged of the most baneful poisons; they saw their institutions unshaken in the storm, their social fabric strained but not torn; and they saw the crucial elements of their ideology still intact and now impregnable.

With undisguised smugness white Middle Tennesseans remarked the frequent affirmations of the loyalty of their black helots, so recently depicted as restive and bloodthirsty. The Clarksville *Jeffersonian* reported in December that free blacks were working cheerfully in the town's army hospital and that "most of them express their satisfaction that they are able there to contribute to the cause of the country." When a group of blacks in

38 Henry C. Yeatman to his wife, August 14, 1861, in Polk-Yeatman Papers.

39 Maury County Court Minutes, May 6, 20, October 7, 1861, Vol. XIII, 450, 462–63, 536, March 6, 1862, Vol. XIV, 95; Davidson County Court Minutes, May 18, July 1, October 7, 1861, January 6, 1862, Bk. H, 657, 665, 668, 702–703, 728, 732.

Fayetteville presented a tableaux exhibition at the Cumberland Presbyterian Church, which raised $40 for the benefit of sick soldiers, the *Observer* announced with satisfaction that "this incident contains a large lesson for Old Abe and his satraps, if they will only heed it."[40]

The flush of contentment that suffused these months was, however, like a drunkard's euphoria. Intoxicated by the heady wine of political independence and ideological triumph, white Middle Tennesseans experienced a blurring of collective vision, a numbing of senses. Many failed utterly to perceive the currents of fear and disunity that flowed—now submerged but still powerful—beneath the surface of their society.

If there were brash assurances of the fidelity of the blacks, there were also more quietly acknowledged misgivings. In December the Marshall County court appended to its routine orders an unusual official recommendation that "the owners of the slaves in this county should keep them at home during the Christmas Hollidays." A Maury County farmer wrote in his journal on Sunday, January 19, that his day's activities had included attending church in the morning, then a visit to a neighboring farm, "where the minute men were examining & whipping negroes supposed to be guilty of burning . . . corn."[41]

If there was outspoken confidence that the social entity was whole and pure, there were also deep, sporadically confessed doubts. The editor of the Shelbyville *Expositor* grudgingly conceded in October the lukewarm patriotism or downright disloyalty of many in that town, though he proffered the unconvincing reassurance that "it will not be long before the people of old Bedford will be of one heart and mind." And Nashvillians at year's end were so panicked by rumors of a plot by Yankees and Southern traitors to infiltrate the city and burn it down that they begged for a military police force and spoke earnestly of instituting loyalty checks to root out subversives among citizens and leaders.[42]

If there was a widespread conviction that secession and independence would bring moral renewal and spiritual resuscitation, there were already hints of war-engendered moral degeneration and weariness of spirit. Newspapers charged as early as October that avaricious speculators were deliberately raising food, fuel, and clothing prices to exorbitant levels, cruelly afflicting the poor, and one editor expressed the hope that this outrage would be corrected "before the wrongs and hatred of the oppressed culmi-

40 Clarksville *Jeffersonian*, December 13, 1861; Fayetteville *Observer*, December 12, 1861.

41 Marshall County, Tennessee, County Court Clerk, Minutes, County Court, December, 1861, Vol. J, 431 (Microfilm copy in TSLA); Matthews Journal, January 19, 1862.

42 Shelbyville *Expositor*, October 11, 1861; Nashville *Patriot*, December 29, 1861; A. S. Johnston to J. P. Benjamin, December 30, 1861, in *OR*, VII, 807–808.

nate in scenes which all would remember with regret and shame." In December an elderly Maury countian, as patriotic as any but now disheartened rather than inspired by the sight of so many neighbors and friends leaving their families to go off to war, laid a curse on both houses: "May god with his infinate Wisdom, severely punish those North & south who was instrimental in bringing on this dredful calamity upon our once beloved & prosperous country."[43]

If there were steadfast public faith and cocksure predictions of victory and absolution, there were also profound personal trepidations about the future. An itinerant Williamson County minister, who rode far and wide with his message of the applicability of biblical prophecies to current events, recapitulated on December 31, 1861, his experiences of the past twelve months: "This year I have traveled two thousand four hundred and sixty miles. . . . I have had more and larger cong[regation]s than I ever have had since I have been preaching. . . . The congs not only large but [exhibiting] the most intence anxiety to hear me upon the prophesies I ever saw."[44]

These undercurrents of apprehension, whose wellsprings were real though dimly discerned perils, were about to come boiling to the surface, exposing and demolishing the flimsy foundations of public complacency and optimism. In early February, 1862, Union army and navy forces invaded Middle Tennessee along the Cumberland and Tennessee rivers, and at Fort Donelson they quickly destroyed a large portion of the Confederate army defending the heartland. Union gunboats continued up the Cumberland and captured Clarksville on February 19. As the remaining Confederate forces hurriedly retreated southward, a second Federal army marched into Middle Tennessee from Kentucky. Nashville fell on February 24. During the next three years, many of the gloomiest premonitions of the dourest prophets of a year earlier would come to pass; the prophecies of the hopeful would be buried with the many other casualties of the war.

---

43 Nashville *Patriot*, October 2, 15, 1861; Fayetteville *Observer*, October 31, 1861; Nimrod Porter Journal, December 16, 1861 (MS in SHC).

44 Jesse Cox Diary, December 31, 1861 (MS in TSLA).

Chapter V

I Wish There Was a River of Fire

The Devastation of the Heartland, 1862–1865

THE INVASION of Middle Tennessee in early 1862 by tens of thousands of armed Yankees evoked stoic resignation from some heartlanders and muted joy from some others. The rest of the populace—including many with a political or financial stake in the Confederacy—stayed at home in dismay or panic or frenetically took to the highways in flight. "At the commensement of the Battle of Fort Donaldson," reported a Clarksvillian on February 20, "the Citizens of this place commensed moving from Town in every direction and are keeping it up to this time. Not more than half of the Families have remained. You can't imagine the said appearance of our City." A Maury County farmer breathlessly described the spectacle that same day in his community, still far removed from the advancing enemy: "great excitement people leaving every where for the south. . . . The strong secessionist[s] leaving every where, oure state bank in Columbia packing up for a run off with all the money Thousands people come from Nashville to Columbia a perfect stampead."[1]

The capital itself witnessed scenes hardly imaginable to its proud citizens. "The whole city of Nashville was in an uncontrollable panic," a Confederate officer recalled in his memoirs; "people were rushing madly about with their most valuable possessions in their arms. . . . It was a supreme

---

1 William Epps Newell to Sallie Ann Newell, February 20, 1862, in Historical Records Survey, Tennessee, *Civil War Records* (Nashville, 1939), III, 116; Porter Journal, February 20, 1862.

pandemonium. . . . Hysterical women, half laughing, half crying, dragged their children behind them." A unionist who remained in the city vowed that "Such Scenes as were enacted in Nashville will never be fully known in this world." Scornfully he described the frenzied exodus of politicians, jurists, editors, and ministers and the disgraceful vandalism by retreating Confederate troops. "The City puts on the appearance to day of Sabbath in cholera times," he wrote five days after the arrival of the Union army. "Not a house in the city open Not *one* Oh but the judgments of Heaven has fallen heavily upon Nashville." [2]

Most Middle Tennesseans, however, believed in their hearts that those judgments, though harsh, were not final. Despite their agitation, many saw the invasion only as a test of faith, not an irrevocable consignment to perdition. They would have agreed with the Murfreesboro girl who declared, as the Union troops entered her town, "I cannot feel yet . . . that God has forsaken us. I do not believe it, he will yet smile upon [us]." The heartland would be soon redeemed, the faithful affirmed, by a revived and reinforced Confederate army. But with the passage of time they were compelled to acknowledge that they had mistaken the will of their Lord. [3]

The Yankee invaders had come to stay. They held Middle Tennessee as long as the war continued and beyond, occupying the important towns except for a time from the fall of 1862 to the early summer of 1863 and a few weeks in late 1864, when Confederate forces reoccupied the southern portion of the region. The Northern army held Nashville for the duration of the war, making the city the center of the Union's western war effort. No other major Southern region, except northern Virginia, endured enemy occupation during the Civil War for as long as Middle Tennessee.

The most conspicuous consequence of three years and more of war and occupation in the heartland was the region's physical devastation. Wartime travelers bemoaned the stark ruination and sterility of the land as impassionedly as their antebellum counterparts had marveled at its lush beauty and fecundity. "This is a dreary, desolate, barren and deserted looking country," wrote a Federal officer who crossed the northern heartland in late 1862. "The houses and stores are either closed or smashed to pieces. Everything is going to utter destruction." A sympathetic Yankee cavalryman described Davidson County in a letter home the following April: "It

2   Adam R. Johnson, *The Partisan Rangers of the Confederate States Army* (Louisville, 1904), 71; Rees W. Porter to Andrew Johnson, March 1, 1862, in Graf and Haskins (eds.), *Papers of Andrew Johnson*, V, 168–69. See also *The Great Panic: Being Incidents Connected with Two Weeks of the War in Tennessee* (Nashville, 1862).

3   Ready Diary, March 22, 1862.

is really sad to see this beautiful country here so ruined. There are no fences left at all. There is no corn and hay for the cattle and horses, but there are no horses left anyhow and the planters have no food for themselves." A Confederate soldier who marched through Bedford and Rutherford at about the same time lamented that "the country wears the most desolate appearance that I have ever seen anywhere. There is not a stalk of corn or blade of wheat growing."[4]

The towns of Middle Tennessee suffered as sorely as the farms and villages. "Our town looks like desolation itself," wrote a Clarksville woman in early 1863. "All its glory has departed." A Union officer described Pulaski the following year as a "nice town but like all Seceshdom gone to Seed." Nashville, as the Federals' primary post, bore the hardest usage. The city "was one of the brightest, most wealthy and prosperous cities of the Union," observed a Northern staff officer in 1864. "Of all this she is now the exact reverse. Her finest buildings . . . are now used as military hospitals and store-houses. Her streets are dirty. . . . Her suburbs are a mournful wreck. . . . As we write, the city of Nashville is stagnant, prostrate, and in the abject position of a subjugated city."[5]

Destruction is the ineluctable spawn of war. But the utter desolation of the heartland demands further explanation. One essential point is evident: the principal agent of destruction in Middle Tennessee was not armed conflict per se but the Union army. Though the region was among the Civil War's most fought-over battlegrounds (Confederate armies contested it 1862–63 and late 1864; smaller military forces and guerrillas did so throughout the war), relatively little damage resulted from actual combat between blue and gray regiments on the battlefield. Instead, the region's roles as breadbasket of the Federal army and strategic gateway to the Deep South brought down upon it the full wrath of war.

Middle Tennessee's prolific farms were called upon to furnish the main Union army in the western theater with food, equipment, and draft animals, even after the greater portion of that army moved on to Chattanooga

4 Jay Caldwell Butler, *Letters Home [by] Jay Caldwell Butler, Captain, 101st Ohio Volunteer Infantry*, ed. H. Butler Watson (Binghamton, N.Y., 1930), 32–34; "Documents: The Shelly Papers," *Indiana Magazine of History*, XLIV (1948), 187, 189–90; Hannibal Paine to his sister, June 4, 1863, in Paine Family Papers, TSLA. Other contemporary accounts of devastation are plentiful, but see especially William D. Bickham, *Rosecrans' Campaign with the Fourteenth Army Corps . . .* (Cincinnati, 1863), 50; Louis to his sister, April 9, 1863, in Talbot and Related Families Papers, TSLA.

5 Sarah Kennedy to her husband, February 2, 1863, in Sarah Ann (Bailey) Kennedy Letters, TSLA; David M. Smith (ed.), "Documents: The Civil War Diary of Colonel John Henry Smith," *Iowa Journal of History*, XLVII (1949), 142; John Fitch, *Annals of the Army of the Cumberland . . .* (Philadelphia, 1864), 643.

and Georgia. Not once or twice but day after day, season after season, year after year, farmers had to stand by impotently as Federal foraging squads helped themselves to horses and pigs, bales of cotton, and barrels of cornmeal. "When we have eaten a place empty," an Indiana cavalryman wrote in 1863, "we go a few miles farther and take everything there we can find." At least as troublesome as formal requisitions was informal pillaging by loosely disciplined troops. "The Federal soldiers have taken every horse mare and mule that I have," a Williamson County planter complained in his diary in 1863. "They have broken into my smoke house repetedly and have taken all my hams. They have taken a goodeal of my corn and all of my hay and near all my fodder. My health is very bad. I will certenly go crazy."[6]

The determination of Federal authorities to hold and defend this rich, strategic region and deny its use to the Confederacy engendered other forms of mayhem. Even after the main field army moved on, large Union garrison forces occupied the heartland's important towns and a few other key points on turnpikes and railroads (Nashville alone had a permanent garrison of ten thousand troops). These detachments served both to keep rebel armies at bay and to cow hostile native whites. Each garrison seized buildings for barracks, hospitals, and supply depots and dug mountains of fortifications, often with the help of local slaves impressed en masse. Wherever troops billeted or camped, fence rails (the soldiers' favorite fuel) disappeared. The occupation authorities strictly limited or simply proscribed civilian travel, correspondence, publishing, trade, and industry. Railroads and bridges, except those the army needed, were destroyed.[7]

To these afflictions incidental to war and occupation was added deliberate, spiteful destruction. The mutual enmity between Yankee invaders and their recalcitrant subjects often provoked retaliatory or simply malicious measures against Middle Tennesseans. Such acts became common as the war went on bitterly and heartlanders remained restive, even rebellious. "It does us good to distroy the greesey belleys property," a Union soldier declared, "when some of the boys get holt of any property of any kind beloning to the rebels they distroy it as fast as they can and then say dam him he was the coss of bringing us here." After his return from a foraging ex-

---

6   "Documents: Shelly Papers," 193; Samuel Henderson Diary, April 13, 1863 (MS in TSLA).

7   Sarah Kennedy to her husband, December 11, 1862, in Kennedy Letters; "Documents: Shelly Papers," 190; C. Johnson to Jefferson Davis, October 17, 1862, in *OR*, Vol. XVII, Pt. 2, pp. 730–31; Clarksville *Chronicle*, July 28, 1865; Peter Maslowski, *Treason Must Be Made Odious: Military Occupation and Wartime Reconstruction in Nashville, Tennessee* (Millwood, N.Y., 1978), 142–43.

pedition that had stripped many Middle Tennessee families to the point of starvation, a Northern officer in Gallatin wrote his wife, "We are obeying your christian exhortation 'to kill them' but prefer to let them die by inches to shooting them down."[8]

Nevertheless, the Union army did not lay waste to Middle Tennessee single-handedly. Much of the demolition of industry, railroads, and bridges and the burning of stored supplies such as cotton was the work of retreating rebel troops in early 1862; and then and afterward many heartlanders came to dread the "friendly" visitations of foraging Confederates as intensely as the depredations of the enemy. Furthermore, as order deteriorated in the countryside from late 1862 on, vicious bandit gangs appeared, preying on defenseless farms and plundering without mercy. And as the bonds of slavery loosened and fell away during the war years, some blacks seized the opportunity to appropriate the comforts of life long denied them. "It is the blacks that are doing most of the stealing at this time," insisted a Maury County farmer in March, 1865, after his wagon disappeared.[9]

Finally, there was an intangible enemy whose work was nearly as ruinous as the spoliations of soldiers, slaves, and bandits. This was uncertainty, a pervasive trepidation about the unknown future, which kept the farmers of the heartland from sowing their fields or multiplying their flocks. "The farmers in this section are not planting much," a Confederate artilleryman wrote from his camp south of Murfreesboro in the spring of 1863. "They are in a bad fix—they do not know whether to plant or not, for if we do not hold the country the enemy will destroy the whole crop." Nimrod Porter of Maury County noted ruefully two years later that "verry few of the citizens are trying to raise a crop in this county."[10]

The furies of rack and ruin careered savagely through Middle Tennessee from 1862 on. Their visitations, however, were not even-handed and impartial but cruelly capricious. The likeliest victims were in and near occupied towns and along main highways. Such heartlanders might suffer daily pillaging whereas others in remote parts went unmolested for months at a time. Nimrod Porter, whose farm was perilously near the important

8 Elias Brady to his wife, November 24, 1862, in Elias Brady Papers, SHC; A. T. Volwiler (ed.), "Documents: Letters from a Civil War Officer," *MVHR*, XIV (1928), 512.

9 Ebenezer Hannaford, *The Story of a Regiment: A History of the Campaigns, and Associations in the Field, of the Sixth Regiment Ohio Volunteer Infantry* (Cincinnati, 1868), 201; Porter Journal, March 20, 1862, January 13, July 23, 1863, January 1, November 27, December 2, 1864, March 2, 11, 1865; Fayetteville *Observer*, March 26, 1863; General Orders No. 10, Army of Tennessee, December 11, 1862, in *OR*, Vol. XX, Pt. 2, p. 446; report of S. Palace Love, May 6, 1863, *ibid.*, Vol. XXIII, Pt. 1, p. 327.

10 John E. Magee Diary, April 9, 1863 (MS in DUL); Porter Journal, March 11, 1865.

town of Columbia, saw hardly a day after the summer of 1862 when he or his close neighbors did not lose food, stock, fencing, or equipment to troops of one side or the other. Jesse Cox, a Williamson County farmer and preacher, was equally tormented: "The yankies hear for something to day," he wrote on March 29, 1863, "every day 2 or 3 times in the day and never pay anything." During a raid five days earlier, Cox wrote, one trooper "galloped up to me presented his gun . . . called me a damn old sun of a bich and said he would blow my brains out," and then rode off with half a bushel of corn. By contrast, however, James W. Matthews, whose farm lay in an out-of-the-way section of Maury County, suffered not a single depredation until December, 1864, when squads of Yankees ransacked his house and barn, stealing his food, horse, and pocket watch.[11]

The rich, the prominent, and the outspoken also drew an unhappily large measure of the havoc of war. Unionists in areas under Confederate control were singled out and onerously levied upon, some of them stripped or even burned out as thoroughly as any rebel was ever scourged by the Yankees. Where Federal power prevailed, military authorities often marked leading secessionists for brutal harassment. George A. Washington, a wealthy and distinguished Robertson County planter, suffered repeated depredations throughout 1864 by ruthless Union troops. During one raid the Yankees tormented Washington with loaded guns for two hours before finally shooting and wounding him, then ransacked his house and burned the outbuildings. Mark Cockrill, the renowned Davidson County planter and stock raiser, had by 1863 lost to the Federal army hundreds of his celebrated sheep, dozens of horses, mules, and cattle, thousands of bushels of corn, and vast quantities of bacon, oats, hay, and firewood. William G. Harding's Belle Meade plantation, perhaps the most famous estate in the heartland and unluckily close to Nashville on a major thoroughfare, was devastated before the war ended—its deer and buffalo shot down in their fabled park, its work animals and food stores plundered, its fields and fences stripped. Harding estimated his losses during the first year of occupation alone at $32,000.[12]

11 Porter Journal, 1862–65, *passim;* Cox Diary, March 24, 29, 1863, and *passim;* Matthews Journal, December 25, 1864, and *passim.* See also John Nick Barker Diary, February 4, 5, 6, 7, 9, March 15, 1863 (Microfilm copy in TSLA).

12 Report of J. J. Reynolds, February 10, 1863, in *OR,* Vol. XXIII, Pt. 2, pp. 54–57; Jane S. Washington to George A. Washington, March 2, May 4, July 25, August 8, 1864, in Washington Papers; Jane S. Washington to her son, December 18, 1864, in Jane S. Washington Letter, TSLA; Fitch, *Annals of the Army,* 641; "Diary of Jacob Adams, Private in Company F, 21st O.V.V.I.," *Ohio Archaeological and Historical Society Publications,* XXXVIII (1929), 639; Randal M. Ewing to William G. Harding, August 28, 1862, in Harding-Jackson

The people of the heartland suffered during the war in body and spirit, but the nature and extent of their suffering varied according to their circumstances. The demons of privation and affliction haunted urbanites and rural folk alike, but those demons assumed different forms in the towns and in the countryside.

From the first days of occupation the Union army's interdiction of trade deprived country people of the few necessities not produced in their predominantly self-sufficient communities. Articles formerly taken for granted suddenly became scarce luxuries. "You have but little idea of the privations that 'Secessh' has brought upon this 'glorious Confederacy,'" a unionist woman wrote sardonically from rural Rutherford County in 1863. "No sugar, no tea, no coffee, no soda, no salt, no kind of cloth but what is made by hand—& finally no nothing."[13]

As the war and occupation continued, however, above these annoyances rose the specter of true suffering in the countryside. The loss of stored food and meat on the hoof, the loss of money and valuables and cash crops with which food might have been purchased, and the diminution of harvests because of the loss of growing crops, work animals, buildings, equipment, fencing, and slaves (not to mention the pernicious effects of uncertainty) all colluded to reduce most rural Middle Tennesseans to the meanest subsistence and some to actual starvation. "I talked to a farmer at whose house I was picketing," wrote a Yankee cavalry trooper near Nashville in 1863. "He told me he had no potatoes to plant and all winter long he lived on corn and a very little smoked meat. . . . Everything they had planted and also their cattle was stolen. . . . I can't see how the people live at all." An officer who rode through Giles County in 1864 beheld shocking scenes of distress, declaring (according to the Nashville *Dispatch*) that "no man who has not visited the localities he has, can form any conception of the great scarcity of every thing necessary to sustain life that exists there."[14]

Want and famine were not the only tribulations of war in the rural heartland. Many country people confronted as well the necessity of arduous and unaccustomed labor. Food shortages, equipment losses, the unavailability of manufactured goods, the dearth of able-bodied white men, and the ever-increasing desertion of slaves all compelled rural people to work as never before. A Union officer in Murfreesboro told of carrying off slaves from every farm he raided, "leaving the women to do their own

---

Papers, SHC; Herschel Gower, "Belle Meade: Queen of Tennessee Plantations," *THQ*, XXII (1963), 213–16.

13 Jane C. Warren to Electa Ames, August 27, 1863, in Ames Papers.

14 "Documents: Shelly Papers," 187; Nashville *Dispatch*, January 12, 1864.

work as do the blessed yankee girls." Jesse Cox, who preferred to let his farm take care of itself while he attended to matters of God, lamented "having to labour for a support" in 1864: "I am compelled to labour," he explained, "as I lost about eight thousand dolars worth of property by the yankeys, for wich I have never received any compesation."[15]

Suffering in the rural heartland was no respecter of class or race. As one Union general observed, "All suffer, rich and poor." The black field hand sweated and anguished along with his white master, the plantation mistress went hungry along with the wagon maker's wife and the tenant farmer's children. Suffering was the common denominator of society in the Middle Tennessee countryside during the Civil War. Hammett Dell, raised as a slave on a Rutherford County farm, described his wartime experiences in passages indistinguishable from many a white narrative: "There couldn't be a chicken nor a goose nor a year of corn to be found. . . . It was sich hard times." Similar privation at the opposite end of society's scale left aristocrats broken and humbled. John W. Burgess, a Giles County unionist who spent the war in Nashville, recalled that "day after day I saw the wives and daughters of the once wealthy and well-to-do planters of my own acquaintance getting out of [railroad] box cars, clad in tatters, carrying bundles of bedding, and staring about themselves vacantly as not knowing where to look for food or shelter."[16]

The awful visages of ruin, violence, and want confronted Middle Tennesseans in the towns, too. Subject not sporadically but daily and unremittingly to the imperious demands of Federal garrison troops, townspeople sustained appalling incidental losses and willful destruction. Houses and public buildings by the hundreds were seized for use as military command posts, barracks, hospitals, or supply depots. Yankee soldiers proved as adept at breaking into homes and buildings while billeted in towns as they were at breaching barns and smokehouses while on the march. An Episcopal rector in Columbia watched heartbroken in May, 1864, as soldiers invaded his church, stole everything they could carry off (including surplices), and even tried to pry loose the church's cornerstone in search of valuables. Seven months later he wrote in his diary, "Saturday—Xmas Eve—Soldiers in the ch[urch] carrying on work of despoilation—The *organ* is a *complete ruin.* 'How long, O Lord!'" A Gallatin girl who witnessed frequent Yankee depredations and bodily violence remarked wryly in her diary in April, 1864, "Well, well, was ever such a time seen before

15 "Major Connolly's Letters to His Wife, 1862–1865," *Transactions of the Illinois State Historical Society* (1928), 248; Cox Diary, April 13, 1864.

16 Maslowski, *Treason Must Be Made Odious*, 132–34; Rawick (ed.), *American Slave*, Ser. Two, Vol. VIII (Ark.), Pt. 2, p. 139; Burgess, *Reminiscences*, 31.

since [Post Commander] E. A. Payne has been here; they have neither burned any houses or killed any body in *three whol[e] days*." [17]

Privation stalked the towns implacably. But there it was not the consequence of direct enemy impressment and pillaging, as in the countryside, but of economic derangement, especially the drastic curtailment of imports from the farms. Stripped of their food surpluses (indeed, hardly able to feed themselves), and fearful of traveling on dangerous highways, the farmers of the heartland could not after 1862 victual the towns anywhere near as copiously as before. And those towns had ever more hungry inhabitants to feed, as soldiers, Northern civilians, runaway slaves, and white refugees poured in. The inevitable results were shortages and high prices in the towns—not just of food but of firewood, which even in the depths of their affliction rural folk could take for granted. Supplies did trickle in under watchful Federal eyes or through smuggling, but on the whole the heartland's urbanites suffered an immense decline in their level of sustenance. [18]

There simply was not enough food and fuel to go around. "I was in Murfreesborough yesterday," a Rutherford County woman wrote in 1864; "times hard and tight every thing sells high . . . eatables very scarce and price high." Sarah Kennedy in Clarksville observed in 1863, "Every day the reins are tightened. . . . I find it next to impossible to get any thing to eat for the family." In Nashville, bursting at the seams with soldiers and civilians, the price of wood rose to $14 per cord by September, 1862, evoking great public concern at a time when a laboring man might earn a dollar or two a day. A year and a half later the price was $30. [19]

Had supplies been plentiful and prices low, however, many townspeople would still have gone hungry and cold because they had no work. Unlike the country folk, whose privations impelled them to desperate exertions, urbanites subsisted on trade and industry, which evaporated at the appearance of the Yankees in early 1862, driving thousands of laborers and tradesmen into idleness. As the occupation forces settled in, some lucky mer-

17   David Pise Journal, May 5, December 24, 1864 (MS in SHC); Alice Williamson Diary, April 23, 1864 (MS in DUL).

18   Nashville *Dispatch*, September 11, October 31, 1862, notes the hesitancy of local farmers to bring food into the city. For evidence of smuggling see W. Williams, "A Reminiscence of Clarksville, Tennessee," *Confederate Veteran*, XXII (1914), 206; Fitch, *Annals of the Army*, 489–98.

19   Nancy B. Smith to James B. Smith, May 26, 1864, in Nancy B. Smith Letters, TSLA; Sarah Kennedy to her husband, March 13, 1863, in Kennedy Letters; Nashville *Dispatch*, September 11, 1862, March 28, 1863, January 8, 1864; Frank A. Handy Diary, December 24, 1864 (MS in DUL); Zeboim Cartter Patten Diary, February 13, 1863 (Microfilm copy in TSLA).

chants received permission to resume business (a few even prospered), and some workers eventually found employment in industries (mostly military-related) revived by the Federals. But neither trade nor industry ever regained during the war anything approaching its antebellum level. Nashville's important publishing houses and newspapers, for example, were all seized by Federal authorities for the duration of the war. Clarksville's tobacco-processing establishments were closed and its iron manufactories demolished. From early 1862 to the end of the war, the townspeople of the heartland endured grossly inflated prices, economic recession, high unemployment, and profound distress.[20]

The agony of the urban poor, however, starkly eclipsed the mere discomfort of the affluent. In contrast to the rural experience, suffering in the towns was a function of wealth. Urban suffering thus underscored the exaggerated class distinctions and extremes of wealth that had long distinguished urban from rural society in the heartland. The urban rich held much of their wealth in currency, securities, gold, or other easily safeguarded valuables. Some lost fortunes in Confederate bonds or in business or bank failures, and Yankee pillaging took its toll on material possessions. But the Federals made no systematic effort to appropriate the assets of the urban wealthy. High prices curtailed conspicuous consumption, but the rich for the most part retained their fortunes and could always afford the necessities of life no matter how high prices rose. And they continued to dwell in their palatial homes while the poor crowded into foul, disease-ridden tenements or simply wandered. In the winter of 1864 a Sumner County official wrote imploringly to the local Federal commander about the poorhouse inmates in Gallatin: "They are now living on nothing but bread . . . some of them are so naked they are very bad objects to look at and [some] . . . are going from place to place begging." While the poor tramped and starved, the well-to-do dined and discussed with genteel concern the high price of bread and the scarcity of black servants to wait on them.[21]

Even the well-fed urban rich, however, endured cruel mental torments. Their gold could not buy sustenance for the spirit, which the war's vicissi-

20 Nashville *Dispatch*, May 6, 18, December 7, 1862, May 31, 1863; Fitch, *Annals of the Army*, 643; Nashville *Daily Times and True Union*, December 12, 1864; W. Harrison Daniel, "The Effects of the Civil War on Southern Protestantism," *Maryland Historical Magazine*, LXIX (1974), 52; Stephen V. Ash, "A Community at War: Montgomery County, 1861–65," *THQ*, XXXVI (1977), 39–42; Maslowski, *Treason Must Be Made Odious*, 131–36.

21 John W. Brooks to E. A. Paine, February 24, 1864, in Andrew Johnson Papers, LC. The destitution and suffering of the Nashville poor, unsurpassed anywhere else in the region, is described in Handy Diary, December 24, 1864; Nashville *Daily Press*, June 5, 1863; Nashville *Dispatch*, September 27, October 22, November 5, 1862, February 3, 1864.

tudes beleaguered as relentlessly as they assailed the body. Thus the war brought hardship in one or more forms to nearly all the people of Middle Tennessee, the rich and the poor, the humble and the exalted. "What dreadful sufferings has been produced by this unnecessary war," wrote one agonized heartlander in 1864, "no one living ever will be able to give a full picture of its consequences and distresses." Physical privation and material loss, grief and anxious uncertainty, all inflicted wounds on flesh and soul, imperiling an entire world-view. By 1864 the ideology sustained by optimism, prosperity, and plenty was in collapse.[22]

Some Middle Tennesseans took the ultimate step, leaving their homes as refugees to follow the retreating rebel army south, or to seek haven in the occupied towns, or even to escape to the North. Others, resolutely staying on as their world crumbled around them, took refuge in deep religious faith. The afflicted but devout Jesse Cox found a measure of peace at the end of 1863: "My dependance is entirely upon the Lord," he avowed, "in this dark and trying hour." The fathers of the First Presbyterian Church of Murfreesboro, meeting in 1864 to chronicle the "many sad events [which] have transpired in our midst & around us," concluded their report with a declaration of undiminished trust: "Having made this sad record the Session would humbly rear an Ebenezer, & render thanks to God for mercies that are still continued, & to the honor of his name acknowledge that we have never yet seen an end to the goodness of the Lord!"[23]

Other heartlanders, unwilling to flee but lacking inner sources of strength, suffered profound emotional traumas which left them helpless and spiritless—a desolation of the psyche as thorough and calamitous as the desolation of the land. A Robertson County widow, ill and rapidly declining into poverty as a result of thievery and the desertion of her few slaves, wrote pathetically to Military Governor Andrew Johnson in December, 1863: "Great God, Sir to think of the relations friends and propety I once had around me, and now this christmas day sitting here alone no one even to whisper a kind word of consolation I have lost what little mind I had and my little remaining strength is fast giving away. I see nothing before me but beggery and suffering." Plagued by violence and unruly blacks as the war neared its end, another Robertson County woman

22   Porter Journal, January 1, 1864.

23   Cox Diary, December 31, 1863; First Presbyterian Church, Murfreesboro, Rutherford County, Records, Session Minutes, July 18, 1864 (Microfilm copy in TSLA). (For the meaning of "rear an Ebenezer" see 1 Sam. 7: 12.) Evidence of refugees from Middle Tennessee is in Nashville *Daily Press*, May 5, 1863; Nashville *Dispatch*, May 21, 1863; James Whiteside to his sister, November 5, 1865, in Whiteside Family Papers, TSLA; Mary E. Massey, *Refugee Life in the Confederacy* (Baton Rouge, 1964), 6, 83–84, 86, 89.

wrote her daughter-in-law in deep despair: "If I am to live long like I am living now and have been I had wrather die and be clear of this troublesome world."[24]

Most Middle Tennesseans simply abided and silently hoped, but on occasion they evoked the pathos of their experience with words of impassioned imagery summoned from the depths of an agonized soul. Thus did elderly, long-suffering Nimrod Porter, a customarily prosaic diarist, voice his distress at the "greate trouble in the country" in one entry made during the last autumn of the war: "I wish there was a river of fire between North & South," he wrote, "that would burn with unquentiable fury for ever more & that it could never be passed, to the endless ages of eternity by any living creature."[25]

The old man's anguished plea for an end to war and affliction would be granted. But it was time, not a fiery river, which would bring that to pass.

The land and people of Middle Tennessee were not the only casualties of war. The region's institutions, those inveterate manifestations of society's deepest convictions and loftiest achievements, also suffered in the years of turmoil following the invasion. At no time were all institutions—schools, courts, government, churches—wholly suspended; but few escaped some disruption, and many sustained crippling and near-mortal wounds.

The institutions of the heartland faced two deadly enemies during the Civil War; one haunted the towns and another the countryside. In the towns constant and pervasive Federal presence was the rule. Thus many institutions fell victim to the expropriation of buildings for army needs and many to deliberate, politically motivated military interference. In the rural areas such tribulations were not unknown, but they were rare. Far more lethal there was the restriction of mobility, and thus social intercourse, imposed by wartime conditions. Fear of Yankee rapine and abuse, fear of rebel conscription, fear of guerrilla and bandit violence kept anxious rural heartlanders at home and away from church, schoolhouse, village, town, and courthouse. "I have only been to Clarksville three times in the last two years," wrote a Montgomery County farm woman in 1864, "and visit but little in the neighborhood"; and when Jesse Cox called on a sick neighbor in June, 1863, he noted in his diary that it was "the first time I have been outside of my farm in three months."[26]

24 Mrs. W. W. Pepper to Andrew Johnson, December 25, 1863, in Graf and Haskins (eds.), *Papers of Andrew Johnson*, VI, 525–27; Mary C. Washington to Jane S. Washington, March 17, 1865, in Washington Papers.

25 Porter Journal, October 22, 1864.

26 Sallie to John Minor, May 15, 1864, in Sailor's Rest Plantation Papers, TSLA; Cox

Most schools in the countryside were abandoned when the Yankees arrived, and subsequent hazards kept pupils and teachers away. A few private academies and subscription schools persisted or later reopened in remote communities luckily free of danger, but rural public schools—such as they were—ceased altogether as county government faltered or disappeared. Urban schools were untroubled by disrupted mobility and aided by the Federals' benign neglect (or in some cases outright encouragement). Many private schools continued and even flourished under the towns' enforced order and relative peacefulness. Most urban schools closed temporarily in the initial panic of early 1862, and occasionally thereafter the army seized school buildings for military use (Stewart College in Clarksville and the famous Clarksville Female Academy, both used as hospitals, were wrecked). And, too, financial distress closed public schools in the towns, most notably in Nashville, whose excellent school system was shut down in 1862 by a nearly bankrupt city council. Nevertheless, urban schools as a whole—insulated from rural turbulence, generally unharassed by Federal authorities (who perceived schools as no threat), and patronized by the still prosperous affluent of the towns—endured war and occupation better than any other of the region's institutions.[27]

The hand of war struck much more fiercely at county government. With few exceptions, county courts closed after the capture of Nashville, even where the Federal army was not present, as terror-stricken magistrates and clerks fled, some taking all their records. In Franklin the Federal commandant encountered a typical predicament in June, 1862: the Williamson County court was dissolved, taxes were uncollected, the treasury held less than $50, the poor fund was gone, many citizens were in destitution, and bridges were out all around the county. Several county govern-

---

Diary, June 16, 1863. The disruption of mobility and communication in the rural areas—a phenomenon with profound social implications, which are explored in Chapter VII—is further documented in Sarah Kennedy to her husband, February 12, 1863, in Kennedy Letters; wife to William G. Harding, August 5, 1862, in Harding-Jackson Papers; Matthews Journal, July 16, 18, 1863; Nashville *Dispatch*, September 11, October 31, 1862; Jane S. Washington to George A. Washington, September 22, 1864, in Washington Papers; James Nolen case, LL 2731, in Court Martial Case Files, 1809–1938, Records of the Office of the Judge Advocate General, Record Group 153, NA.

27   The closing of rural schools is indicated in Matthews Journal, July 17, 1862, July 10, 1863. Their occasional persistence is evidenced in *ibid.*, April 6, 1863, March 7, 1864. On the survival or revival of urban schools see Sallie F. McEwen Diary, May 6, 1862 (MS in TSLA); Henderson Diary, September 21, 1863; Williamson Diary, March 30, 1864. Military seizure or destruction of school buildings in the towns is noted in Kate S. Carney Diary, June 19, 1862 (MS in SHC); Ash, "Community at War," 37–38. On the fate of the Nashville public schools see Nashville *Dispatch*, August 13, 19, 1862, August 12, 1863.

ments in the southern heartland resumed under Confederate control for a few months after the summer of 1862, when the Union army withdrew to Nashville. But thereafter, to the end of the war, the fate of government in each of the region's thirteen counties was determined by a combination of local circumstances, the caprices of the local commandant, the broader military situation, and the political maneuvers of Military Governor Andrew Johnson in Nashville.[28]

It was Johnson's devout belief that the white masses of Middle Tennessee were true patriots at heart who had been hoodwinked into secession by a handful of villainous leaders. His policy, therefore, was to reestablish civil government in the region as quickly as possible after purging the body politic of the truly disloyal and disenthralling the rest of the populace. In pursuit of this goal he was willing, initially at least, to let local office-holders remain until elections could be held if they would take an oath of allegiance to the Union. Some army commanders denounced this policy as overly lenient, but many upheld it because a functioning civil administrative body could relieve military occupation forces of many burdens. Courts were most easily revived where a stalwart nucleus of unionists was already on hand to assist. Such was the case in Davidson and in Bedford, and thus county government there, and in Robertson as well, resumed soon after the invasion with the blessing of the Yankees.[29]

Other counties enjoyed no such smooth resumption of government. In Lincoln, for example, every officeholder left the county with his records, or just went home, when Fayetteville was occupied; the post commander vainly exhorted all to return. Confederate military threats hamstrung the Federals' efforts as severely as did civil defiance. Little reconstruction of government could be accomplished while the Confederate army contested Middle Tennessee. And even after that, small rebel units and guerrilla bands continued to challenge civil government under Yankee aegis. Slowly, however, courthouse by courthouse, local government returned to the heartland—although in three counties (Montgomery, Cheatham, and Sumner) it did not reappear until very near the end of the war.[30]

28   William B. Cassilly to Andrew Johnson, June 28, 1862, in Graf and Haskins (eds.), *Papers of Andrew Johnson,* V, 511–12.

29   Ormsby M. Mitchell to Andrew Johnson, April 5, 1862, *ibid.,* 269; Shelbyville *Tri-Weekly News,* June 19, 1862. Military control of Bedford County changed hands at least five times during the war. The travails of the county court, alternately taken over by unionists and secessionists, are interestingly documented in Bedford County, County Court Clerk's Office, County Court Minutes, May, August, 1863, Vol. A, 6, 14 (Microfilm copy in TSLA).

30   Curran Pope to Andrew Johnson, April 19, 1862, in Graf and Haskins (eds.), *Papers of Andrew Johnson,* V, 311. The Wilson County court reopened under Federal control in October, 1862; Marshall in October, 1863 (after the initial Federal withdrawal in the late summer

Army cooperation with these county governments ranged from generous to null. Some local commanders resented the frequent reappearance of old, familiar faces among the newly seated officeholders, denounced them as unreconstructed rebels, and declined to assist them. But other Federal officers worked faithfully to supervise local elections, administer oaths to voters and elected officials, and get the wheels of local government turning again, however creakily. And until the courts were operating, army officers acted—often at the behest of citizens—as administrators, judges, and even welfare commissioners. The Fayetteville provost marshal recounted in his memoirs how he frequently redressed grievances and alleviated hardships among the local folk, who came to his office because they had nowhere else to turn: "Some had had horses taken by our army, or by bushwhackers; some had been robbed of money or other valuables . . . and others needed assistance from the Government to keep from starving."[31]

Nevertheless, even where Federal authorities were most helpful and the courts were soon meeting, persistent problems prevented the restoration of county government to anything like prewar efficacy. Taxes were generally uncollectable, records were often missing, and courthouses were sometimes damaged or occupied by troops. Many lawyers and litigants were off in the army or in refuge elsewhere. Vexatious legal questions arising from the war stymied the resolution of what business the courts did undertake: how to divide among heirs an estate whose slaves had run off, for example, or whether to accept Confederate money in payment of debts. On top of all these obstacles, the Confederate invasion of late 1864 threw every county court south of Nashville into turmoil and shut down some for months—magistrates and clerks now, in an ironic turnabout, dodging rebel troops as resolutely as they had the Yankees not three years earlier.[32]

---

of 1862 this court had remained open under Confederate control until November, 1862); Williamson in October, 1863 (open under Confederate control from October, 1862, until January, 1863); Maury in February, 1864 (open under Confederate control from probably the late summer of 1862 until July, 1863); Lincoln in April, 1864 (open under Confederate control from October, 1862, until June, 1863); Rutherford in May, 1864; Montgomery in February, 1865; Sumner in March, 1865; Cheatham in June, 1865. Giles County court records for the war years are unavailable, but that county's experience probably paralleled Lincoln's. County court records are on microfilm in TSLA. See the bibliography for a complete list of those consulted.

31 Hinkley, *Narrative of Service*, 109–11. Fitch, *Annals of the Army*, 282–83, gives a colorful description of the role of the provost marshal in Middle Tennessee. A perusal of the lists of county court justices appointed or elected under Federal rule reveals, in every county, many names familiar from antebellum lists.

32 Practical problems involving estates, slaves, taxes, and debts, as well as disruption

A deeper problem was that Federal cooperation, even at its most magnanimous, was always qualified. Andrew Johnson's enthusiasm for speedy political reconstruction notwithstanding, Federal authorities for the most part viewed local government and local functionaries warily. Although many Union commanders were willing to revive the county courts to help administer conquered territory, they regarded the courts jealously as competing institutions of power (unlike the schools), and they supervised them closely. And they were rarely well disposed toward resuscitating the chancery and circuit courts because from a strictly military standpoint the provision of civil and criminal justice was a frill, contributing little to the practical administration of a subject land and people. Whether the local folk were able to transfer title to real estate, or sue a neighbor for welshing on a contract, or legally prosecute a swindler were matters of supreme indifference to most army officers. In only four counties—Maury, Rutherford, Williamson, and Davidson—were both chancery and circuit courts functioning before the war ended, and only in Davidson were they operating before mid-1864 or with close to a normal volume of business. All the same problems that plagued the county courts afflicted the courts of civil and criminal justice, too, with the added vexation of having to rely on hard-to-convene and usually recalcitrant juries composed of local men.[33]

More stultifying to every reopened court than any other difficulty, however, was that no matter how formidable the court's arm, its reach could not extend far beyond the limits of town. As long as the countryside remained chaotic and dangerous to travelers, rural folk had no recourse to the courts, nor could the courts exert their authority over the rural citizenry. Law, justice, and government had by 1863 ceased to exist in the rural heartland.

The experience of sixty-year-old magistrate Isaac Ivy of Williamson

---

resulting from the Confederate invasion, are illustrated in Davidson County Court Minutes, July 7, 29, 1862, July 6, 1863, Bk. I, 82, 87–88, 152; Rutherford County Court Minutes, March, 1865, Bk. DD, 669–70; Williamson County, County Court Clerk's Office, Minutes, January, 1867, Vol. XX, 244–46 (Microfilm copy in TSLA); Lincoln County, County Court Clerk's Office, Minutes, April, 1864, to July, 1865, *passim*, Vol. A, 1–63 (Microfilm copy in TSLA).

33   Except in Davidson County (where they reopened in April, 1862), no chancery court in the region reopened before September, 1864, and no circuit court before April, 1864; most did not reopen until 1865. Problems with juries are illustrated in Nashville *Daily Times and True Union*, October 7, 1864. In addition to the circuit and chancery court records (see bibliography), information on the reopening of the courts may be found in Nashville *Daily Times and True Union*, May 13, 1864; Andrew Johnson to George H. Thomas, September 26, 1864, in *OR*, Vol. XXXIX, Pt. 2, p. 482. In a few cases military officials did encourage the reopening of courts of justice, especially where it relieved the army of the burden of trying civil-

County is poignantly illuminating. Ordered in 1864 to enroll every man in his district in the state militia, Ivy explained plaintively to Governor Johnson that the district was "very large, & thinly settled . . . a large portion of it mountains, Hills & timber, Generally thick Set with undergrowth, in which bands of Guerrilas & Robers are frequently Seen. . . . Some of them have threatened me, and other Justices of the Peace. . . . The Cituation . . . is Such, that no protection would be of benefit to me that could or would be given. Now I hope the above will be Sufficient excuse for not enrolling [the citizens] . . . and your excellency will appoint some young man." Ivy's ordeal was reenacted many times across the rural heartland.[34]

The towns, by contrast, bustled with the activity of government throughout the war (save just after the initial panic), even where county, chancery, and circuit courts were functioning meagerly or not at all. Federal authorities keenly desired order in the towns, their bases of operation. Thus they often tolerated and even encouraged urban government. And though chronically short of funds, town governments (unlike the county courts) enjoyed an accessible and readily coerced citizenry by virtue of protected mobility within their dominions. Town streets, however full of pickpockets and drunken soldiers, were far safer than country roads. In Murfreesboro, for example, government went on for weeks after the invasion before military authorities demanded so much as an oath of allegiance from the officeholders. When they finally did so, only the mayor, recorder, and two aldermen refused; those officers were removed and quickly replaced by others chosen by the remaining aldermen. Town government thereupon proceeded as usual. Nashville city government, nearly overwhelmed by newly aggravated problems of crowding, crime, disease, and poverty, found itself busier than ever before. With army assistance (and after a thorough political purgation by Andrew Johnson), it set about to police the unruly, warm and feed the poor, and bury the dead, all at a pace that made antebellum Nashville seem sleepy by comparison.[35]

---

ians by military commissions on criminal charges. See Nashville *Daily Times and True Union*, April 13, 1864; Maslowski, *Treason Must Be Made Odious*, 64–66.

34 Isaac Ivy to Andrew Johnson, September 30, 1864, in Johnson Papers.

35 Murfreesboro *Union Volunteer*, May 20, 1862; Nashville *Dispatch*, October 22, November 5, December 7, 11, 21, 30, 1862, November 3, 1863; *Nashville Daily Times and True Union*, May 12, 1864; Maslowski, *Treason Must Be Made Odious*, 53–54, 121–37. See also Shelbyville *Tri-Weekly News*, June 19, 1862. Clarksville was an exception to this rule. Antagonism between citizens and the army there resulted in the suppression of town government and its replacement by military rule. See Clarksville *Weekly Chronicle*, September 22, 1865, February 16, 1866.

The churches of the heartland saw harsh trials and knew deep anguish from 1862 to 1865, for the house of God was no sanctuary from the all-permeating pestilence of war. Urban churches, like urban schools, did benefit from the preservation of order in the towns by Federal bayonets. Many continued services uninterrupted, or nearly so, through the war (some even received substantial additions to their weekly congregations in the form of blue-uniformed worshipers). But an urban location was no guarantor of serenity and safety for any church. The First Baptist Church of Nashville, for example, was abruptly dissolved in 1863, when the army seized its house of worship for a hospital and ultimately wrecked it. The fathers of the First Presbyterian Church of Murfreesboro recorded sadly in July, 1864, on the occasion of their first meeting in two and a half years (and their last until 1865), "There has been an unprecedented destruction of property . . . & even the *resting-place* of the dead . . . & the Sanctuary itself . . . have been & still are *desolated* & *desecrated!*" But even without deliberate Yankee vandalism or expropriation, many churches of the heartland's towns found the tribulations of war insurmountable. The large Cumberland Presbyterian Church of Lebanon, for example, was disorganized through the entire period of occupation. As its minister explained in 1866, "The w[o]nts of war—armies, battles, alarms and woes, broke up not only regular session meetings, but regular services."[36]

Along with all the familiar "alarms and woes" of war, another affliction plagued the urban churches. Like local government but unlike the schools, churches were institutions of power and influence in the towns, real or potential rivals of the jealous Yankee conquerors. But the churches offered no service of practical value to the occupiers comparable to that provided by local government, no tribute to propitiate a distrustful ruler. Thus the merest hint of sedition or disobedience from the pulpit was usually enough to provoke the Federals to close a church's doors or lock up its minister. Such political retaliation probably disrupted as many urban churches from 1862 to 1865 as did all the other exigencies of war together. In Murfreesboro in the first weeks of occupation army authorities closed every church until clergymen agreed to take the oath, then jailed the recalcitrant and required permits of the rest even to hold a funeral. The wealthy and

---

36 Rufus B. Spain, "R. B. C. Howell: Nashville Baptist Leader in the Civil War Period," *THQ*, XIV (1955), 338; First Presbyterian Church, Murfreesboro, Session Minutes, July 18, 1864; Historical Records Survey, *Cumberland Presbyterian Records*, II, 51–52. Instances of Union soldiers attending urban churches are in Ready Diary, March 31, 1862; Carney Diary, May 25, 1862; Handy Diary, February 19, 1865. For an example of an urban church undisrupted by the war, see Presbyterian Church, Lewisburg, Marshall County, Records, Session Minutes, 1862–65, *passim* (MS in TSLA).

defiant First Presbyterian Church of Clarksville was closed by military edict from the arrival of the Yankees until very near the end of the war. In Nashville, Andrew Johnson wasted little time before rounding up all the leading ministers, including R. B. C. Howell of the First Baptist Church and C. D. Elliott of the Nashville Female Academy, to demand the oath from them. Those who refused he banished to the south or imprisoned; Howell and Elliott, for example, spent months in a penitentiary.[37]

Most ministers in Middle Tennessee's towns escaped harassment only by treading very lightly, or by actually embracing the Union cause. Philip Fall of the Disciples of Christ, who conscientiously preserved strict neutrality during the war and preached a pure Gospel devoid of politics, was perhaps the only Nashville minister allowed to carry on unmolested by Andrew Johnson. In Murfreesboro soon after the invasion another clergyman quietly omitted at Sunday services the customary prayer for the Confederacy, and a week later—with numerous Federal soldiers in attendance—"preached a sermon more in accordance with their feelings than of the Southern portion of his congregation," as one reproachful member wrote. Not long afterward the Baptist minister in that town declared himself a unionist and prayed outright for the Yankees. In Nashville that year the Second Presbyterian Church witnessed a virtual palace revolution when a unionist faction of the church elders (deposed in 1861), after intriguing with Federal authorities, occupied the church building with a squad of armed troops, seized records and funds, and reclaimed control of the church.[38]

Violence, not politics, determined the fate of the heartland's rural churches. As the war continued inexorably and the countryside grew ever more perilous for wayfarers, rural congregations (particularly those dependent on circuit-riding ministers) despaired of keeping up regular Sunday preaching and session meetings. Sadly, unwillingly, but nonetheless surely, the churches one after another defaulted on their sacred obligations to nurture the spirit, correct the errant, and sustain the community of believers.

The extent of rural church disruption, as well as its chronology, varied with local circumstances. The important determinants were the relative

37   Carney Diary, May 16, June 18, July 3, 1862; First Presbyterian Church, Clarksville, Session Minutes, Vol. II, 1862–65, *passim*; Spain, "R. B. C. Howell," 335–37. See also Pise Journal, 1862–65, *passim*, which details the persistent Federal harassment of an unyielding Episcopal rector in Columbia.

38   Herman A. Norton, *Tennessee Christians: A History of the Christian Church in Tennessee* (Nashville, 1971), 99–100; Ready Diary, March 23, 31, 1862; Carney Diary, June 22, 1862; Mrs. Roy C. Avery (ed.), "The Second Presbyterian Church of Nashville During the Civil War," *THQ*, XI (1952), 356–75.

isolation of the neighborhood, the propinquity of Union troops, and the magnitude of guerrillaism and banditry. But few country churches escaped disruption at some point after the occupation began. A Disciples of Christ minister who rode circuit in Rutherford County traveled unhindered until 1863 but thereafter was so frequently harassed and robbed (of his horse, for example) that he gave up his work until the spring of 1865. The fathers of Enon Primitive Baptist Church of Bedford County gathered in September, 1863, for the first time in nine months, ascribing their long absence to "bad weather and troublesome times." They met next in April, 1864, and resumed regular monthly sessions for a time, but then again failed to meet from October of that year until the war was nearly over. The New Hope Primitive Baptist Church congregation in Bedford assembled but twice in 1862, "on account of the federal soldiers being among us," and did not meet again during the war. Even Zion Church of Maury County, the Presbyterian community whose "oneness" was proverbial, suffered anguishing interludes of suspension. "Owing to the disturbances in the country," the church clerk recorded in April, 1864, "we have had no communion since October 1862; & Session have had no meeting since that time."[39]

Most striking and evocative are the wartime minutes of West Station Primitive Baptist Church of Sumner County. From July to December, 1862, each month is simply marked "No conference," followed by the terse explanation "war"; similar notations appear for every month of 1863, along with the scribbled entreaty "Lord save us"; the record for all of 1864 consists of but one entry: "No meetings (Lord have mercy and revive us[)]"; for the conflict's last months in 1865 there is the epigraph, in a penciled scrawl, "War War War War War War."[40]

Only a few fortunate congregations, remotely sequestered and safe from

39   Norton, *Tennessee Christians*, 100; Enon Primitive Baptist Church, Bedford County, Session Minutes, 1862–65, *passim*, especially September, 1863; New Hope Primitive Baptist Church, Fairfield, Bedford County, Records, Session Minutes, 1862–66, *passim*, especially October 4, 1862 (MS in TSLA); Zion Presbyterian Church, Columbia, Maury County, Records, Session Minutes, April 10, 1864 (Microfilm copy in TSLA). For other examples of the disruption of rural churches and ministry (the important social consequences of which are discussed in Chapter VII), see Cedar Lick Baptist Church, Wilson County, Records, Session Minutes, 1865 (Microfilm copy in TSLA); Robertson Fork Church of Christ, Marshall County, Records, Session Minutes, 1862–65, *passim* (MS in TSLA); Silver Creek Society of the Cumberland Presbyterian Church, Maury County, Records, Session Minutes, 1862–65, *passim* (MS in TSLA); Cox Diary, April 6, August 24, 1862, December 31, 1863; Matthews Journal, October 11, 1863, April 17, 1864.

40   West Station Primitive Baptist Church, Sumner County, Records, Session Minutes, 1862–65, *passim* (Microfilm copy in TSLA).

roaming pillagers and murderous brigands, sustained their fellowship throughout the war. Bethlehem Baptist Church of Robertson County, for one, dutifully carried on its work without interruption. Throughout 1863 and 1864, as violence and ruin convulsed the heartland and churches everywhere were empty and their worshipers scattered, Bethlehem Church was meeting regularly to exalt the Lord, conduct church business, and discipline wayward members for their drinking, dancing, swearing, and other acts of debauchery—all seemingly unabated by the war. In April, 1863, for example, the church took time to expel two women for "acting the Harlot," another for "having an unlawful child," and one hapless brother "For his repeated conduct in showing his Secrets to the Ladies."[41]

Even when a church endured, however, war brought absences and loss that threatened its heart and soul: the circle did not abide unbroken. Often when congregations did assemble, white women, children, and older men constituted the whole of the faithful: young white males were away in the army or in fearful hiding; black brothers and sisters of every age were seeking new lives. Surviving church minutes sometimes transcend their routinism to convey poignantly a sense of the congregation's grief. When the Yankee occupation kept Brother Watson of Wilson Creek Primitive Baptist Church of Williamson County from joining his anxiously waiting congregation in October, 1862, the clerk dolefully reported that "after reading a chapter the church sung & p[r]ayed with & for each other & also for our beloved pastor & retired in pensive silence." A month later Watson was again absent, and the faithful sang, prayed, and "retired in silent gloom trusting in a merciful God for better times." Still without its preacher in December, the congregation "retired with sadness of hearts."[42]

Brother Watson eventually returned to his flock, but many another church suffered losses that could not be redeemed on earth. One was McCains Cumberland Presbyterian of Maury County, which in August, 1862, mourned the death of Brother Robert H. Maxwell, Confederate volunteer, of pneumonia in a Yankee prison camp. "While we deeply deplor our loss," the congregation resolved, "we will bow in submission to the divine and mysterious dispensation of God in this our sad bereavement."[43]

Mysterious indeed must God's dispensations have appeared to all the people of Middle Tennessee in the three years following the Northern in-

41   Bethlehem Baptist Church, Robertson County, Records, Session Minutes, Vol. I, 1863–65, *passim*, especially April, 1863 (Microfilm copy in TSLA).

42   Norton, *Tennessee Christians*, 101; Wilson Creek Primitive Baptist Church, Williamson County, Session Minutes, October, November, December, 1862.

43   McCains Cumberland Presbyterian Church, Maury County, Session Minutes, August 13, 1862.

vasion; terrible, too, did they seem, dark and wrathful. Those heartlanders who endured saw their rich land ravaged, their handiworks smashed
and burned. They saw the grandest living symbols of their culture—their
institutions of learning, of law, and of worship—gutted and trampled or
grievously wounded. They saw their countrymen suffer and die. Yet amid
the pain and ruin, certain of these people joyously perceived a glorious
boon: freedom. Of all the cataclysms of war, only this one—emancipation—evoked any cheers from the people of the heartland. But among the
majority who cheered it not, no church's demise, no village's obliteration,
no patriot's martyrdom, was ever so agonizingly apprehended and deeply
mourned as was the death of slavery.

Chapter VI

Jubilee

Slaves, Masters, Yankees, and Freedmen, 1862–1865

MANY A YANKEE soldier's most vivid impression of the march into Middle Tennessee in the first months of 1862 was not of verdant fields and fat cattle but of rapturous black faces at every point along the route. As the 6th Ohio Infantry passed through Williamson County its men saw "gangs of slaves . . . clinging to the fences by the road side, whence they watched the marching column with wondering eyes and unmistakable delight, as long as it remained in view." In Clarksville, one resident recalled, "The negroes were all excited by the near approach of the men in blue. They were gathered on the water front, watching eagerly . . . and of all the population, they alone were to welcome the invaders." An Ohio officer en route to Murfreesboro with his regiment wrote that "at every plantation negroes came flocking to the roadside to see us. They are the only friends we find. They have heard of the abolition army, the music, the banners, the glittering arms . . . [and they] welcome us with extravagant manifestations of joy. They keep time to the music with feet and hands and hurrah 'fur de ole flag and de Union,' sometimes following us for miles." [1]

When the troops and the excitement had passed, however, the slaves of the heartland dutifully returned home, picked up their hoes, and went back to the fields. Slavery in Middle Tennessee did not dissolve at the mere

---

1 Ebenezer Hannaford, *The Story of a Regiment: A History of the Campaigns, and Associations in the Field, of the Sixth Regiment Ohio Volunteer Infantry* (Cincinnati, 1868), 227; Williams, "Reminiscence of Clarksville," 206; Beatty, *Memoirs of a Volunteer*, 93.

touch of the enemy. The "abolition army" whose paeans the jubilant blacks sang was far from being that in 1862. The general disposition of the army high command in the region during the first year and more of occupation was an earnest desire to avoid unsettling the institution of slavery, and especially to avoid being annoyed by slaves. Strict orders went out to field and post commanders limiting the military employment of slaves and forbidding the harboring of fugitives. These edicts were for the most part well received and faithfully obeyed by subordinate officers, for this citizen army had a strong streak of conservative Democracy—to the pleasant surprise of many white Middle Tennesseans, who had long viewed every blue-coated brigade as an arm of Radical Republicanism. A Rutherford County woman complimented the Murfreesboro commandant on his moderation and his willingness to aid local whites whose slaves had run off to the army. "I know of one or two he has sent home," she added, "& instructed their owners to chastise them." In Nashville the military authorities vowed not to interfere with the city's enforcement of the slave code and enthusiastically joined the civil police in cracking down on black vagrancy. Military Governor Andrew Johnson's typically outspoken remark on Lincoln's preliminary Emancipation Proclamation in late 1862 summed up the attitude of many of his subordinates: "Damn the negroes," he declared; "I am fighting these traitorous aristocrats, their masters!"[2]

Most of those bondsmen who so joyfully greeted the arrival of the supposed army of liberation were soon disillusioned. Typical was the experience of a Murfreesboro slave who with high expectations visited the Union occupiers soon after they entered the town in March, 1862. The next day his mistress wrote, "Our negro returned this afternoon—he went into the Camp with a confederate coat on—they called him a secesh negro and put him to hard work—about noon . . . he gave them the slip and came home perfectly satisfied says he will never leave his master again." Slaves in Nashville, too, came to believe that the Yankees were best avoided, especially after a surprise raid in September in which hundreds of blacks were rounded up to work on fortifications. "The colored population of that city," chuckled a Union officer some time after, "have probably not yet forgotten the suddenness with which [the army] gathered them in from barber-shops, kitchens, and even churches." Several bloody encounters

2   D. C. Buell to O. M. Mitchell, March 11, 1862, in *OR*, Vol. X, Pt. 2, p. 31; testimony of Lovell H. Rousseau, *ibid.*, Vol. XVI, Pt. 1, pp. 350–51; Sarah Ridley Trimble (ed.), "Behind the Lines in Middle Tennessee, 1863–1865: The Journal of Bettie Ridley Blackmore," *THQ*, XII (1953), 63; Nashville *Dispatch*, December 30, 1862, February 14, 1863; John Cimprich, "Military Governor Johnson and Tennessee Blacks, 1862–65," *THQ*, XXXIX (1980), 461.

between blacks and soldiers in the city also taught Nashville's slaves and free blacks the sad lesson that the soldiers of the Union were not necessarily the friends of the oppressed. In one incident early in September, soldiers hunting seats in a crowded theater beat up and evicted blacks in the audience, then spilled out into the street after the show, assaulting every black man they could lay hands on.[3]

Such evidence of personal hostility and official conservatism persuaded many slaves in this early period of occupation that life under the Stars and Stripes held no more promise of freedom than that under the Stars and Bars. Most therefore abandoned their initial exultation, readopted their habitual masks of insouciance, and resumed their accustomed toil, to the profound satisfaction of their masters and mistresses. Every indication of slave loyalty and contentment was seized upon and flaunted by relieved whites. A Murfreesboro slaveowner proudly recounted in May, 1862, how a drunken soldier had accosted her female servant and demanded to know if she was for the South or the North: South, the slave replied (in the presence of her mistress). The eminent Davidson County planter William G. Harding received welcome news from his family about affairs at his Belle Meade plantation that spring. "Every one [slave] seems determined to do his or her best," his wife wrote on May 2, "and there has been no trouble, and you know how gratifying it is to me to make such a report."[4]

More perspicacious observers were less sanguine. Subtle counterevidence was there for those who noticed it. A young Murfreesboro woman observed in July, 1862, that the mood of local slaves rose and fell with the movements of the Union army. Confederates recaptured the town on the thirteenth and released all the jailed secessionists: "They looked so happy," she wrote, "but, who did not except the dusky forms that hovered around our front steps." The rebels soon departed and the Federal troops returned, only to pull out again on the twenty-second: "I can see the spirits of the servants are ebbing low since the Yankees are pushing along." The next day, however, another Union force passed through: "The ebony images were overjoyed to see them return." A sharp-eyed Northern officer in Murfreesboro, studying the black multitude that turned out to watch troops parade in March, 1862, concluded that every slave would readily desert his master if he could get away with it.[5]

The circumstances of war would soon give the slaves of Murfreesboro and all Middle Tennessee that opportunity. The war had its own liberating

---

3   Ready Diary, March 24, 1862; Fitch, *Annals of the Army,* 182; Nashville *Dispatch,* September 2, 9, 1862.

4   Carney Diary, May 25, 1862; wife to William G. Harding, May 2, 1862, in Harding-Jackson Papers.

5   Carney Diary, July 13, 22, 23, 1862; Beatty, *Memoirs of a Volunteer,* 96.

momentum, scarcely impeded by the conservatism and apathy of the Union army or by the determination of native whites to keep their slaves in bondage, but mightily reinforced by the desire of black heartlanders to be free. Even as the mass of bondsmen went placidly about their work in field and kitchen under the contented gaze of their masters, hairline cracks appeared in the edifice of slavery, gradually widened, and ultimately crumbled the institution, freeing its captives.

In the first place, the Federal army—however intolerant its commanders were of idle slaves and runaways around the camps—needed strong black arms and backs and usually welcomed Negroes as teamsters and spade-wielders. When they did not appear voluntarily in sufficient numbers, as they did not in these early months, the Yankees did not hesitate to go out and seize them. The army took in or impressed many hundreds, perhaps thousands, of black laborers throughout the heartland during 1862, and many of those slaves did not return home. Some, reckoning that working for the Yankees was no worse than working for their old masters, willingly stayed with the Union army when it retreated from southern Middle Tennessee in the fall. "Large crowds of them were on the railway trains," an officer remembered, "and I saw a great many going north in wagons by the country roads." Others, who ran away from digging trenches or were released or expelled from the Federal camps without being sent home, wandered at large, their fate a matter of indifference to the Federals as long as they did not burden the army.[6]

These first months of occupation witnessed also a few deliberate acts of liberation unconnected with the army's need for labor and in direct contravention of the wishes of the high command. Sometimes the motive was a Union soldier or officer's compassion for the slave; more often it was revenge against slaveholding secessionists. Sympathetic Illinois soldiers in Fayetteville forged passes in June, 1862, to help a Lincoln County slave girl escape to Kentucky. An Ohio officer in Nashville that spring professed his concern about "trouble with escaped negroes" but then confessed slyly that those coming into the lines "in some mysterious way are so disposed of that their masters never hear of them again." In September, Federal soldiers bent on retaliation ransacked Clarksville and led away not less than two hundred slaves. "The negroes were induced by both private persuasion and shameless public invitation," wrote outraged townspeople, "and often compelled to join the ranks and flee from their masters."[7]

6 Testimony of Lovell H. Rousseau, in *OR*, Vol. XVI, Pt. 1, pp 350–51; testimony of Francis Darr, *ibid.*, 617; Nashville *Dispatch*, August 12, 1862; sister to William G. Harding, August 14, 1862, in Harding-Jackson Papers; Bickham, *Rosecrans' Campaign*, 87.

7 Alexander P. Smith to Andrew Johnson, June 27, 1862, in Graf and Haskins (eds.), *Papers of Andrew Johnson*, V, 510–11, 511 n.; Beatty, *Memoirs of a Volunteer*, 91–92; Clarksville,

Even those slaves who found the Yankees unhelpful, inhospitable, or downright malevolent (and they were certainly the great majority of slaves before 1863) came to recognize that in a subtle way the mere fact of military occupation compromised their masters' authority. Instances of black disaffection and disobedience—all in some way connected to the presence of the Yankees—multiplied during 1862 and early 1863, even as slave-owners assured one another of their bondsmen's steadfast fidelity.

Often the slaves were displaying a furtive impudence or disloyalty, well hidden from the eyes and ears of a potentially furious master but nonetheless corrosive to their "proper" subordination. As the Yankee army approached, blacks in Giles County composed wickedly insubordinate ditties and sang among themselves with spiteful glee:

> Ole massa runned away,
> And de darkey stayed at home . . .
> Dere's wine and cider in de cellar,
> And de niggers must hab some.

> Oh black gal, you can't shine,
> I done quit foolin' wid de kinky-headed kin';
> First of July and de las' of May,
> I've had a white gal on my min'.

Others secretly provided the invaders with information withheld by uncooperative whites. "The white people are treacherous and unreliable, all lying to deceive us," a Union officer reported in March, 1862. "We can only depend on the statements of negroes."[8]

In growing numbers, however, the blacks of the heartland—with a glance over their shoulders at the nearby Yankees—dared to flaunt their contumacy and infidelity in overt, openly defiant acts. A Davidson County slave went boldly to the Federals in May, 1862, and charged his owner and two other men with keeping forbidden weapons; the three were promptly arrested and turned over to the Nashville provost marshal. In Williamson County that spring, Sam, a fifteen-year-old slave of Jesse Cox, had been "doing bad for some time," according to his master's breathless report, "refuse[d] to be corrected by me, jerked me down I being very weak, and then took the ax and started off I sent the other [slave] after him, he presently returned with the ax and said the yankey cavelry had taken Sam

---

Tennessee, citizens to Ulysses S. Grant, September 15, 1862, in Confederate Collection, TSLA.

8   Bell I. Wiley, *Plain People of the Confederacy* (Baton Rouge, 1943), 74–76; report of John Kennett, March 8, 1862, in *OR*, Vol. X, Pt. 1, p. 6.

behind one of them." Washington, a Nashville slave married to the slave of another owner, so persistently harassed his wife's mistress in January, 1863, that she banned him from her house. He thereupon cursed her, went off, returned with an armed soldier and a wagon, and proceeded to haul away furniture and bedclothes from the woman's home over her loud but unavailing objections.[9]

Washington received thirty-nine lashes from the city police and a term in the workhouse, then returned to the custody of his master. The same day he ran off, Sam reappeared at Cox's farm and went back to work. But many slaves who deserted their owners in these early months of occupation had no such qualms as Sam and did not go home again. And, increasingly, those slaves (following in the footsteps of antebellum free blacks) made their way to the towns, especially Nashville, in hopes of losing themselves in the black urban subculture and dodging the determined searching of an angry master. By the end of 1862 Nashville was filling up with these "contrabands," and civil authorities and white residents of the city grew concerned. The editor of the *Dispatch* declared that the contrabands mistakenly thought themselves free, and he urged the authorities to round them up, put them to work, and relieve the city of "an intolerable burden and nuisance."[10]

The citizens of Nashville sided with the *Dispatch*, but history sided with the contrabands. Slavery in Middle Tennessee, already under stress in 1862, fractured in 1863 and disintegrated in 1864. What can account for this momentous, nearly incredible turn of events?

The death of slavery in the heartland can be concisely (though perhaps facilely) explained thus: rural chaos permitted it, the Union army encouraged it, and the slaves desired it and perpetrated it. Physical devastation and the breakdown of order and social intercourse in the countryside destroyed not only the coercive power of master and state over the slave but the entire web of human and institutional relationships that bound the slave to his master and defined him as a slave. Where ruin and disorder reigned, the rural community could not extend its broad embrace, the rural church could not unite the faithful and discipline the errant, the conscientious master could not feed and protect his "people," the abusive master could not whip his, and the gun-toting sheriff with his dogs could not track down a runaway. But such social and institutional disruption meant only that slaves could leave their masters if they so chose. That they did

9   Wife to William G. Harding, May 15, 1862, in Harding-Jackson Papers; Cox Diary, April 16, 1862; Nashville *Dispatch*, January 10, 1863.
10   Nashville *Dispatch*, November 1, 1862, January 18, 1863.

leave in ever-growing numbers after 1862 was a consequence of the Union army's increasingly antislavery policy and of the slaves' unquestionable urge to be free. These two forces fed each other reciprocally: the more the slaves liberated themselves from bondage, the more the Federal army was inclined to treat them as free men and women; the more the Federal army considered them free, the more the slaves deemed themselves so. It may be said that if Yankee soldiers made the slaves of Middle Tennessee freedmen, the slaves of Middle Tennessee made the Yankee soldiers abolitionists.[11]

By 1863 slaveholders and civil authorities realized that the Union army was not a reliable ally in preserving slavery. Rather than remaining neutral, that army was becoming an active agent of emancipation, motivated less by sympathy for the slave than by a growing desire to punish the recalcitrant rebels. In February the Nashville city council, in the midst of formulating a sterner policy toward contrabands, received a letter from the army provost marshal decreeing that if city police made any further attempts to return black runaways to secessionist slaveholders, "I will take the case into my own hands, and give [the policemen] a term in the city prison." Around the region military officials increasingly ignored civil law, standing army directives, and even direct orders to return fugitives. The officer in charge of contrabands in Gallatin from September, 1863, to August, 1864, routinely turned away fugitive-hunting masters, even those bearing official authorization from army headquarters. Another officer who took charge of contrabands in the region in June, 1864, testified afterward that during his tenure he always treated the blacks as though they were free, whatever the legal technicalities, because Tennessee was an "insurrectionary district."[12]

The army did not confine itself merely to preventing the reenslavement of runaways. Increasingly, field officers seized slaves outright, going far beyond the early, restrained impressment policy. Before long they were taking every black they could find, whether they needed them for labor or not. The policy by 1864 was, in the words of one officer, "keep all we get, and get all we can." A high-ranking Union commander in Nashville reported that year that "it is . . . the practice of soldiers to go to the country and bring in wagon-loads of negro women and children to this city, and I suppose to other posts." An Illinois officer wrote his wife describing his raids through the countryside, during which his troops routinely took every horse and slave they could find: "Now what do you think of your husband," he teased, "degenerating from a conservative young Democrat

11 Rural social disruption is fully analyzed in Chapter VII.
12 Nashville *Dispatch*, February 27, 1863; *Senate Executive Documents*, 38th Cong., 2nd Sess., No. 1209, p. 11; *House Reports*, 39th Cong., 1st Sess., No. 1273, pp. 120–22.

to a horse stealer and 'nigger thief,' and practicing his nefarious occupation almost within gun shot of the sacred 'Hermitage' and tomb of Andrew Jackson? Yes, while in the field I am an abolitionist."[13]

Many of the slaves led away by the Yankees were handed not pick and shovel but musket and bayonet. The recruitment of black troops became official Federal policy in 1863, and that summer a regiment was raised in Nashville from among laborers impressed in 1862 and still in the army's hands. By September, army officials had regularized the procedure and hired a corps of white recruiters and black assistants. Zealously these agents, along with officers of black regiments, scoured city streets and countryside, making speeches, enrolling volunteers and sometimes conscripting others, and reinforcing their appeals with the promise of government care for wives and children. So successful were they (new regiments soon mustered at Gallatin, Shelbyville, Clarksville, and Murfreesboro) that officers responsible for black work details complained that the recruiters were siphoning off needed labor.[14]

As they forcibly released fugitive blacks from their masters' clutches and gathered in others by the thousands to work or fight, Federal authorities brushed aside legalities and issued their own proclamations of de facto emancipation. In July, 1863, the Nashville provost guard arrested Manson M. Brien, a prominent jurist and unionist, who had waylaid his recently runaway servant on the street, pounced on her, and locked her up in his house. Releasing the woman, the provost marshal politely but firmly informed Judge Brien that "*the time had passed when negroes could be whipped in this country.*" In September the officer supervising black recruitment in Middle Tennessee gave orders promising freedom at the end of service to slave volunteers fleeing secessionist masters. Two months later the same official declared flatly before a government commission on contraband policy, "Slavery is dead; that is the first thing. That is what we all begin with here, who know the state of affairs." By 1864 even the conservative army high command was echoing those words. The major general commanding the District of Nashville conceded in January that "slavery is virtually dead in Tennessee."[15]

13 Fitch, *Annals of the Army*, 270; Lovell H. Rousseau to W. D. Whipple, January 30, 1864, in *OR*, Vol. XXXII, Pt. 2, pp. 267–68; "Major Connolly's Letters," 247–48.

14 George L. Stearns to E. M. Stanton, September 25, 1863, and enclosure, in *OR*, Ser. III, Vol. III, 840; R. D. Mussey to C. W. Foster, October 10, 1864, *ibid.*, IV, 762–64; Lovell H. Rousseau to W. D. Whipple, January 30, 1864, *ibid.*, Ser. I, Vol. XXXII, Pt. 2, pp. 267–69; G. M. Dodge to U. S. Grant, December 9, 1863, *ibid.*, Vol. XXXI, Pt. 3, pp. 366–67; John Hope Franklin (ed.), *The Diary of James T. Ayers, Civil War Recruiter* (Springfield, Ill., 1947), xvi, 38, 106.

15 Nashville *Dispatch*, July 28, 1863; George L. Stearns to E. M. Stanton, September 25, 1863, and enclosure, in *OR*, Ser. III, Vol. III, 840; testimony of George L. Stearns,

Yankee pronouncements were superfluous, however, because by late 1864 most of the black men and women of the heartland had declared themselves free. Those authorities who announced the death of slavery were reacting less to the government's armed emancipation of the slaves than to the slaves' spontaneous self-liberation. Their own recognition of freedom marked the turning point of the slaves' Civil War, and they reached it in their own minds and hearts, not as a result of Federal decrees. The popular image of emancipation—a group of field hands gathered by the cabins at the end of the war listening with hushed excitement as their master or a blue-uniformed officer reads aloud from an official document pronouncing them free—has no place in Middle Tennessee history. Emancipation in the heartland is best exemplified by the story of Joel, a trusted Rutherford County slave, who in 1864 accompanied his mistress to a store in Murfreesboro and held her horse while she went in. When she emerged a few minutes later, Joel was gone. She found him nearby at army headquarters: "The little rascal was perfectly insolent & defiant," she reported indignantly; "—told me 'you have no business to take me out of town—I intend to stay and go to school & be free. I won't go.'" Unable to get any help from the indifferent Yankees, Joel's mistress rode home alone and Joel became a free man.[16]

Freedom took many forms, however, for not every beneficiary of emancipation or self-emancipation ran off to town or donned an army uniform. Freedom was not a place or a pursuit but a state of mind and a set of human relationships, just as slavery had been. Freedom came when slaves realized that their masters no longer held the power of compulsion over them, that is, when they understood that they could leave without fear of recapture or could refuse orders and resist punishment without fear of ultimate retribution. Before the Civil War, of course, slaves could and often did run away or refuse a whipping. But these were always desperate acts, committed with the knowledge that punishment was certain because, even if the master had been foiled, the fury of the white community would quickly be leveled at the refractory servant. After 1862, however, as social disarray, institutional disruption, and Federal interposition destroyed the coercive power of master and community, and as the slaves grasped this fact and acted upon it, they ceased to be slaves.

The black people of the heartland came to perceive their new status intuitively. A few observant whites also noted it. At the end of 1864 two

American Freedmen's Inquiry Commission Report; Lovell H. Rousseau to W. D. Whipple, January 30, 1864, in *OR*, Vol. XXXII, Pt. 2, pp. 267–68.

16   Trimble (ed.), "Behind the Lines," 70–71.

Federal commissioners reported to the U.S. Senate that a government camp established near Clarksville for contrabands "by its moral influence, has greatly weakened and almost broken the bonds of the slave in all [the] surroundings. The master knows his slave has the power to leave him and to reach this camp, where he will be secure, and consequently the tasks and punishments he has been accustomed to exact, or to inflict, are greatly reduced and ameliorated." Slaves who knew they could lay down the plow and walk away were no longer slaves, even if they kept on plowing. Masters who knew that their slaves could walk away were not masters, even if they still gave orders.[17]

A few blacks renounced slavery in spirit even while the white community still held dominion over their bodies. Thus did Edmund, a Maury County slave owned by an estate and awaiting assignment to an heir, declare himself free in the summer of 1862 when the Union army marched through. Edmund ran off with the Yankees but was recaptured when they retreated and, according to the county court's report in May, 1863, he "has since been . . . confined in jail where the administrator has [been] compelled to keep him to prevent his running away again . . . he still persists in his determination of returning to the Federals and has repeatedly expressed his intention of doing so."[18]

The actions of Edmund, Joel, and thousands of others obviously gave the lie to all the old white affirmations of the loyalty and contentment of the heartland's slaves. Those masters who had convinced themselves that paternalism was a mutual bond of affection and allegiance were proved wrong countless times. The disruption of slavery frequently brought out long-suppressed bitterness and anger within slaves. Asked teasingly by a soldier in 1864 if she was afraid of the Yankees, a Rutherford County black woman replied sincerely, "Oh no sah . . . hadent bin for the yankees dey a done had me used up afor dis time." Even when personal ties between master and slave were strong, they were (unbeknown to the master) usually neutralized by the slave's resentment of physical and social subjugation. When the whites' power of compulsion dissipated, bonds of affection and inveterate habits of obedience were rarely adequate to sustain the master-slave relationship. The war revealed that the true foundation of slavery was not nature or paternalistic and filial devotion but force. A Yankee officer came to this realization during a slave-gathering sweep through Wilson County in 1863, when an elderly white woman begged him not to take her servant Mollie, with whom she had been raised and

17 *Senate Executive Documents*, 38th Cong., 2nd Sess., No. 1209, p. 10.
18 Maury County Court Minutes, May 4, 1863, Vol. XIV, 234.

whom she loved. The officer noticed that the slave "seemed to give no attention" to this declaration of affection and that she remained silent even after further pleading by the old mistress's daughter. He thereupon led the unprotesting Mollie off with the other slaves.[19]

A few blacks, however, deeply attached to their owners, remained loyal. Tales of slave fidelity in wartime are not merely the rosy-hued myths of a later generation of Lost Cause votaries. Some of the slaves on the plantation of George A. Washington in Robertson County, for example, faithfully stayed on even during their owner's long absence in the latter part of the war: "Granville [is] very anxious to see his Master," the plantation mistress wrote in March, 1865. Slaves on occasion selflessly protected their master's property and even saved their master's life. When a Yankee tried to rob Nimrod Porter at gunpoint in November, 1864, his slaves came to the rescue and subdued the soldier; Porter noted with satisfaction that the would-be thief was "bad used up" by the blacks. In an episode with all the elements of romantic fiction, a Giles County farmer about to be lynched by bushwhackers was saved—with the rope literally around his neck—by his slave Angeline, who convinced them that her master was a loyal Confederate.[20]

A very few slaves were not only faithful but servile long after the compulsions of slavery ceased. These blacks, perhaps ruled by deeply ingrained habits of deference or naturally dependent personalities, remained slaves in spirit even after the white community relinquished physical mastery of them. Isham, owned by Maury County farmer James W. Matthews, stayed with his master through the war and as late as May, 1865, submitted to a whipping for sneaking off on a "fishing spree" during working hours. Some blacks returned themselves to white control after involuntary emancipation. A youth who had accompanied his master in the Confederate army showed up at Nimrod Porter's farm in the last days of 1864, asking for permission to remain there because his master was a Federal prisoner; "he seamed to be quite uneasy," Porter wrote, "until I give him liberty to stay."[21]

Most blacks, however, abandoned submissiveness by 1865 because it had never suited them and now no constraints necessitated it. But they did not have to run away to express their freedom. Many chose to stay on at

19   "Documents: Civil War Diary of Jabez T. Cox," *Indiana Magazine of History*, XXVIII (1932), 47; "Major Connolly's Letters," 263–64.
20   Mary C. Washington to Jane S. Washington, March 15, 1865, in Washington Papers; Porter Journal, November 12, 1864; L. C. Ewell to Campbell Brown, June 4, 1865, in Polk-Brown-Ewell Papers, SHC.
21   Matthews Journal, May 8, 1865; Porter Journal, December 25, 1864.

their former master's farm or town house, where they evinced their free-dom in other ways. Slavery had meant, above all, obedience and work. Thus disobedience and refusal to work were the most common manifesta-tions of black freedom. By 1863 these attitudes were epidemic in town and country alike. Nimrod Porter observed in August that the blacks on his Maury County farm "are all getting along as usual only there is but verry little doing in the way of working." A year later the situation had further deteriorated: "Nothing doing around the plantation," Porter wrote; "I am verry tyered of it." A Pulaski man wrote in March, 1864, to an absentee slaveowner about the "deadhead negroes you have on your lot." As the war neared its end the mistress of the Washington family's vast plantation in Robertson County complained that "I do not know what to do with those negro devils they will not work." [22]

A Rutherford County plantation mistress's journal chronicles the dis-solution of slavery in microcosm. Bettie Blackmore recorded in Septem-ber, 1863, that "the servants had become very demoralized during the summer, they would not work, were becoming insolent. . . . [They] would sleep until the sun was high, then saunter out hands in their pockets look around & get to their work about 9 or 10. Then take a nap in the evening & come home early." By November the blacks were "growing more and more unruly. They are not only indolent & perfectly trifling every way, but, are very insolent & disobedient." In early 1864 she reported "Negroes doing badly. Hulda & Celeste have not done one day's work since Christmas. . . . *All* negroes have lost their respectful manner & they generally seem to dis-like their owners more than anyone else." By the last winter of the war, no pretense of servility lingered: "My negroes refractory and insolent and not supporting themselves," wrote another woman on the plantation who con-tinued the journal in December, 1864. "The negroes are so utterly worth-less they will not put up fences and [they] burn the rails to keep from cut-ting wood." [23]

Theft, vandalism, and disloyalty were further manifestations of the black heartlanders' new freedom, for slavery had denied slaves the posses-sions they had sweated to secure for others and had demanded strict pro-priety and fidelity while they toiled. Nimrod Porter complained fre-quently of thievery by local blacks as slavery disintegrated; horses and mules were especially popular booty, he observed, for they could be read-ily sold. Bettie Blackmore railed against similar malefaction in Rutherford

22   Porter Journal, August 16, 1863, September 19, 1864; W. Rivers to Sarah Trotter, March 25, 1864, in Pope-Carter Family Papers, DUL; Mary C. Washington to Jane S. Wash-ington, March 11, 1865, in Washington Papers.

23   Trimble (ed.), "Behind the Lines," 62–63, 65, 70, 77.

County: the slaves "steal anything they can and sell it," she declared in 1863; "they find it easier to steal at home, than work with the Yankees." Other blacks saw the end of slavery as an opportunity not for personal gain but for vengeance. Albert, the slave of a Davidson County lawyer, was apprehended in 1864 after setting fire to his master's barn and causing thousands of dollars in damage. Similar acts of arson and sabotage multiplied around the region.[24]

Black pilferage and vandalism were, of course, not new to Middle Tennessee slaveholders; it was the volume of such mayhem after 1862 that made it remarkable. More novel, and even more galling to whites, was the loss of property to the Yankees through black treachery. A young Wilson County slave woman walked six miles through darkness and rain to inform Union troops that her master had cached barrels of salt behind a garden fence and horses, mules, and guns in a cave. Old Humphrey, a slave on the Washington plantation, deliberately betrayed to Yankee foragers the hiding place of his owner's last remaining horses. "Oh how enraged I was at the old wretches perfidy," his mistress wrote in exasperation.[25]

A few blacks challenged slavery's holiest injunction by threatening or even physically assaulting their masters or other whites. A Williamson County planter reported in March, 1863, that the slaves of a neighboring woman had tried to poison her. In Sumner that year Federal soldiers were awakened at midnight by a woman's screams. Rushing to her nearby home, they found her "scared most to death," as one soldier wrote: "She had been assaulted By a negro the colored person could not be found." A Union general asserted in 1864 that "many straggling negroes have arms obtained from soldiers, and by their insolence and threats greatly alarm and intimidate white families." At least one slave perpetrated the ultimate act. Henry, of Williamson County, trailed his master, who was fleeing the Yankees with his valuables, caught the man asleep in the woods, axed him to death, then fled to Nashville with his property.[26]

Most conspicuously, however, slaves acknowledged their freedom by running away: since slavery had meant confinement, freedom would mean mobility. A Union officer with a literary bent colorfully limned a scene

24   Porter Journal, August 29, December 24, 1863, January 1, 1864, March 2, 11, 1865; Trimble (ed.), "Behind the Lines," 62, 63, 65, 70; Nashville *Dispatch*, January 13, 1864.

25   Fitch, *Annals of the Army*, 236–37; Jane S. Washington to George A. Washington, August 8, 1864, in Washington Papers.

26   Henderson Diary, March 31, 1863; D. M. Ransdell Diary, January 30, 1863 (MS in SHC); Lovell H. Rousseau to W. D. Whipple, January 30, 1864, in *OR*, Vol. XXXII, Pt. 2, pp. 267–68; Frank H. Smith, *Frank H. Smith's History of Maury County, Tennessee* (Columbia, Tenn., 1969), 183.

being repeated over and over in the heartland after he observed contrabands making their way into Murfreesboro in 1863: "They are on foot,
and early travellers. . . . The women invariably toil along with their babies
in their arms; the men and the larger boys and girls trudge past, laden
with bundles of grotesque form and appearance; while the little pican-
ninies mix in and patter on as would a flock of young quails in a wheat-
field. Perhaps . . . [the] fugitives [have] *borrowed* 'ole massa's' best horse, or
mule, or yoke of cattle, and the large farm-wagon, in the night-time, and
are coming in, bag and budget in hand."[27]

Most Middle Tennessee slaves voluntarily left their masters before the
Civil War ended. Slaveowner Sarah Kennedy in Clarksville reported in
June, 1863, that "Negroes are leaving daily," and in October, "Every day or
two we hear of several leaving"; four months later she wrote that "almost
every family have been deprived of *every one* they had." At the Giles
County plantation of William Stoddert, which may be typical of the
largest holdings, seventy blacks had absconded by the end of the war, leaving only thirty-four.[28]

Several impulses drove Middle Tennessee slaves from their masters'
homes and farms. One was the urgent desire to escape rural privation and
suffering, which blacks in the countryside shared in full measure with
whites. But sometimes more immediate perils sent blacks fleeing. For example, in 1863 and again in 1864, Nimrod Porter saw hundreds run off to
the Federals or to the woods when the imminent arrival of Confederate
troops sparked fears that blacks would be gathered up and sent south.
More often, though, slaves were persuaded to desert by other blacks, who
had already renounced their bondage. A Robertson County slaveholder
complained in late 1863 that her blacks "have been happy and contented
untill that old Negro came here from Cincinnati." At the Washington plantation in the same county, a number of local runaways appeared at the slave
quarters in 1864, urged all who wanted to to come along, and led away
several.[29]

The most potent influence on the slaves, however, was the conviction
that true freedom entailed a fresh beginning in a new home. One slave-

27 Fitch, *Annals of the Army*, 283.

28 Sarah Kennedy to her husband, June 17, October 6, 1863, February 11, 1864,
in Kennedy Letters; L. C. Ewell to Campbell Brown, June 4, 1865, in Polk-Brown-Ewell
Papers.

29 Porter Journal, August 13, 1863, December 16, 1864; Mrs. W. W. Pepper to Andrew
Johnson, December 25, 1863, in Graf and Haskins (eds.), *Papers of Andrew Johnson*, VI,
525–27; Jane S. Washington to George A. Washington, March 2, 1864, in Washington
Papers. Burton, *Diary*, 6, notes the arrival in Pulaski of a large group of contrabands who fled
the rural areas in 1864 to avoid starvation.

holder testified before a Federal commission of inquiry in Nashville in late 1863 that she had seven slaves, who were "well clothed and fed, their rooms nicely carpeted, and their beds comfortable, and . . . she would be willing to pay them wages, but they were unwilling to stay, because they thought they would not be free unless they went away."[30]

Many of those who walked or rode away from their masters' homes relocated nearby, a few roamed aimlessly, but many others had a destination. Thousands, for example, headed for contraband camps hurriedly established by the army at several points around the region in 1863 and 1864. Many thousands more trekked to the black enclaves of the towns. Whether they went to camp or town, these blacks sought not only to realize their immediate freedom but to assure their future security and advancement. Over and over again they spoke of their desire for education: slavery had meant ignorance, and they were determined that freedom would mean knowledge. A sympathetic Union army chaplain in Nashville, pondering the future of the Negro race, concluded in 1863 that "the anxiety of these people for education is an omen for good." The prospect of schools and liberty within a black community was a powerful force, drawing the freedmen to the towns and government camps as vigorously as rural privation and their own aspirations for new lives propelled them from the countryside.[31]

Freedom—that is, the self-defined emancipation not only of slaves who ran off but of those who stayed with their masters but refused any longer to act like slaves—came at different times in different places. Indeed, since slavery was a frame of mind and a personal relationship as much as a legal and social institution, it is fair to say that there were as many acts of emancipation in the heartland as there were slaves. The chronology of freedom was determined by the complex interaction of factors internal and external to the bondsmen. Two of these stand out as critical determinants of the advent of freedom.

The first was the presence of the Union army. Though a few dauntless spirits such as Edmund of Maury County proclaimed themselves free while still in Confederate hands, most slaves realized their freedom only after Northern ascendancy was incontrovertibly established and Union troops were on hand. Thus blacks far from Federal army camps and permanent installations in the towns, and those in the southern part of the

30 Testimony of Mrs. De Moville, American Freedmen's Inquiry Commission Report.
31 Lovell H. Rousseau to W. D. Whipple, January 30, 1864, in *OR*, Vol. XXXII, Pt. 2, pp. 267–68; Daniel Chapman to Brother Whipple, November 18, 1863, in American Missionary Association, Tennessee Records, Amistad Research Center, Dillard University; Burton, *Diary*, 6.

heartland in general (where Confederate control was reestablished for a time after the invasion), tended on the whole to find their freedom later than did others more happily situated.

Of equal or greater consequence was the precise nature of the master-slave relationship in each case. In households with few slaves or only one, the master's authority and the slave's subordination were swathed in an atmosphere of intimate personal association. If that association was affectionate, freedom usually came later, but if there was bad blood, freedom came sooner. Thus, Hammett Dell, who lived with four other slaves on a small Rutherford County farm and loved his master dearly, had no transcendent experience of self-liberation and stayed with his master in a relationship that evolved only gradually into freedom. Mary Scott, on the other hand, the young house servant of an abusive Williamson County woman whom she despised, left gladly when her father came from a neighboring farm to take her away. As Mary departed she sabotaged her mistress's spinning wheel because, she explained, the woman had "been so mean." [32]

On large plantations familiar interracial relationships were less common: the distance from slave quarters to big house was far greater than the sum of its linear parts. Plantation slavery relied on the dominating presence of an aloof patriarch and on the whip he or his overseer wielded. Where such an imposing white personality was absent during the war, freedom tended to appear; where such a figure abided, freedom was suppressed. For example, during the long absence of their planter-patriarch George A. Washington, most slaves on the Washington estate ceased work and deference altogether. But when another forceful white man arrived at the plantation he aggressively reinstituted some of the old compulsions. "If he was not here I do not know what we would do," wrote a young boy on the plantation; "he has spread terror abrod among the Negros." [33]

A second determining factor in slaves' self-emancipation concerns not timing but tactics. With few exceptions, freedom derived not from an institutional or legal mechanism but from a personal stroke. The black people of the heartland had long known that institutions—government, court, and church—were instruments of the white man's subjugation of blacks as surely as were the whip and chain. When the time came to seize freedom, blacks shunned institutions (even where they were functioning) in favor of the individual coup. Sometimes such coups employed the threat

32   Rawick (ed.), *American Slave*, Ser. Two, Vol. VIII (Ark.), Pt. 2, pp. 137–44, and Vol. X (Ark.), pt. 6, pp. 124–26.

33   Joseph E. Washington to Jane S. Washington, March 11, 1865, in Washington Papers.

of physical force, for Middle Tennessee's slaves understood force and its efficacy as only the long-suffering victim can know his oppressor. Over and over again a scene was enacted in the wartime heartland: a black man (sometimes armed) would appear with an escort of armed Yankees whom he had cajoled into accompanying him at the home of a slaveowner who held the man's wife or child or lover or friend and would attempt to rescue the other from slavery. Bettie Blackmore witnessed one such visitation at her Rutherford County plantation in early 1863, when a black man arrived with seven soldiers to claim his wife and child: "The negro had a very haughty consequential air," she reported, "wore a brace of pistols—strutted about the house with great freedom, talking loudly and boldly and altogether the incident alarmed us a good deal."[34]

A great many white people were alarmed by such incidents, which seemed to presage that gory servile uprising whose specter had terrorized the South for generations. But no such bloodbath stained the soil of Middle Tennessee, despite the opportunity ostensibly offered by war and occupation. Long after Appomattox a former slaveholder of Montgomery County commended the slaves for their wartime comportment: "Any other race known to history," he declared, "would have spread devastation over the land, waylaid and murdered the ruling classes and shocked the world by their crimes." This man attributed the blacks' laudable conduct not only to their humanity, which was certainly a factor, but to their masters' temperate treatment of them, which is dubious. There was another reason: the early invasion and occupation of Middle Tennessee offered the region's enslaved blacks an unprecedented opportunity to realize their long-desired freedom simply by walking away from their bondage, or at most by breaking their masters' weakened hold through a show of force. No guns had to be fired, no axes bloodied. Thus, ironically, it may be that at no time in the history of Middle Tennessee was a slave insurrection there *less* likely than after the Northern invasion. In their haste to vilify the detested Yankees for ushering in the destruction of slavery, the white people of the heartland never thought to thank them for delivering white society from its own bondage of fear.[35]

The slaveholders of Middle Tennessee refused to bow graciously to fate. They resisted vigorously, even desperately, the dissolution of their peculiar institution and the loss of their valuable black bondsmen. More eclectic (from necessity) than their slaves, whose self-emancipation was almost

34 Trimble (ed.), "Behind the Lines," 50.
35 Killebrew Autobiography, I, 176.

wholly personal and pacific, slaveholders resorted to an array of devices to preserve slavery, including government and law, suasion and subterfuge, but above all violence. And on this single issue unionists and secessionists joined hands, for not even the divisive politics of the Civil War could dilute the potency of slavery and race as a unifying ideological force in Middle Tennessee.

Few whites understood during the first year and more of occupation that slavery was dying. As late as November, 1863, a Union officer in Nashville judged that "the bulk of the people here are not yet exactly satisfied that the slaves are to be free. Many of them give it up, but there is a lingering hope that by some hocus-pocus things will get back to the old state." In this early period whites perceived only temporary disruptions of the institution and random incidents of insubordination, not a pattern of ineluctable decline; and they met each challenge with fierce determination. Slaveowners pursued the growing number of wartime runaways as energetically as they had chased down antebellum fugitives, availing themselves whenever possible of the aid of friendly, conservative army officers and railing loudly against those who were less than helpful. A Davidson County slaveowner whose runaways were forcibly liberated by soldiers when he tried to fetch them home beseeched Andrew Johnson for assistance, appealing in his outrage to law and justice: "There not having been any Law of Congress or Proclamation of the President to deprive me of them," he declared, "[I am] as much entitled to the controll & injoyment of them as you or I am to our Horses & Cattle & Houses."[36]

Violence against slaves redoubled as masters anxiously sought to maintain their grip. The familiar whip appeared even more frequently. One master lured his fugitive slave woman, Maria, from the Union army camps by kidnapping the child she had taken with her and then paying a soldier to coax her back home with the promise of help in rescuing the child. When Maria did return, her master seized her, locked her up for four days, and beat her until she was scarred. When owners could not constrain their fractious bondsmen, guerrilla bands lurking in the countryside sometimes acted in the master's stead, catching and punishing delinquents.[37]

Whites exacted the ultimate price in these months from those few slaves

36 Testimony of George L. Stearns, American Freedmen's Inquiry Commission Report; Thomas B. Johnson to Andrew Johnson, August 8, 1863, in Graf and Haskins (eds.), *Papers of Andrew Johnson*, VI, 318–19.

37 Thomas Cotton to Andrew Johnson, October 19, 1863, in Graf and Haskins (eds.), *Papers of Andrew Johnson*, VI, 426–27. See also Cox Diary, May 13, 1862. Guerrilla violence against blacks is documented in Chapter VII, which explores guerrillaism as a social phenomenon.

who dared to strike back at their oppressors. After Gilbert Dowell burned the barn of his wife's Maury County master in late 1862 (in retaliation for selling off Dowell's wife and child to Louisiana), dogs tracked the slave down, and, even though the county government was operating, a shotgun-wielding kangaroo court expeditiously tried, convicted, and lynched him. Henry, the Williamson County slave who axed his sleeping master to death in the woods, was captured by Confederate troops after being turned away by the Federals at Nashville. The rebels put a noose around Henry's neck, stood him on a rail fence, and kicked out the rails.[38]

In the towns, as before the war, institutions of authority helped maintain slavery in place of the personal supervision of slaves which urban life had always obstructed—now more than ever. By keeping order in the towns, the Federal presence helped indirectly to safeguard slavery there even as it increasingly disrupted it. Urban slavery withered from daily contact with Yankee soldiers, to be sure, but urban slaveholders did not have to contend with the social and political chaos that vitiated the coercive power of their rural brethren. Nashville's civil officials, though loyal unionists to a man, stood squarely for the preservation of slavery in this early period of occupation. The municipal whipping post and workhouse saw constant service as the police apprehended unruly blacks and masters turned incorrigibles over to the authorities. The masses of contrabands crowding into the city could not be regulated by government, however, because of their ambiguous legal status and their sheer numbers. White Nashvillians therefore turned to other institutions. They pleaded with the army to round up black vagrants and put them to work and called on black churches to carry out their responsibility for "making and keeping [blacks] honest, sober, industrious, and well-conducted in all respects." The contrabands, however, persisted in asserting their freedom, and as officials continued their crackdown on the city's slaves, bondage and liberty flourished side by side in Nashville.[39]

In their determination to preserve slavery, some slaveowners in both town and country resorted to precautions unknown before the invasion. A few, rather than tightening discipline, relaxed it for fear of triggering an incident that might turn a loyal servant into a disgruntled fugitive. A fellow planter advised George A. Washington early in 1863 to "look closely after those who are still at home and direct your overseer to abstain, as far as possible, from giving them any excuse for leaving you." A Giles County

38   Smith, *Frank H. Smith's History of Maury County,* 183, 239–41.
39   Nashville *Dispatch,* December 11, 14, 27, 1862, January 14, 16, February 14, March 6, June 24, 25, 1863.

plantation mistress wrote at the same time that "overseers generally are doing very little good and they complain of the negroes getting so free and idle, but I think it is because most every one is afraid to correct them. I tried to correct our negroes for a thing last summer; it would frighten Mr. Ashford [the overseer] out of his wits almost."[40]

Persuasion and soft words, whether from their own lips or those of a trusted black, also availed uneasy masters. George A. Washington's correspondent told his own slaves that "the very best thing they can do for themselves is to remain quietly at home and attend to their work, and wait until it is known what disposition is to be made of the negroes generally, and in case they shall all be emancipated, *mine also will be set free.* . . . This advice seemed to them reasonable and I think they are disposed to follow it." Two months later, he dispatched a slave man to Washington's plantation, ostensibly on an errand. "But my principal object in sending him," the planter admitted, "was that he might see and talk with your negroes. I think his advice to them may have a good effect upon them." Other slaveowners, fearing positive inducements would not keep their slaves loyal, spread horror stories detailing the abuse the blacks could expect at the hands of the Yankees if they were foolish enough to run off to the Federal camps.[41]

Some masters, lacking confidence in their powers of persuasion, physically restrained their slaves. Others hid their slaves along with other valuables at the approach of the Yankees, asserting (not always truthfully) that their fear was not their slaves' disloyalty but Federal labor impressment. Many left nothing to chance and carried their slaves south out of the region and safe from both Yankees and aspirations for freedom. "Very General efforts is being made by oweners & drivers to Run [slaves] South," a Union officer reported from Nashville early in 1863, "and Large Numbers Have been Taken from the City."[42]

If such precautions seemed to insinuate misgivings about their slaves

40   William B. Lewis to George A. Washington, March 6, 1863, in Washington Papers; Bell I. Wiley, *Southern Negroes, 1861–1865* (New Haven, 1938), 76.

41   William B. Lewis to George A. Washington, March 6, May 1, 1863, in Washington Papers; Fitch, *Annals of the Army*, 651.

42   Chief of Police of Nashville to the Commander of the Department of the Cumberland, March 7, 1863, in Ira Berlin *et al.* (eds.), *The Destruction of Slavery* (Cambridge, England, 1985), 301, Ser. I, Vol. I of Berlin *et al.* (eds.), *Freedom: A Documentary History of Emancipation, 1861–1867*, 5 series projected. Further evidence of slaves being run south is in Hannibal Paine to his sister, April 26, 1863, in Paine Papers; Thomas T. Smiley to Andrew Johnson, June 15, 1863, in Graf and Haskins (eds.), *Papers of Andrew Johnson*, VI, 252–53. The hiding of slaves from the Federals is documented in "Major Connolly's Letters," 262–63; Rawick (ed.), *American Slave*, Ser. One, Vol. VI (Ind.), 43–47.

and anxiety about slavery's survival, few masters in the early period of occupation would have openly admitted it. The slaveholders' ideological devotion to slavery remained as firm as their trust in God, and they repeatedly affirmed the dogma of their faith: slavery was a positive good; masters and slaves shared mutual obligations; slaves were fundamentally loyal and contented. Masters continued to trumpet their trust in the good sense and docility of their pampered bondsmen. A Davidson County planter declared confidently, "My negroes . . . have no great liking to a camp life—they saw enough of it when the troops were camped close around their houses for some five or six weeks, to satisfy them that they were much better of[f] at home, and in their own houses, than in the care and under the protection of their *northern friends*." On New Year's Day, 1863—the date of presidentially declared freedom for slaves in most of the Confederacy outside Tennessee—a Nashville woman gloated in her diary: "The day so long looked for by the North in which the 'poor oppressed race' would rush to their northern bretheren has dawned upon us, and yet we have witnessed no insurrections no massacres, but all moving quietly along. Harvey and Jeff left us when the Yankees first entered but both are at home. The rest seem perfectly contented."[43]

Other slaveowners proudly proclaimed their paternalistic solicitude for their bondsmen. "Just come from a negro funeral," a Murfreesboro woman wrote in April, 1862; "—a parson by the name of Willis preached & one by the name of Miles had service at the grave—O Yankee what would you say to that." A Fayetteville slaveowner in the Confederate army instructed his wife in 1863 to "say to the servants that I hope to hear that they have been kind and attentive to you and the children. . . . I have endeavored to do my duty towards them but if they are dissatisfied & should leave you all I can say to them is what I have often said viz. if they can do without me, I can do without them. They know how I have labored to make them comfortable."[44]

The slaveholders dismissed evidence impugning their protestations of black fidelity as temporary aberrations caused by unsettled conditions or, more often, as the villainies of outside agitators and "bad niggers." The latter ascriptions were, of course, the stock in trade of antebellum slavery apologists, and in Middle Tennessee from 1862 on every day brought new contradictions to be thus rationalized. "Oh! these wretched-wicked Yankees," exclaimed Bettie Blackmore in 1863, refusing to believe that her in-

43   William B. Lewis to George A. Washington, March 6, 1863, in Washington Papers; Harriet Ellen Moore Diary, January 1, 1863 (MS in SHC).

44   Elvie Eagleton Skipper and Ruth Gove (eds.), "'Stray Thoughts': The Civil War Diary of Ethie M. Foute Eagleton," ETHS*P*, No. 40 (1968) and No. 41 (1969), Pt. 1, p. 136; James R. Bright to his wife, August 26, 1863, in Douglass-Maney Family Papers, TSLA.

creasingly disobedient blacks were self-motivated. "If they would only see the terrible effect of their teachings, upon the negroes." A Montgomery County slaveowner accused the Northerners of attempting to "excite insurrection & seduce the slaves from their masters." The Nashville *Dispatch* complained frequently in 1863 about the erosion of slave discipline and morality in the city, which it blamed on the insidious influence of contrabands and Northern free blacks. "It is a well known fact," the editor aphorized, "that one bad negro will corrupt many." After vigilantes lynched Gilbert Dowell for barn-burning in the fall of 1862, white Maury countians agreed that Dowell had always been a "bad darkey" and that his owners had a reputation for not controlling their slaves.[45]

As black deference and allegiance deteriorated, however, ideology collided with reality and the slaveholders' serene professions of faith turned shrill and tremulous. Fear and distrust, long submerged, began to surface. Whites grew cautious about their words and deeds in front of blacks. A Murfreesboro girl whose family briefly harbored some escaped, disguised rebel soldiers in June, 1862, confided in her diary that she felt obliged while in her slaves' presence to pretend that the men were Yankees. A Williamson County man, plotting a secret expedition late that year, warned a confederate to "say nothing to any one, especially w[h]ere negroes are, as to our destination."[46]

Before long, voices of concern could be heard across the heartland—faint at first, nearly drowned out by the loud avowals of confidence, but swelling as the months passed. A Maury County woman wrote, "I have sent Louisa off to the country to be hired out. She has acted in such a way lately as to destroy my confidence in her." The Murfreesboro girl who cautiously dissembled in front of her servants in June, 1862, declared flatly in July, "I don't trust the negroes now. They have too much of the yankees about them, to suit me." Sarah Kennedy of Clarksville, apprehensively scrutinizing her slaves' demeanor as the date of presidential emancipation neared, confessed, "I feel . . . quite anxious sometimes, at the events which are likely to take place the first of January."[47]

As reality continued to hammer away at their faith, whites evidenced shock, disbelief, and dismay. Convinced that their complacent servants

45 Trimble (ed.), "Behind the Lines," 65; Tennessee Planter to the Commander of a Tennessee Confederate Regiment, December 1, 1862, in Berlin *et al.*, (eds.), *Destruction of Slavery*, 799; Nashville *Dispatch*, January 18, 1863; Smith, *Frank H. Smith's History of Maury County*, 241.

46 Carney Diary, June 13, 1862; Edward C. Bain to James B. Crockett, November 1, 1862, in Andrew Crockett Papers, TSLA.

47 Sarah Trotter to Cynthia Carter, n.d. (probably 1862), in Pope-Carter Papers; Carney Diary, July 21, 1862; Sarah Kennedy to her husband, December 22, 1862, in Kennedy Letters.

could never prefer the vile Yankees over their benevolent masters, slave-owners watched uncomprehending as blacks left in droves for the army camps. "The negroes will run to them from good homes of kind masters," sputtered an incredulous Bettie Blackmore in late 1863, "& bear more oppression than they ever knew before, get *no pay* & yet love the Yankee for his meanness." Persuaded that slaves needed their masters even more than the reverse, slaveholders choked on the emerging bitter truth that masters were superfluous but slaves indispensable. A Shelbyville unionist begged Andrew Johnson in 1863 to protect his two slave men from conscription: "These servants of mine . . . [are] *absolutely necessary* for my comfort and convenience—if taken away I do not know how I would supply their place—and I would be compelled to break up Housekeeping."[48]

As slavery unraveled, ripples of doubt and consternation turned to waves and then torrents, and the slaveholders of Middle Tennessee faced a crisis of ideology. The incontrovertible fact that the Yankees were there to stay destroyed all assurance that the disorder was transitory, to be endured and afterward rectified. The mass desertion of slaves exploded the myths that slavery was a decree of nature and that slaves reveled in their bondage. The withering away of black deference and obedience turned "good darkeys" by the tens of thousands into "bad darkeys," refuting the slaveholders' doctrine that black miscreancy was the work of a few bad apples. Black self-assertion gave the lie to notions about outside agitators. Nothing remained of slavery's ideological edifice but the slaveholders' credos that slavery was a necessary good and that masters had a duty to their bondsmen. These cornerstones could not stand alone against the tidal wave of events. The consequence was nothing less than the intellectual abandonment of slavery and paternalism by the slaveholders of the heartland.

This was the turning point of the slaveholders' Civil War, the opposite side of the coin from the slaves' realization of their freedom. Much as slaves apprehended that they were no longer slaves, their masters came to understand that they were no longer masters. The evanescence of the slaves' servility found its counterpart in the dissolution of their masters' paternalistic ethos: just as the slaves rejected their masters as oppressors they no longer had to endure, so the masters renounced their slaves as burdens they no longer had to bear.

The first signs of the disintegration of the slaveholders' ideology appeared in 1863, as masters in growing numbers acknowledged the inevitability of slavery's death and declined to retrieve runaways or hold on to

48   Trimble (ed.), "Behind the Lines," 65; Edmund Cooper to Andrew Johnson, November 1, 1863, in Graf and Haskins (eds.), *Papers of Andrew Johnson*, VI, 446–47.

slaves who wished to leave. In January the Nashville police arrested Dan, a local slave who had run off the previous November; when they prepared to turn Dan over to his owner, the latter announced that he would take the slave back only if he wanted to return. In the summer of 1864, Cherry, owned by James Matthews, ran off from her master's Maury County farm; she soon returned, only to announce that she would be staying less than a week: "I am not willing for her to stay on her terms," Matthews huffed in his diary, "so she packed up with her child and left." "I wish you would look at the stern reality of facts," a Pulaski man advised a Maury County slaveholder that same year. "In my own opinion slavery has run its race in Tennessee, in no contingency is it likely to be revived or profitable, no use then in electioneering around negroes to stay with us *unless* they can be made *profitable*, or at least be made to pay their *own expense*. . . . [I] symply suggest that you divest your sel[f] of all negroes that are not able & willing to make ther own support."[49]

More and more, slaveowners did take steps to divest themselves of unproductive blacks. In scenes that would have been incredible two or three years earlier, masters across the heartland ordered away their former slaves. James Childress, a Davidson County slave, later recalled that his master commanded all hands to leave the farm and make their own homes after self-emancipation had rendered them "too excited to work in the fields or care for the stock." James A. Garfield, a Federal officer (and future president) sympathetic to the blacks, described how "thousands have been abandoned by their masters, who have lost all hope of gain by keeping them and now cruelly turn them out. . . . It is one of the saddest pictures I ever witnessed." As often as not, however, the newly liberated and now defiantly assertive blacks simply ignored orders to vacate, leaving their former masters to fume impotently or seek help in evicting them. The Union officer supervising black recruitment asserted late in 1863 that "numerous applications have been made to me by planters . . . to take their slaves by force, as they say they have become a nuisance to them."[50]

The ordeal of the wealthy Washingtons of Robertson County epitomizes the decline and fall of the slaveholders' world-view. Slaves on the

49   Nashville *Dispatch*, January 22, 1863; Matthews Journal, August 1, 1864; W. Rivers to Sarah Trotter, March 25, 1864, in Pope-Carter Papers. See also Porter Journal, February 23, 1864; Chancellor (ed.), *Englishman in the Civil War*, 135–36; Rawick (ed.), *American Slave*, Supplement, Ser. Two, Vol. I (Ala. *et al.*), 101.

50   Rawick (ed.), *American Slave*, Ser. One, Vol. VI (Ind.), 55–56; James A. Garfield to Salmon P. Chase, April 12, 1863, in Frederick D. Williams (ed.), *The Wild Life of the Army: Civil War Letters of James A. Garfield* (East Lansing, Mich., 1964), 257; testimony of George L. Stearns, American Freedmen's Inquiry Commission Report. See also A. A. Smith to B. H. Polk, April 19, 1864, in Letters Sent, 1863–65, No. 192, E3023, RCC.

family's huge plantation began running off to Nashville and the Federal camps in early 1863. George A. Washington pulled every string possible that year to retrieve his fugitive blacks, fretted constantly about those still at home, and took precautions to keep them there. But slaves continued to depart through 1863 and 1864, and those who remained began to exhibit the familiar symptoms of "impudence," disloyalty, and refusal to work. The determination of the Washingtons to hold on to their bondsmen dwindled concomitantly. "Henry Terry and his whole family took their departure last night," Washington's wife, Jane, reported in July, 1864, "—a good riddance." By early 1865, blacks and whites alike agreed that slavery was finished on the Washington plantation. Most blacks declined either to work or to leave: "Monroe . . . has not done a solitary thing," a white family member wrote; "Cousin P has told him that he could not & should not stay here, but he does not regard it any more than if she did not speak to him." A provoked white woman on the plantation reported in March that "no negroes [have] left will never leave until their houses are thrown down or burned down I wish they were all gone." Those whites who, like the Washingtons, had built their world around patriarchal and paternalistic racial ideals were the most vehement in their repudiation of those ideals when that world crumbled.[51]

Slavery, as the Washingtons and thousands of lesser slaveholders discovered, was the weak link in the heartland's patriarchal society, a link forged by force and violence, not by nature or internalized values. The slaves of Middle Tennessee, like those all across the South, were free as soon as that frangible bond was broken. But slaveholders in other parts of the South were not so quickly freed from the chains of ideology as those in the heartland. Why did the slaveholders of Middle Tennessee so decisively abjure slavery and paternalism by 1865, while those elsewhere attempted to hold fast to their bondsmen and their peculiar, moribund institution for years after Appomattox?[52]

The explanation lies in Middle Tennessee's uniquely shattering Civil War experience, which was as lethal to ideology as it was to lives and for-

---

51   William B. Lewis to George A. Washington, February 24, March 6, 1863; George A. Washington to "Major," December 14, 1863; Jane S. Washington to George A. Washington, February 29, July 25, August 15, 1864; Joyce A. Davis to Jane S. Washington, February 19, 1865; Mary C. Washington to Jane S. Washington, March 1, 29, April 1, 1865; Joseph Washington to Jane S. Washington, February 9, March 27, 1865; William Washington to Jane S. Washington, March 11, 1865, all in Washington Papers.

52   The war did not extinguish every trace of paternalism, of course, just as it did not destroy close and affectionate black-white relationships. For an example of continued paternalism see William Stoddert to R. S. Ewell, May 24, 1865, in Polk-Brown-Ewell Papers.

tunes. Certainly no other part of the South was battered more furiously by the war than the heartland, and few regions even approached the degree and duration of physical devastation, institutional disruption, and human suffering which the heartland endured. The planter in southern Georgia or Alabama who never saw a Yankee soldier until the war was over or nearly so, whose fields remained green and prolific, and whose slaves toiled diligently with no opportunity of escape until the last armies of the Confederacy laid down their arms might cling stubbornly to an ideology that, though superseded by reality, had not been wrested from him by violence. The slaveholders of Middle Tennessee were as forcibly stripped of their ideology after 1862 as they were of their corn and cattle. No one who watched columns of armed Yankees pass by daily, plundering and destroying without hindrance, could deny that the war was a palpable, transforming entity. No one who beheld black men and women in great numbers throw down their scythes and hoes, stand tall, denounce their masters to their faces, and defiantly walk away could fail to understand that slavery was dead and paternalism repudiated.

Slavery as an institution of law followed a similar course from tenacity to uncertainty to ultimate dissolution. The deteriorating legal status of slavery during the war can be traced through the judicial decrees of Judge Manson M. Brien of Nashville, a native unionist and influential leader of wartime reconstruction. Presiding over the Davidson County criminal court in February, 1863, Brien instructed the grand jury to enforce strictly all existing slave codes and laws governing free blacks. But by the time court met in December, Brien's policy had changed markedly. Speaking of the slave code and laws governing free blacks the judge remarked that "the new state of things . . . had rendered [them] inoperative in many respects." By May, 1864, when he opened the Rutherford County circuit court, Brien was insisting that "we must recognize the rebellion and war as it is," which meant acknowledging the Federal policy of encouraging runaways: "So this slave code and slave policy of Tennessee is virtually repealed," he concluded, "at least it is not practicable or expedient to enforce it." Finally, in March, 1865, as he opened court in Williamson County, Judge Brien—who not two years earlier had clashed with Federal authorities after waylaying and forcibly restraining his own runaway slave—read slavery's obituary. Blacks would be deemed free, he ordered, slavery would be considered abolished, and any blacks still coerced by their former masters could sue for damages.[53]

53 Nashville *Dispatch*, February 10, December 8, 11, 1863; Nashville *Daily Times and True Union*, May 13, 1864, March 17, 1865. Slave sales and other legal transfers of slave property in Middle Tennessee were disrupted in 1862 and 1863 because of runaways and nearly

The threat of militant freedmen hauling their stubborn former masters into court was anathema to white Middle Tennesseans. So, too, were the spectacles of black men in uniform shouldering muskets, black field hands stuffing weekly wages into their pockets, and black children at school desks laboring over *McGuffey's Reader*. Having disavowed slavery and their obligations to the slave, most whites took not another step. They denounced all the manifestations of black legal, economic, and social equality that followed in freedom's wake: "They will do nothing recognizing that the negro is entitled to anything," wrote an outraged Northerner in the spring of 1864. Whites in Columbia raged furiously that year when authorities announced that black testimony would be admitted in the trial of a white man, and some turned violent after a black man opened a school in the town. When a number of blacks began working for wages in Murfreesboro, an observer reported that their former masters "will not hire the slaves themselves. . . . They will not consent to see others hiring them . . . and [they] predict with pleasure the hoped for failure of the new experiment." White violence against black soldiers was common (three were murdered in a ten-day period in Nashville in the spring of 1864), and army recruiters of blacks met enormous white animosity across the region. "Destructive vengeance is everywhere to be seen and felt in this country," declared a Northerner who had heard native whites excoriate every token of black equality. The intransigence and violent racial hostility of Middle Tennessee whites that would mark the Reconstruction era represented simply the rank proliferation of an ugly weed that had sprouted while the armies still battled.[54]

Whatever exultation and revelry the heady wine of first freedom provoked, other, grimmer realities of the war years kept the black men and women of the heartland sober, determined, and steady on their feet. The joy and hope that accompanied deliverance from thralldom were tempered by the agonies of getting along in a world still inimical, still brutal. Hardship and uncertainty confronted the freedmen wherever they turned. Whether they remained in the countryside, fled to town, or sought their fate with

---

ceased in 1864. In the latter part of 1864 Military Governor Johnson decreed that in any case before the civil courts involving blacks, they must be deemed free (see R. D. Mussey to C. W. Foster, October 10, 1864, in *OR*, Ser. III, Vol. IV, 772). Slavery was formally abolished in Tennessee in February, 1865, by state constitutional amendment. For examples of the disruption of slave sales and other legal transfers see Bedford County Court Minutes, September, November, December, 1863, January, 1864, Vol. A, 18–19, 32–34, 44, 55.

54 Nashville *Daily Times and True Union*, April 18, 25, May 10, 20, 1864; Porter Journal, April 16, 22, July 23, 1864; Franklin (ed.), *Diary of James T. Ayers*, xvi–xvii.

the Northern invaders, the newly emancipated blacks soon apprehended that the epoch of freedom would be no millennium.

Many who traded Southern owners and overseers for Yankee bosses very quickly discarded any lingering notions about Northern benevolence. The army's mass roundups of unwilling black laborers in town and country continued through the war, and many a black man thus seized must have sought in vain to define the distinction between such involuntary servitude and the slavery he had just left behind. The abuse of impressed blacks and others employed by the army became so common and so scandalous as to provoke condemnation from blacks, Northerners, and native whites alike. "The colored men here are treated like brutes," a Federal officer wrote from Nashville in September, 1863. Rations for impressed blacks were usually scanty and poor, shelter inadequate, conditions unhealthy, the work difficult, and the pay meager or nonexistent. Some contrabands were hired out to private contractors who cheated them of their provisions and ignored their welfare, not feeding them for days. These freedmen "dye by dozens from there neglect," one witness declared, and he concluded with some justification that they "are in a much wors condition than in a state of slavery." A Davidson County man who observed contrabands in an army camp characterized them as "the most miserable wretched looking creatures I ever saw—lousy, ragged, dirty, half starved devils . . . [and] when sick no more att[ent]ion was paid to them than if they were so many dogs, and, in fact, five of them died in camp." [55]

Abuse was not confined to those working for the army. Blacks suffered at the hands of malevolent soldiers wherever they encountered them, whether in army camps, on city streets, or on country roads. An Indiana soldier in Murfreesboro remarked that "the darkies are . . . really the only friends we have yet whenever they come to camp the boys curse them and threaten them." Verbal hostility was but the mildest of the Yankees' misdeeds, however. Armed robbery and physical violence became commonplace before the war's end. On at least two occasions while at work in the fields, Nimrod Porter's blacks were robbed at gunpoint by Federal soldiers. The sexual abuse and exploitation of black women by white soldiers were prevalent enough to prompt condemnation by Northern humanitarians and military commanders. Reports of unprovoked assaults on blacks by soldiers proliferated throughout the region. [56]

55 George L. Stearns to E. M. Stanton, September 25, 1863, and enclosure, in *OR*, Ser. III, Vol. III, 840; John W. Birdwell to Andrew Johnson, November 4, 1864, in Johnson Papers; William B. Lewis to George A. Washington, March 6, 1863, in Washington Papers.
56 "Documents: Civil War Diary of Jabez T. Cox," 52; Porter Journal, March 25, No-

The freedmen of Gallatin were the victims of probably the worst sustained military brutality against blacks in the region, at the hands of the 13th Tennessee Cavalry—a regiment of East Tennessee unionists and by all odds the most malicious band of Negrophobes among the Federal occupiers. Entering Gallatin in May, 1864, and apprehending scornfully (as one soldier recalled) that the previous garrison troops "had made the 'colored man and brother' think he was the whole thing," the soldiers of the 13th set about to teach the town's contrabands a lesson. "They are the meanest men I ever saw," wrote a Gallatin girl, whose diary chronicles their terrorism, "but they have one good trait they make the negroes 'walk a chalk.'" Within a day of their arrival the troopers burned down a black school, vowing that "they will have none of that while they stay here." Two days later, a soldier shot and killed a contraband, and soon thereafter other soldiers vowed to "kill every negro in G[allatin]" as soon as they could get away with it. A few weeks later, the troopers set fire to a new schoolhouse which the blacks had courageously opened. The travail of the freedmen of Gallatin was simply the ugliest manifestation of a phenomenon prevalent throughout Middle Tennessee from 1862 to 1865.[57]

To be sure, not every Union soldier was a Negro-baiting bully. The black men and women of the heartland had much to thank the Yankees for before the war was over: acts of kindness, generosity, protection, and dedicated mission by a few idealistic soldiers who desired to use the war to set the future of the black race on a sound foundation. By late 1863, local commanders had orders to provide food and shelter for every contraband woman and child coming into the lines (men were to be impressed for work or enlisted), whether by offering direct aid at army expense, by quartering the blacks on abandoned or secessionist-owned farms, or simply by returning the blacks to their former masters with instructions to feed and house them. The very worst abuses of blacks by native whites often met a quick response: more than one white man who dared to whip or kill a freedman found himself in the guardhouse awaiting military justice.[58]

Much succor and justice for the freedmen, of course, emanated from the

---

vember 12, 1864. Interracial sex between soldiers and black women (which was common during the occupation) and the sexual abuse of black women are noted in "Documents: Shelly Papers," 196–97; Joseph G. McKee and M. M. Brown to Andrew Johnson, November 3, 1863, in Graf and Haskins (eds.), *Papers of Andrew Johnson*, VI, 450–51.

57   Samuel W. Scott and Samuel P. Angel, *History of the Thirteenth Regiment Tennessee Volunteer Cavalry U.S.A.* (Blountville, Tenn., 1903), 140–41; Williamson Diary, May 2, 3, 4, 5, 6, 9, June 5, 1864.

58   A favorable assessment of military treatment of blacks in Nashville (written by a Northern missionary) is David Chapman to Mr. Editor, December 9, 1863, in American Mis-

mundane desire of the Federals to preserve order and punish rebels. But a strain of high-mindedness was also at work, well represented by Colonel R. D. Mussey, whose formal report on the recruitment and training of black soldiers in Middle Tennessee concluded with a personal note: "I regard . . . the organization of colored troops as a very important social, humanitarian, as well as military measure, and as a providential means of fitting the race freed by this war for their liberty. . . . I have now, after a year's labor in this department, more hope and more faith than ever in the capability of the negro to make a good soldier and a good citizen."[59]

The best and the worst of Yankee intentions were mirrored in the contraband camps, which harbored thousands of Middle Tennessee freedmen during the war. The Gallatin post commander established one informally in 1863, but by early 1864 the army high command began to systematize the procedure and soon founded other camps at Nashville, Clarksville, Murfreesboro, and Pulaski. Official policy envisioned these as temporary shelters to house the women and children and the elderly who came into the lines until they could be settled under contracts on the farms of loyal whites or on secessionists' abandoned lands.[60]

The Clarksville and Pulaski camps, however, became something more than depots. Under the direction of idealistic and energetic officers, blacks in these two camps (numbering more than a thousand in each) farmed their own acres, built their own cabins and barracks, operated a blacksmith and other trade shops, cut lumber and firewood, pooled money earned from their labor and crop sales, and moved toward self-sufficiency. Northern missionaries conducted well-attended schools in both camps, and the government provided medical care. Camp authorities endeavored to keep families together, to exempt young children from heavy work, and to ensure that blacks who hired out to local whites were well treated and fairly remunerated. Federal inspectors who visited the Clarksville camp in the summer of 1864 lauded it as a well-managed enterprise generating profound social repercussions throughout its environs by safeguarding the black family and severing the last bonds of slavery.[61]

---

sionary Association, Tennessee Records. Federal policy on providing for contrabands is outlined in Circular, Headquarters Left Wing, Sixteenth A.C., November 19, 1863, in *OR*, Vol. XXXI, Pt. 3, p. 198. Instances of Federal protection of freedmen or punishment of whites who mistreated them are in Hinkley, *Narrative of Service*, 101–102; Porter Journal, May 16, 1864, March 8, 1865; A. A. Smith to B. H. Polk, April 19, 1864, in Letters Sent, 1863–65, No. 192, E3023, RCC.

59 R. D. Mussey to C. W. Foster, October 10, 1864, in *OR*, Ser. III, Vol. IV, pp. 762–74.

60 *Ibid.*, 770–71; *Senate Executive Documents*, 38th Cong., 2nd Sess., No. 1209, pp. 1–3, 11.

61 L. Pettijohn to S. S. Jocelin, March 8, 1864, in American Missionary Association,

The same observers proffered no such encomia for the Nashville camp. "It would be difficult to imagine," they indignantly reported, "a more deplorably destitute condition of things than we found here to exist." The officers in command, whom the inspectors charged with unconscionable lack of humanity and disregard of duty, had ignored orders to build barracks and instead crowded their black charges into a few leaky tents. They similarly shirked other responsibilities: a number of the women and children were in rags, schooling was neglected, and the blacks did not get enough to eat. Many were sick and many others had died. "We are free to say," the inspectors concluded, "we have never witnessed an aggregate of wretchedness and misery equal to that we were here called to look upon."[62]

Most freedmen, however, never saw a contraband camp, good or bad. Far more of those who left the countryside headed for towns than camps, for the quasi-autonomous black urban communities continued to beckon seekers of independence as in antebellum days. By the thousands blacks poured into the towns. But the economic calamities of war had rendered those towns incapable of absorbing such swarms without drastic consequences—crowding, unemployment, poverty, and all their attendant evils. There were simply too many freedmen, too few jobs, and too little housing.[63]

Blacks in every town confronted these hardships by 1863, but those in Nashville faced the most severe trials. Most could find no regular, gainful work. They took such odd jobs as they could find; they scrambled for meager army handouts; they begged. Some stole goods they had no money to buy. Some black women worked in army hospitals simply for board because there was no provision for paying them wages. Many others turned to prostitution. In the winter, most Nashville contrabands were cold, and in every season they were hungry. Some black men, after weeks or months of dodging army impressment squads, finally allowed themselves to be taken just to get a meal. Desperate for shelter, blacks crowded into decrepit buildings, dank cellars, and even outhouses. As many as a dozen or even twenty could be found crammed into a twenty-feet-square room.

Tennessee Records; Burton, *Diary*, 8; *Senate Executive Documents*, 38th Cong., 2nd Sess., No. 1209, pp. 9–10.

62 *Senate Executive Documents*, 38th Cong., 2nd Sess., No. 1209, pp. 3–9.

63 On conditions in Columbia, Clarksville, Murfreesboro, and Shelbyville, see General Orders, No. 12, Headquarters, U.S. Forces at Columbia, February 28, 1865, in General Orders, 1865, No. 191, E3018, A. A. Smith to B. H. Polk, February 8, 1864, in Letters Sent, 1863–65, No. 192, E3023, H. P. Van Cleve to B. H. Polk, March 9, 1864, in Letters Sent, 1863–65, No. 196, E3071, all in RCC; Thomas H. Coldwell to Andrew Johnson, June 25, 1864, in Graf and Haskins (eds.), *Papers of Andrew Johnson*, VI, 755–56.

These were the lucky ones, for many had no roof at all over their heads and languished in streets or alleys in cold weather and hot. City officials found one homeless black woman in May, 1863, asleep on a manure pile. Disease ran rampant among the contrabands under these conditions—smallpox was a persistent menace—and they died by the hundreds.[64]

Besides cold, famine, and pestilence, contrabands in Nashville and elsewhere endured intolerance and gross mistreatment. The death of slavery did not end formal or informal discrimination against blacks. Civil authorities segregated them on railroad cars, prosecuted them for buying liquor, and harassed and punished them for every petty offense. Native whites in the towns abused contrabands even more severely than Federal soldiers did. Violent interracial hostility, aggravated by the fierce competition for jobs, triggered numerous scuffles and bloody brawls.[65]

Why, then, did the freedmen flock to the towns, and why did they remain in the face of such tribulations? One reason, of course, is that for many the suffering and violence they left behind in the rural areas were even worse. But the freedmen understood that the towns, oppressive as they were, offered the best opportunity for black self-expression, for liberation from white control, and for a safe future in the postemancipation era. Though no overseer would ever again brandish a whip over black chattels in the field, and no black family would ever again be relegated to the slave quarters, life in the countryside still pivoted around the white man's farm, village, and church—or would so pivot again, once peace had restored social equilibrium. Only in the towns could black people live in a world all—or nearly all—their own. Concentrated numbers ensured not only greater personal safety but a more independent and secure black community.

The black urban communities that were well established before the war endured because military occupation sheltered them from rural chaos. They flourished—despite the terrible hardships in the towns—when emancipation brought in new constituents by the thousands and freed the communities from many of the old constraints. Crowded black tenements and taverns and noisy black house parties and street celebrations were the most conspicuous emblems of the fructification of black community and consciousness during the war. Quieter but nonetheless significant mani-

64 Joseph G. McKee and M. M. Brown to Andrew Johnson, November 3, 1863, in Graf and Haskins (eds.), *Papers of Andrew Johnson*, VI, 450–51; Nashville *Dispatch*, November 1, 26, 27, 1862, April 26, May 23, July 9, November 27, December 9, 1863.

65 Chancellor (ed.), *Englishman in the Civil War*, 135; Joseph G. McKee and M. M. Brown to Andrew Johnson, November 3, 1863, in Graf and Haskins (eds.), *Papers of Andrew Johnson*, VI, 450–51.

festations went mostly unremarked: the semi-independent black mission of Nashville's First Baptist Church, for example, doubled its membership during the war years (while the enrollment of white churches declined); in March, 1865, the mission petitioned for and received full independence from its parent church.[66]

The privileges most stringently denied them as slaves were those the freedmen most avidly seized in the heartland's towns, especially those that might help safeguard their future. Most notably, black education and political activity had their genesis in the towns during the war. By late 1863, at least twelve hundred Nashville blacks were attending nine schools (some of them Northern missionary schools, some private), and many other blacks in the city received less formal instruction from Union army chaplains. Clarksville, Springfield, Columbia, Edgefield, Murfreesboro, Gallatin, and Pulaski also boasted schools before the war ended. Black political demonstrations kept the streets of Nashville and other towns crowded in the last months of the war. The freedmen paraded, concocted memorials to government leaders, and held mock plebiscites to demonstrate their fealty to the Union cause and their eagerness for legal freedom and civil and political rights. The abolition of slavery by state constitutional amendment evoked an immense celebration in the capital in March, 1865, featuring processions, speeches, and regimental bands, a day-long black festival the like of which the city had never seen before. "The Darkies here seem to think 'De year ob Jubilee am cum,'" wrote a Federal lieutenant who witnessed the affair, "and I expect they are about right in regard to the matter."[67]

Those freedmen who remained in the countryside during the war had scant opportunity for schools, politics, or parades. Until the summer of 1865 their lives perforce centered on evading rebels, robbers, guerrillas, and starvation. Not all succeeded. Nimrod Porter, his neighborhood plagued by larcenous black vagrants in the early weeks of 1865, com-

66   Nashville *Dispatch*, April 9, 1863; Nashville *Daily Times and True Union*, July 11, 1864; Porter Journal, July 4, 1864; Mechal Sobel, "'They Can Never Both Prosper Together': Black and White Baptists in Antebellum Nashville, Tennessee," *THQ*, XXXVIII (1979), 306.

67   Handy Diary, March 20, 1865. On education see Daniel Chapman to Brother Whipple, November 18, 1863, and Daniel Chapman to Mr. Editor, December 9, 1863, in American Missionary Association, Tennessee Records; Jane C. Warren to Electa Ames, August 27, 1863, in Ames Papers; Williamson Diary, May 9, 1864. On black political activity see Nashville Blacks to the Union Convention of Tennessee, January 9, 1865, in Ira Berlin *et al.* (eds.), *The Black Military Experience* (Cambridge, England, 1982), 811–16, Ser. II of Berlin *et al.* (eds.), *Freedom: A Documentary History of Emancipation, 1861–1867*, 5 series projected; Nashville *Dispatch*, January 2, 1864; Nashville *Daily Times and True Union*, October 25, November 14, 1864, February 23, 1865.

mented that "many of them . . . seems much like starved." Hammett Dell, who remained with his former master in Rutherford County when the war ended, remembered "droves [of] darkies just rovin' round. Said they huntin' work and homes. Some ask for victuals." Nevertheless, despite chaos and suffering in the countryside, some rural blacks managed to take a few first steps toward independence, and most often those steps manifested the same universal ambitions which Hammett Dell heard the vagabonds speak of—work and homes.[68]

Slavery had meant living in the quarters or a back room of the master's house. Thus, the freedmen reasoned, freedom would have to mean living under their own roofs. A Marshall County farmer described how a "stray negro" came by the farm during the war, worked for a day, decided to stay, and subsequently moved not into the farmhouse but into an unoccupied cabin nearby. As the war neared its end, Nimrod Porter noted that his man Caleb, having determined to rent a plot of Porter's land, was busy building his own house. All across the region, wherever conditions were safe enough, rural blacks abandoned their old quarters in favor of new homes beyond the white man's scrutiny.[69]

Slavery had also meant working without recompense for a master not of one's own choosing. Freedom would mean very different working conditions. Economic reality, Federal injunctions, and the resolute determination of the freedmen soon compelled even the most obstinate white to capitulate and commence paying his black farmhands and servants with wages or crop shares. One Giles County planter began as early as 1863 to divide the harvest among himself and the thirty or so blacks remaining on his plantation. As spring planting time approached in 1865, Nimrod Porter agreed to pay his laborers $10 per month. March found the blacks all hard at work and their employer well pleased: "The plowers are braking up in the field next the garden where the wagons have been runing over the ground," Porter wrote, "the girls are cutting stalks in the field next to Town[,] Press & Alfred making a . . . fence in the orchard[,] Green fixing the plows, &c, all doing something."[70]

Some rural freedmen worked under Federal aegis. The Treasury Department and the army seized a number of abandoned farms in the region and leased them to loyal native whites or to Northern "carpetbaggers." Blacks on those estates made contracts and received monthly wages under

68   Porter Journal, January 22, 1865; Rawick (ed.), *American Slave*, Ser. Two, Vol. VIII (Ark.), Pt. 2, p. 143.

69   Duling Memoir; Porter Journal, February 28, March 7, 1865.

70   L. C. Ewell to Campbell Brown, June 4, 1865, Polk-Brown-Ewell Papers; Porter Journal, March 21, 1865. See also Nashville *Daily Times and True Union*, October 29, 1864.

explicit government regulations. By the spring of 1864, as many as fifteen such farms were operating near Murfreesboro alone, employing perhaps hundreds of former slaves. Blacks in the contraband camps who hired out in the neighborhood were similarly protected and supervised by army officials.[71]

Three salient points emerge respecting the conduct of Middle Tennessee blacks in their earliest months and years of freedom during the war. The first concerns perspective. In the eyes of most Southern whites, prepared to grant the freedmen legal freedom and little else (Nimrod Porter was an exception), blacks in the early period of emancipation were lazy, insolent, and outrageously unreasonable. The exasperated outburst of a Rutherford County woman in January, 1865, exemplifies the white viewpoint: "I am annoyed to death with the negroes," she wrote. "Wash is hired to Mr. Doves, but talks of leaving. Hardin wants to make a new bargain every week—Henry gets drunk and is impertinent to everybody."[72]

A very different tableau appears, however, from the viewpoint of the freedmen, who had resolved to test the limits of their freedom. "Unreasonableness" was merely a rational calculation of the blacks' own interests and a determination to bargain for the best terms while withdrawing as far as possible from white control; "insolence" and "laziness" were a refusal to act or work like slaves—an insistence on more than mere technical, legal freedom. Freedmen in the towns for the most part did work if work was available. The prevalence of idle contrabands on the sidewalks owed more to economic derangement than to black sloth. Freedmen on the farms worked, too, as conditions permitted, but they declined to render the laborious, sunup-to-sundown toil which their former masters had routinely extorted, and they insisted on some payment for their labor.

The second point about the earliest days of black freedom is that the freedmen, who had already demonstrated their initiative through self-emancipation, continued to demonstrate it in a thousand ways—proving beyond cavil that slavery had only suppressed, not destroyed, much black ambition and talent. The militant politicking of the urban freedmen was only the most arresting manifestation of black self-assertion. Other blacks, more quietly but nonetheless resolutely, went about confirming their ability to make their own future as free men and women. Northern observers, not prejudiced by experience with slavery, remarked often in this period on the freedmen's zeal for education and their proficiency at making their

71 Nashville *Daily Times and True Union*, April 14, May 30, 1864; *Senate Executive Documents*, 38th Cong., 2nd Sess., No. 1209, pp. 1–3.

72 Trimble (ed.), "Behind the Lines," 78.

own living. Natural qualities of leadership, unleashed by emancipation, emerged in some blacks. Those contrabands who worked in labor gangs for the Union army chose their own officers, who proved thereafter their ability to command. Altered conditions in the countryside also opened up new opportunities for black aptitude. After Nimrod Porter reorganized his farm on a wage system in the spring of 1865, he noted with satisfaction that his employee (and former slave) William "has been issuing out the rations for the blacks & feed for the horses & is attending to that branch of business which requires a good deal of attention." In the towns a number of blacks came forward to organize political associations or to establish their own schools for the freedmen. Notable among them was Cap Jordan, a Columbia preacher, who began a school in a church building soon after the town first fell to the Union army and steadfastly continued classes through the war despite threats and brutal physical abuse at the hands of Confederates, Yankees, and local whites alike.[73]

The final point is that during this earliest period of freedom the blacks of the heartland manifested an attachment to family, community, and place which confirmed their essential Southernness, however much they differed from their former masters in other ways. The first step for many upon emancipation was to reunite separated parents and children, brothers and sisters, husbands and wives. Many black men avoided enlistment or army labor until assured their families would be cared for, and once in the service they remained keenly solicitous for the welfare of loved ones left behind in towns or camps or on farms.[74]

The majority of blacks left their masters' homes during the war, of course, but some stayed, and probably most who left remained in the neighborhood, or at least in the wider community. A Davidson County slaveowner noted in December, 1864, for example, that most of those who had abandoned his plantation still resided in the vicinity. After Winger Vanhook's master ordered Vanhook and family off his Wilson County plantation, the freedmen packed up their clothes and moved only about four miles away, taking up work at another farm in the community. Blacks in Middle Tennessee had always been partners—albeit subordinate ones—in

73 Daniel Chapman to Mr. Editor, December 9, 1863, in American Missionary Association, Tennessee Records; Nashville *Daily Times and True Union*, April 18, May 30, 1864; Fitch, *Annals of the Army*, 665; Porter Journal, March 24, 1865; *Century Review, 1805–1905, Maury County, Tennessee* . . . (Columbia, Tenn., 1905), 24.

74 Rawick (ed.), *American Slave*, Ser. Two, Vol. X (Ark.), Pt. 6, p. 126; testimony of George L. Stearns, American Freedmen's Inquiry Commission Report; Urbain Ozanne to William G. Brownlow, April 10, 1865, in Letters and Reports Received, 1863–66, No. 184, E2922, RCC.

the culture of town and country. Though no longer bound to their masters by loyalty and law, they remained tied to their native communities by bonds of blood, faith, and custom. Even those who ran off to the towns generally chose the nearest town; those who fled to distant parts did not often leave the region, though many had the opportunity to do so. Middle Tennessee was the homeland of its black denizens, too, and their roots ran deeply into its soil.[75]

The full expression of black community, however, like the unhindered release of black energy and ambition, had to await peace. Until the summer of 1865 the freedmen's land—save for the occupied towns—remained a place of danger and disorder, an inhospitable clime in which to nourish the seedlings of a liberated black society. The harsh winter of discontent and war took its toll, too, on white society. The white men and women of the heartland, whose story is the subject of the next chapter, witnessed a transmutation of their society during the war years as startling as the metamorphosis of slaves to freedmen. But their ordeal conferred none of the rewards for body and spirit which the black experience proffered.

75   William D. Gale to his wife, December 9, 1864, in Gale-Polk Papers, SHC; Rawick (ed.), *American Slave*, Supplement, Ser. Two, Vol. X (Tex.), Pt. 9, p. 3905.

Chapter VII

Lamentations

White Society, 1862–1865

I N T H E three years following the Northern invasion, the tranquil social landscape of the antebellum heartland became a dark and bloody
ground, a tumultuous arena of violence and anarchy. Men and women
who had lived their days in an orderly world of familiar faces, inveterate institutions, manageable or at least comprehensible forces, broad
prosperity, and unbroken rhythms of life were hurled into a murky, ungovernable wilderness in which few of the old rules and none of the old
certainties prevailed, a storm-wracked wasteland with no recognizable
landmarks. The horrifying ordeal of a Clarksville family graphically epitomizes the agony of Middle Tennessee society in the war years. "Of all the
Sad Seans that any Mortal Man was ever Called to witness on earth,"
wrote John W. Gorham in January, 1865,

> I suppose mine is the most Heart rending
> I have a farm upon the opiset Side of the River from this place about Two
> miles distent upon which my Negroes lived, with a plenty of all the Cumforts
> of life Surrounding them. On Monday Night One Weak ago A lot of ruffians
> Came to the House and forced the doors and verry illey treated the Negroes
> by Beating One a women over the Head with a Pistoll &c taking off with
> them a *dead* Negroes Cloathing &c &c, but did not disturb any thing else, the
> Negroes becoming uneasy My Son a Boy about 18 years of age went to
> the Farm to protect them. they felt Secure but *alas alas* how Mistaken. On
> the following Monday Night *last* a band came and forced the doors again
> after Shooting throw the Shelter Killing a Negro Woman and wounding my
> Son badly, he Killing one of them and wounding another their conduct after

then was too horrible to tell, they then Shot My Son Several times and cut his ears off with a knife & otherwise maimed him and left him for dead they then Shot the Old Negro Woman in the feat and body and Set the House Beads &c on fire left the House & went to My Barnes Set fire to them Containing Some 750 bushes Corn A Considerable quantity of Hay &c. &c. taking 2 Horses Set the Hay Stacks on fire a short distance off and left. to day they returned about . . . 1 oclock and Burnt the Dwelling and all other Buildings, belonging to the Place.[1]

A land where such blind atrocities become routine, without hindrance or retribution, is one whose social fabric has been ravaged, a nightmarish bedlam wherein the customary personal, communal, and institutional constraints on human behavior are vitiated or annihilated—a land in social chaos. Before the Civil War ended, rural Middle Tennessee had become just such an earthly abyss. But the people of the heartland did not reach that dreadful judgment overnight. The disintegration of their society proceeded gradually, though inexorably, in the months and years following the invasion.

The first contacts with the invaders underscored the cohesion and profound conservatism of white society in Middle Tennessee. Determined to preserve their society and institutions intact, and not yet convinced that the Federal occupation would be permanent (indeed, patriotically confident that it would prove ephemeral), whites conquered their initial panic and then stood shoulder to shoulder in resolute hostility and resistance to the Yankees. As the enemy troops approached in February, 1862, a Nashville woman defiantly declared, "I hope to be able to entertain a large number. I would with pleasure give each a cup of coffee and I think it would be the last any of them would ever drink." A magistrate in the city swore two months later that he would "have his neck streached as long as a clothes line" before he would take the loyalty oath demanded of him. After two Federal officers visited her home and called for music, Kate Carney vowed, "I would cut my hands off, before I would play for Yanks. . . . The very idea, I hope I will die before I am found receiving Yankees. They said they had never received a single kind word from anyone in Murfreesboro." When Federal foragers visited minister Jesse Cox's Williamson County farm, Cox recorded, "I talked very plain to the officers I told them they were all rogues and that God would punish them." Brashly continuing his pro-Confederate preaching despite warnings and harassment, Cox darkly denounced the Yankees as "anti christ, the Beast that assend from the bottomless pits."[2]

1 John W. Gorham to Andrew Johnson, January 15, 1865, in Johnson Papers.
2 Annie Sehon to Bettie Kimberly, February 8, 1862, in Kimberly Papers; Hugh C.

Women, as many observers remarked, seemed to be more outspoken and uncompromising in their animosity than men. Undoubtedly their brashness reflected the popular assumption, in that age of chivalry, that even the abominable Yankees would not dare retaliate against a lady, whereas a man might risk liberty or even life with an intemperate word. A Federal general in Columbia, for example, pronounced the women there "intense bitter & unbearable." Gentlewomen in Nashville held their noses when passing Union officers on the street, and some, in a most unladylike display, would stop at the house of an officer whose wife was at home, spit over the gate, and yell "Yankees!" Diehard female pugnacity was exemplified by an elderly Murfreesboro woman who, according to an acquaintance, "refused to take the oath. Said the Yankees might blow her brains out, & bury them, before she would take it as she had 3 sons & 7 grandsons in the Southern army. Hurrah! for her."[3]

More exasperating to the Federals than scathing words and insulting gestures were the outright aid and comfort which the unsubmissive heartlanders gave to Confederate troops during their periodic forays through the region. When rebel cavalry passed through Sumner County in March, 1862, its commander noted that "the whole country . . . turned out in masses to welcome us. I have never before witnessed such enthusiasm and feeling: men, women, and children never wearied in their efforts to minister to [our] wants." During 1862 Confederate forces briefly retook Clarksville, Murfreesboro, and Gallatin, and in each instance local men turned out with guns and joined in the attack. Other heartlanders more covertly served the cause as guides, scouts, and spies for the Southern army. "Clothed in the peaceful garb of the citizen," complained one Union officer, "they enter our camps and pass through our lines, and the citizen's dress is generally but the disguise of a spy."[4]

Thompson to Andrew Johnson, April 28, 1862, in Graf and Haskins (eds.), *Papers of Andrew Johnson*, V, 346–47; Carney Diary, May 24, 1862; Cox Diary, May 17, June 29, August 10, 1862, March 15, 1863. Among many other such examples see Daniel Leib Ambrose, *History of the Seventh Regiment Illinois Volunteer Infantry* . . . (Springfield, Ill., 1868), 45; Wilbur F. Hinman, *The Story of the Sherman Brigade* . . . (Alliance, Ohio, 1897), 316; testimony of Thomas J. Wood, in *OR*, Vol. XVI, Pt. 1, p. 156.

3 J. S. Negley to Andrew Johnson, August 10, 1862, in Graf and Haskins (eds.), *Papers of Andrew Johnson*, V, 605; Beatty, *Memoirs of a Volunteer*, 91; Bell I. Wiley, "Southern Reaction to Federal Invasion," *JSH*, XVI (1950), 508; Carney Diary, May 9, 1862. See also Henry H. Eby, *Observations of an Illinois Boy in Battle, Camp, and Prisons—1861 to 1865* (Mendota, Ill., 1910), 56; Sir Arthur J. L. Fremantle, *Three Months in the Southern States: April–June, 1863* (New York, 1864), 140.

4 Report of John H. Morgan, March 19, 1862, in *OR*, Vol. X, Pt. 1, pp. 31–32; report of John G. Parkhurst, July 13, 1862, *ibid.*, Vol. XVI, Pt. 1, p. 805; report of Rodney Mason, August 27, 1862, *ibid.*, 864; report of William H. Sidell, August 13, 1862, *ibid.*, 844; report of Edward M. McCook, December 14, 1862, *ibid.*, Vol. XX, Pt. 1, p. 51.

Resistance was not only a personal commitment but a communal affirmation, reflecting and at the same time reinforcing traditional bonds among whites. For example, when Federal troops in Gallatin set out in the summer of 1862 to seize tools from citizens in the countryside, word spread so quickly through the network of neighborhoods and communities that the impressment squads came up nearly empty-handed. After the army arrested Maury County farmer James W. Matthews and sent him to the guardhouse at Columbia, friends visited his cell daily to succor and encourage him.[5]

Such positive communal reinforcement for the afflicted faithful was complemented when necessary by negative sanctions against the perfidious. A frequent phenomenon in the early months of occupation was the social ostracism of unionists and collaborators. Outright unionists were rare in occupied Middle Tennessee (except in Shelbyville), but every town had its stalwart handful; and as the occupation continued a few other heartlanders gave up the struggle from weariness or practicality and cooperated or even socialized with the Federals. These turncoats earned the bitter enmity of the entire community and suffered the lonely fate of the pariah. The editor of a Shelbyville newspaper remarked in late 1862 on the "utter non-intercourse, and in many cases, the bitter recriminations" with which townspeople punished those who fraternized with the enemy. A poor widow in Clarksville who sewed a Union flag for an officer just to earn a little money was visited soon after by local women who informed her that she should no longer expect any charity, or even civility, from them. A Columbia minister publicly denounced brethren of his church who had invited the post commander to tea; and when three members of the First Baptist Church of Nashville declared for the Union soon after the city fell, their fellow worshipers were "immeasurably mortified," according to their pastor, and shunned the three along with their families "as if they had been infected with leprosy."[6]

5   Statement of J. R. Boone, August 12, 1862, in *OR*, Vol. XVI, Pt. 1, pp. 853–54; Matthews Journal, July 31, August 1, 2, 3, 4, 5, 1862.

6   Shelbyville *Reveille*, December 4, 1862; Lizzie to Andrew Johnson, July 10, 1862, in Graf and Haskins (eds.), *Papers of Andrew Johnson*, V, 547–48; John A. Campbell to Andrew Johnson, June 6, 1862, *ibid.*, 447; Rufus B. Spain, "R. B. C. Howell: Nashville Baptist Leader in the Civil War Period," *THQ*, XIV (1955), 334. See also R. A. Shackleford to his brother, February 27, 1863, in R. A. Shackleford Letters, TSLA. The fervent unionism of many or most Shelbyvillians, which never failed to astonish and gratify Federal soldiers in the town, is illustrated in Beatty, *Memoirs of a Volunteer*, 98; Fitch, *Annals of the Army*, 449, 654; W. L. Gammage, *The Camp, the Bivouac, and the Battle Field . . .* (1864; rpr. Little Rock, 1958), 72–73; "Major Connolly's Letters," 271. The dearth of unionists elsewhere in the region (see Chapter IV) is documented in B. R. Peart to Andrew Johnson, June 5, 1862, in Graf and

Social sanctions like these were the only recourse for heartlanders in the immediate presence of the occupation forces. But where Union troops were not on hand, the community could more harshly enforce its decree of solidarity. Many unionists and apostates were threatened, persecuted, or even physically abused by their neighbors or by Confederate soldiers. Some fled their homes at the first opportunity from fear for their lives. A Davidson County unionist reported in April, 1862, that a group of his "used to be friends" accosted him soon after the invasion and asked him menacingly if he liked the Yankees; when he answered affirmatively, they told him "very well old fellow we will jerk you off the ground when they go away from here." A Cheatham County man who suffered punitive pillaging that spring at the hands of the rebels declined to go to the Federal authorities in Nashville because, as he explained, "being a union man I have to stay close in order to avoid suspicion and perhaps cruel assassination." A unionist in Franklin, who had been assaulted by a drunken secessionist in broad daylight on the public square, begged Andrew Johnson for protection: "I am quite uneasy I know nothing about the use of fire arms & am too old to learn it. . . . [Such men] are a terror to timed men. He has nothing against me except that from the beginning of this rebellion I have adhered to the union and am hated and dispised."[7]

Nothing more cogently illustrates the communal nature of resistance in the occupied heartland than the emergence of guerrillaism. Within weeks of the invasion of the region in 1862, armed guerrilla bands began to harass the Federal occupiers, and they continued to plague them to the end of the war. Never strong enough to assault the main fortified posts in the towns, the guerrillas struck at isolated outposts, railroad and wagon trains, telegraph lines, couriers, foraging squads, and other small parties of soldiers on detached duty. As their disruptive sorties multiplied over the months, the guerrillas seriously jeopardized the maintenance of Federal power in Middle Tennessee; and as the war continued relentlessly, the violence of their attacks reached a brutal intensity. In December, 1863, for example, near the village of Mulberry in Lincoln County, guerrillas cap-

---

Haskins (eds.), *Papers of Andrew Johnson*, V, 443–44; Cornelius C. Peacher case, OO1188, Court Martial Case Files.

7   Thomas A. Faw to his wife, September 22, 1862, in Walter Wagner Faw Papers, TSLA; report of William W. Lowe, September 10, 1862, in *OR*, Vol. XVI, Pt. 1, p. 956; Amanda to Mary, September 12, 1862, in Clarksville, Tennessee, Correspondence Concerning Civil War Guerrillas, TSLA; Hugh C. Thompson to Andrew Johnson, April 28, 1862, in Graf and Haskins (eds.), *Papers of Andrew Johnson*, V, 346; J. B. Williams to Andrew Johnson, May 20, 1862, *ibid.*, 407–408; Thomas W. Spivey to Andrew Johnson, June 5, 1862, *ibid.*, 444–45.

tured five Yankees who were straying from the main body of their foraging detachment, then led the soldiers off the road and into the woods, tied their hands, lined them up, and shot them all down in cold blood.[8]

The guerrillas of Middle Tennessee were not, however, merely footloose partisans waging ruthless war on the Yankee invaders. They were men (and boys) of the rural communities, known to their families and neighbors, harbored and supported by them, and committed to safeguarding their world. Federal authorities misinterpreted guerrillaism in the region as evidence of anarchy, an irony because it was in fact just the contrary. An extension of rural society, the guerrillas of the occupied heartland became the surrogate instruments of communal integrity and discipline when the customary instruments faltered or disappeared under the stress of war; and they enforced with loaded guns the deeply conservative values of the communities they embodied.[9]

Tapping (and simultaneously helping to sustain) the nervous system of rural society—the traditional network of neighborly contacts and communication, the communal sharing of news, rumor, and opinion—the guerrillas, acting now in place of the generally defunct churches, courts, and less formal bodies, identified deviants and transgressors who jeopardized the purity, the unity, or the very existence of the community. Then, with threats and violence, they endeavored to bring the wayward back into the fold or, failing that, to expel them, so that the community might retain its virtue and cohesion. Those who took the oath, sold goods to the Yankees, in any way cooperated with the invaders, or opposed guerrillaism were deemed enemies of the community. In one illustrative incident during the summer of 1863, Nimrod Porter was accosted on his farm by a guerrilla who had heard rumors that Porter had encouraged another man to take the

8   Report of Silas Colgrove, December 26, 1863, in *OR*, Vol. XXXI, Pt. 1, pp. 623–24. Guerrilla attacks on military targets and the concern they inspired among Federal commanders are documented in D. C. Buell to E. M. Stanton, May 12, 1862, *ibid.*, Vol. X, Pt. 2, p. 183; testimony of E. M. Cook, *ibid.*, Vol. XVI, Pt. 1, pp. 326–29; J. S. Negley to J. S. Fry, July 30, 1862, *ibid.*, Pt. 2, p. 233; W. H. Sidell to J. B. Fry, August 23, 1862, *ibid.*, 402–403; Nashville *Dispatch*, July 30, 1863; Thomas F. Carrick file, Civil War Questionnaires (Confederate); B. F. Ramsay case, OO1227, Court Martial Case Files; John S. Daniel, "Special Warfare in Middle Tennessee and Surrounding Areas, 1861–62" (M.A. thesis, University of Tennessee, Knoxville, 1971).

9   For evidence of the relationship of the guerrillas to their local communities see Nashville *Daily Times and True Union*, November 28, 1864; testimony of Francis Darr, in *OR*, Vol. XVI, Pt. 1, pp. 613–14; report of Robert H. Clinton, February 12, 1865, *ibid.*, Vol. XLIX, Pt. 1, pp. 38–39; A. A. Smith to B. H. Polk, October 15, 1864, in Letters Sent, 1863–65, No. 192, E3023, RCC; James Nolen case, LL2731, Court Martial Case Files. This last citation indicates that on one occasion guerrillas in Montgomery County held a dance in a rural neighborhood.

oath. Porter explained himself to the satisfaction of the guerrilla, who thereupon affirmed that he would spread the word to his cohorts, all of whom had taken note of Porter's alleged misconduct. Similarly, Jeptha Pilant of Robertson County testified that a guerrilla leader and twenty-five of his men rode up in the fall of 1863, demanded horses, and said that Pilant "was a damned Lincolnite and they intended to strip me. Says I 'how do you know I am a Lincolnite' says he 'your neighbors say so.'"[10]

Some unionists and collaborators received blunt orders to leave the community. A Maury County man described a nighttime raid by guerrillas, all of whom he recognized as local men and who "were very abusive and threatened to kill [their victims] and burn their house and gave them until the next day to get out of the house and leave the neighborhood." A band of guerrillas, who in early 1864 ran a Giles County unionist out of the county, subsequently, in a perhaps symbolic gesture, auctioned off the victim's property to his neighbors.[11]

When suasion did not suffice, guerrillas resorted without hesitation to destruction, assault, and even murder. Six guerrillas visited a Giles County woman in 1864, and, according to her testimony, their leader "asked if my husband was in the Federal Army, and told me to come out as he was going to burn up my damned old 'shebang.' I left the house with my children. They set fire to the beds and throwed everything topsy-turvy and ransacked the whole house. . . . [The leader] said he ought to burn the house with the whole family in it." A Union officer reported that thirteen guerrillas attacked the home of a Sumner County unionist one night in April, 1863, wounded and captured the man, dragged him away from his horrified family to a spot some miles away, and there killed him, "literally hewing him to pieces." Near Pulaski in 1862 guerrillas lynched two unionists and left their bodies dangling publicly as a grisly warning of the consequences of disloyalty.[12]

Such brutal violence, or the threat of it, generally achieved its purpose, sending fearful unionists into hiding or exile. "Mother sent word to father

10 Porter Journal, July 18, 1863; Cornelius C. Peacher case, OO1188, Court Martial Case Files. See also Michael Carpenter case, LL2476, *ibid.*; and Hinkley, *Narrative of Service*, 107–108, which indicates that guerrillas in Lincoln County knew and communicated with one another and that one was caught with a list containing the names of others.

11 Winn G. McGrew case, OO873, Court Martial Case Files; Special Orders No. 42, Headquarters, Left Wing, 16th Army Corps, February 15, 1864, in *OR*, Vol. XXXII, Pt. 2, pp. 400–401. See also John A. Hamilton to Andrew Johnson, November 26, 1862, in Graf and Haskins (eds.), *Papers of Andrew Johnson*, VI, 73–74.

12 Powhatan Hardiman case, OO847, Court Martial Case Files; A. J. Cropsey to Phelps Paine, April 27, 1863, in *OR*, Vol. LII, Pt. 1, p. 355; testimony of Marc Mundy, *ibid.*, Vol. XVI, Pt. 1, p. 636.

not to come [home]," a young Cheatham County man testified in 1864, "knowing there were a good many Guerrillas in the neighborhood. She always sends him word when there are suspicious persons about. Father is a Union man, and has to lay out from home a good deal." Those not compelled to flee were at the very least cowed and silenced. A Montgomery County man said that guerrillas in his community "shot everybody that interfered with them. If they didn't kill the people they would beat them on the head with a pistol or anything they could get hold of and every body was afraid of them. . . . I would not report them . . . if I did I would get my house burned down and everything destroyed." [13]

Slaves had always been an integral part of the rural communities, and their subjugation was one of the cornerstones of Middle Tennessee society. Thus the guerrillas endeavored to safeguard slavery and white supremacy as vigilantly as they did white unity. Roving guerrilla bands pounced on and whipped or otherwise chastised black miscreants and fugitives, filling at least partially the vacuum left by the demise of the court-administered slave patrols and the weakening of masters' authority through Federal interference. Nimrod Porter reported in 1863 that guerrillas had recaptured several local runaways and thus "some of the rest have taken a scare." A Montgomery County slave testified that guerrillas patrolled his neighborhood so thoroughly that "the colored people were afraid to pass around much at night." Not only blacks but anyone who transgressed racial mores might become the target of guerrilla reprisals. One guerrilla showed up near the village of Cairo, Sumner County, in 1864 and announced his intention of burning a mill belonging to a white man named Allen, who, according to rumor, "had an 'outhouse' [*i.e.*, outbuilding] occupied by Negroes . . . [and] had refused to let white men occupy it." [14]

Guerrillas defended their communities not only against defectors within but against intruders from without. A Northern carpetbagger who leased a farm near Franklin, hired fifteen blacks, and began planting early in 1865 became a prime target of local guerrillas, who so persistently bedeviled the man that he very nearly had to give up the enterprise. At the same time in Maury County guerrillas raided a farm operating under Federal auspices,

13   William Russell case, NN3272, E. H. Dean case, MM1743, Court Martial Case Files.
14   Porter Journal, August 17, 1863; E. H. Dean case, MM1743, William S. Pollard case, OO1181, Court Martial Case Files. See also Nashville *Daily Press*, May 23, 1863; John C. Starkweather to B. H. Polk, May 25, 1864, in Letters Sent, 1864–65, No. 190, E3011, RCC; Jane S. Washington to George A. Washington, July 27, 1864, Mary C. Washington to Jane S. Washington, March 25, 1865, in Washington Papers.

thoroughly stripped it, and made threats against others; "[their] destruction is expected," Nimrod Porter wrote.[15]

The guerrillas were the guardians of rural society in its hour of peril, but they were also its faithful subjects. They yielded to the traditional authority of family and folk, and they affirmed the collective will of their people. (Near the war's end a number of guerrillas, about to surrender to the Union army, requested that it be made to look like capture so that they might avert opprobrium in the eyes of their community.) The guerrillas loyally championed the local aristocracy (which in turn patronized the guerrillas in their role as watchdogs of the social order), and, as the Federal army soon apprehended to its benefit, they remained dutifully obeisant to patriarchal sovereignty.[16]

Resistance in its various manifestations—the insult hurled at a Yankee soldier, the cold shoulder turned toward an oath-taker, the midnight ambush of a passing troop train, the rope tightened around a kidnapped unionist's neck—denoted the dogged persistence of traditional ideology in the heartland and the adamant determination of the region's whites to preserve their society and shield it from the corrosive storms of war and occupation. The implacable defiance of white Middle Tennesseans, some of whom became ruthless, unpardonable terrorists and killers in defense of their world, suggests how serious they deemed the invasion as a threat to their way of life—a mortal threat far more dire than that posed even by the shattering political events of 1859–61, which had moved heartlanders then to panic and violence. As in that earlier period of terrified reaction, Middle Tennesseans after the invasion identified political defection with social disintegration and therefore reckoned unionists and collaborators a menace to the survival of the community, a malignancy in the social body to be remedied or excised. Retribution against transgressors, which included social sanctions and physical violence aimed at coercing the wayward back into the fold or driving them away, harked back to the traditional methods of control in the rural social-religious communities and served nearly as effectively as those methods, now vitiated by the war. Thus through the first year and more of occupation, Middle Tennessee's white society held essentially intact its structure and its ideological foundations (if not all of its institutional instruments), stubbornly perpetuating the status quo ante bellum under the enemy's very nose.

15 R. Pierce Beaver, "An Ohio Farmer in Middle Tennessee in 1865," *THM*, Ser. 2, I (1930), 31–36; Porter Journal, March 31, 1865.
16 W. J. Clift to E. T. Wells, February 7, 1865, in *OR*, Vol. XLIX, Pt. 1, p. 665; J. S. Negley to J. B. Fry, August 9, 1862, *ibid.*, Vol. XVI, Pt. 2, p. 300; Shelbyville *Tri-Weekly News*, June 21, 1862.

The Federal high command was at first disinclined to challenge that status quo. Just as they refused to interfere with slavery in the early months of occupation, Union commanders generally declined to meddle with white society beyond ousting prominent secessionist political leaders, quashing overt resistance, and encouraging what they were convinced was the latent unionism of most Middle Tennesseans. The "rose-water" policy pursued by Major General Don Carlos Buell, commander of the army of occupation that first spring and summer, strictly prohibited troops from pillaging or entering private homes and encouraged civilians to report such incidents, eschewed the arrest or harassment of minor secessionist leaders and peaceable citizens, and relied on the advice of local unionists, who for the most part magnanimously urged a lenient course of action toward their deluded fellow heartlanders. "We are in arms," Buell admonished his soldiers after the fall of Nashville, "not for the purpose of invading the rights of our fellow-countrymen anywhere, but to maintain the integrity of the Union and protect the Constitution."[17]

From the lips of Union commandants in these months came propitiatory speeches more often than harsh edicts. Most favored positive inducements, such as public pro-Union meetings and indulgent supervision of the citizens' business and social activities, over such negative sanctions as mass arrests and administering of oaths. The Fayetteville provost marshal reported in April, 1862, that his command was doing its best to "conciliate the Citizens" and suggested that "mild yet firm measures in the course of two or three months will bring the people back to their allegiance." A secessionist woman who came to know the Federal officers stationed in Columbia felt compelled to admit in May that "some of them I liked. . . . Taking all things into consideration, the Yankees have treated us very well." Elite heartlanders, in particular, often received cordial treatment from senior officers who felt a patrician kinship with those conquered gentlefolk, whatever their political persuasion. "I have no reason to complain of the higher officers of the Federal Army," a Davidson County aristocrat wrote. "They have treated me, I am happy to say (without an exception) with great kindness and respect."[18]

17   General Orders No. 13a, Department of the Ohio, February 26, 1862, in *OR*, Vol. VII, 669–70; D. C. Buell to George McClellan, February 28, 1862, *ibid.*, 671; James B. Fry to O. M. Mitchell, March 1, 1862, *ibid.*, 675–76; testimony of Lovell H. Rousseau, *ibid.*, Vol. XVI, Pt. 1, pp. 350–55; William B. Campbell and Jordan Stokes to Andrew Johnson, April 23, 1862, in Graf and Haskins (eds.), *Papers of Andrew Johnson*, V, 322–23.

18   Testimony of Russell Huston, in *OR*, Vol. XVI, Pt. 1, pp. 497–504; testimony of Marc Mundy, *ibid.*, 632–36; Marcellus Mundy to Andrew Johnson, April 23, 1862, in Graf and Haskins (eds.), *Papers of Andrew Johnson*, V, 325–26; Curran Pope to Andrew Johnson, April 19, 1862, *ibid.*, 311; Lizzie Rogers to G. W. Gordon, May 18, 1862, in Gordon and Avery

The honeymoon was brief, however. Before long it became obvious that Middle Tennesseans would not be easily coaxed back to the bosom of the republic. The continuing stiff-necked defiance manifested even by those in towns under the army's thumb, the utter failure to spark an appreciable grass-roots unionist movement in the region, and the accelerating, bloody armed resistance in the unsubjugated countryside all conjoined to convince most Union commanders to discard the carrot and take up the stick. Buell and his policies came under political fire in Washington, too, and he was replaced in the fall of 1862. Thereafter it was generally understood among the Federal occupiers that the citizens of the heartland were to be subdued, not cajoled. "These people are proud, arrogant rebels," wrote a brigadier general in Pulaski in late 1863. "I propose, so far as I can, to let these people know that we are at war." Andrew Johnson decided as early as the summer of 1862 that his own conciliatory policy had failed, and he subsequently concluded that disloyal citizens "must be made to feel the burden of their own deeds."[19]

That burden weighed more and more heavily upon the people of Middle Tennessee as the war went on. Having abandoned their attitude of hopeful indulgence toward the rebellious in spirit, military authorities after 1862 ruled with a naked iron hand. The arrest and punishment of outspoken secessionists became a matter of routine. Guardhouses and provost marshals' offices grew crowded with sullen citizens summoned at bayonet point to atone for their contumacy. Jesse Cox, who all through 1862 had continued his rebel preaching in Williamson County pretty much unmolested, was arrested in March, 1863, and thereafter strictly prohibited from leaving his farm to ride his pastoral circuit. In April the Nashville provost guard rounded up more than seventy-five people with secessionist sympathies and locked most of them up in the state penitentiary. Eventually the occupation authorities ordered citizens across the region to take the oath or go south.[20]

The recalcitrant endured not only sterner regulation but destruction and violence. Not satisfied that edicts alone would cow the audacious Jesse Cox, soldiers came to his farm in April, 1863, and "threatened to burn

Papers; William B. Lewis to George A. Washington, February 24, 1863, in Washington Papers.

19 G. M. Dodge to Henry R. Mizner, November 27, 1863, in *OR*, Vol. XXXI, Pt. 3, pp. 261–62; W. H. Sidell to J. B. Fry, August 1, 1862, *ibid.*, Vol. XVI, Pt. 2, pp. 242–43.

20 Cox Diary, March 25, December 31, 1863; Nashville *Dispatch*, April 18, May 6, 1863; Nashville *Daily Press*, May 12, 1863; James S. Negley to Andrew Johnson, August 13, 1862, in Graf and Haskins (eds.), *Papers of Andrew Johnson*, V, 614; General Orders No. 43, Department of the Cumberland, March 8, 1863, in *OR*, Vol. XXIII, Pt. 2, p. 121.

[my house] and drive me off. We are packed up as well as we can not knowing what will be the result, will the Lord help us to bare it with patience,
no tunge can describe the intence anxiety." A cavalry expedition through
Rutherford and Wilson counties that same month methodically stripped
all the secessionists' farms and redistributed the goods to unionist families.
In neighborhoods where guerrillas had attacked Federal troops or unionist
citizens, the army sometimes wrathfully punished secessionists. Soldiers
in Giles County, for example, put an entire village to the torch in 1864
after guerrillas ambushed an army detachment nearby. Guerrillas and
spies captured by the military could expect swift and fatal retribution,
often without the formality of a trial.[21]

The Yankees' efforts to crush the individual spirit of resistance eventually converged to touch white society as a whole. The military government instituted strategies directed deliberately against the cornerstones of
Middle Tennessee society. Reinforced and furiously accelerated by the
blind momentum of war, this calculated campaign swelled to an overwhelming force, which battered that society relentlessly and jarred it to its
foundations. Stout but not indestructible, the edifice of society ultimately
collapsed into ruins.

Among the first targets of peremptory military rule was the ruthlessly
enforced unity of white society in opposition to the invaders. Unionists
and collaborators coerced by social pressure or violence were protected by
the Yankees, encouraged by them, placed in positions of power, and even
armed, permitting many at last to confront the despotic majority without
submitting or fleeing. Some used the opportunity to avenge old wrongs.
Unionists in Shelbyville, for instance, seized control of the county court
after the rebel army retreated from the heartland in 1863 and promptly
cashiered the sheriff, who had helped raise troops for the Confederacy. A
Murfreesboro collaborator took power in 1862 with the aid of Northern
bayonets and proceeded to persecute his secessionist neighbors mercilessly
(at least in their eyes). One denounced him as a "wicked man" and moaned
that "tyranny stalks in open day, & private grudges of years standing are
brought to light, & revenge is considered sweet." A group of Maury County
unionists, "driven from our homes by a lawless band of rebel ruffians because we refused to fight in their unholy cause," petitioned Andrew Johnson in 1863 for a supply of double-barreled shotguns and permission

21 Cox Diary, April 13, 1863; Fitch, *Annals of the Army*, 430; journal of Jacob D. Cox,
November 14, 1864, in *OR*, Vol. XLV, Pt. 1, p. 356; Hans C. Heg to Gunild, June 19, 1863,
in Theodore C. Blegen (ed.), *The Civil War Letters of Colonel Hans Christian Heg* (Northfield,
Minn., 1936), 218; William D. Gale to his wife, October 17, 1862, in Gale-Polk Papers;
Williamson Diary, June 16, 1864.

to return to their communities, reclaim their homes, and punish the "outlaws."[22]

Eventually the government did organize and equip unionists to fight rebel resistance in their counties. Implacably these "home guards" tracked down guerrillas and their abettors: "They are killing many of the worst men in this part of the State," a Union officer wrote after scouting through Wilson County in 1864, "& will soon drive all the Guerrillas out. . . . I am convinced of their usefulness." A number of unionists, emboldened by the triumph of Federal power in the heartland, enlisted in the Union army. The better part of an entire Federal regiment—the 1st Middle Tennessee Cavalry—was recruited in the region in the summer of 1862, and its members served to the end of the war as scouts, guides, and avenging angels in their homeland. Thus as the omnipotence of the heartland's obdurate white majority withered, the long-stifled dissenters, few in number but formidable in their righteous wrath, took up arms and turned on their oppressors, with the result that white Middle Tennesseans faced for the first time not just the threat but the dreaded reality of an unleashed enemy within their own ranks.[23]

As the Yankees remained in the heartland, their understanding of its people grew. Just as they came to appreciate the crucial significance of white unity, so, too, they became aware of the immense influence of patriarchal authority and communal bonds in that society. Eventually they sought to use those hierarchical and communal forces for their own ends. By pressuring both local leaders, who in turn exerted their social authority downward against their deferential liegemen, and "significant others," who then exerted their persuasiveness outward toward kith and kin, the army found it could curtail overt local resistance and more readily work its will on the populace.

The Federal authorities found this tactic notably successful against guerrillaism. Abandoning their initial assumption that the guerrillas were footloose anarchists unassimilated by the community (an "idle floating population," one officer had called them, with "no habitation . . . here today and in another place to-morrow"), the Yankees came to recognize and exploit the communal nature of guerrillaism. As one enlightened official wrote after the telegraph wire was cut near Clarksville in September, 1862, "The secesh attend their farms in the day-time and go bushwhacking

22 Bedford County Court Minutes, August 1863, Vol. A, 14; Carney Diary, May 12, 1862; Maury County refugees to Andrew Johnson, July 8, 1863, in Johnson Papers.

23 Fayetteville *Union Herald*, June 18, 1862; David A. Briggs and James P. Brownlow to Andrew Johnson, August 9, 1863, Alvan C. Gillem to Andrew Johnson, August 9, 1864, in Johnson Papers; Fitch, *Annals of the Army*, 213–15.

at night." If such culprits could not be apprehended, local commanders found it efficacious to apply pressure at sensitive points in the guerrillas' communal or familial context. In localities where guerrillas had destroyed the property of unionists, the Federals often forced every secessionist family in the neighborhood to pay stiff fines. Where unionists or soldiers had been killed, Federal troops would march in and burn the homes of secessionists and sometimes take neighbors hostage until the perpetrators were caught or their attacks ceased. "Bring in all the disloyal citizens around about where Briggs was killed," a Union commander in Giles County ordered. "They must be made to suffer for this Bushwhacking business."[24]

If, as was sometimes the case, the guerrillas could be specifically identified, even more direct pressure was brought to bear. For example, after a Bedford County guerrilla and his gang murdered ten home guardsmen in 1864, the district commandant wrote his superior for permission to arrest and banish the guerrilla's wife, who lived in Shelbyville, and to burn down the guerrilla's house. In Sumner County that same year, occupation authorities arrested the wife and four neighbors of a guerrilla chieftain believed responsible for the kidnapping of a local unionist and held them hostage for the victim's safe return.[25]

The Federals also attacked guerrillaism vertically downward through the local aristocracy. This was an equally effective expedient, based on the army's growing awareness that guerrillaism was an extension of the community, that the community bowed to the aristocracy, and that the aristocracy supported guerrillaism. "The wealthy secessionists of this neighborhood are undoubtedly aiding & sympathizing" with the guerrillas, a Union general in Maury County told Andrew Johnson in August, 1862. The officer was certainly correct, but Johnson needed no such reminders. As early as May, 1862, the governor had ordered the arrest and punishment of five prominent secessionists in any neighborhood where guerrillas assailed loyal citizens or soldiers. This edict and similar later ones were enforced with a vengeance—many a patrician found his plantation stripped, his

24   Testimony of R. W. Johnson, in *OR*, Vol. XVI, Pt. 1, pp. 266–67; C. Dwyer to J. B. Fry, September 5, 1862, *ibid.*, Pt. 2, p. 484; General Orders No. 199, Department of the Cumberland, August 15, 1863, *ibid.*, Vol. XXX, Pt. 3, pp 33–34; General Orders No. 6, Department of the Cumberland, January 6, 1864, *ibid.*, Vol. XXXII, Pt. 2, pp. 37–38; Nashville *Dispatch*, November 14, 1863; A. A. Smith to Lovell H. Rousseau, December 5, 1863, in Letters Sent, 1863–65, No. 192, E3023, H. P. Van Cleve to B. H. Polk, June 13, 1864, in Letters Sent, 1863–65, No. 196, E3071, John C. Starkweather to Funkhousen, July 3, 6, 1864, in Letters Sent, 1864–65, No. 190, E3011, RCC.

25   R. H. Milroy to G. H. Thomas, October 12, 1864, in *OR*, Vol. XXXIX, Pt. 3, p. 238; Walter T. Durham, *Rebellion Revisited: A History of Sumner County, Tennessee, from 1861 to 1870* (Gallatin, Tenn., 1982), 208–209. See also Hinkley, *Narrative of Service*, 105–107.

valuables confiscated, and himself behind bars after local guerrillas murdered a unionist or ambushed a foraging party—and they very often achieved their intended effect, as harried patriarchs quietly but sternly passed orders to the community that guerrilla attacks must cease. The Fayetteville provost marshal claimed, for example, to have wiped out guerrillaism in Lincoln County in 1864 by assessing rich rebels for every penny of loss or damage caused by guerrillas.[26]

While with one hand the Yankees thus strove to use the power of the patriarchy against the common folk, with the other they endeavored to turn the common folk against the patriarchy. It was an article of faith among most Federals—in particular Andrew Johnson—that secession had been an aristocratic coup carried out insidiously against the true interests of the masses, who were intrinsically loyal but deluded by their overbearing superiors, "coaxed and browbeat," as one unionist declared to Johnson, "by their devilish aggressive leaders—the Secession disease being in the *thin* upper Stratum of society." If told the truth, Johnson and others assumed, the people would surely see their error, reembrace the Union, and renounce the villainous slaveholding patriarchy that had brought upon them such travail and woe. A Union commander in Fayetteville advised Johnson early in the occupation that the suffering of the plain folk—especially the soldiers' families, whom aristocrats had promised to care for when they encouraged volunteering in 1861—was a "fruitful . . . Cause for future prejudice and disaffection—if wisely used." Thereafter anti-aristocratic propaganda became a staple of Federal policy in Middle Tennessee. The Nashville *Daily Times and True Union*, for example, which articulated the sentiments of many of the occupiers, regularly denounced the "rapacious slaveocracy" and "heartless, domineering aristocracy," called for the abolition of slavery and the redistribution of land, and exhorted poor whites to consider the need for "social revolution."[27]

The Yankees were not content merely to incite the masses to insurrec-

26 James S. Negley to Andrew Johnson, August 10, 1862, in Graf and Haskins (eds.), *Papers of Andrew Johnson*, V, 605; Governor's Proclamation, May 9, 1862, *ibid.*, 374; Hinkley, *Narrative of Service*, 105–107. For examples of the burdensome effect of Johnson's order on patricians, see Rutherford County citizens to Andrew Johnson, May 22, 1862, in Graf and Haskins (eds.), *Papers of Andrew Johnson*, V, 410–11; wife to William G. Harding, July 13, 1862, in Harding-Jackson Papers. Guerrillaism was not, of course, completely quashed everywhere in the region until the war was over. But it was significantly curtailed by such measures as those described here.

27 W. H. Sidell to J. B. Fry, August 1, 1862, in *OR*, Vol. XVI, Pt. 2, pp. 242–43; Alexander W. Moss to Andrew Johnson, April 28, 1862, in Graf and Haskins (eds.), *Papers of Andrew Johnson*, V, 344–45; Curran Pope to Andrew Johnson, April 19, 1862, *ibid.*, 311; Nashville *Daily Times and True Union*, February 22, 26, May 4, 1864.

tion. While the occupation was still young they embarked on a campaign whose ultimate aim was nothing less than to crush the patriarchy. As one officer declared in June, 1862, "The bad rich men must feel our power." Indeed, some occupation authorities in Middle Tennessee came to see this use of force as the crux of their mission. A major general wrote after scouting the region in 1863 that "the only effectual mode of suppressing the rebellion must be such a one as will conquer the rebellious [leaders] now at home as well as defeat their armies in the field; either accomplished without the other leaves the rebellion unsubdued." [28]

One way to neutralize the pernicious sway of the patriarchs, the Federals discovered, was to uproot them from their social context through imprisonment or expulsion. (Many, of course, had already uprooted themselves by enlisting in the rebel army in 1861 or fleeing in 1862.) Beginning in the summer of 1862, the army rounded up many prominent leaders, especially wealthy planters and outspoken politicians and ministers. Those who refused the oath were locked up in the guardhouse or ordered to Northern penitentiaries (the grand patriarch of the heartland himself, William G. Harding, spent months in a prison in Michigan) or were exiled beyond rebel lines. After learning from some of the local folk how deeply they feared the revenge of the aristocracy should they openly embrace the Union cause, the Pulaski commandant arrested twenty Giles County bigwigs in June, 1862, and threatened them with banishment if they declined the oath. Six who did were promptly escorted to Confederate territory. Some Union commanders favored the wholesale expulsion of the elite rather than selective measures against the recalcitrant alone. "If they are [all] sent away," one officer explained in 1863, "their presence and their influence are gone." [29]

Those patriarchs who remained in their homes and communities suffered harassment, ruination, impoverishment, and violence at the hands of the Yankees. One officer leading his men on a devastating "clean sweep" through Rutherford County in 1863 deplored the plight of the poor but remarked, "For the rich rebels I have no sympathy." Troops despoiled Belle Meade plantation over and over, and authorities in Nashville persecuted its owner, William G. Harding. Another famous Davidson County planter, Mark Cockrill, likewise sustained huge losses of crops, livestock,

28 Marcellus Mundy to Andrew Johnson, June 8, 1862, in Graf and Haskins (eds.), *Papers of Andrew Johnson,* V, 456–58; report of J. J. Reynolds, February 10, 1863, in *OR,* Vol. XXIII, Pt. 2, pp. 54–57.

29 Herschel Gower, "Belle Meade: Queen of Tennessee Plantations," *THQ,* XXII (1963), 213–15; testimony of Marc Mundy, in *OR,* Vol. XVI, Pt. 1, pp. 632–33; report of Joseph J. Reynolds, April 30, 1863, *ibid.,* Vol. XXIII, Pt. 1, pp. 269–70.

equipment, and dignity. Dragged before the military police in 1863 for further reprisals, the exasperated, seventy-four-year-old Cockrill lost his composure and screamed his denunciation of his tormentors: "Kill 'em! Plant 'em out! Manure the soil with 'em!" Many large plantations in the region were so ravaged by looting, impressment, and slave desertions that their owners abandoned farming. Wealthy secessionists in town and country alike were heavily levied upon by the Federals throughout the war, some to the point of penury, to help care for indigents and unionist refugees or as retribution for rebel and guerrilla attacks. In some cases the government seized entire plantations and evicted the owners.[30]

Draconian measures against patriarchal property and pride were sometimes accompanied by physical violence. During a viciously destructive Yankee raid in 1864, the great planter-patriarch George A. Washington of Robertson County stoically endured two hours of "threats, curses, jeers and taunts . . . pistols . . . snapped in his face and shaken over his head," only to be shot and wounded in a scuffle with one of the pillaging soldiers. Federal cavalry troops near Fayetteville in 1864 furtively trailed and then cold-bloodedly murdered a prominent local man, Judge Chilcothe, who earlier had bravely confronted them to demand the return of the horse they had stolen from him.[31]

Three years of havoc and punishment brought the exalted patriarchs of Middle Tennessee to their knees. Assailed bodily and spiritually by the Yankees, stripped of their wealth and their slaves and their aristocratic ornaments, compelled in many instances to labor like plain folk, the heartland's elites were left humbled and defeated, the abject detritus of a once lordly class.

Witnesses and victims alike vividly and sometimes poignantly depicted the humiliating debasement of the patriarchy. In 1862, for example, authorities ordered a group of Nashville's eminent ministers to appear before Andrew Johnson for refusing the oath. The governor proceeded to deliver a "violent and vituperative" harangue, tongue-lashing the astounded clergymen (as one of them recalled) like "an angry overseer speaking to a herd of grossly offending slaves." The ministers were afterward arrested and marched at gunpoint through the city's streets to the provost marshal's

30   Beatty, *Memoirs of a Volunteer*, 217; Gower, "Belle Meade," 213–16; Fitch, *Annals of the Army*, 626–43; Nashville *Daily Times and True Union*, March 23, April 14, 1864; Nashville *Dispatch*, December 13, 1862; General Orders No. 4, Military Division of the Mississippi, November 5, 1863, in *OR*, Vol. XXXI, Pt. 3, p. 58; R. W. Johnson to Spalding, March 12, 1865, in Letters Sent, 1864–65, No. 190, E3011, RCC.

31   Nashville *Daily Times and True Union*, December 13, 1864; Jane S. Washington to her son, December 18, 1864, in Washington Letter; Hinkley, *Narrative of Service*, 114–15.

office. That same year a relative at Belle Meade wrote to William G. Harding, "I am of opinion that you are happier in your Northern prison than we are here. . . . Imprisonment is hard to bear, but degradation and misery is still harder." An aristocratic Shelbyville woman whose slaves had run off lamented her own degradation and misery, as well as helplessness: "I cannot see how we are to get through the winter," she wrote. The war against the upper class left some of its tormented members literally begging for anonymity. "It is a happy thing these days to be obscure," Mrs. William G. Harding wrote her imprisoned husband, "and a man's safety now depends on his insignificance . . . and if I could you would find, on your return, Belle Meade and all it's appurtenances occupying as unfindable a place as possible."[32]

Facing invincible power, once-imperious aristocrats prostrated themselves before the Northern conquerors. "The tone of this class in February," a Union general remarked wryly in April, 1863, "was quite defiant; they were determined to persevere in their rebellion until they secured their rights. They have since that time lost no little property. . . . The tone of this class is now changed. They have discovered their mistake. They had been misled. They have found their rights, and they are now anxious to take the non-combatant oath, give bonds, and stay at home." Later that year, an officer in Nashville asserted that next to the death of slavery the "most distinguishing feature in this country . . . is the manner in which these people are cowed by the force of the Gov't. Slaveholders of all classes—the common farmer, the most aristocratic man and the most aristocratic lady—come . . . to talk with me about their slaves, and are the most polite people I ever saw."[33]

The mortification of the proud patriarchs who once bowed to no one but their Creator is exemplified in the travail of Gideon J. Pillow, Confederate general and eminent Maury County planter, master of eighty-one slaves and a vast plantation worth more than half a million dollars. His estate confiscated and his family impoverished and evicted from their home by the Yankees, Pillow swallowed his pride and from behind Confederate

32   Spain, "R. B. C. Howell," 335–37; Randal M. Ewing to William G. Harding, August 17, 1862, in Harding-Jackson Papers; Agnes Whiteside to E. E. Peacock, November 30, 1863, in Whiteside Papers; wife to William G. Harding, June 16, 1862, in Harding-Jackson Papers.

33   Report of Joseph J. Reynolds, April 30, 1863, in *OR*, Vol. XXIII, Pt. 1, pp. 269–70; testimony of George L. Stearns, American Freedmen's Inquiry Commission Report. Other examples of aristocratic submission to the Federals are in James H. Negley to Andrew Johnson, August 13, 1862, in Graf and Haskins (eds.), *Papers of Andrew Johnson*, V, 614; William B. Lewis to George A. Washington, May 1, 1863, in Washington Papers.

lines wrote to Union General William T. Sherman in late 1864, beseeching him to permit Pillow "as a personal courtesy, amenitory of the harshness of this war," to travel to Middle Tennessee and take his distraught wife and seven children south. "If the application is not allowed in the form presented," Pillow continued, "you will confer a favor on me to allow a personal interview with yourself."[34]

Dispossessed of dignity, property, and position, or exiled, the patriarchs of the heartland forfeited their majesty and saw their power and moral authority evaporate. Compounded with institutional disarray and with the eruption of black self-assertion at the opposite end of the social scale, the assault on the patriarchy shattered the hierarchical structure of Middle Tennessee society. No longer could the lofty planter influence his humble neighbors by word, by example, or by political or economic coercion; no longer could the fatherly pastor tend his white and black flock, encouraging some, scolding others, ministering to all; no longer could the local magistrate punish the community's scofflaws; no longer could the master beat his fractious slave into submission; no longer could whites of whatever class tyrannize blacks with impunity. Middle Tennessee had become an alien and bewildering land to its white inhabitants, a land where aristocratic trappings were a curse, where rank had no privileges, where white skin conferred no prerogatives—a world turned upside down and violently shaken.

The society of the heartland had not just one dimension, however, but two: a dimension not only of height and hierarchy but one of breadth and community. But the forces of war touched that aspect of society as well and smashed the bonds of communalism. Danger, disruption, and ruin in the countryside stifled the activities and institutions through which rural culture exerted its powerful embrace. The burgeoning violence all around them kept most rural folk fearfully at home, isolated from their neighbors and estranged from the churches, courthouses, schools, and village taverns where they had always gathered in solemn attendance or noisy revelry; and even where traveling was safe, Yankee interference often shut down those institutions for reasons of politics and war. Destruction and uncertainty disintegrated the unifying fellowship of agrarian life and work: where there was no cotton or tobacco to be picked, no corn to be shucked, no horses to be shod, no barns to be raised, and no quilts to be sewn, no neighbors came together to share labor and leisure and gossip. Moreover, the suppression of guerrillaism by the Federals wrecked the last remaining

34 Gideon J. Pillow to William T. Sherman, November 2, 1864, in *OR*, Vol. XXXIX, Pt. 3, pp. 639–40; Chase C. Mooney, *Slavery in Tennessee* (Bloomington, Ind., 1957), 198–99.

instrument of communal integrity in many areas. And even as these plagues of war withered society's sinews and vital organs, death and flight removed many of that society's constituents—white and black—and thus drained its lifeblood.[35]

War and occupation devastated not only the corpus of society but its psyche as well. Before the war ended, the ideological underpinnings of Middle Tennessee society were destroyed. Among the cluster of common assumptions and revealed truths constituting the social credo of white heartlanders were three essential tenets whose widespread acceptance had done much to define and shape that society: first, that the salutary relationship of person to person, class to class, and race to race depended not only on authority and submission but on the faithful performance of mutual obligations; second, that survival required society to close ranks and present a staunch and united front against all threats; third, that natural abundance and widespread affluence were enduring facts of life in Middle Tennessee, helping to ensure harmony and a bright future. But the scourge of war laid waste to ideological consensus. Looking around aghast after 1862 amid the blazing ruins of their land, heartlanders saw their countrymen of high rank and low defaulting on or abjuring their sacred obligations to one another. They saw some of their fellows, white and black, allying with the mortal enemy and taking up arms against their own people. They saw prosperity and optimism consumed in the awful conflagration.

The demise of authority and deference, the dissolution of communal bonds, and the collapse of society's ideological foundations toppled the props of social order in the rural heartland. By 1864 the Middle Tennessee countryside was a moral as well as geographical no-man's-land, a world without accepted verities and shared convictions, without collective obligations and common rewards, without all the customary formal and informal instruments for commending the virtuous, reproving the wayward, and punishing the wicked. Subject no longer to coercion from authorities above or from peers around, or in many cases from conscience within, individual volition was cast adrift on a turbulent sea of social anarchy. "I can see every day people are for them selves and no boddy else," a Robertson County woman wrote. "I think . . . most of [the] people have turned out to steal and lie not many that care for any one but themselves." A bitter Giles County planter declared in 1865, "I have gone through centuries of experience in human villainy during the last two years. . . . Society in a moral aspect is in extreme beyond any I ever knew. . . . I have been robbed, perse-

35   For detailed documentation of institutional disorganization, economic devastation, and the disruption of mobility in the rural areas, see Chapter V.

cuted, slandered, threatened." The experience of a Maury County woman exemplifies the obliteration of social constraints and the unfettering of passion and will in the once tightly disciplined rural communities. When a Union foraging squad set fire to her house in January, 1865, she rushed outside and, to her astonishment, found one of her neighbors accompanying the Yankees. He "said he had joined them," she reported, "[and said] that he had been broken up twice, once by the Rebels and once by the Federals, and he was going to have revenge and didnt care who it was off of." [36]

The most striking manifestation of the fracturing of Middle Tennessee society was the proliferation of crime. During the latter part of the war, the region was engulfed by an indigenous crime wave of tidal proportions, a deluge of villainies committed by heartlanders against heartlanders, which left no high ground for refuge. The first signs appeared early. In October, 1862, Lincoln County citizens met publicly to denounce the "lawless persons [who have taken] advantage of the exigency of the times . . . committing gross offenses against the peace and good order of society." The following April, a Union officer in Sumner County reported that robberies there were an "Almost nightly" occurrence. Crime continued to mushroom. In the fall of 1864, for example, there were ten highway robberies in a single day near Clarksville. A group of Rutherford County residents described their land that year as one "where crime of every grade unrebuked, runs riot at noonday, where there is neither safety for the person or protection for the property of the citizen." In Maury County, Nimrod Porter woefully chronicled the burgeoning incidence of lawbreaking. "Midnight roberies . . . on the high ways are the order of the day," he wrote at the beginning of 1864, "in every part of the country committed in every neighborhood & every day." By the last months of the war, lawlessness was epidemic. "There are sore trouble[s]," Porter wrote in November, 1864, "thefts, roberies & murders every day all round us"; and early in 1865 he noted, "Many house brakings & robing going on all over the country it is truly distressing to hear of so much lementations coming up from all round the country of robing & plundering &c." [37]

36 Mary C. Washington to Jane S. Washington, March 18, 31, 1865, in Washington Papers; William Stoddert to R. S. Ewell, May 24, 1865, in Polk-Brown-Ewell Papers; James Garner case, OO1235, Court Martial Case Files. See also Zion Presbyterian Church, Maury County, Session Minutes, August 22, 1865; Nashville *Daily Times and True Union*, August 25, 1864.

37 Fayetteville *Observer*, October 9, 1862; A. J. Cropsey to Phelps Paine, April 27, 1863, in *OR*, Vol. LII, Pt. 1, p. 355; Nashville *Daily Times and True Union*, October 6, August 25, 1864; Porter Journal, January 1, November 20, 1864, January 20, 1865.

Crime in every form was rampant by 1864, but that which most cogently epitomized the disintegration of society was the emergence of bandit gangs. Banditry was almost unknown in the antebellum heartland. By 1864 it was rife in the seething rural areas. Banditry arose almost simultaneously with guerrillaism, coexisted with it in many places, but progressively overshadowed it everywhere across the region as guerrillaism was checked and disorder grew. Federal authorities consistently mistook bandits for guerrillas, and labeled them as such, because bandits often attacked military targets. Nevertheless, crucial distinctions separated the two.[38]

Unlike the guerrillas, bandits had no ultimate social or political purpose. They acted not to keep their society unified and their world intact but to pillage and scourge their fellow heartlanders from the basest of personal motives, notably greed and vengeance. Guerrillaism, though far from exemplifying any lofty idealism, at least symbolized the persistence of community, hierarchy, and ideology. The rise of banditry represented the obliteration of all three. Its victims were not just the unionists, Yankees, and runaway slaves who threatened the integrity of the community. The mayhem of the bandits was undirected, or rather, directed against all—unionists and secessionists, Yankees and rebels, slaves and contrabands, plebeians and patricians, men, women, and children. These were not the "social bandits" of western lore; instead, they were rapacious, egocentric, conspicuously asocial or antisocial brigands. Arising from and feeding on social chaos, they were completely unresponsive to social coercion from above or around. Thus Federal attempts to quash banditry through the standard antiguerrilla tactic of pressuring local aristocrats, neighbors, or kinfolk failed utterly. Where rural anarchy was worst, bandit gangs roamed without hindrance and in some cases continued their depredations for months after the war had ended and all justification for political or military resistance had vanished.[39]

Bandits did, however, share with the guerrillas two characteristics: they

38   The appearance of bandit gangs is noted in report of S. Palace Love, May 6, 1863, in *OR*, Vol. XXIII, Pt. 1, p. 327; Nashville *Dispatch*, December 11, 1862, July 28, 1863; Nashville *Daily Times and True Union*, April 2, 1864; George A. Washington to Jane S. Washington, September 12, 14, 1863, in Washington Papers.

39   Personal vengeance as a motive behind banditry is illustrated in Nashville *Dispatch*, March 7, 1863. The indiscriminate nature of bandit violence is noted in *ibid.*, February 20, 1863. Depredations against secessionists are documented in Lincoln County *News*, September 26, 1868, and Nashville *Daily Times and True Union*, July 25, 1864; against blacks in James Buchanan case, MM3028, Court Martial Case Files, and Henderson Diary, May 7, 1864; against the rich and against Yankees in Nashville *Daily Times and True Union*, October 1, 1864; against itinerant ministers in Herman A. Norton, *Tennessee Christians: A History of the Christian Church in Tennessee* (Nashville, 1971), 100; and against women and children in Nashville *Daily Times and True Union*, March 5, 1864. Persistent banditry beyond the end of the war is noted

were for the most part men of the community, often known to their neighbors, and they did not hesitate to use brutal violence to attain their ends. In fact, as chaos spread, many guerrillas metamorphosed into bandits and proceeded to plunder the communities they had once protected. Others became quasi-bandits, still selectively attacking unionists and soldiers but also robbing them or stripping their corpses. Some of the bandit gangs, however, were made up of Confederate deserters or rural social outcasts who had had no part in guerrillaism.[40]

Whether degenerate guerrillas or merely opportunistic desperadoes, the bandits routinely terrorized their communities with a viciousness that beggars description. Nimrod Porter recorded in 1864 that the local bandits' favorite expedient was "attacking [a] house in the dead of the night gitting the doore open & punishing the inmates by partially hanging & choking them until they tell where there moneys & valuables are." Early in 1865 in another part of Maury County, a bandit gang robbed a wealthy secessionist, James Coughran, who promptly complained to authorities in Columbia. When the bandits learned that he had done so, they returned, burst into Coughran's home, dragged his wife upstairs and put a bullet through her head, then murdered Coughran, ransacked the house, and rode off. Near the end of the war, a Union officer reported that a notorious bandit chieftain plaguing the southern counties of the heartland had, in one recent night of savagery, "murdered two of my scouts, shot a number of loyal men, robbed them of everything they had . . . ravished one loyal lady, with fifteen of his gang, and made a similar attempt on an orphan girl sixteen years of age in the same room with the corpse of her cousin, whom they had killed. . . . I consider him and his gang demons incarnate."[41]

---

in Special Orders No. 104, Sixth Division, Cavalry Corps, Military Division of the Mississippi, May 21, 1865, in *OR*, Vol. XLIX, Pt. 2, p. 863; and W. D. Whipple to John E. Smith, July 25, 1865, *ibid.*, 1090.

40   That bandits were residents of their communities (many of them teenage boys) and often known by name there is shown in James Buchanan case, MM3028, Hervey Whitfield case, MM2054, William Perdue case, NN3272, Henry Stolzy case, NN3687, and Oscar S. Fraley case, OO873, Court Martial Case Files. Examples of guerrilla bands that took up banditry are in Reason Perdue case, LL2694, and William H. Walker case, OO1235, *ibid.* Attacks on soldiers, unionists, military outposts, and other traditional guerrilla targets that featured robbery as well are noted in Hans C. Heg to Gunild, June 19, 1863, in Blegen (ed.), *Civil War Letters of Colonel Heg*, 218; Nashville *Daily Times and True Union*, July 26, 27, 1864; Durham, *Rebellion Revisited*, 206; Nashville *Daily Press*, June 20, July 17, 1863; Winn G. McGrew case, OO873, Court Martial Case Files. That some bandits were Confederate deserters is documented in Powhatan Hardiman case, OO847, *ibid.* The W. R. H. Matthews file, Civil War Questionnaires (Confederate), indicates that some bandits had been notorious social outcasts before the war.

41   Porter Journal, February 6, 1864; Nashville *Daily Times and True Union*, February 8,

The proliferation of these and similar atrocities all across the heartland in the latter part of the war, hand in hand with unremitting Yankee violence, left rural Middle Tennesseans vulnerable and terror-stricken. "What will we do," pleaded an anguished Nimrod Porter as bandit outrages convulsed his neighborhood in 1864. "We cant defend our selves." Even the mighty Washingtons of Robertson County, masters of hundreds of slaves and thousands of acres, cowered before the merciless fury of the bandits. Menaced in the summer of 1864 by a local gang whose leader had sworn vengeance against all who had testified against him, men, women, and children of the Washington clan gathered their belongings, stockpiled pistols and ammunition, and barricaded themselves inside the big house, boarding up windows and fortifying doorways. "We have everything so concentrated," the plantation mistress pluckily wrote her absent husband on July 27, "that I think it would take a battery of 12 pounders to capture our citadel." But a few days later she confessed anxiously, "I do not think that we can live here much longer."[42]

Brutalized and plundered to the point of desperation, some heartlanders eventually counterattacked. Nothing more compellingly attests the antisocial nature of banditry and its fundamental distinction from guerrillaism than the determined efforts of Middle Tennesseans of all classes and political persuasions to destroy the bandit gangs. Late in 1862, Robertson County citizens arrested, on their own initiative, three men they identified as "nothing moore or less than thieves travling through the Country Committing depredations upon quiet Citizens." The Robertson countians asked Andrew Johnson for armed guards to escort the bandits to Nashville to be "dealt with as they deserve." The following summer, provoked Shelbyvillians mounted their horses and went after a bandit gang that had been preying on travelers in Bedford and Lincoln counties. "The Citizens are becoming aroused," one of the gang's victims reported exultantly, "and feele a determination to put down bushwhackers & thieves." Near the end of the war, a Union general organized local home guard companies in the southern portion of the heartland and ordered every white male over fourteen years old to enroll. He found to his gratification that many of these men and boys cooperated willingly, armed themselves with shotguns and

---

1865; R. H. Milroy to George H. Thomas, May 12, 1865, in *OR*, Vol. XLIX, Pt. 2, p. 737. Other instances of extreme brutality are in Henry Mullins case, OO1227, and James H. Hill case, OO802, Court Martial Case Files. See also John W. Gorham to Andrew Johnson, January 15, 1865, in Johnson Papers, quoted at the beginning of this chapter.

42   Porter Journal, January 25, 1864; Jane S. Washington to George A. Washington, July 27, 31, 1864, in Washington Papers.

squirrel rifles, and set out without military assistance to track down and kill the bandits who had been wantonly sacking their communities. Familiar with the bushwhackers' haunts and thirsty for vengeance, these citizens wiped out banditry in Bedford and Lincoln by April, 1865, and won the gratitude of nearly all the populace, who, as the general reported, "now feel more freed from apprehension and terror of lawless men than at any time since the beginning of the war." These home guard units went beyond the suppression of banditry to attack rural anarchy at its roots by setting up in their communities informal courts that resolved neighborhood problems of every variety—the first institutions of order and justice in months or even years to make their power felt in the Middle Tennessee countryside.[43]

Order in the rural areas, though earnestly desired by the people of the heartland, was not the paramount concern of the Northern invaders. The occupiers had a more imperative object: to crush the will of the people to resist. Despite the continued suffering of Middle Tennesseans and the preponderance of Federal power, this was a difficult task. Confederate sentiment in the region represented not just political predilection but allegiance to a peculiar ideology and an entire way of life, which the deeply conservative white heartlanders were loath to renounce. Moreover, lacking the benefit of modern hindsight, no one in Middle Tennessee before late 1864 could be certain of ultimate Union victory. Until then, Confederate morale in the region persisted, its intensity rising and falling in response to the proximity of rebel troops and the war news from other fronts. As late as September, 1864, Andrew Johnson complained that "the raids . . . [by Confederate units] in this section of the country have a great tendency to keep a rebellious spirit alive." A Montgomery County woman wrote her brother in the spring of 1864 that "we are more hopeful than we have been for a long time, indeed we are full of hope. We are expecting a great deal from [Robert E.] Lee."[44]

The deteriorating Confederate military situation, however, and especially the repulse of rebel commander John B. Hood's invasion of Middle

43 E. M. Reynolds to Andrew Johnson, November 25, 1862, in Graf and Haskins (eds.), *Papers of Andrew Johnson*, VI, 71; R. P. Shapard to Andrew Johnson, August 23, 1863, *ibid.*, 340; R. H. Milroy to B. H. Polk, April 9, 1865, and enclosure, in *OR*, Vol. XLIX, Pt. 2, pp. 291–93. Other examples of citizen opposition to banditry are in Williamson County citizens to Andrew Johnson, December 25, 1863, in Johnson Papers; Nashville *Dispatch*, March 4, 1863. The home guards referred to here are not to be confused with the exclusively unionist home guard units organized earlier to combat guerrillaism.

44 Fitch, *Annals of the Army*, 130; Andrew Johnson to George H. Thomas, September 26, 1864, in *OR*, Vol. XXXIX, Pt. 2, p. 482; Sallie to John Minor, May 15, 1864, in Sailor's Rest Plantation Papers.

Tennessee in December, 1864, blasted the last shreds of faith that the enemy would yet be driven from the land. As heartlanders realized that their enormous sacrifices would never be rewarded with victory and that the Yankees were there to stay, Confederate morale collapsed. Few of these discouraged Middle Tennesseans embraced the Union cause outright, and most continued to hate the invaders with all their hearts; but before 1864 ended, nearly all bowed to the inevitability of Northern victory. Even as Hood's army entered the region jubilantly in November, hundreds or perhaps thousands of local men—already convinced that the Confederate cause was lost and determined not to be conscripted into its service—fled to the safety of Nashville and its Federal occupiers. And in the wake of Hood's decisive defeat, Andrew Johnson remarked that "its withering influence upon rebels [in Middle Tennessee] is more decided than anything which has transpired since the beginning of the rebellion." The former Confederate governor of Tennessee, Isham G. Harris, who was traveling with Hood's army, admitted that "the unfortunate result [of the campaign] was very discouraging to our people."[45]

Signs of defeat began to appear all around. Citizens by the thousands consented to take the oath and submit to a reconstructed state government. Guerrillas still active in the rural areas surrendered to Federal authorities. Some of the refugees of 1862, seeing now the handwriting on the wall, ended their self-exile and returned to the heartland. Many Middle Tennessee soldiers deserted their commands, came home to their long-suffering families, took the oath, and endeavored to get on with their lives. "If we judge the Confederacy by this section," wrote a Clarksvillian after seeing a number of returning rebel soldiers in January, 1865, "the army must be greatly depleted."[46]

As heartlanders forsook the struggle but continued to endure the tribulations of war, their prayers for glorious victory turned to pleas for simple peace. As early as January, 1864, a Union general declared that most civil-

45   Andrew Johnson to George H. Thomas, January 1, 1865, in *OR*, Vol. XLV, Pt. 2, p. 471; Isham G. Harris to Jefferson Davis, December 25, 1864, *ibid.*, 732. Refugees from Hood's invasion are mentioned in Handy Diary, December 24, 1864; Nashville *Daily Times and True Union*, December 2, 1864; Porter Journal, December 16, 1864.

46   [?] to John Minor, January 25, 1865, in Sailor's Rest Plantation Papers. The surrender of guerrillas is noted in James Gilfillan to B. H. Polk, May 10, 1865, in Letters Sent, 1864–65, No. 194, E3048, RCC; A. A. Smith to B. H. Polk, April 20, 1865, in *OR*, Vol. XLIX, Pt. 2, p. 418; H. D. Brown to B. H. Polk, May 10, 1865, *ibid.*, 710. The return of many citizens who had fled the region in 1862 or 1863 to escape Federal occupation is documented in Nashville *Daily Times and True Union*, July 13, 1864. The account of a Middle Tennessee Confederate soldier who deserted after Hood's defeat is in William V. Mullins file, Civil War Questionnaires (Confederate).

ians in the district around Nashville had recently evidenced a "very marked and decided" change of attitude: sick of anarchy and affliction, they were now ready for peace "on almost any terms." Nimrod Porter articulated the thoughts of many a Middle Tennessean in the last months of the war: "O will that time ever come that . . . the country [is] once more in peace," he wrote in November, 1864; "what would I give yes all I have to effect it." Three months later, more desperate still, he wrote, "I would agree to go any where to live in any kind of government that would stop our troubles. . . . O for a change Some way I feel like agreeing to any thing to stop the war."[47]

Such sentiments marked the watershed of white society's Civil War in Middle Tennessee. The persistence of Confederate patriotism had signified the heartlanders' profound commitment to preserving the world they knew in 1861. The abandonment of it signified not only war-weariness and the admission of military defeat but ideological surrender on the enemy's terms and the acknowledgment of a new and transformed world. Though most whites were determined to retain as much of the old world as they could, all understood that the new one would inevitably stand in stark contrast to that which they had known all their lives and for which many had died and many had killed. "It is now pretty well understood the Southern Confederacy has gone up," Nimrod Porter wrote in resignation three weeks after Lee's surrender, "& peace of some sort either for well or for woe, will take place . . . shortly."[48]

Defeatism appeared earliest in the towns, where Federal power was most palpable and irrefutable. Well before rural heartlanders laid down their ideological arms, most urbanites had acknowledged Northern victory and conceded the futility of resistance. Many came to rely on the army for subsistence and protection and eventually identified their own interests with those of the Yankee occupiers. Some began to fraternize openly with the enemy without fear of social disgrace. Before the war ended, it was common for heartlanders in the occupied towns to attend church services, picnics, balls, and teas with Federal soldiers, on the most affable terms. An officer in Fayetteville recalled in his memoirs that by 1864 "almost every family in town had its friends among the soldiers. They were very sociable, and always seemed glad to have the Federal officers call on them. The young ladies would sing and play the piano beautifully, and make things quite homelike for us after the routine of the day's

47 Lovell H. Rousseau to W. D. Whipple, January 30, 1864, in *OR*, Vol. XXXII, Pt. 2, pp. 267–68; Porter Journal, November 20, 1864, February 19, 1865.
48 Porter Journal, April 29, 1865.

work." When his regiment was finally ordered elsewhere, he continued, "I think that [the townspeople] really were . . . sorry at our going." Similar instances could be found in other towns, and it was not unknown for townspeople to issue a formal commendation of their occupation troops or to petition to keep a particular unit which they had grown fond of. Perhaps the most remarkable indication of the mellowed sentiments of urban Middle Tennesseans appeared in Clarksville—long known as the most rabidly secessionist town in the region—when a great crowd of citizens gathered in April, 1865, to express formally and publicly their sorrow at Lincoln's assassination.[49]

Well might the vanquished heartlanders of the occupied towns feel some measure of gratitude toward their Federal conquerors, for the muskets and cannons and fortifications of the Yankee garrisons held rural anarchy at bay and spared urbanites the horrors of social disintegration that ravaged the countryside. To be sure, military authorities could be brutal in suppressing resistance in the towns, and unofficial violence and pillaging by undisciplined or vengeful soldiers plagued every town throughout the war. Moreover, townsfolk suffered as surely as their rural brethren most of the other personal, social, and ideological disasters spawned by the war—dire privation, the loss of loved ones, the degradation of the patriarchy, the decline of prosperity and optimism, and most conspicuously the proliferation of moral degeneracy and crime. Nashville, in particular, brimming with drunks, murderers, thieves, confidence men, smugglers, and prostitutes, was condemned by one outraged Northerner as "rotten, morally and socially," and by another as "about as disorderly a place as I ever resided in." A third pronounced the city absolutely insufferable and blamed the war, which had "undermined and demoralized the whole foundation of society in Tennessee." These three witnesses reacted understandably enough to the evident moral decay in the towns, but all three misread the essential fact about urban society in the wartime heartland.[50]

49 Hinkley, *Narrative of Service*, 108–13; *83rd Illinoisan* (Clarksville), April 21, 1865; R. M. Baldwin to Andrew Johnson, April 18, 1865, in Johnson Papers. Resignation to Confederate defeat among citizens of occupied towns is illustrated in Nashville *Daily Times and True Union*, May 20, 1864. Social mingling of Yankees and townspeople is further evidenced in Hans C. Heg to his wife, May 14, 1863, in Blegen (ed.), *Civil War Letters of Colonel Heg*, 211; Handy Diary, March 4, 1865; J. C. Harwood Diary, November 29, 1863 (Microfilm copy in TSLA); Betsy S. Underwood, "War Seen Through a Teen-Ager's Eyes," *THQ*, XX (1961), 183. Resort to and reliance on army authority by civilians in the towns is shown in Fitch, *Annals of the Army*, 282–83; James Gilfillan to Andrew Johnson, January 28, 1865, in Johnson Papers. Expressions of goodwill and gratitude toward occupation troops and officers are noted in Nashville *Dispatch*, June 10, 1863; Porter Journal, March 21, 1864.

50 Fitch, *Annals of the Army*, 350; Johnson, *Soldier's Reminiscences*, 304; Allan Nevins, *The War for the Union* (4 vols.; New York, 1959–71), II, 297–98.

The war had indeed "undermined and demoralized the whole foundation of society" in the rural areas, because rural society was built upon
personal bonds, which after 1862 were shattered, bringing chaos to the
countryside. But urban society rested more on formal institutions of authority than on personal relationships; and most of those institutions (town
councils, courts of law, police departments, highly structured churches
and schools) carried on their work under Yankee rule (and Yankee protection) or were supplanted by equally authoritative and effective ones, such
as provost marshals' offices, military guardhouses, and Northern humanitarian agencies. The poor might starve in their filthy tenements, lordly
merchants and ministers might languish behind bars, and urbanites might
swindle, rob, and assault one another with scandalous frequency, but urban life remained structurally intact, morally but not socially "rotten,"
noxious and boisterous and dangerous but not in essence "disorderly."
Vice, venality, and suffering, rampant though they were in the towns, did
not fundamentally threaten the institutions of authority that governed urban society. They merely pointed up the need for more police, bigger jails,
better-organized relief services, and other extensions of formal administration. On a social scale, individual volition in the towns remained subordinate to the ordained powers. In the countryside, by contrast, where personal ties and obligations knit society, widespread immorality, disaffection,
and violence represented the dissolution of social order and the wholesale
untethering of individual volition. Middle Tennessee after 1862 was a kind
of social archipelago, a dozen or so little islands of quasi-normality (the
occupied towns, with institutions and order more or less intact) surrounded by a stormy sea of anarchic rural communities.

It remains to set this miniature of Middle Tennessee's white society at
war alongside a broad-canvas portrait of the entire white Confederacy and
to compare the two subjects' features. Such a comparison reveals two very
different visages. In general outline, of course, there are certain likenesses:
Confederates everywhere sooner or later endured invasion, occupation,
and emancipation. But beneath the superficial resemblances there are fundamental dissimilarities, all because invasion came so early in Middle Tennessee and occupation lasted so long. The experience of the heartland defies or exaggerates nearly every important generalization about Southern
white society in the Civil War. The degree of devastation and human suffering in the wartime heartland—equaled in few Southern regions and
probably exceeded in none—has been documented in a previous chapter,
which also explored the ideological consequences thereof. Another chapter has contrasted the traumatic nature of emancipation in Middle Tennessee with that in most other parts of the South and has shown that the
shock of slavery's rapid dissolution forced slaveholders in the heartland to

abandon the institution intellectually while their fellows elsewhere clung to it. Three further points remain to be examined.

In the Confederacy as a whole, wartime exigencies opened up the restricted, aristocratic Southern leadership class to a limited but appreciable number of aspirants from below, plebeian or nouveau riche arrivistes, who made their way to the top through merit rather than old wealth, family connections, and cultured manners. No such democratization occurred in Middle Tennessee because after Federal control was secured in the towns and order broke down in the countryside, no native leadership class remained in power anywhere to accept new members, from whatever rank.

More conspicuous was the exacerbation of class tensions in the Confederacy arising from the unequal sharing of the terrible burdens of war among patricians and plain folk. In most parts of the Confederacy behind the lines, these animosities led to popular indignation against what was perceived as "a rich man's war and a poor man's fight" and ultimately to widespread political disaffection among the yeomanry. A few areas witnessed overt, armed insurrection against aristocratic hegemony. But in wartime Middle Tennessee no such class hostility emerged, no red flags or mutinous mobs materialized (despite the efforts of Federal authorities to provoke lower class resentment)—for the plain reason that the rich as well as the poor suffered there. The small farmer of the heartland and his family endured unspeakable privation and brutality from 1862 to 1865, to be sure, but they could look down the road and see the great planter's fields similarly stripped, his mansion plundered, his children ragged and hungry. In this respect, then, the war did bring a kind of democracy to the heartland; but it was a democracy of devastation, which mitigated class discord among whites by punishing and humbling high and low alike. There was indeed class conflict in Middle Tennessee during the Civil War but it pitted insurgent slave against master, not angry yeoman against planter. Thus the social experience of the wartime heartland was in a sense the antithesis of that behind Confederate lines, where slaves remained comparatively quiescent and yeomen grew restive.[51]

The essential fact about Southern white society in the Civil War is that even though its structure was in some degree challenged or altered, as an entity it remained intact. But the rural heartland's white society had by 1864 virtually ceased to exist as an entity, its fragments drifting chaotically after the bonds of hierarchy, community, and ideology had been snapped.

---

51 Chapter V of this study did suggest that in the heartland's towns the poor suffered physical privations which the rich escaped. There is no evidence of the development of lower-class resentment in the towns, however, perhaps because the Federal assault on the aris-

In no other respect does Middle Tennessee stand so starkly apart from the Confederacy as a whole.

Severed from their Confederate brethren, the white people of the occupied heartland were unable to judge their own experience within its wider context. They knew only that theirs was a land of ruin and suffering. Their ordeal provoked a multiplicity of bitter explanations, pathetic pleas, and plaintive laments. But increasingly such expressions drew upon the precepts and words and metaphors of biblical faith—for many the last remaining truth in a world of vanishing certainties. An anguished Robertson County woman wrote Andrew Johnson in December, 1863: "God knows why he has allowed this horrable War to afflict the country. May his wrath be appiesed and piece be restored I feel that unknow[n] callamities are now su[s]ppended as if by a thread over the heads of the Wicked rulers of this land, that had to do in bringing it on. . . . They have fanned [the people's] zeal into fanitisism and made them mad. The wind they have sown has become a whirlwind . . . God help the innocent and helpless." Another in Rutherford offered the governor a different interpretation of the war and a personal admonition: "I think it is a fulfillment of the bible, as the learned of all denominations admit that their is some important event to take place between this and 1866 the melenial year. . . . And if that be a correct opinion we all should be ready to appear before the juge to receive our final doom. . . . Mr. Johnson you have power now but recollect the bible says whatsoever measure we meete out it will be measured back again." [52]

As the war ended, the fearful prophecies of 1861 had come to pass and were bewailed in the lamentations of 1865. That spring Nimrod Porter looked sadly around and saw his neighbors "with many aking hearts for the loss of there friends & there *All*. We will set down & mourn in Sack Cloathes & ashes for many days, weeks, months & years to come." Those who read carefully and with faith the words of the Prophets, however, found therein cogent expression and deep understanding of their own travail and some measure of comfort to assuage their grief. "Your country is desolate," the Lord told the impenitent people of Israel through Isaiah; "your cities are burned with fire: your land, strangers devour it in your presence." The author of Lamentations gave voice to the sufferers after

---

tocracy in Middle Tennessee humiliated and humbled urban patricians even if it did not starve them.

52   Mrs. W. W. Pepper to Andrew Johnson, December 25, 1863, in Graf and Haskins (eds.), *Papers of Andrew Johnson*, VI, 525–27; Narcissa R. Hall to Andrew Johnson, June 27, 1862, *ibid.*, V, 509–10.

God's punitive devastation of Jerusalem, and vividly he presaged the fate of white society in Middle Tennessee:

> Our inheritance is turned to strangers, our houses to aliens.
> We are orphans and fatherless, our mothers are as widows. . . .
> Our necks are under persecution: we labour, and have no rest. . . .
> Servants have ruled over us: there is none that doth deliver us out of
> their hand. . . .
> Princes are hanged up by their hands: the faces of elders are not
> honoured. . . .
> The joy of our heart is ceased; our dance is turned into mourning.

But through His spokesman Jeremiah, the Lord delivered not only prophetic judgment against the sinful but lasting hope to the faithful:

> Lo, I will bring a nation upon you from far . . . it is a mighty nation. . . .
> Their quiver is as an open sepulchre, they are all mighty men.
> And they shall eat up thine harvest, and thy bread . . . they shall
> impoverish thy fenced cities. . . .
> Nevertheless in those days, saith the Lord, I will not make a full end
> with you.[53]

Like the children of Israel, the white men and women of the heartland were direly punished but ultimately permitted to abide. Subdued and chastened but not destroyed, they turned in the spring of 1865 to the task of reconstructing their shattered world according to the sublime will of their Lord and the dictates of worldly necessity.

---

53 Porter Journal, April 29, 1865; Isa. 1: 7; Lam. 5: 3–15; Jer. 5: 15–18.

Chapter VIII

Resurrection

Economic and Institutional Recovery, 1865–1870

N ATURE'S resplendent self-renewal in the spring of 1865
veiled but could not altogether conceal the ugly scars of war
in Middle Tennessee—scars on society and landscape alike. A
Union officer in Nashville rode a few miles into the Davidson
County countryside on April 1 and found spring "fully inaugurated,"
with beautiful peach, pear, and apple trees blossoming and forest trees and
clover already green. But his gaze took in also ruined fences and barren
fields, and he could only conclude that this land "must have been almost
an earthly Paradise before Secession set its seal of desolation upon it." A
returning Murfreesboro preacher found his church "an utter wreck, nothing standing but the cupola, and the graveyard is also a desolation." Another minister in Williamson County likewise beheld spring's glorious arrival and the land's devastation, but he was preoccupied with the loss of his
slaves and livestock, which prevented him from riding his preaching circuit: "I am undertaking to make a crop by myself this year," Jesse Cox
wrote, "so I canot travel far during crop time having only one blind mair to
do it with." A Fayetteville exile who returned home optimistically that
summer was disappointed to find the town dilapidated and its citizens "not
altogether as bouyant and hopefull of the future as I had hoped to have
found them."[1]

---

1   Handy Diary, April 1, 1865; William Eagleton to Martha Pride, March 17, 1865, in
Pope Papers, TSLA; Cox Diary, entry dated January 1, 1865, but, as internal evidence indi-
cates, written the following spring; G. W. Jones to Andrew Johnson, July 26, 1865, in Letters
Received, First Special Agency, Records of Civil War Special Agencies of the Treasury,
Record Group 366, NA.

If the land was pervaded by gloom and ruin that spring, however, there were also signs of hope and restoration. Black heartlanders exuberantly celebrated their newly won liberty and anticipated in the postwar era of freedom a greater share of life's rewards than slavery had permitted them. Whites acquiesced, if grudgingly, in black emancipation and in the defeat of the Confederate nation manqué. Men and women of both races mourned the loss of dead friends and kin but joyously welcomed the return of the survivors from the battle front or from exile. A Nashville woman remarked in May that the city had begun "to assume its old air again—the streets are not so bare of familiar faces and on yesterday I could hardly listen to the sermon at Church for recognizing old friends whose places have so long been filled by strangers." The more sanguine Middle Tennesseans detected evidence of a popular willingness to forsake the past and to get on enthusiastically with the business of living in the present. The editor of the Shelbyville *American Union*, for one, espied "returning enterprize and energy . . . every where around—the people seem to have forgotten almost that such a 'thing' as Rebellion ever visited our country."[2]

That editor may perhaps be forgiven his hyperbole, because in some respects the heartland's postwar recovery was indeed remarkably rapid and thorough. To be sure, the war had resulted in immense destruction of property. Buildings, implements, and other tangibles that had formed the material basis of the region's institutions and economy were in ruins, and their replacement would demand great effort. But those institutions and that economy also consisted of people and their knowledge, skills, needs, and passions, and these had not been destroyed but merely held in abeyance through the disruptions and uncertainties of war. Once peace was restored, trade, production, cultivation, and institutions could rebound. With a new roof and pews for the church, a new door and a coat of white-wash for the courthouse, a new bridge for the turnpike, and a new fence for the cornfield, but above all with men and women able and willing to do the work, recovery could proceed swiftly.

Restoration of order in the rural areas was the key to economic and institutional revival in Middle Tennessee. Wartime violence and chaos had kept country folk fearfully at home, thus sundering their social bonds, strangling their economy, and maiming or wrecking their institutions of government, education, religion, and community. Rural anarchy and danger—a consequence not just of Yankee pillaging and brutality but of the mayhem of the murderous bandit gangs that infested the countryside after

2   Lady Ewing to [?], May 29, 1865, in Polk-Brown-Ewell Papers; Shelbyville *American Union*, August 19, 1865.

1862—could not be suppressed until Union authorities were convinced that white heartlanders had ended their resistance so further Federal repression was unnecessary and that Confederate troops no longer threatened Northern control of the region so attention could be focused on subduing banditry. Those conditions were met by the spring of 1865, and the Federals ended their punitive harassment of the citizenry and moved vigorously out of their fortified urban enclaves to quell rural disorder. As soon as the country people perceived that travel was again safe, that brigands, cutthroats, and vengeful Yankee soldiers no longer lurked on every trail and turnpike, they hitched up their mule teams or mounted their horses (if they had any left) and rode off to resume their interrupted fellowship through their traditional activities and institutions.[3]

The first stop for many was the long-vacant country churches, for second only to their livelihoods, farm and village folk valued their Christian sodality. Freedom to ride the country roads without fear brought rural families of high rank and low together again on Sunday mornings and allowed circuit preachers once more to bring comfort and salvation to their waiting flocks. The restoration of rural mobility also permitted church elders to reconvene, bringing long-delayed judgment against transgressors of God's laws and society's mores and thus helping to reknit the shredded bonds of community.[4]

Some urban churches, too, quickly revived (many had not even been disrupted), but others were resuscitated only very slowly and laboriously. A number of outspokenly secessionist town churches had been closed by Federal authorities, and many of those and others had been seized for army use and reduced to wreckage by 1865. With the end of the war political sanctions were lifted, but destitute congregations found it difficult to repair extensively damaged buildings. Thus some urban churches remained boarded up for months after Appomattox. The elders of the First Presbyterian Church of Gallatin, which was closed throughout the war, met for business in July, 1865, only to admit that they could not pay the pastor's salary and could not hold services until the church building was

3   Evidence of the waning resistance of rural dwellers to Federal authority is in J. O. Shackleford to Andrew Johnson, May 28, 1865, in Johnson Papers; and Pulaski *Citizen*, March 30, 1866 (see also Chapter VII). A good sense of the gradual return of normal activities among the country people is conveyed in Matthews Journal, 1865, and Porter Journal, 1865. The efforts of Union troops and home guards to quash banditry are discussed in Chapter VII.

4   For examples of the rapid recovery of rural churches see Mt. Olivet Baptist Church, Mt. Juliet, Wilson County, Records, Session Minutes, Vol. II, June 1865 (Microfilm copy in TSLA); Enon Primitive Baptist Church, Bedford County, Session Minutes, March, 1865; West Station Primitive Baptist Church, Sumner County, Session Minutes, May, 1865.

repaired. A Cumberland Presbyterian church in Pulaski was still closed as late as January, 1866, because of wartime damage and the poverty of its small congregation. Another in Clarksville reopened its doors only in April, 1866; and one in Lebanon held no services until even later that year. Whether swiftly or slowly, however, nearly all urban and rural churches ultimately regenerated, and the faithful gave thanks. "We have all mourned," the Reverend David Pise told his Episcopal parishioners in Columbia at their first gathering since Federals took over the church in December, 1863, "over the temporary alienation of this House from the holy purpose to which it was . . . set apart—and with pious hands hastened to efface the scars that the ungloved hand of War had left upon its walls. To day we rejoice over its restitution. . . . Here again will the voice of prayer and praise be heard." [5]

Formal learning had never stoked the zeal of Middle Tennesseans as religious faith and fellowship had done, and thus in the difficult years of postwar institutional and economic reconstruction schools progressed more slowly than churches. Among the plain folk, in particular, education languished after the war, for hard times and public indifference hindered the rehabilitation of both subscription schools and county-administered public schools, nearly all of which had closed during the occupation. The sorely pressed yeoman farmer who willingly gave up a day of work to help repair his church and gladly donated a few bushels of corn to pay the minister was loath to do as much to secure a schoolhouse and teacher for his children, who at any rate were desperately needed on the farm. County magistrates, too, could hardly justify spending tax money for schools when roads and bridges were out and the courthouse was in ruins. The Lincoln County court, for example, did not even begin to consider reorganizing its public schools until August, 1866. Ironically, the only public education in Middle Tennessee in the immediate postwar period was that provided for the freed blacks, through the efforts of the Union army, Northern humanitarian agencies, and the newly established Freedmen's Bureau. [6]

5   First Presbyterian Church, Gallatin, Sumner County, Records, Session Minutes, July 25, 1865 (Microfilm copy in TSLA); Pulaski *Citizen*, January 12, 1866; Clarksville *Weekly Chronicle*, April 20, 1866; Historical Records Survey, *Cumberland Presbyterian Records*, II, 52; Pise Journal, June 11, 1865; Historical Records Survey, Tennessee, *Records and Histories of Certain Episcopal Churches in Tennessee* (Nashville, 1938), St. Peter's Episcopal Church History, 3–4. The generally strong recovery of churches across the region is documented in Herman A. Norton, *Tennessee Christians: A History of the Christian Church in Tennessee* (Nashville, 1971), 139–47; and Journal of Conferences, Methodist Churches in Middle Tennessee District, Records, 1866–70 (Microfilm copy in TSLA).

6   Lincoln County Court Minutes, August, 1866, Vol. A, 436–37.

The private academies and colleges that had served the region's elite before the war also struggled against postwar economic woes, but they enjoyed certain advantages over the common folks' schools. For one, many were located in towns and had been disrupted not at all, or only briefly, by invasion and occupation. Too, many of the patrons of these private schools were well-to-do urbanites who had not been stripped of their prosperity during the war as had the planters. But among all the elite, even the rural gentry whose wealth had been decimated by the war, there persisted an ethic of education that made schooling for them not a luxury or a frivolity but a necessity, an element of their social constitution as essential as wealth and position. Thus the academies and colleges revived in time, though that time was often measured not in weeks or months as with the churches but in years. For instance, although both schools were relinquished by military authorities in 1865, the Clarksville Female Academy did not reopen until the fall of 1866, and Stewart College in the same town remained closed until 1869. Union University in Murfreesboro, its library and other buildings wrecked during the occupation, reopened only in 1868. Nevertheless, private education in postwar Middle Tennessee not only recouped but surpassed its antebellum glory. The number of academies and colleges in the region increased several fold between 1860 and 1870, and student enrollment more than doubled.[7]

Public education in Middle Tennessee did manage to take some strides forward by the end of the decade, though it enjoyed no such boom times as private education. Under the energetic direction of Radical Republican John Eaton in Nashville, a new statewide school system appeared in the late 1860s. Better funded than its predecessor, demanding higher standards of its teachers, and most notably providing schools for the freedmen, the new system was a vast improvement over the old and attracted much public attention in its inaugural months. Nevertheless, on the whole, education in Middle Tennessee ended the decade much as it had begun it—skewed by elitism and racism and debilitated by apathy among the white masses, for whom public schooling remained as much a stigma as a prize.[8]

7   Clarksville *Chronicle*, September 1, 8, 1865, September 18, 1869; Clarksville *Weekly Chronicle*, September 7, 14, 1866; Carlton C. Sims (ed.), *A History of Rutherford County* (Murfreesboro, Tenn., 1947), 152; Ninth Census, 1870, Manuscript Returns of Social Statistics, Tennessee, in NA; Eighth Census Social Statistics. On the dearth of private schools just after the war, see Pulaski *Citizen*, June 15, August 17, 1866; J. T. Trowbridge, *A Picture of the Desolated States: and the Work of Restoration, 1865–1868* (Hartford, Conn., 1868), 273.

8   Robert H. White, *The Development of the Tennessee State Education Organization, 1796–1929* (Kingsport, Tenn., 1929), 78–113; Killebrew Autobiography, 186–87. John Eaton, Jr., *First Report of the Superintendent of Public Instruction for the State of Tennessee* . . . (Nashville,

Nowhere was institutional recovery swifter and continuity more evident than in local government. Most county courts were already functioning, with Federal assistance and supervision, before the war's end. The remainder were operating by the summer of 1865, as were nearly all the circuit and chancery courts and town governments. As the countryside was gradually pacified the courts were able to extend their reach beyond the towns, to which they had been confined by wartime rural chaos. And by the same token, rural people were able to take their business to the courthouse for the first time in years.[9]

Although administrative and judicial machinery was readily resurrected, social, economic, and political derangement in the postwar months complicated the full restitution of local government and justice. For example, when the Cheatham County chancery court opened in June, 1865, the judge and sheriff were obliged to pick a grand jury from among bystanders because there had been no opportunity to summon jurymen. Only after the jury was seated and deliberations had begun was it discovered that one of the jurors was a criminal defendant in the very case under consideration, and another juror was his relative. More serious still was the fiscal plight of town and county governments. Most had not collected taxes for years, treasuries were empty, few citizens could pay even current assessments, and financial records were temporarily missing or lost forever. Moreover, taxable property was vastly reduced in value because of wartime destruction and emancipation. The Clarksville mayor and city council, for example, found themselves in September, 1865, with only $6,705 to pay current expenses and interest past due of $74,000. Nevertheless, the gradual return of social and economic stability in the region permitted local governments eventually to get back on their feet. Most raised taxes from prewar levels, worked to pay current expenses first, and then turned to long-term debt. All were solvent within a few years or even months.[10]

1869), xli, clxxxv, shows that the number of students of both races attending free public schools in 1869 was but a small proportion of the total number of school-age children. Evidence of white apathy toward the free school system is in Joseph B. Killebrew *et al.*, *Introduction to the Resources of Tennessee* (Nashville, 1874), 827. Much of the new system was undone after Conservatives recaptured control of the state legislature in 1869.

9   Details of the reorganization of the courts in the last months of the war are in Chapter V. See also John H. Wright to John F. Grill, September 14, 1865, in Letters Received, 1865, No. 192, E3029, and H. D. Enry to Robert D. Reed, August, 1865, in Letters Sent, 1863–65, No. 196, E3071, RCC.

10   Cheatham County, Chancery Court Minutes, June 19, 1865, Vol. 1857–67, p. 172 (Microfilm copy in TSLA); Clarksville *Weekly Chronicle*, September 22, 1865, February 16,

Vexing legal questions arising from the war plagued local government, however, even after the resolution of administrative and financial problems. Debts, contracts, and wills made before the war, especially those involving slaves, presented problems. And what was to be done about obligations that had been paid during the war in Confederate money? In general, the courts took a practical approach to such conundrums, refusing to acknowledge any tabula rasa. Prewar debts and contracts and other legal obligations were deemed still valid. Criminal acts committed before or during the war were prosecuted afterward, if the culprits could be apprehended, and civil suits based on wartime or antebellum actions were accepted by the courts. Slaves were of course free, however, so provisions of wills bequeathing slaves were simply ignored. But slavery was not treated as if it had never existed. Thus, for example, an unpaid debt incurred for the purchase of a slave in 1861 was held to be still due in 1865. Payment of taxes, debts, and all other liabilities in Confederate money during the war was (with some qualifications) declared valid, thus avoiding a potential bottomless morass of suits and countersuits.[11]

More troublesome still was the matter of the freedmen. Many were now indigent or in jail, but their legal status was uncertain. There were no longer any masters to assume responsibility for such blacks as before the war, but the prerogatives of local government were unclear. A committee of the Williamson County court, arduously grappling in 1866 with the legal, financial, and humanitarian questions raised by the problem of black paupers, pronounced the issue "one of perplexity and difficulty." The army and the Freedmen's Bureau stepped in forcefully at first, but those institutions gradually faded into the background. Local government ultimately solved the issue by incorporating the blacks into its traditional functions, that is, by taxing black property owners, apprenticing black or-

1866. Confusion surrounding the opening of courts is further documented in Williamson County, Chancery Court Office, Minutes, April, 1865, Vol. J, 144–45 (Microfilm copy in TSLA). Financial problems are also illustrated in Williamson County Court Minutes, January, 1867, Vol. XX, 244–46. Most county and town governments simply wrote off uncollected taxes for 1862–64. See, for example, Marshall County Court Minutes, July, 1865, Vol. L, 157. The restoration of missing records is indicated in Cheatham County Court Minutes, October 2, 1865, Vol. B, 315.

11   The prosecution of prewar and wartime civil and criminal cases is illustrated in Cheatham County Chancery Court Minutes, October 16, 1865, Vol. 1857–67, pp. 180–85; and Giles County, Circuit Court, Minutes, Civil and Criminal, August 9, 11, 1865, Vol. 1865–66, n.p. (Microfilm copy in TSLA). For an example of how the postwar courts dealt with estate and other property cases involving slaves, see Bedford County, Clerk and Master's Office, Minute Books, March 8, 1865, Bk. 1859–65, p. 572 (Microfilm copy in TSLA). On debts paid in Confederate money see Fayetteville *Observer*, March 21, 1867.

phans or authorizing guardianships for them, imprisoning black law-breakers, and putting black indigents into black poorhouses. But the freedmen were not merely acted upon by the courts. More and more they exercised their new legal rights by filing lawsuits, writing wills, and so on, though with few exceptions they were denied seats of power or responsibility in local government.[12]

Even with all the dilemmas raised by Reconstruction, however, the heartland's local governments revived rapidly, in part because, despite the subsumption of the freedmen, government remained small and unobtrusive. Notwithstanding the many revolutionary changes wrought by war, the people of Middle Tennessee in 1870—black as well as white—were for the most part a traditional, self-reliant people, as they had been in 1860. The government that served them continued to be a simple apparatus, offering few services to its constituents and demanding little of them in return. Taxes remained low (despite increases), public debt small, public charges few. Moreover, the dramatic power struggles between Radicals and Conservatives that wracked government at the state level during Reconstruction rarely threatened the county courthouses, where continuity, quiet routinism, and minimal activity prevailed.[13]

The towns that accommodated those county courthouses had, paradoxically, both suffered and thrived as a result of war and occupation. The presence of Federal troops had kept urban society and most of its institutions intact but also had exposed townspeople to constant punishment and despoliation. Furthermore, military occupation had simultaneously stimulated the urban economy, by bringing in thousands of blue-coated consumers, and strangled it, by cutting the towns off from their rural hinterlands and extraregional markets. By 1865 Middle Tennessee's towns seemed whole and vibrant only by contrast with the devastated countryside; compared with their condition in 1861, they were mutilated and prostrate. A Fayetteville man who returned home in the summer of 1865 reported that "our once beautiful village I found with all the evidences of

12   Williamson County Court Minutes, August, 1866, April, 1867, July, 1868, Vol. XX, 163–64, 285, 431; Wilson County, County Court Clerk's Office, County Court Minute Books, January 8, 1867, Vol. 1864–67, pp. 431–32 (Microfilm copy in TSLA). On the anomalous legal position of the freedmen see also Fayetteville *Observer*, November 30, December 21, 1865. Instances of legal actions and officeholding by blacks in Middle Tennessee are cited in Chapter IX.

13   Continuity is evidenced by the large number of postbellum local officials who had also served before the war. Postwar county court records for every county reveal many names familiar from antebellum records. An effort by the Radical-dominated state legislature to modernize the county court system was overturned by Conservatives in 1869, and the new 1870 state constitution did not materially change the traditional structure of county government.

the evils, of that terrible scourge of nations, present on all sides and on all hands, Ruin and devastation all around." A Maury County farmer who rode into Columbia that fall pronounced it a "poor dull place."[14]

The restoration of peace breathed life into the towns, however, and the rapid resuscitation of the urban economy seemed a marvel to many heartlanders. The decline of violence and uncertainty in the countryside brought rural folk once again into the towns, which thereupon resumed their role as local entrepots; and the revocation of military restrictions permitted the renewal of interregional trade. "Our town is entirely free from soldiers," a Franklin newspaper reported in the fall of 1865. "Everything is moving along [at] something like the ante-bellum pace. . . . Our merchants are doing a prosperous business. . . . So on the whole, we are getting along amazingly." The editor of the Clarksville *Weekly Chronicle* observed that in the few months since the "incubus of restricted trade" was removed, "a new life and energy have characterized our population." Business houses in Clarksville were being repainted and refurbished and tobacco warehouses were reopening; Northern insurance companies were returning to the town for the first time since their hasty exodus in 1861. In December, 1865, the first shipment of Montgomery County tobacco since 1861 left Clarksville for New Orleans, and by the following summer postal routes were reestablished in the county, the Cumberland River bridge was rebuilt, and rail service to Memphis was resumed. The scars of war were literally and symbolically erased in Clarksville and every town as gangs of workmen took up picks and shovels to level the earthworks left behind when Yankee regiments decamped.[15]

Accompanying the remarkable physical and economic restoration of the towns was a striking social phenomenon: a radical change in the heartland's urban constituency. In 1860 hardly 8 percent of Middle Tennessee blacks (free and slave) had resided in towns, and the region's urban population had been only about 19 percent black. Contrabands and freedmen poured into the towns during and just after the war, however, and many whites departed. By 1870, 20 percent of blacks lived in towns, and the region's urban population was 44 percent black. Nashville alone saw its

14   G. W. Jones to Andrew Johnson, July 26, 1865, in Letters Received, First Special Treasury Agency; John Orr Diary, October 31, 1865, in Orr Family Diaries (Microfilm copy in TSLA).

15   Franklin *Review*, quoted in Gallatin *Examiner*, November 11, 1865; Clarksville *Weekly Chronicle*, October 27, November 3, 24, 1865, January 5, March 23, July 27, August 17, 1866; Clarksville *Chronicle*, August 4, 11, September 8, 1865; Stephen V. Ash, "Postwar Recovery: Montgomery County, 1865–1870," *THQ*, XXXVI (1977), 211. See also Shelbyville *Republican*, October 16, 1866; Fayetteville *Observer*, January 31, 1867, February 25, 1869; Sumner County *Republican*, July 4, 1868.

black population more than double over the decade, climbing from 3,945 to 9,709.[16]

Nevertheless, the region's inhabitants as a whole did not experience increased urbanization. The urban population (white and black combined) grew between 1860 and 1870 from about fifty thousand to about sixty thousand, but the rural population kept pace. In 1860 about 16 percent of all Middle Tennesseans were townspeople; in 1870, about 17 percent. Nashville grew considerably during those years, its population swelling from seventeen thousand to twenty-six thousand, but that increase by itself nearly accounted for the region's entire urban population increase. Most other towns experienced little growth or stagnated. Nashville's boom times testified only that urbanism was becoming more focused in Middle Tennessee, not more significant.

Besides urbanism, another measure of modernization suggests that Middle Tennessee's Civil War experience had not propelled—or even nudged—the region toward the future. The heartland's industry, which was ravaged during the war, languished in the postwar years. Large-scale manufacturing had been a notable (if not preeminent) feature of the antebellum economy, though it had been largely confined to two counties (Montgomery and Davidson) and had been dominated by four products: iron, tobacco, cotton cloth, and machinery. But Montgomery County's iron and tobacco industries (which in 1860 had accounted for nearly all the region's output of those two products) were for all intents and purposes wiped out by the war. The number of hands employed in the county's ironworks fell from 261 in 1860 to 46 in 1870, and capital investment decreased 97 percent; in the tobacco factories, the number of hands dropped from 344 to 6, and capital investment decreased 99 percent. Davidson County's machinery industry, which had accounted for virtually all machinery production in the region, likewise declined precipitously over the decade: the number of hands fell from 442 to 101, and capital investment decreased 26 percent. Cloth production, however, emanating mostly from the southern counties and benefiting from increased cotton cultivation, enjoyed moderate growth: the number of hands rose from 244 to 282, and capital investment increased 16 percent. Those "industries" in the heartland that experienced substantial growth from 1860 to 1870 (notably flour and lumber mills) were rural enterprises of small scale, tied closely to their local communities—adjuncts of agriculture rather than hubs of industrialization.[17]

16 The urban population statistics given here and below are based on the census samples discussed in Appendix A. Nashville's population figures are in *Statistics of Population, 1870*, 262.

17 *The Statistics of Wealth and Industry of the United States* . . . (*June 1, 1870*) . . . (Wash-

Agriculture, not industry or commerce, was of course the heart of Middle Tennessee's economy; and it was toward agriculture that all eyes turned in 1865 to diagnose the true extent of the region's injuries and to judge the outlook for recovery. Despite the devastation of the heartland's farms—the fences and barns in ashes, the fields stripped or abandoned, the herds and flocks slaughtered—optimism abounded among the agrarian folk in the months after Appomattox. Uncertainty and Yankee soldiers had caused most of the desolation, but peace would banish both and agriculture would rebound—or so many believed. "In the country the farming business is going on with renewed energy," one exuberant observer wrote from a village in Lincoln County in March. "I have rented out all my land. I have got the most of my pasture land that was thrown out by the Armies refenced." Enthusiasm was unabated as the 1866 planting season began: "There seems to be a new spirit here in farming," he wrote in February; "every body seems to be exerting themselves to make large crops." [18]

The farmers' faith went unrewarded, however. Though buildings and fences were quickly rebuilt and fields replanted, disappointing harvests after 1865 proved the visions of bountiful crops to be mere chimeras. Nature cruelly added its own punishment in the postwar years to the scourging that the region's farms had endured from 1862 to 1865. Crop disease, storms, and floods ravaged many of the heartland's fields and turned optimism to pessimism and sometimes to despair. The same Lincoln County man who saw such bright prospects for agriculture in early 1866 wrote the following June to chronicle the intervening natural disasters, concluding that "upon the whole the crops are more unpromising than I ever knew." As 1866 ended, the editor of the Fayetteville *Observer* reviewed the year's events and judged three the most momentous: "pestilence, famine, and Radical misrule." By December, 1867, as the Pulaski *Citizen* reported, the "unprecedented failure of every kind of cultivation" had re-

---

ington, D.C., 1872), 569 70, 732–35; *Manufactures, 1860,* 560–78; Clarksville *Chronicle,* March 13, 1869. The region's considerable industrial growth over the decade as implied in these census aggregates (the number of hands employed in all industries rose from 4,326 to 6,863, and total capital investment increased 12 percent) is accounted for in great part by flour and lumber milling and similar small-scale, rural production and by manufactories such as carriagemaking and printing shops in Davidson. None of those postwar industries in Davidson, however, rivaled the size and importance of the four major antebellum industries. The average number of hands per manufacturing establishment in the region as a whole declined between 1860 and 1870 (from 6.24 to 4.15), as did the average capital investment (down 53 percent), suggesting that the many new manufactories arising after the war were small-scale operations.

18 Lucius Bright to Elizabeth Elliot, March 5, 1865, February 9, 1866, in Collins D. Elliott Papers, TSLA.

sulted in "the increasing poverty, desolation and de[s]peration of the [rural] people and especially of the negroes," some of whom were "on the verge of starvation." [19]

Natural calamities were not the only, or even the primary, cause of the agricultural depression that struck the heartland after 1865, however. These years also witnessed the evolution of a new and less efficient system of labor. Immediately after the war, agricultural prices were high. The larger farmers were able to hire laborers (white and black) for cash. Prices crashed after 1865, however; many farmers were left with little cash and felt compelled to spread their risk. The result was the share-wage system, by which workers were paid with shares of the crops harvested. Whether they paid with cash or shares, however, these farmers all sought a disciplined, reliable, and dependent labor force. They therefore insisted on employing their workers in strictly supervised gangs, just as they had employed their slaves and hired help before the war. But the new realities of the postwar society and economy soon modified this traditional system. [20]

The crucial factor was the scarcity of rural labor. In the postbellum years blacks continued their exodus from the farms which they had begun during the Yankee occupation. Some rural areas were considerably depopulated: the rural districts of Sumner County, for example, lost 10 percent of their black population between 1860 and 1870, those of Robertson 13 percent, those of Wilson 15 percent, and those of Cheatham 22 percent. Furthermore, those freedmen who remained in the countryside refused to toil any longer like slaves. They demanded shorter work days, less laborious tasks, and more days off; and they declared that black women would no longer work in the fields but in their own homes and gardens as white women did. No complaint was more common in these years among white farmers than the "uncertain and unreliable" nature of black labor, as one observer put it. Numerous white men took up farm work, but critical labor shortages persisted through the Reconstruction era. [21]

    19   Bright to Elliot, June 10, 1866, *ibid.;* Fayetteville *Observer,* December 20, 1866; Pulaski *Citizen,* December 13, 1867. See also James R. Bright to Charles Bright, March 29, 1867, in Douglass-Maney Papers.
    20   Killebrew, *Introduction to Resources,* 350–51; Lincoln County *News,* July 7, 1866; Pulaski *Citizen,* April 17, 1868; report of Moses West, February, 1866, in Narrative Reports of Operations and Conditions, Records of the Assistant Commissioner for the State of Tennessee, Records of the Bureau of Refugees, Freedmen, and Abandoned Land, 1865–69, Record Group 105, NA; hereinafter cited as FB Records.
    21   *Statistics of Population, 1870,* 61–63, 261–69; James P. Brownlow Autobiography, TSLA; Lincoln County *News,* July 20, 1867; Fayetteville *Observer,* October 24, 1867, February 27, 1868; report of George Judd, May 3, 1866, in Narrative Reports, FB Records; Pulaski *Citizen,* November 22, 1867; Killebrew, *Introduction to Resources,* 742, 824.

One result of the lack of labor was a decline in the region's agricultural output and the abandonment of many once prolific fields. But more remarkable was the shift of bargaining power in favor of the laborers, white and black alike. Some took advantage of the seller's market to demand higher cash or share wages. But many others went a step further by quitting rigorous gang work and securing small tenant farms to cultivate on their own, paying the owner in cash or, more often, crop shares. In succeeding decades, of course, this sharecropping system—in conjunction with the credit monopolies of local merchants, a pernicious crop-lien system, and state laws limiting tenants' rights and freedom—entangled sharecroppers in a web of poverty and dependence. But in the immediate postwar years tenancy was a true liberation for the agrarian working class, providing many of the landless with some measure of control over their own livelihoods and a significant degree of independence from the landowners.[22]

As the years passed, renting and sharecropping of small holdings became common. In 1860 the heartland had contained fewer than nineteen thousand farms, averaging 100 improved acres apiece; two out of ten of those farms (22 percent) were rented (sharecropping was rare at that time). By 1870 there were nearly thirty thousand farms, averaging 71 improved acres; four out of ten (41 percent) were rented or sharecropped (30 percent by white tenants, 11 percent by blacks). Of that increase of approximately eleven thousand farms, more than eight thousand were tenant farms. Between 1860 and 1870 the share of the region's improved acreage accounted for by tenant farms rose from 11 to 19 percent, the share of corn production from 15 to 27 percent, and the share of livestock value from 11 to 22 percent. As farm owners rented out parcels of their land, the average improved acreage of owner-operated farms declined from the 1860 level of 113 to 97 by 1870. Tenant farms, which had averaged 52 improved acres in 1860, by 1870 averaged just 36 for farms worked by whites and 26 for those worked by blacks.[23]

22   Killebrew, *Introduction to Resources*, 824, 835–36; Lincoln County *News*, February 10, 1866; Fayetteville *Observer*, December 26, 1867, February 24, 1870; report of M. Walsh, November 4, 1867, in Narrative Reports, FB Records. Improved acreage in the region declined only 4 percent from 1860 to 1870 (see note 25 below), but contemporary sources indicate that many of those acres, though fenced and cleared, were left uncultivated after the war. See, *e.g.*, Clarksville *Chronicle*, March 13, 1869. An important concomitant of the development of sharecropping was the rise of the country store as the local supplier of the small tenant farms, replacing the large furnishing and supply houses in the towns, which had served the big farmers before the war. See Killebrew, *Introduction to Resources*, 842; and Thomas D. Clark, "The Country Store in Post-Civil War Tennessee," *ETHSP*, No. 17 (1945), 3–21.

23   These statistics are derived from the census samples discussed in Appendix A. See also Killebrew, *Introduction to Resources*, 908, 1007.

Astute contemporary observers recognized that both share wages and tenancy resulted in reduced agricultural yields and deteriorated farm land. The laborer who was paid with share wages, as one commentator remarked, was inclined to work only from planting time through the harvest, then would "spend his time during the fall and winter months to no profit to himself or employer." Thus, "fences rotted down, [and] noxious weeds and shrubs grew without limitation over the farm." The annual renter or sharecropper, another writer noted, likewise neglected to maintain and improve his small plot: "He does not know when he goes on a place whether he is to reap the advantage of any improvement he might be disposed to make; he does not know who is to cultivate the fields next year; he thinks a tumble down gate will 'maybe' get through this year, and he does not know who would enjoy a good one, if placed there . . . and thus it goes on year after year, the landlord getting his rent it is true, but his place is going down." But though many critics concurred on the deleterious long-term effects of this system, none could devise a practical alternative.[24]

The corn and livestock economy that formed the nucleus of Middle Tennessee's agriculture was sorely damaged by the war and did not fully recover by 1870. Corn was easily replanted, of course, but stolen or slaughtered livestock took many years to replace, and skilled stock handlers became very scarce after blacks began leaving the farms. Agricultural census statistics are striking. In 1870 the total value of all livestock in the heartland was 18 percent lower than in 1860. (Maury County in particular—the state's leading livestock producer before the war—experienced a grievous decline of 40 percent.) The total number of horses in the region was 16 percent lower, mules and jackasses 30 percent lower, and swine 36 percent lower. Because there were fewer animals to feed and fewer fields to plant, corn production declined 20 percent over the decade. Thus the rich surplus of grain and animals, which the farmers of the antebellum heartland had traditionally sold south at considerable profit, disappeared almost entirely after the war.[25]

The decimation of the corn and livestock economy left most farmers in a quandary, for they knew no other kind of agriculture. High cotton prices in 1865, however (the result of pent-up Northern and European demand), encouraged many to try their hand at that staple, which had not been plentiful in the region before the war. Moreover, cotton culture did not

24   Killebrew, *Introduction to Resources*, 350–51, 835–36; Fayetteville *Observer*, February 24, 1870. See also report of M. Walsh, December 15, 1866, in Narrative Reports, FB Records.

25   Killebrew, *Introduction to Resources*, 841–42; report of S. B. Barr, May 3, 1866, Narrative Reports, FB Records; *Agriculture, 1860*, 132–39; *Statistics of Wealth, 1870*, 242–49. These last two sources also provide the acreage figures given in note 22.

demand the skill that livestock raising did, and thus laborers were more easily found. Many observers remarked on the switch to cotton in Middle Tennessee in 1865 and thereafter. But the region was not prime cotton land; and, too, the fiber's price plummeted after 1865. Thus few fortunes were made in cotton in the heartland, and production probably peaked before 1870. Output that year was only about 11 percent above that of 1860, although the proportion of farms that grew cotton that year was two and a half times greater than in 1860 (46 versus 18 percent, considering only farms in the major cotton-growing counties). Nevertheless, in some districts cotton remained king. As late as January, 1870, the Columbia *Herald* reported that farmers around Santa Fe, in Maury County, were "going to put in all the cotton they can manage."[26]

The movement to cotton and the unremitting labor problems affected the region's other important staple, tobacco. Production of the weed in Middle Tennessee dropped 38 percent between 1860 and 1870, mostly in counties where cotton production substantially increased. In Williamson County in particular, the second largest tobacco producer in 1860, output fell an incredible 97 percent. But even in the three northern counties (Montgomery, Robertson, and Sumner), where cotton could hardly grow and tobacco had long reigned supreme, production of the weed declined 9 percent.[27]

The prospects for Middle Tennessee's agrarian folk in the postwar years were not totally gloomy. Certainly by 1870 agriculture had come a long way from the desolation of 1865. Furthermore, many prewar agricultural societies and fairs revived after the war and new ones sprang up across the region, offering farmers opportunities for education and improvement. Modern labor-saving machinery—mule-driven separator threshers, Woods and McCormick reapers, and so on—made their appearance in these years and were eagerly adopted by farmers who could afford them. Yet no Middle Tennessean in 1870 could rightfully have denied that the decade just ended had been one of agricultural decline rather than progress. Wartime destruction, the end of slavery and its replacement by a less productive labor system, crop failures, and soil depletion had all sapped the strength of Middle Tennessee's nurturing heart. Vibrant and robust in 1860, the region's agriculture entered the 1870s languid and frail.[28]

26 Killebrew, *Introduction to Resources*, 841–42; *Statistics of Wealth, 1870*, 242–49; report of J. H. Gregory, May 3, 1866, report of Moses C. West, May 8, 1866, in Narrative Reports, FB Records; Trowbridge, *Picture of the Desolated States*, 280; Pulaski *Citizen*, April 5, December 13, 1867; Columbia *Herald*, January 21, 1870.

27 *Statistics of Wealth, 1870*, 242–49; *Agriculture, 1860*, 132–37.

28 Agricultural societies and fairs are noted in Fayetteville *Observer*, May 23, 1867; Pulaski *Citizen*, May 10, June 28, 1867, October 16, 1868. The introduction of new machinery is indicated in Lebanon *Record*, July 3, 1869; Jordan, "My Recollections."

The derangement of agriculture reverberated throughout the whole of the region's postwar economy and society, for hardly a man or woman in Middle Tennessee did not share directly or indirectly in the fortunes of the farmer and the land. No matter how the towns seemed to bustle with commerce, their prosperity rested fundamentally on agriculture, now weakened. The physical reconstruction of both town and countryside had progressed remarkably, of course. The editor of the Fayetteville *Observer* justifiably boasted near the end of the decade, "If a traveler had passed through this county in 1865, and again in 1869, he would hardly recognize it as the same." But he admitted in the same breath that the people as a whole had never regained their antebellum affluence; and on another occasion he noted the spread of poverty since 1861: "Families that cannot look back to the time when, before the war, they were not well housed, well fed, well clad," he wrote, "are now squalid with privation." The broad prosperity that had distinguished the antebellum heartland and had been a cornerstone of its society was not resurrected from its wartime grave.[29]

War and Reconstruction transformed Middle Tennessee society in other ways as well. Thus the apparent continuity of the region's institutions— the speedily revived courts, schools, and churches—was in some respects deceptive, for those institutions functioned in a new social context. It remains to delineate more fully the social world of the postbellum heartland.

In 1867 a Northern woman took a train from Nashville to Chattanooga. She passed through the towns and countryside of Davidson, Rutherford, and Bedford counties and left a colorful account of her journey. Poverty and stagnation impressed her most deeply. She saw

lands rich in promise and possibility, but wretched and squalid. . . . The station-villages show a huddle of dirty-white frame houses, small, disorderly, mean. . . . Groups of unkempt, unshorn, unwashed men lounge on the stoops; men and village are dirty-white together.

But this is the better class of houses. By far the larger number on the road . . . are huts, cabins. . . . One shudders to think of human beings living in such houses, and content to live there. . . . Black and white live side by side . . . looking even more wretched and squalid than their houses. One door is adusk with swart faces . . . and a few feet away another hovel overflows with tow-heads. The whites seem by far the most pitiable. They have a gray,

---

29 Fayetteville *Observer*, November 12, 1868, August 5, 1869. See also *ibid.*, December 21, 1865, May 7, 1868; Clarksville *Weekly Chronicle*, October 13, 1865. The average value of real and personal property holdings per white family in Middle Tennessee declined from $8,957 in 1860 to $4,763 in 1870 although the decade was one of considerable inflation nationally.

earthy look, as if the Lord God had formed them of the dust of the ground
. . . but had hardly yet breathed into their nostrils the breath of life.[30]

Like similar accounts by other Northern visitors in the South in those
years, this woman's often trenchant observations were distorted by prejudices, stereotypes, and ignorance. Riding through the villages, she could
see little more than stoops and faces. Had she only stepped off the train at
one of the stops, entered some of those hovels, and conversed a while with
the inhabitants, she might have come away with a better understanding of
the people. She might have sensed the deep divisions between the two
races, which the juxtaposition of their equally humble cabins obscured.
She might have come to appreciate the bonds that united black with black
and white with white—bonds subtler and more powerful than mere shared
skin color, whether swart or dirty-white. She might, indeed, have ultimately come to understand that the common wretchedness she saw disguised the coexistence of two very different peoples in one land. Those
two peoples are the subjects of the chapters that follow.

30   Mary Abigail Dodge [Gail Hamilton], *Wool-gathering* (Boston, 1868), 207–10.

Chapter IX

Isaiah's Time

Race Relations and Black Society, 1865–1870

O N MARCH 20, 1865, the black population of Nashville turned out en masse to celebrate the formal abolition of slavery in Tennessee by constitutional amendment. The awesome magnitude and dignity of the occasion impressed many witnesses. "Towards noon," a Union officer wrote, "an immense procession of colored people marched through the principle Sts of the City. . . . The procession was composed of both sexes and all ages—on foot and riding in carriages, hacks and vehicles of all kinds Two fine Brass Bands were with them Business and labor generally was suspended among the colored people and the principle thorough-fares of the City were *black with Darkies* dressed in their best *go to meetin' clothes* during a considerable part of the day—They were generally very orderly and well behaved."[1]

The jubilation of the freedmen was justified, to be sure, but as many of them recognized, their celebration marked not only a recent triumph but the inauguration of a new struggle. The black people of the heartland were determined, now that their shackles had been broken, to raise themselves up as a people and to do so on their own terms. But other groups, composed of whites, were just as determined to guide the freedmen's fate. To a great extent, the black experience of the succeeding five years would be shaped by that bitter clash of wills.

The most formidable of those who expected to control the blacks were the native whites. By the war's end, virtually all white Middle Tennesseans

1 Handy Diary, March 20, 1865.

bowed to the reality of black freedom, but that was the only concession most wished to grant. Almost to a man they resolved that blacks, though no longer slaves, must remain powerless, poor, legally inferior, and submissive—beasts of burden, hewers of wood, and drawers of water for the conquered but still superior Southern white race. "We would not raise the negro to a social level with the white man," the Pulaski *Citizen* announced in its first postwar issue. "We believe social equality a humbug and an impossibility." The Lincoln County *News* told its readers, "The area of usefulness which nature has fitted Sambo for, is a very limited one. As a field hand, with some white man to do the thinking for him, he is useful; as a house servant to a degree he may be made serviceable; as a leading working man, a 'boss,' he is, and ever was a failure." The Clarksville *Weekly Chronicle* likewise consigned the black man to eternal servility, insisting that "the God of nature never made him the equal of the white man."[2]

Whites bristled at every assertion of black independence and were particularly rankled by the freedmen's demands for social privileges. "It may be an unreasonable prejudice," the editor of the Fayetteville *Observer* confessed sarcastically in 1868, "but we *are* prejudiced against the view that [blacks] are fit companions for us at the table, in the domestic circle, in the theatre and concert room, and so on." The freedmen's campaign for political rights likewise provoked the scorn of whites. Another editor declared in 1866 that "ours is a white man's government, so intended by our fathers, the framers of our Constitution." One white spokesman ridiculed the idea of black suffrage by likening it to another equally unthinkable proposition: "We would prefer to see women vote, at once," he wrote, "to bestowing the right of suffrage upon the colored people, and we should look on either as the accomplishment of one of those absurd notions that haunt only effete and morbid imaginations." Blacks who bought land, or who sought education, or who wore army uniforms, or who stepped forward to lead their people, or who dared to look the white man in the eye and speak to him as man to man all were anathema to the intransigent native whites, who vowed not to rest until blacks were again subjugated. "The people of the country will never be on good terms with the negroes," a Freedmen's Bureau agent reported in 1868, "until they have got them in their power."[3]

2 Pulaski *Citizen*, January 5, 1866; Lincoln County *News*, August 6, 1870; Clarksville *Weekly Chronicle*, May 18, 1866. See also Fayetteville *Observer*, January 31, 1867; Clarksville *Chronicle*, August 18, 1865.

3 Fayetteville *Observer*, October 1, 1868, August 16, 1866; Lincoln County *News*, February 10, 1866; report of George E. Judd, February 1, 1868, in Narrative Reports, FB Records. White opposition in general toward the freed blacks is further illustrated in report of R. Caldwell, February 28, 1866, *ibid*. White hostility toward black political rights in particular is apparent in Murfreesboro *Monitor*, October 7, 1865. Opposition to the renting or purchase of

A corollary of the whites' denial of black equality was their insistence on treating the freedmen as high-handedly and brutally as they had treated slaves. "The [white] people do all they can to degrade them," another Freedmen's Bureau agent wrote, "and keep them down to what they see fit to call their proper place." An army officer in Murfreesboro reported that "complaints are daily made to me by colored men and women of acts of fraud, cruel treatment, and oppression practiced upon them by white citizens." Whites assaulted blacks for trivial causes, or none at all, and when challenged by Federal authorities claimed the right to do so. Moreover, flagrant sexual abuse of black women by white men continued, leading one visiting Northerner to declare that "the mulatto girl has as little protection against white ruffianism now as she had while a slave." When blacks were accused of heinous crimes, whites assumed the right to dispatch the culprits without benefit of formal justice, just as they had before the war. In 1868, for example, after a group of whites lynched a black man accused of raping a white woman, the Fayetteville *Observer* nonchalantly affirmed that such retribution was sometimes necessary for the "safety of society" and defended the perpetrators as "instruments of Divine vengeance in carrying out His holy and immutable decrees." Whites wantonly assailed not only blacks but whites who sided with them. "They act as if they would like to kill any man who hints that the negro has the same rights that they have," a Freedmen's Bureau agent remarked. A Pulaski newspaper warned white renegades bluntly in 1868: "The line is drawn—you must be a white man or a nigger. No middle ground."[4]

A third tenet of white racial dogma that survived the war concerned the Negro character. Forgetting or ignoring the wartime explosion of black self-assertion which had shattered slavery, whites persisted in their inveterate belief that most blacks were meek, passive, and contented with inferior status unless stirred up by inside or outside agitators. "Bad niggers" were still around to instigate mischief, of course; and the loathsome abolitionists of the old days had disappeared only to be replaced by equally pernicious

land by blacks is noted in report of John Laurence, February 28, 1866, in Narrative Reports, FB Records. Black troops are denounced in Clarksville *Chronicle*, September 8, 1865. Animosity toward black education is noted in B. H. White to John Eaton, January 18, 1868, in John Eaton Correspondence, TSLA.

4 Report of J. K. Lewis, October, 1866, in Reports of Outrages, Riots and Murders, FB Records; H. P. Van Cleve to W. D. Whipple, June 21, 1865, in Letters Sent, 1863–65, No. 196, E3071, RCC; report of M. Walsh, February 18, 1867, in Narrative Reports, FB Records; Lebanon *Record*, September 19, 1868; Fayetteville *Observer*, June 18, 25, 1868; report of J. K. Lewis, August 28, 1866, in Reports of Outrages, FB Records; Pulaski *Citizen*, May 1, 1868.

Radical Republicans. Thus white heartlanders easily found scapegoats for their unremitting problems with the freedmen. "The white men from the North are at the bottom of the whole trouble," one heartlander declared in 1868. "If bad men get a hold of [the freedman] and fill his mind with all sorts of ideas as to his rights, and induce him to look upon his old masters as so many monsters who should be killed at sight, what can you expect of him?" And yet many whites continued to believe also, in the curiously paradoxical Southern manner, that these same docile blacks were addicted to theft, rape, arson, and conspiratorial rebellion—the old, familiar phantasms of the slave South.[5]

One crucial component of the ideology of slavery did not abide, however, and that was paternalism. The shock of slavery's rapid dissolution and the slaves' peremptory rejection of their masters had demolished the paternalistic ethos to which most slaveholders had in greater or lesser degree subscribed. A few traces did linger after the war: it was not unknown for whites to care generously for aged or orphaned former slaves, for example, or to remember faithful blacks in their wills. But as black people as a whole continued to seek autonomy, even the most altruistic whites renounced paternalistic obligations, abandoned their role as protective lord or indulgent father, and became the freedmen's indifferent boss. "The negro is now free," the Fayetteville *Observer* stated in 1866 after reporting rumors that some needy blacks had applied to their old masters for succor, "and his former owner will not be likely to again assume the responsibility of [his] maintenance and protection." A Wilson County resident who since the war had provided for a blind black man and two black orphans went before the county court in 1868 to ask that he "be relieved from the care and expense of all of said paupers"; the court thereupon turned the adult over to the poorhouse and bound the children out as apprentices. While supervising the signing of contracts between planters and black workers in Sumner County in 1866, a Freedmen's Bureau agent lamented the reluctance of the employers to consent to provisions requiring them to support whole families. The whites, he said, deemed black children unprofitable and "troublesome as well as expensive. I have had great difficulty persuading the farmers & others to take families & have been mortified and deeply grieved to learn how little sympathy & kind feeling was felt for this unfortunate class of people; self interest seems to be the ruling passion."[6]

5 Fayetteville *Observer*, October 15, 1868. See also A. R. Wynne to Andrew Johnson, September 8, 1865, A. O. P. Nicholson to Andrew Johnson, July 24, 1868, in Johnson Papers; Columbia *Herald*, July 30, 1869.

6 Fayetteville *Observer*, August 2, 1866; Wilson County Court Minutes, May 4, 1868, Vol. 1867–70, p. 241; report of T. C. Trimble, February 28, 1866, in Narrative Reports, FB

Despite the stinginess, the insouciance, or the downright malignity of some employers, however, relations between former slaveowners and slaves were not totally rancorous. Several contemporaries pointed out that former masters were considerably more likely than other native whites to deal decently with the freedmen because, some insisted, the former slave-holders understood the Negroes and retained a humanitarian if no longer paternalistic concern for them. "They need our friendship now," one newspaper editor proclaimed in 1866. "We know them better than any others can, and when left to their own impulses they naturally rely upon their former masters." The Pulaski *Citizen* likewise noted that freedmen generally got along best "with their old masters, who are, after all, their best friends." More objective observers understood that such bonhomie on the part of whites of the "better sort" owed less to their empathy or be-nevolence than to their urgent need for farmhands and servants. Not only were many of the white gentry willing to extend the hand of amity and fairness to the blacks to get them to work, but they were ready to make tangible concessions. Some planters, for example, seeing that schools were a powerful magnet to the freedmen, abandoned their opposition to black education and even built schoolhouses on their land to attract workers. Many swallowed their pride and sought the help of the Freedmen's Bureau, and some came to rely on it. "Many of the best farmers have been to me," a bureau agent wrote from Williamson County in 1866, "saying they did not know what they should do if the power of enforcing contracts was taken from the [bureau] Superintendent of the County."[7]

No such harmony characterized relations between blacks and poor

---

Records. Instances of continued paternalism are in petition to Maury County court, Febru-ary 23, 1867, in Slave Scrapbook, Jill K. Garrett Collection, TSLA; Rawick (ed.), *American Slave*, Ser. Two, Vol. XI (Mo.), 373–75; Williamson County Court Minutes, March, 1866, Vol. XX, 57–58.

7 Columbia *Herald*, May 12, 1866, May 20, 1870; Pulaski *Citizen*, January 18, 1867; re-port of George Judd, May 31, 1866, in Narrative Reports, FB Records. For further evidence of good relations between blacks and upper-class whites see report of R. Caldwell, April 4, 1866, *ibid*. Favorable attitudes of elites toward black schools, which were not in every case motivated solely by self-interest, are documented in E. H. Truman to Samuel Hunt, June 28, 1866, in American Missionary Association, Tennessee Records; Trowbridge, *Picture of the Desolated States*, 289; Pulaski *Citizen*, March 30, 1866; Killebrew Autobiography, I, 186–87; report of George Judd, January, 1868, in Monthly Reports from Subassistant Commissioners and Agents, Records of the Superintendent of Education for the State of Tennessee, Bureau of Refugees, Freedmen, and Abandoned Land, 1865–70, Record Group 105, NA (here-inafter cited as FB Education Records). Upper-class cooperation with the Freedmen's Bureau is further shown in Trowbridge, *Picture of the Desolated States*, 287; report of William J. Bryan, March 1, 1866, in Narrative Reports, FB Records.

whites. Lower-class hostility toward the freedmen and their few white advocates during Reconstruction was venomous and violent. One Freedmen's Bureau agent declared flatly in 1868, "the poor whites are the freedmens worst enemy." Another agent agreed, noting that there was "a large number of low degraded and brutal whites, who prefer to sit around grogeries and abuse freedmen to earning an honest living." A third contrasted the cooperativeness of white elites with the virulent antagonism of the plebeians: "All the animosity and hatred of the Bureau and its officers," he said, "seems to be among those who have the least at stake." The most spiteful antipathy was reserved for black schools and teachers. "Among the uneducated whites," an agent wrote in 1866, "the prejudice against the education of the negro is extremely bitter." Racism among poor whites was vividly personified by a man whom a Northerner met on a train heading into Murfreesboro in late 1865: "an ignorant brute," the scandalized Yankee wrote, "with his shirt bosom streaked with tobacco drizzle, who was saying in a loud, fierce tone, that 'we'd better kill off the balance of the niggers,' for he had 'no use for 'em now they were free.'"[8]

Such hostility was not new, of course. Its roots were in the antebellum period, when slaves frequently endured brutal violence at the hands of lower-class whites. But Reconstruction aggravated that traditional—and mutual—enmity. The educational and economic progress of the freedmen forcibly reminded poor whites of their own ignorance, penury, and powerlessness. A bureau agent in Lincoln County unwittingly identified a prime cause of racial troubles when he reported that the condition of the blacks in his district was "as good as that of the poor class of white persons and perhaps better in many instances." Furthermore, Radical rule and the disfranchisement of former rebels embittered the white masses, who took out their frustrations on the most obvious reminder of their own political impotence—the freedmen, who by 1867 had won the franchise and become a powerful force in Tennessee politics. Many observers in Middle Tennessee noted that white antagonism toward blacks waxed and waned in response to political news from Nashville and Washington. The major sources of intensified racial discord in the postwar heartland, however, were the in-

8 Report of George Judd, February, March, April, 1868, in Monthly Reports, FB Education Records; report of M. Walsh, April 8, 1867, in Reports of Outrages, FB Records; report of George Judd, May 31, 1866, report of John Laurence, February 28, 1866, in Narrative Reports, *ibid.*; Trowbridge, *Picture of the Desolated States,* 272. See also report of M. Walsh, October 3, 1866, in Reports of Outrages, FB Records; report of George Judd, March 31, 1866, in Narrative Reports, *ibid.*; F. Ayer to M. E. Strieby, October 2, 1865, in American Missionary Association, Tennessee Records; report of McQuiddy, March, 1868, in Monthly Reports, FB Education Records.

creasing physical proximity and the growing economic interrelationship of blacks and poor whites. The thousands of freedmen moving into villages and towns rubbed shoulders with white residents and competed with them for unskilled work. Many a white laborer must have fumed bitterly in 1865 and later as blacks took up residence all around him and then took his job at lower pay. Conflict burgeoned in the countryside as well. Some white tenant farmers sublet plots of land to blacks or hired blacks as farmhands. The results were incessant bickering, mutual accusations of cheating and negligence, and frequent clashes, all on a scale unknown before the war, when contacts between slaves and poor whites were limited.[9]

With few dissenters the native white community—aristocrats as well as plebeians, old unionists as well as former rebels, planters who dealt kindly with blacks as well as thugs who brutalized them—agreed that the black man must remain, if no longer the white man's slave, at the very least his submissive servant. To secure the utter subordination of the freedmen, whites in the postwar era resorted to every weapon and artifice at their command; and they did so with a single-minded determination that rivaled or surpassed their aggressive efforts to retain their slaves in the months following the Union invasion of 1862. Acknowledging only that blacks could no longer be legally bought, sold, or whipped, whites resolutely set about devising substitute methods of control.

Native whites generally maintained a firm grip on the county courthouses during Reconstruction, and they used those institutions as instruments of racial repression. Though forced to honor the letter of postwar state law establishing black legal rights, many judges and justices of the peace subverted the spirit of the law by willfully resolving every interracial case to the blacks' disadvantage. "The idea of negroes getting justice before the magistrates of this county is perfectly absurd," an indignant Freedmen's Bureau agent wrote from Giles in 1866. "They will hear the testimony of the blacks but will give it no weight unless it happens to suit their purposes."[10]

Traditional administrative and judicial powers of the courts were dusted off and polished up in the postwar years and then brought to bear against

9   Report of Alfred Bearden, June 30, 1866, in Narrative Reports, FB Records. The influence of national and state politics on race relations is noted in report of J. W. Gelray, September 10, 1868, and report of S. Barr, March 1, 1866, *ibid.* For evidence of economic conflicts between blacks and poor whites see report of M. Walsh, January 16, October 7, December 7, 1867, *ibid.*

10   Report of J. K. Lewis, August 1866, in Reports of Outrages, *ibid.* See also report of M. Walsh, January 16, 1867, in Narrative Reports, *ibid.;* report of Fred S. Palmers, June 13, 1866, in Inspection Reports, *ibid.*

the freedmen. One of the most important of these powers was apprenticing. The county-supervised indenturing of free orphans had been infrequent in the antebellum period because white families usually had some property with which an orphan could be supported. But the number of apprenticeship agreements multiplied after the war, and the vast majority bound a black orphan to a white adult (who was often, on the evidence of surnames, the child's former master). To the minds of most magistrates, undoubtedly, apprenticeship was not a calculated method of racial subjugation but merely a practical solution to a serious problem, for numbers of young blacks were wandering homeless in the region at the end of the war. With that judgment, moreover, the Freedmen's Bureau concurred. Some black children were bound out to other blacks rather than to whites. Furthermore, the law required (and the justices generally insisted) that black apprentices receive the same benefits that white apprentices always had, that is, humane treatment, a small amount of property at the end of their service, and a basic education in the three R's. But the young freedmen's apprenticeship bonds also enjoined strict obedience to the master, often in language noticeably sterner than that customarily used when apprenticing whites. When, for example, ten-year-old Harriet Louisa was bound out to a Marshall County white man in July, 1865, the court decreed that she "shall obey the lawful commands and faithfully serve said Thomas Hardison, and be *in all* respects subject to his authority and control." Whatever its intent, the ultimate effect of the apprenticeship system was to subject considerable numbers of freed black youngsters to the direct command and supervision of whites.[11]

A second traditional legal instrument that assumed a new role after the war was imprisonment. Few slaves in the antebellum era ever saw the inside of a jail, for the punishment of their miscreancy was customarily the master's prerogative. Emancipation, however, forced local government and law to step in; and they did so with a vengeance. Granted, the courts and law officers faced a deluge of black crime after the war, particularly in the urban black communities, and something had to be done with the numerous black lawbreakers. The Columbia *Herald* took note in 1869 of the "fre-

11   Marshall County Court Minutes, July, 1865, Vol. L, 153–54. Other examples are abundant in the county court records. See, *e.g.*, Lincoln County Court Minutes, September, 1866, Vol. A, 467–68, February, 1869, Vol. B, 202–205. For an example of a black bound to a black master see Giles County, County Court Clerk's Office, County Court Minutes, February 1, 1869, Vol. II, 103 (Microfilm copy in TSLA). The Freedmen's Bureau's advocacy of the apprenticing of blacks and subsequent limited supervision of the system are evidenced in report of R. Caldwell, February 28, 1866, in Narrative Reports, FB Records; Alfred Bearden to Joseph G. Carrigan, October 23, 1865, in Legislative Petitions, 1866.

quent and alarming shedding of colored blood by negroes. . . . Indeed, the heading, 'A Negro Killed,' might be left standing in our columns with a fair prospect of being used each week." But jails became more than just a place of legal custody for black felons; they became also an agent for the social control of the black race. Authorities invoked vagrancy laws, for example, against urban blacks reluctant to sign work contracts with white employers, and they frequently imprisoned blacks for other "crimes" for which no white man ever served time. A Davidson County Freedmen's Bureau agent complained in 1867 that "freedmen are committed to jail on the most frivolous grounds and are compelled to lie there until they become lousy, dirty and demoralized." "Uppitiness" toward whites was a common excuse for incarceration. The *Herald* reported with some satisfaction in 1870, for example, that a certain Miles Stokes, "whose skin is the color of the Fifteenth Amendment," had received a sentence of six months in prison for the high crime of insulting some white women.[12]

Labor contracts, which had come into use even before the war ended, offered a third means of legally controlling the freedmen. By 1866 nearly all black workers (in the rural areas at least) were earning their wages or crop shares under formal, written agreements. These ostensibly guaranteed the faithful performance of obligations by both employer and employee, and they were welcomed by blacks and whites alike and required by the Freedmen's Bureau, which for a time supervised their signing and enforcement. But many employers took advantage of the freedmen's ignorance to force bad terms on them. As black workers gained experience and became more wary, some whites resorted to outright fraud. A bureau agent in Giles County accused farmers there of quickly selling their harvested crops and then telling their black employees "to whistle for their pay." Another agent estimated in 1867 that across the region fully one-third of all black contract workers had in one way or another been "mulct[ed] out of their years labor or had to settle on very disadvantageous terms." "The freedmen are generally industrious and struggle under great disadvantage to perform their part [of the contract]," an agent in Columbia affirmed. "If they could be met in the same spirit much good would result therefrom." Unfortunately, that spirit did not animate all whites, and through the Reconstruction period blacks remained as much the victims as the beneficiaries of the contract system.[13]

Social as well as legal instruments availed the white community in its

12   Columbia *Herald*, October 29, 1869, April 29, 1870; Pulaski *Citizen*, January 18, 1867; report of M. Walsh, April 8, 1867, in Reports of Outrages, FB Records.

13   Report of S. B. Barr, May 3, 1866, report of M. Walsh, December 15, 1866, report of D. D. Holman, June, 1866, report of J. H. Gregory, July 10, 1866, all in Narrative Reports, FB Records; report of M. Walsh, April 8, 1867, report of John Seage, January 1866, report of

postwar crusade to bring the freedmen to heel. In particular, whites attempted to control blacks through the authority of the churches. White churchmen tended their black brethren closely in these years, as they had done during past periods of fear and uncertainty over slaves. When representatives of Middle Tennessee Presbyterian churches met in Murfreesboro in 1867, for example, they resolved to establish special black Sunday schools and decreed that every minister must preach to the freedmen at least once a month. That same year the elders of Zion Presbyterian Church in Maury County began a Sunday school for black members and held grave discussions with the freedmen concerning their relationship to the church. They also updated the church's black membership rolls and, as the session minutes recorded, "set on foot [measures] to reclaim if possible those [blacks] who have backslidden and gone back to the world." The Columbia *Herald* urged churches to take up the task of "training . . . young negroes and fitting them for the duties and responsibilities that now devolve on them" and thus counteract the "pernicious and dangerous influence" of Yankee teachers.[14]

Despite the earnest efforts of white church leaders, however, harmony was conspicuously absent in the interracial churches of the heartland after 1865. Black worshipers in increasing numbers grew restive under white control, and ultimately most withdrew to form separate churches. Whites fumed at this loss of mastery and blamed the usual "evil influences." But they soon recognized that they were helpless to prevent the black exodus, and they took practical steps to make the best of a bad situation. Reckoning that the moral authority of black churches over their members was better than no moral authority at all, the white community eventually came to support those churches. Whites in Franklin, annoyed by black children running around unrestrained on Sundays, openly gave thanks when the town's freedmen organized a Sunday school in 1866. In Fayetteville whites helped blacks erect a church building in 1869, and the following year the Montgomery County magistrates turned their courthouse over to the town's black Baptists "for the purpose of giving a supper for the benefit of their Church."[15]

J. K. Lewis, August 28, 1866, all in Reports of Outrages, *ibid.* Other accounts of white chicanery are in Campbell Brown to Mrs. R. S. Ewell, August 31, September 3, 1865, in Polk-Brown-Ewell Papers; Trowbridge, *Picture of the Desolated States*, 287. For examples of white advocacy of labor contracts and a sample contract, see Clarksville *Chronicle*, September 1, 1865; Murfreesboro *Monitor*, September 9, 1865.

14 First Presbyterian Church, Clarksville, Session Minutes, Vol. II, April 17, 1867; Zion Presbyterian Church, Maury County, Session Minutes, April 8, July 8, 1867; Columbia *Herald*, May 12, 1866.

15 E. H. Truman to Samuel Hunt, June 28, 1866, in American Missionary Association,

Even as they aggressively wielded every device of racial subjugation at their disposal, however, whites knew that their coercive power was vitiated by their fundamental economic dependence on free black labor. This awareness led to much discussion of ways to reduce that dependence. Some spokesmen advised farmers to plant more grass and less cotton so that they might get by with fewer black farmhands. Others urged whites in town and country to invest in labor-saving machinery. The editor of the Fayetteville *Observer*, for example, commended to his readers the new-fangled Doty's Washing Machine and Universal Wringer, which he judged an absolute necessity "under our uncertain system of labor—or, rather, our system that is certain to be unsatisfactory." Eventually such sentiments culminated in a ludicrous campaign to replace black workers with imported foreigners (Germans and Chinese were most often mentioned). The *Observer* exhorted farmers in 1868 to "bestir yourselves" to bring in Europeans: "We want no more *black* labor—we must obtain the white." The Columbia *Herald* warned blacks that if they continued to misbehave and to repudiate white authority, "they may expect that their former masters . . . will turn them over to the tender mercies of their friends across the Ohio and try John Chinaman awhile." [16]

Most whites, however, were realistic enough to see that immigration schemes were folly and that black labor was there to stay. Their solution was not to make labor less black but less free—thus the apprenticeship and contract systems. As whites gained economic power over the freedmen they used that power as a club against those who dared to step out of line, particularly those who voted the wrong way. Quietly at first, but before long blatantly, whites threatened and harassed their black workers who sided with the Radicals. They fired black farmhands, evicted black tenants, and boycotted black tradesmen. "We are glad to say," the Clarksville *Chronicle* remarked after the August, 1867, state election, "that many of the Radical darkies in town waked up this morning without a job." A Northern newspaper correspondent who toured the heartland in 1868 reported that "planters repeatedly told me . . . that if their 'croppers' . . . did not vote just as they told them, they would drive them off the place." Whites in Pulaski blacklisted a Negro barber who was active in Radical politics, leaving him with only a handful of white Radical customers. The

Tennessee Records; Lincoln County *News*, February 20, 1869; Montgomery County, County Court Clerk's Office, County Court Minutes, April 4, 1870, Vol. XXVII, 251 (Microfilm copy in TSLA). See also Columbia *Herald*, February 25, 1870.

16   Fayetteville *Observer*, October 24, 1867, February 27, March 26, 1868, December 15, 1870; Pulaski *Citizen*, October 11, 1867; Columbia *Herald*, July 30, 1869.

editor of the Lincoln County *News* spoke for most native whites when he warned in 1867 that "it is a bold presumption upon our patience and interest" for the freedmen to vote Radical and yet assume that whites "will continue to countenance and employ them."[17]

When legal, social, and economic sanctions failed to stifle black assertiveness, white threats turned more sinister. "The negroes of this State have done all in their power," the Fayetteville *Observer* declared in 1867, "to forfeit the good opinion of the white race, and, as a consequence, their day of trouble is just dawning. . . . They will have their reward." Another newspaper ominously prophesied that blacks who espoused Radicalism would "create an antagonistic element in our midst that sooner or later will grow into a bloody conflict between the races, and the fate of the Indians will assuredly be theirs." One white Middle Tennessean—an old unionist—put it more bluntly: if Federal troops were withdrawn, he avowed, "the buzzards can't eat up the niggers as fast as we'll kill 'em."[18]

With increasing frequency there came reports of violence against blacks. A freedmen's church and school were burned in Shelbyville in the fall of 1865, and at least two other schoolhouses in Columbia met the same fate. In Clarksville that year white youths exchanged blows and gunfire with black troops during a Christmas Day clash. Angry whites in Robertson County in early 1867 burned down several cabins that were to be occupied by black families who intended to quit wage labor and begin farming independently. That summer armed whites in Franklin attacked a group of black political marchers, likewise armed, and the resulting melee swelled into a huge, bloody shoot-out between the town's Radicals and Conservatives. Similar incidents multiplied around the region.[19]

Random white violence persisted through the Reconstruction era, but

17 Clarksville *Chronicle*, quoted in Fayetteville *Observer*, August 15, 1867; Lebanon *Record*, September 19, 1868; report of M. Walsh, September 6, 1867, in Narrative Reports, FB Records; Lincoln County *News*, May 4, 1867. See also Killebrew Autobiography, I, 191–92; Pulaski *Citizen*, November 20, 1868; Shelbyville *Republican*, November 6, 1868; "Special Report of colored laborers discharged from employment . . . on account of voting for certain candidates in the election of August 1st 1867," in Subdistrict of Nashville, Miscellaneous Reports, 1866–67, FB Records (this source documents in detail more than two hundred cases of blacks fired by employers in six Middle Tennessee counties).

18 Fayetteville *Observer*, August 15, 1867; Lincoln County *News*, July 20, 1867; *House Reports*, 39th Cong., 1st Sess., No. 1273, pp. 120–21.

19 S. P. Anderson to John Ogden, October 3, 1865, in American Missionary Association, Tennessee Records; E. M. Mears to John Ogden, October 14, 1865, *ibid.*; Clarksville *Weekly Chronicle*, December 29, 1865; Jane S. Washington to Joseph Washington, February 3, 1867, in Washington Papers; report of M. Walsh, July 15, 1867, in Reports of Outrages, FB Records. See also "List of Outrages perpetrated by the whites upon the Freedmen in the State of Tennessee from April 1865 to March 1866," *ibid.*

by 1867 it was overshadowed by the rise of massive, organized violence through the agency of the infamous Ku Klux Klan. Middle Tennessee—specifically, Pulaski—holds the dubious distinction of being the birthplace of the Klan, which spread terrorism across the South in those years. With its clandestine meetings and secret oaths, its ritual and regalia, the Klan won the loyalty of thousands of white men; with its high-flown rhetoric of white supremacy and anti-Radicalism it captured considerable popular support; and with its frequent resort to the gun and the whip it visited fear, mayhem, and death upon "uppity" blacks, white Radicals, and anyone else who piqued its wrath.[20]

The first Klan incidents cropped up in 1867, when blacks gained the franchise and political excitement in the region intensified. These earliest manifestations were ostentatious (but generally nonviolent) processions of silent, hooded horsemen, intended to scare black and white Radicals away from the polls. When that stratagem failed, the Klansmen went for their guns. In large or small bands they roamed the countryside—sometimes in broad daylight—dragging their black and white victims from their homes and beating or murdering them on the spot. "Every turnpike and cross-road is nightly patrolled by the Klan," a Northerner wrote from Nashville in 1868. "Peaceful and inoffensive white men, as well as negroes, have been seized at night by these disguised bands and outraged in the most cruel manner." Near Shelbyville Klansmen broke into the cabin of a white man whose crime was being "an associate of negroes and . . . a professor in a negro school," whipped him, and ordered him out of town. Another gang in Maury County attacked several members of a black family and cruelly scourged them with stirrup straps and buckles because one was a "big-feeling nigger" active in Radical politics.[21]

It was lynching, however, that became the hallmark of the Klan, the symbol of its purpose and its power. Over and over again, in a ghastly ritual that would become even more familiar to subsequent generations of Middle Tennesseans and all Southerners, black men accused of arson or

20   Evidence of popular support for the Klan in Middle Tennessee is in Pulaski *Citizen*, August 2, 1867; report of M. Walsh, February 29, 1868, in Narrative Reports, FB Records.

21   Lebanon *Record*, September 19, 1868; Pulaski *Citizen*, July 10, 1868; Alrutheus Taylor, *The Negro in Tennessee, 1865–1880* (Washington, D.C., 1941), 61. See also Fayetteville *Observer*, September 10, 1868; Sumner County *Republican*, August 8, 1868; Shelbyville *Republican*, October 23, 1868; "List of Murders in Counties of Maury and Marshall Tenn. from July 1st 1867 to July 1st 1868," and special report of W. P. Carlin (1868), in Reports of Outrages, FB Records; report of M. Walsh, September 6, 1867, reports of George Judd, February 1, May 1, June 9, November 30, 1868, and Register of Outrages, October, 1865 to July 1868, in Narrative Reports, *ibid.* Nonviolent Klan demonstrations are noted in Pulaski *Citizen*, June 7, July 26, 1867.

(more often) the rape of a white woman were taken from jail by disguised gangs and shot or hanged in a public spectacle. In the early morning of June 30, 1868, for example, a well-organized group of about one hundred men surrounded the Pulaski jail and forcibly removed a freedman awaiting trial on charges of raping a white woman and her daughter. Two hours later the town omnibus ran over the black's dead body, which lay face down on Main Street, as the newspaper reported, "literally riddled with bullets." No one, of whatever race or even sex, was safe from the vengeance of the white South's ignoble champions. "The Ku Klucks Can hung a negro woman yesterday," Nimrod Porter noted in his diary in April, 1868; "she had beat up a white woman This is 4 they have hung 2 whites & 2 blacks in the course of a month or so." Lethal violence surged to an awesome, bloody apogee during that spring, summer, and fall of 1868, as the national elections neared and popular agitation grew white-hot. "The general tenor of all the reports of Agents in this Sub Dist[rict]," wrote a Freedmen's Bureau supervisor in Nashville, "is terror and oppression to the Freedmen and violence and contempt for law on [the] part of the whites." By July, as growing numbers of blacks resisted white attacks, many people were convinced that all-out war between the races was imminent.[22]

More than any other instrument of racial subjugation in the postwar heartland, the white campaign of violence achieved its ugly purpose. It was not wholly successful, however, for in the towns where the freedmen congregated under the protection of the army, the Freedmen's Bureau, and on occasion the Radical state militia, blacks to a large extent defied white thuggery and worked, attended school, paraded, and voted as they pleased. But in the rural areas, outside the sanctuary of the urban communities and beyond the reach of their white friends, blacks were often at the mercy of native white terror. Some observers who commented on the progress of black schools in the towns, for example, noted that few such schools could be established in the countryside for fear of white retaliation. On election days Klansmen patrolled the rural precincts and in some places prevented the casting of a single Radical ballot, despite the presence of large numbers of black voters. Blacks on the farms were informed peremptorily that whites would countenance no such bold claims to equality and independence as urban blacks asserted; those who flouted these commandments

22 Pulaski *Citizen*, July 3, 24, 1868; Porter Journal, April 23, 1868; report of J. B. Coons, April 6, 1868, report of J. W. Gelray, September 10, 1868, in Narrative Reports, FB Records. Other Klan lynchings are documented in E. H. Truman to M. E. Strieby, August 3, 1868, in American Missionary Association, Tennessee Records; Lebanon *Record*, September 26, 1868.

too flagrantly were often beaten, murdered, or sent fleeing to the towns. The results were apparent to all: as a white Maury countian said in the fall of 1868, urban blacks were troublemakers, but those on the farms "look up to us with the same deference as they did when bound to us as slaves." This was hyperbole, of course, for even rural blacks had long since cast off their chains, rejected paternalism, and seized many of freedom's rewards. But the remark nevertheless contained a grain of truth. Even at the height of Radical dominion and black power in postwar Middle Tennessee, native whites ruled the countryside.[23]

Besides the intransigent natives, the postbellum heartland accommodated three other groups of whites, each with its own ideas about the freedmen's rightful destiny. Each group was small but to some degree influential. One of these was the Radicals, a mixed bag of Northern newcomers and native Middle Tennesseans, most of the latter being former unionists. The Radicals' common point of reference was the administration of civil governor William G. Brownlow in Nashville, which succeeded Andrew Johnson's military governorship in April, 1865. Their common goal was to organize the freedmen, secure their political rights, lead them to the polls, and make sure that they voted correctly and in sufficient numbers to keep the Radical party in power. Radicals confined their activities primarily to the towns, where they could live and work in comparative safety. They nevertheless endured—sometimes with admirable nobility—the animosity, the threats, and not infrequently the physical assaults of the native white community. In most cases, however, their nobility did not comprehend a broad, liberal vision of the social and economic elevation of the freedmen.[24]

A different spirit moved the region's Northern missionaries. These ide-

23 Fayetteville *Observer*, October 15, 1868. The dearth of rural schools for blacks is noted in report of George Judd, March 31, 1866, in Narrative Reports, FB Records; report of George Judd, March, 1868, in Monthly Reports, FB Education Records. Interference with black voters in the countryside is illustrated in Shelbyville *Republican*, November 6, 1868; Fayetteville *Observer*, August 15, 1867. Terrorism against rural blacks resulting in their flight or submission is evidenced in Cheatham County Republicans to William G. Brownlow, June 3, 1867, in Petitions, 1865–69, Governor William G. Brownlow Papers, TSLA; reports of George Judd, July 9, August 6, 1868, in Narrative Reports, FB Records; "Consolidated Report of Outrages, State of Tennessee, September, 1866," in Reports of Outrages, *ibid.*; Fayetteville *Observer*, January 21, 1869.

24 A notable exception to the rule that white Radicals had little interest in the freedmen's advancement was William A. Peffer of Clarksville. See Peter H. Argersinger, "The Conservative as Radical: A Reconstruction Dilemma," *THQ*, XXXIV (1975), 168–87. Examples of Radical-led political activities are in Pulaski *Citizen*, January 10, 1868, May 7, 1869; report of M. Walsh, September 6, 1867, in Narrative Reports, FB Records.

alistic reformers—many of them women, most of them former abolitionists—came to the heartland during or after the war under the spon-
sorship of humanitarian agencies. They worked hard to fill hungry black
stomachs with food, but their true mission was to imbue the freedmen's
characters with rectitude and their minds with learning. In the manner of
many nineteenth-century liberals, the missionaries presumed that if the
freedmen could only be provided with the formal schooling and moral
training denied them as slaves, they would be able to raise themselves up
in the world. As a committee of Northern Methodists in Murfreesboro affirmed in 1866, "The more ignorant and degraded men are, the worse
members of society they are, and the more troublesome do they become.
So will it be with these children of oppression, unless they are elevated
and refined by culture." That the self-advancement of the race might depend not only on the sacred qualities of virtue and knowledge but on the
profane powers of the ballot and the purse did not enter into the missionaries' thinking. They were zealous moral reformers and generally shunned
politics. Their aspirations for the freedmen were, moreover, highly culture-
bound. Fundamentally, they hoped to make the heartland's blacks over in
their own Northern, middle-class image, that is, to teach them (among
other things) to stop smoking and drinking and swearing and to adopt a
solemn, "dignified" Christianity in place of the frenetic emotionalism that
characterized black religion. The missionaries braved the hostility of native
whites, but their limited goals did not directly challenge white power, and
they suffered considerably less abuse than did the Radicals.[25]

The smallest group of all, yet in some ways the most important, was
made up of the Freedmen's Bureau agents. Established by Congress in
1865 to oversee freedmen's affairs in the South, the bureau was the only
agency of Federal authority on which the heartland's blacks could rely
after the army withdrew in 1866. Considering its accomplishments, the
bureau in Middle Tennessee was an astonishingly diminutive operation.
There were never more than thirteen field agents (eventually fewer), none
with even a clerk to assist him. Agents had legal authority to use the courts
and at first had army force behind them; but justice for the freedmen was
hard to come by in the local courts, and the army was soon gone. Most
agents therefore mediated difficulties between blacks and whites on a personal basis, relying on suasion to coax both parties. In 1867, for example,

25 Journal of the Tennessee Annual Conference of the Methodist Episcopal Church,
Vol. I, vi, 2–8 (MS in TSLA). The teaching and preaching of the missionaries and their
unpopularity among native whites are illustrated in Edward P. Smith to M. E. Strieby, October 11, 1865, and report of C. A. S. Crosby, May 1, 1866, in American Missionary Association, Tennessee Records.

the Robertson County agent admonished a white man whose black employee had complained of being cheated of her wages: "Now these things must not be *and shall not be*. You must settle with this woman. I prefer having these things done in a friendly, upright manner, and will be much obliged if you will settle with her like a man." Not long after, however, the same agent sympathetically counseled another white man whose black farmhand had walked off the job: "I wish you would talk to him as I would could I see him and advise him that if he wishes to establish his character as a good hand he had better go to work and behave himself. . . . Sometimes a little kind advice will do more good than harsh treatment but if he [insists on quitting] do not pay him one cent."[26]

Thus each Freedmen's Bureau office tended to assume the character of the individual county agent who ran it, and these agents were a motley group. Some were Northern-born Radicals who mobilized the blacks, stood up for them against white employers, and won the enmity of native whites. Others were Conservatives (some of them longtime residents of the community) who sided with the whites and won their support while denigrating the freedmen and endeavoring to keep them under white control. Blacks in Lincoln County, for example, were doubtless put on their guard when Fayetteville's Conservative newspaper lauded the local bureau agent as "honest and faithful," and the county court formally resolved that he was "the right man for the place." The eclectic nature of the bureau, whose representatives ranged from tolerant to bigoted and from broadly reformist to narrowly bureaucratic, explains the diversity of opinions about the agency voiced by native whites across the region: if the Freedmen's Bureau was not everywhere welcomed by whites, neither was it universally despised.[27]

The influence of the bureau dwindled rapidly after reaching its peak in 1865–66. At first its agents were empowered to provision and shelter needy blacks, regulate labor contracts and apprenticeship agreements, resolve interracial disputes in their own informal courts, coordinate educational efforts for blacks, and exercise broad, general authority over all matters concerning the freedmen. One by one, however, these powers

26   "List of Civilian Employees in Nashville Subdistrict . . . 1867," in Subdistrict of Nashville, Miscellaneous Reports, FB Records; James Stickney to W. J. Dunn, February 23, 1867, and James Stickney to W. A. Buntin, March 2, 1867, in Letters Sent, Springfield Office, *ibid.*

27   Fayetteville *Observer*, June 14, 1866; Lincoln County Court Minutes, October, 1865, Vol. A, 166. The conservatism of some agents is illustrated in report of H. W. Barr, April, 1867, in Letters Sent, Springfield Office, FB Records. Bureau activism is evidenced in Pulaski *Citizen*, August 30, September 6, 1867. Popular opposition to certain bureau agents is noted in report of George Judd, July 9, 1868, in Narrative Reports, FB Records. Popular support of the bureau is shown in report of D. D. Holman, June 14, 1866, *ibid.*

were revoked and put into the hands of local authorities, and the bureau ceased to be anything more than a general advisory body to the freedmen. Under such circumstances even the most activist and well-intentioned agent had to compromise or back off from confrontations, leaving the freedmen at the mercy of obstinate whites. The bureau achieved commendable success in its early years, especially in promoting black education and limiting fraudulent practices against black employees. Overall, though, the conservatism of some of its agents and the eventual powerlessness of the agency as a whole meant that the bureau was not a potent instrument for black advancement in Middle Tennessee.[28]

The most powerful instrument and the most progressive vision of the future were to be found within the freedmen themselves. To the black men and women of the heartland, emancipation was more than just a passage from slavery to freedom. It was the dawning of a new epoch in their history. They endowed the experience of emancipation with mystical import and sought to define it with metaphors drawn from their Christian faith. The chatty editor of the Columbia *Herald* offhandedly passed along a bit of gossip in 1869, which could have given reflective readers considerable insight into the meaning of emancipation in the black mind: "The negroes of this county," he wrote, "when referring to the period of their slavery, call it 'Paul's Time,' and when speaking of the present, say, 'Isaiah's Time.'"[29]

The freedmen hailed Isaiah's Time with festivals of joyous thanksgiving and celebration. "There is one continual excitement from day to day with the negroes," Nimrod Porter wrote in August, 1865, "there meetings & schools so much so the negroes seem to be half crazy." But they also consecrated Isaiah's Time, resolving that in this new age they would forge beyond mere legal freedom and break all the shackles of their heritage, raising themselves up individually and collectively and becoming a born-again nation. "We want our colored race to be a people," a black speaker earnestly told the freedmen of Giles County in 1866, "we want our colored race to be able to do their own business. I want our colored race [to] rise and come up to the top of the Hill . . . let us not be pilgrims and hirelings all our days, we must come out and make men of ourselves."[30]

---

28   Examples of the bureau's broad powers over contracts and other matters in the early period of Reconstruction are in Fayetteville *Observer*, January 4, 1866; Trowbridge, *Picture of the Desolated States*, 339–41. One agent's comment on his loss of power is in report of M. Walsh, November 1, 1866, in Narrative Reports, FB Records. The lack of justice for blacks in local courts after the closing of the bureau's courts is noted in report of D. D. Holman, June, 1866, and report of M. Walsh, October 7, 1867, *ibid.*

29   Columbia *Herald*, October 29, 1869.

30   Porter Journal, August 24, 1865; Pulaski *Citizen*, September 14, 1866.

To achieve that ultimate purpose the freedmen adopted a bold strategy and practical tactics. They seized every opportunity for advancement but compromised realistically when their path was blocked. They challenged their enemies when they had any chance of victory but skillfully retreated when they had none. They accepted aid from others who were helpful, rejected it when they became meddlesome, but mostly relied on themselves. They did not merely react to events but moved forward affirmatively to execute their strategy.

That audacious strategy was nothing less than to build an independent black society. Although paternalism was dead—a war casualty, spurned by both former masters and slaves—other manifestations of the antebellum heartland's organic biracial society lingered past Appomattox. Between 1865 and 1870, however, Middle Tennessee blacks moved to divorce themselves in every respect from whites and to fructify the nascent black communities that had germinated in the days of slavery. Their success at doing so within the suffocating context of postwar political, economic, and social oppression was, next to self-emancipation, their greatest triumph of the decade.

The promise of emancipation was most unequivocally fulfilled in the confirmation of the black family. Slavery had by no means obliterated the black family, but it had fettered it and rendered it a provisional and dependent institution, unrecognized by law, liable at any time to separation, and subsumed ideologically (at least in the white mind) within the broader patriarchal family headed by the master. As freedmen, Middle Tennessee blacks immediately set about to establish their families on a firm and independent foundation. Reunions of separated family members were among the most touching scenes of Reconstruction and were anxiously sought by the freedmen. Slave marriages were deemed valid under common law after the war, but blacks insisted on formal ceremonies, and a flood of weddings ensued. In July, 1865, for example, the Bedford County court issued 422 marriage licenses, of which 406 were to blacks; in Rutherford County that September, 431 black couples were married in a single week. Not a few black men legally legitimated children they had fathered under slavery. The freedmen insisted further on adopting surnames, and they declined to refer to themselves as the former slave of so-and-so, a practice whites continued for years after the war. The most conspicuous emblem of the autonomous black family, however, was the detached, single-family cabin. Blacks continued after the war to abandon slave quarters and masters' back rooms, and in great numbers they moved into homes of their own. Black women withdrew from white families' fields, kitchens, and nurseries and busied themselves managing their own households, planting their own gardens, and raising their own children. By 1870 the freedmen of Middle Tennessee had achieved very nearly full familial independence: in 1860 only 2 percent of the region's blacks had (by virtue of their free status) dwelled apart from whites; a decade later the figure was 88 percent.[31]

The freedmen also rejected the embrace of the white church. Though they had long shared in the biracial Christian fellowship proffered by the heartland's churches, blacks understood that those churches were instruments of white dominion. In the first months of peace the celebration of deliverance brought the freedmen together in large, revivalistic, ecumenical gatherings, led sometimes by Northern missionaries but often by their own preachers. Their religious zeal did not subside in the succeeding years, but their holistic worship fragmented. Black churches sprang up everywhere, competing with one another for the devotion of the black faithful. "Morality & religion is taking deep hold in the minds of the freedmen," a bureau agent reported in 1867. "Churches are being erected, Ministers employed who are teaching their hearers the precepts of virtue & Godliness." "Let each and every one go to work," a black minister exhorted the freedmen of Pulaski, "find some responsible man to collect money to purchase land to erect churches for the enlightenment of our race." Freedmen all over the heartland heard such injunctions and obeyed. By 1866 Pulaski had three black churches; Columbia boasted five within a few years after emancipation. By the end of the decade every town and rural community had its own.[32]

31   Black marriages are noted in Shelbyville *American Union*, August 5, 1865; Murfreesboro *Monitor*, September 9, 1865; Fayetteville *Observer*, January 18, 1866; Leona Taylor Aiken, *Donelson, Tennessee: Its History and Landmarks* (Nashville, 1968), 24. On family reunions see report of C. A. S. Crosby, May 1, 1866, in American Missionary Association, Tennessee Records. Legitimation of children is documented in Rutherford County Court Minutes, October, 1869, Bk. FF, 279. The choosing of surnames is illustrated in Rawick (ed.), *American Slave*, Supplement, Ser. Two, Vol. IX (Tex.), Pt. 8, p. 3,844. An instance of a black referred to as the former slave of a certain master is in Fayetteville *Observer*, January 3, 1867. The movement of blacks to separate family housing is noted in Mary Washington to Joseph Washington, January 1, 1867, in Washington Papers; Pulaski *Citizen*, March 30, 1866. On the withdrawal of women from field work see report of George Judd, May 3, 1866, in Narrative Reports, FB Records.

32   Report of M. Walsh, October 7, November 4, 1867, in Narrative Reports, FB Records; Pulaski *Citizen*, August 17, September 14, 1866; Columbia *Herald*, January 21, 1870. Early nondenominational religious meetings are noted in Matthews Journal, June 25, August 20, 1865; F. Ayer to M. E. Strieby, October 2, 1865, and E. H. Truman to Samuel Hunt, June 28, 1866, in American Missionary Association, Tennessee Records; Pulaski *Citizen*, January 25, 1867. The establishment of sectarian black churches and their subsequent activities are noted in Jane S. Washington to Joseph Washington, November 16, 1868, in Washington Papers; W. W. Mallery to S. S. Jocelyn, November 26, 1866, in American Missionary Association, Tennessee Records; Carlton C. Sims (ed.), *A History of Rutherford County*

Every black worshiper who took a seat in the pew of a black church meant one severed from the bosom of a white church. Sometimes the break came soon after emancipation, sometimes only after years. Sometimes it proceeded smoothly and with mutual goodwill, but usually it happened only after agonizing agitation and wrangling. The elders of Mount Moriah Primitive Baptist Church of Lincoln County, for example, debated all through 1866 a black brother's request to preach separately to black members; when they finally denied it, the freedmen began to depart. The fathers of Wilson Creek Primitive Baptist Church of Williamson County struggled earnestly to keep their large black congregation intact after the war, but the blacks nevertheless drifted away. In 1869 the church session "resolved that only those of our colored members who give their attendance at our monthly meetings be regarded as members of this church, namely Neptune Pettus, Linny Hyde, Sarie Hyde, & Louisa Hyde,—all others are hereby excluded." The Cool Springs Primitive Baptist Church in the same county lost all its black worshipers: in September, 1869, the elders moved to "exclude all of our Black Bretherin and Sisters for a Breach of Church Covenant in not atending Meting." Whether painful or not, however, the withdrawal of the freedmen from white churches was very nearly complete. The white Methodist churches in the districts surrounding Nashville, Lebanon, Murfreesboro, Columbia, and Clarksville, for example, which before the war had had thousands of black members, found themselves in 1866 with just 786; four years later the total was 51.[33]

The freedmen's self-imposed exile from the interracial communion of the white churches did not, of course, leave them drifting aimlessly, for their own churches offered a safe and welcome anchorage. The new black churches exercised all the functions of the old biracial churches, uplifting

---

(Murfreesboro, Tenn., 1947), 188–90; Rawick (ed.), *American Slave*, Ser. Two, Vol. XVI (Tenn.), 35; Fayetteville *Observer*, February 28, May 16, 1867; History Associates of Wilson County, *The History of Wilson County: Its Land and Life* (Nashville, 1961), 284; Pulaski *Citizen*, April 16, 1869.

33   Mount Moriah Primitive Baptist Church, Fayetteville, Lincoln County, Records, Session Minutes, Vol. I, March, 1866, Vol. II, May, 1865, January, October, 1866 (Microfilm copy in TSLA); Wilson Creek Primitive Baptist Church, Williamson County, Session Minutes, July, 1868, April, 1869; Jordan, "My Recollections"; Cool Springs Primitive Baptist Church, Peytonsville, Williamson County, Records, Session Minutes, September, 1869 (Microfilm copy in TSLA); Journal of Conferences of Methodist Churches in Middle Tennessee. See also Zion Presbyterian Church, Maury County, Session Minutes, April 5, May 28, July 5, 1870. For an example of a church that dismissed black members, that is, granted them formal permission to join a black church, rather than expelling them, see Fall Creek Baptist Church, Lebanon, Wilson County, Records, Session Minutes, October, 1867, September, 1868 (Microfilm copy in TSLA).

the faithful, correcting the wayward, and providing a nucleus of community. Like the white churches, they were social arbiter and social adhesive—but in an all-black world.

That world came to life with the birth of autonomous black communities. Just as they abandoned the white family and the white church, which had simultaneously assimilated and subordinated them, so the freedmen seceded from the rural community, which had deemed them at once partners and helots. Thousands of blacks headed for the towns, propelled by the persistence of white power and violence in the countryside after 1865 and drawn by the lure of the preexisting black subcommunities, which had been mightily reinforced by the wartime influx of contrabands. By 1870 one black family in five lived in a town, and blacks as a whole had become considerably more urbanized than whites (see Table VI). Before the war, of course, not one slave in ten had been a town resident, and whites had been far more urbanized than blacks (see Table II, Chapter II). To the black newcomer fresh from the plantation, the towns were as unfamiliar and intoxicating as the experience of freedom itself. One newspaper editor remarked that the freedmen found "something novel and fascinating in city life"; another observed that "many of them seem to think that the whole of human happiness consists in 'keeping house' in town." But to the black men and women of the postwar heartland the towns were not simply places of safety, fellowship, and excitement but a symbol of the potentiality of black self-realization in Isaiah's Time.[34]

The urban blacks often congregated in separate settlements, shantytowns centered around a black church, school, or saloon (Macedonia, on the outskirts of Columbia, and Hell's Half Acre in Nashville were two of the best known). These were self-contained communities nestled in the broader, more impersonal urban context, and safe inside them the freedmen celebrated their liberty and struggled to raise their people up. For their shelter and their nurturance the urban communities did exact a stiff price, however, in the form of crime, poverty, crowding, and disease. There were not enough jobs to go around and not enough decent housing. Drunkenness, theft, and murder were commonplace. In Columbia, as Nimrod Porter wrote in the winter of 1866, there was "a verry great scuffle with the blacks to get houses & places to live they are in a pitiful condition & many of them almost starving & naked." A Freedmen's Bureau agent reported about the same time, "There are to day many [black] women & children in and around Gallatin, who are in a destitute condition, having no means & no employment, but ekeing out a miserable existence, as best

34 Columbia *Herald*, May 20, 1870; Fayetteville *Observer*, March 7, 1867.

Table VI. Race of Family Head by Residence, 1870 (total population)

| Residence | Percentage of families, by race of head | | N | Percentage of total families |
	White	Black		
Town	15	20	203	17
Village	11	19	166	14
Farm	74	61	831	69
	White	*Black*		
N	784	416		
Percentage of total families	65	35		

$\chi^2 = 21.9$ with 2 d.f., signif. $= .0000$ N $= 1,200$
C $= .13382$

they can. Many have been taken down with small pox and other diseases & have suffered and died." Nevertheless, the towns remained for the freedmen shining beacons, beckoning the hopeful and illuminating the advancement of the race.[35]

Difficult as it was to escape the presence and influence of whites in the rural areas, freedmen there also succeeded in establishing black communities. Most of the tens of thousands who left the farms did not migrate to towns but took up skilled or unskilled work in villages. (By 1870 fully 19 percent of all freedmen lived in villages; in 1860 only 1 percent of all slaves had been villagers—compare Tables VI and II. The region's village population as a whole, which in 1860 had been 5 percent black, by 1870 was 48 percent black.) Some of these freedmen did not go to existing settlements but clustered in new all-black hamlets (such as Big Springs and Mt. Africa in Maury County), which sprang up all over the heartland's countryside in the postwar years. Even those rural blacks who did not stake out such ter-

35 William S. Fleming, *A Historical Sketch of Maury County* . . . (Columbia, Tenn., 1876), 57; Porter Journal, January 4, 1866; report of T. C. Trimble, February 28, 1866, in Narrative Reports, FB Records. On urban living conditions see also Clarksville *Weekly Chronicle*, October 20, 1865; Gallatin *Examiner*, October 21, 1865; report of J. Cobb, February 28, 1866, and report of George Judd, June 9, 1868, in Narrative Reports, FB Records; report of M. Walsh, October 22, 1866, in Reports of Outrages, *ibid.* Epidemics of smallpox and cholera are documented in William F. Cooper to W. D. Cooper, October 10, 1866, in Cooper Family Papers, TSLA; Sumner County, County Court Clerk's Office, County Court Minutes, June, November, 1865, Vol. 1858–66, pp. 403, 534–35 (Microfilm copy in TSLA). Saloons, street celebrations, political and temperance societies, and other symbols of the black urban community are noted in Columbia *Herald*, May 27, 1870; Sumner County *Republican*, July 4, 1868; Pulaski *Citizen*, August 10, 1866, January 10, 1868; report of M. Walsh, February 18, 1867, in Narrative Reports, FB Records; Porter Journal, July 4, 30, 1865, July 4, 1866, April 20, July 4, 1867.

ritorial communities but lived in isolated cabins on their employers' land managed to sustain spiritual and social communities through their church functions and other gatherings. The freedmen of Maury County, for example, continued and elaborated the old tradition of the "June Meeting," which brought blacks from all over the county together in a day-long festival; and they devised new informal institutions of communal labor and leisure such as the "cotton-picking," which were separate from the biracial corn shuckings and barn raisings they had attended as slaves. Black barbecues, hoedowns, and camp meetings soon became familiar features of the Middle Tennessee countryside, exuberant symbols of rural black communalism. "There is a picknick among the blacks to day down at the creek," Nimrod Porter wrote in the spring of 1867. "I suppose there will be several thousand blacks there, considerable to do, there are about 3 days in the week they have a gathering some where."[36]

By 1870 the freedmen of the heartland, rural and urban alike, lived in a black world within a world. As slaves they had enjoyed a certain separateness in towns and on the larger farms, but it was an unconsummated autonomy, for it was stifled by the enforced biracialism of antebellum life. Emancipation permitted them to fulfill their yearning for independence and to bring their budding society to full bloom. Though they continued to rub shoulders daily with their white neighbors and to pick the white man's cotton and live under his government, the freedmen defined themselves after 1865 through their discrete black communities. Those communities assumed all the responsibilities of the antebellum biracial communities—disciplining the errant, caring for the helpless, gathering all within their custody, and sustaining them from the cradle to the grave. In Rutherford County in 1866, for example, black farm workers caught one of their fellows stealing, convicted him in an informal trial, whipped him, and ordered him off the farm. In Pulaski self-appointed black vigilantes punished a freedman accused of abusing his mother and also apprehended and whipped a black prostitute. In the towns, where its independence was most fully realized, the black community as a whole was able to bring its powerful moral authority to bear against blacks who voted Conservative, branding them pariahs.[37]

36 Columbia *Herald*, October 15, 1869, February 25, June 10, July 29, 1870; Alice S. King, "Intra-County Shift in Negro Population in Maury County, Tennessee, 1860–1870" (M.A. thesis, George Peabody College, 1968), *passim;* Lincoln County *News*, July 7, 1866; Matthews Journal, July 8, August 26, 1865; Jane S. Washington to George A. Washington, June 27, 1869, in Washington Papers; Porter Journal, May 25, 26, November 8, 15, 1867, November 6, 7, 1868, June 6, 1869.

37 Murfreesboro *Monitor*, quoted in Fayetteville *Observer*, March 29, 1866; Pulaski *Citizen*, August 28, November 6, 1868, October 22, 1869.

The generosity of the black communities in ministering to their needy constituents was frequently remarked upon by observers in these years. Newspapers noted that freedmen in Nashville and Pulaski, for example, had formed their own associations for poor relief and that others in Gallatin had organized a burial society. A Freedmen's Bureau agent wrote in 1868 that the blacks in his district manifested a notably selfless spirit of charity, aiding the destitute among them in a way that "their more fortunate Brethren might well emulate." Census statistics on pauperism further suggest the beneficence and self-sufficiency of postwar black society: across the region in 1870 the number of black indigents forced to turn to local government for help hardly exceeded one hundred. The profound sense of community that animated the freedmen was picturesquely embodied in the preamble to the constitution of the aforementioned Pulaski relief association: "We, the Colored Citizens of Pulaski, have united ourselves in an association to be known as the 'Christian Aid Society.' . . . And we trust never to see its desolation until the sun is blown out, the stars disappear and the moon puts on her robe of blood." [38]

In one crucial respect, however, the black community differed from the white. In contrast to the inequality and hierarchy prevailing in the white world, black society was one of relative equality and classlessness. There was no resplendent black plutocracy, no powerful black occupational elite of professionals and planters, no exalted and refined black patrician class monopolizing property and position—none of the social, political, economic, or ideological hegemony of the few over the many that had long marked white society and infused it with a profoundly rank-conscious tone. Black society was no monolith, to be sure, for its own leadership class arose. But unlike white aristocrats, black leaders were men of the people, poor, uneducated, and unpolished, most of them accustomed to working with their hands just as their followers did. This was an equality of poverty and oppression, certainly, but it was an equality that nonetheless helped unify black society.

As they came together to establish communities apart from the white world, the freedmen also moved to secure the present and future autonomy of those communities. Among the chief means they adopted to achieve that goal was the pursuit of education. Literate and broadly educated black men and women would, they knew, constitute a strong society capable of self-advancement rather than a weak and dependent appendage

38   Trowbridge, *Picture of the Desolated States*, 287; Pulaski *Citizen*, January 5, 1866; Gallatin *Examiner*, October 21, 1865; report of M. Walsh, February 6, 1868, in Narrative Reports, FB Records; report of C. A. S. Crosby, May 1, 1866, in American Missionary Association, Tennessee Records; Ninth Census Social Statistics.

of white society. The enthusiasm of the freedmen for schools in the post-war years was nothing short of overwhelming, especially when contrasted with the apathy of the white masses. Indeed, it often influenced their most important decisions, such as where to live and with whom to contract. Blacks generally endeavored to move to towns and rural communities that had schools and to avoid those with none, and they dickered with employers to get them to build schools on their farms. Northern humanitarians and Freedmen's Bureau agents cooperated to establish black schools, which by 1866 numbered dozens in the region. As some of those agents admitted, however, the bulk of the effort and much of the funding for those schools came from the freedmen themselves. Many black parents went to night classes and insisted that their children attend regular classes as often as possible. "Let us go to work and educate our children," a black leader told his people in 1866, "and bring them up like Gentlemen and Ladies." When the new public school system went into operation in the latter part of the decade, the freedmen wholeheartedly supported it. A state official in Nashville reported in 1869 that "the earnestness and zeal of the colored people in acquiring knowledge, and their quiet and orderly deportment, have elicited the praise of all." By the fall of that year there were 229 black public schools in the heartland, many employing black teachers, with a total enrollment of nearly eleven thousand pupils.[39]

The freedmen also took steps to win economic independence. This was an arduous struggle, for despite the war's revolutionary upheavals, land and wealth remained firmly in the grip of the white community. Nevertheless, the freedmen made progress. A few, especially former soldiers who received Federal veterans' bounties, purchased their own homes and small farms. Others started small businesses to serve the urban black communities or, using skills learned as slaves, took up trades in town or village and did business with whites and blacks alike. Davidson County, for example, boasted eleven black merchants and restaurateurs by 1869. Even before that date the town of Pulaski (Giles County) had four black dry goods and grocery stores, three black restaurants, and one black saloon, as well as ten black carpenters, eleven blacksmiths, two wagon makers, and ten brick-

39   Pulaski *Citizen*, August 17, September 14, 1866; Henry Lee Swint, "Reports from Educational Agents of the Freedmen's Bureau in Tennessee, 1865–1870," *THQ*, I (1942), 56, 58, 68; Eaton, *First Report*, cxliv, cxlvii, clxxxxv. See also Jane S. Washington to Joseph Washington, November 16, 1868, in Washington Papers; Columbia *Herald*, May 20, 1870; F. Ayer to M. E. Strieby, October 2, 1865, and report of E. A. Easter, February 12, 1866, in American Missionary Association, Tennessee Records; report of M. Walsh, November 1, 1866, in Narrative Reports, FB Records; R. W. Humphreys to John Eaton, March 24, 1868, in Eaton Correspondence.

layers and plasterers. All told, Pulaski's freedmen in 1867 owned property worth $27,000.[40]

Even the great majority of blacks not fortunate enough to own a farm or business or practice a trade achieved a measure of economic power, for their strong arms and backs were a commodity much in demand in the postwar years—especially in the rural areas, plagued by chronic labor shortages. With experience, black workers grew cannier about trading away that precious commodity. They learned to shop around for the best terms, highest wages, and most reasonable employers, and they sometimes forced white bosses to compete among themselves for black labor. As the 1867 planting season neared, one bureau agent reported that black farm laborers were becoming "shrewder in making bargains and more economical with their hard earnings." Another asserted that the freedmen were doing well making contracts because "they have learned by hard experience to look out for themselves"; and he put his finger on the crux of the matter when he noted (as did several other agents) that white employers "have to treat [blacks] well to get them to work for them." Depending on local circumstances, such leverage often permitted blacks to defy whites who tried to coerce them with threats of dismissal. Thus even the poorest black farmhand or servant came to see that, despite the great economic disappointments of Reconstruction, emancipation had brought with it tangible economic rewards.[41]

The most exciting and potentially most telling weapon in the freedmen's battle for autonomy, however, was politics. For two years—from 1867, when they gained the franchise, to 1869, when Conservatives recaptured control of the state government—disfranchisement of former rebels gave the freedmen the balance of political power in Middle Tennessee. (In Giles County, for example, of 2,600 registered voters in 1867, 2,050 were black.) They supported the Radical party with the understanding that its white leaders would advance black interests, and with their widespread grassroots participation they ensured that the Radicals reigned for as long as possible.

The freedmen's exuberant politicking was the most vivid manifestation of black freedom and black power in the postwar heartland. The Montgomery County Freedmen's Bureau agent, for example, wrote in the summer of 1867 that blacks there were completely absorbed by politics, had

40   Report of M. Walsh, October 7, 1867, and report of Charles Simpson, September 2, 1868, in Narrative Reports, FB Records; Davidson County Court Minutes, February 1, 1869, Bk. K, 44–53; Pulaski *Citizen*, August 17, 1866; Taylor, *Negro in Tennessee*, 165.

41   Report of M. Walsh, December 15, 1866, January 16, August 6, 1867, February 6, 1868, in Narrative Reports, FB Records; Pulaski *Citizen*, August 14, 1868.

talked of nothing else for weeks, and were eagerly learning the ins and outs of the game. In the face of massive white hostility and violence, Middle Tennessee freedmen boldly organized political clubs, paraded in support of their candidates, and lined up by the thousands at the ballot boxes. They were most militant in the towns, where their concentrated numbers gave them more safety, but even in the countryside some actively campaigned under the very noses of their angry white neighbors and employers. A few blacks won local political offices—a right they gained through a state legislative act of 1868—especially in Nashville, where blacks held a number of city posts. (The capital was the center of black political activity in postwar Middle Tennessee. It boasted the region's only black newspaper, the *Colored Tennessean*, and hosted an annual convention of black political leaders from all over the state; moreover, it was home to many of the most prominent blacks of Tennessee's Reconstruction era, including Peter Lowery and Nelson Walker.) As their power grew, the freedmen of the heartland were treated to the spectacle of white Conservatives courting their votes with barbecues, speeches, and grand promises. But they knew their friends from their enemies, and, except in those rural areas where they were intimidated by rampant white violence, the freedmen remained solidly in the Radical camp.[42]

The establishment and advancement of an independent black society in postwar Middle Tennessee demanded more than simply bringing black families together in their own churches and communities, more than exercising the power of the written word, the purse, and the franchise. It demanded also the resolute defense of that society against the attempts of outsiders—whether allies or adversaries of the freedmen—to dominate it. Recognizing that the leadership proffered by their white friends, no matter how well-intentioned, was not necessarily in their best interests, the freedmen declined to follow blindly, or in some cases to follow at all. They played politics astutely, sustaining the Radical party but refusing to be used unfairly or taken for granted. In return for their support the freedmen demanded and won specific state legislation securing black civil and political rights; and in a general way, through their vigorous political activities, they constantly reminded the Radical leaders of their presence, their strength, and their aspirations. They likewise availed themselves of

---

42 Pulaski *Citizen*, May 17, July 26, 1867, May 7, 1869; report of M. Walsh, August 6, September 6, 1867, report of George Judd, November 30, 1868, in Narrative Reports, FB Records; Stanley F. Rose, "Nashville and Its Leadership Elite, 1861–1869" (M.A. thesis, University of Virginia, 1965), 46–49, 68; Columbia *Herald*, February 18, 1870; Lincoln County *News*, June 1, 1867. The wooing of black votes by Conservatives is documented in Fayetteville *Observer*, July 11, 1867; Pulaski *Citizen*, April 5, July 26, 1867.

the aid of sympathetic Freedmen's Bureau agents, but they defied the unsympathetic and for the most part came to depend on themselves in making contracts, caring for the indigent, and obtaining education. As one disapproving and uncomprehending agent wrote in 1868, "Unfortunately there is a disposition gaining ground among the freedmen to manage their own affairs entirely independent of the whites. . . . The course they are taking drive[s] off many whites who would be glad to give them good advice, and work for their interest."[43]

Furthermore, the freedmen ignored the pleas of Northern missionaries to adopt a more sedate style of worship under white aegis. They abandoned the Northerners' somber churches and turned to their own fervent ministers and rousing religious meetings. "The African Methodists are going to sweep the field," a disgruntled missionary reported from Nashville in 1865; "the Methodist brothers north cannot hold the churches they have organized, against the tide towards Africa—The ebony preacher who promises perfect independence from white control & direction carries the col'd heart at once." Another wrote the following year that blacks had spurned Northern churches in favor of "the old time religion as they fondly call their ignorant bluster in the pulpit & wild frenzy in the pews. . . . The louder the noise one can make & the more violent his stampede the more richly imbued with the Spirit of Holiness do they conceive him to be. . . . In deed the common pulpit phrase is God has no still born children." Northern missionaries and Freedmen's Bureau agents alike complained that their temperance efforts among the freedmen were opposed and undermined by black ministers.[44]

The freedmen of course rejected out of hand leadership tendered by native whites. But white force could not be so readily brushed aside. Political and economic pressure and the intervention of the Freedmen's Bureau enabled blacks to obtain a limited degree of formal justice in the courts. A bureau agent noted that magistrates dependent on black votes seemed attentive to the freedmen's grievances and that lawyers came to respect the freedmen's cash: "As the negro comes to have money at his command," he wrote, "he is able to force matters and to secure his rights, for there are no lawyers, who are not as ready to receive their fee from a negro as from a white man, and they will do their best for them, for their reputation (even among the negroes) is of value to them." Though some blacks were impa-

43   Report of George Judd, July 9, 1868, in Narrative Reports, FB Records.

44   Edward P. Smith to M. E. Strieby, July 21, 1865, W. W. Mallery to S. S. Jocelyn, November 26, 1866, and S. S. Potter to John Ogden, June 25, 1866, all in American Missionary Association, Tennessee Records; report of M. Walsh, July 8, 1867, in Narrative Reports, FB Records.

tient with court proceedings, many did not hesitate to haul whites before a judge when it appeared that justice was available. Such cases—particularly lawsuits charging whites with contract fraud, bastardy, or holding black children against the will of the parents—were common in the postwar courts.[45]

Where legal recourse was unavailable, blacks resisted in informal ways. When whites insisted that blacks continue to work like slaves, the freedmen declined to cooperate and adopted a work ethic (whites called it laziness) which mimicked that of whites: "When Saturday comes," Nimrod Porter complained in 1868, "all hands is no account." When whites demanded servility, blacks demurred; those who could get away with doing so repudiated deference, looked whites straight in the eye, and insisted on respectful treatment. The outraged editor of the Fayetteville *Observer* reported in 1868, for example, that a notorious local black man had been insulting white people and "boasting that 'no d——d white man should run over him,' he 'had been at the bottom, but was now a top rail.'" When whites used apprenticeship to subordinate black children, the young apprentices often grew so unruly that their masters abandoned all attempts to control them. In 1870, for example, the Maury County court set aside at the master's request the indenture of a black apprentice who had become "unmanageable and uncontrollable" and of another who "has frequently ran away and is now and has been for some time past indolent and ungovernable, and will not comply with reasonable requests." And when whites employed wholesale incarceration as a method of racial subjugation, the freedmen responded by adopting an ethic that attached no ignominy to imprisonment. "It is a noticeable fact," one newspaper editor wrote reprovingly, "that numbers of colored men who have been in the Penitentiary, come back and live among their fellows without receiving contumely or social disgrace."[46]

When white coercion turned violent, however, some blacks resolved grimly to load their guns and reply in kind. As armed white terrorism mounted between 1867 and 1869, so did armed black resistance. Many

45   Report of M. Walsh, April 8, 1867, in Reports of Outrages, FB Records; report of George Judd, June 30, 1866, July 9, November 30, 1868, in Narrative Reports, *ibid*. Examples of court proceedings brought by blacks against whites are in Cheatham County Court Minutes, January 6, 1868, Vol. B, 613–14; Rutherford County Court Minutes, February, 1867, Bk. EE, 368; Wilson County Court Minutes, July 6, 1869, Vol. 1867–70, p. 461, September 5, 1870, Vol. 1870–72, p. 114.

46   Porter Journal, May 9, 1868; Fayetteville *Observer*, August 13, 1868; Maury County Court Minutes, January 5, May 2, 1870, Vol. XVI, 113, 184; Columbia *Herald*, October 29, 1869.

black men began carrying weapons openly, especially when marching in political demonstrations or going to the polls. Whites, trembling at the long-dreaded, nightmarish sight of angry black men with guns, demanded that they be disarmed. Some were; but, as one Freedmen's Bureau agent warned, if whites went too far the freedmen would fight back "and fight hard, too, if they are crowded to it." This was not an idle threat. Many a Klansman bent on mayhem found himself staring into a gun barrel with a determined black face behind it. A Bedford County black woman, for example, told what happened the night the Klan harassed her father for voting Republican in 1868: "My father was a settin' on de bed," she recalled, "I 'member he had a shot gun in his han'. Well, dey broke de do' down, an' then father he shoot, an' dey scattered all ovah de fence." Similar incidents multiplied all over the region, some of them escalating into full-scale battles.[47]

Armed resistance, black power, and indeed the freedmen's most ambitious aspirations all died abruptly with the Conservative political victory of August, 1869. Whites and blacks alike recognized at once the end of the era of shining promise for black society, the passing of Isaiah's Time.

A stillness descended upon Middle Tennessee, a quiet calm that the land had not known in a decade. Whites contentedly toasted their triumph and, like victors of a bitter battle standing over a fallen foe, they sheathed their swords and spoke righteously of their duty to be magnanimous. In September the editor of the Columbia *Herald*, for example, decried the few continuing instances of Klan violence in the region because, as he explained, white supremacy had been unequivocally reestablished, civil law should now succeed extralegal coercion, and blacks need no longer suffer for their past "mistakes"; "Treat them kind[l]y and Christianly," he urged with benign grace, "and never like pagans."[48]

Blacks acknowledged their defeat on the battlefield and ended their overt defiance. Many whites, however, blindly misinterpreted the sudden quiescence of the freedmen. "The negro is working better and is more contented now than at any time since his liberation from slavery," the *Herald* announced in 1870. "The truth of the matter is that the negroes work

47   Report of M. Walsh, September 6, 1867, in Narrative Reports, FB Records; Rawick (ed.), *American Slave*, Supplement, Ser. Two, Vol. IV (Tex.), Pt. 3, pp. 955–56. Armed freedmen and shoot-outs between blacks and whites are noted in Fayetteville *Observer*, August 8, 1867, March 12, June 25, September 10, 1868; Lincoln County *News*, June 29, July 13, 1867; Pulaski *Citizen*, August 2, 30, 1867.

48   Columbia *Herald*, September 3, 1869. Indications of the return of peace to the region are in *ibid.*, December 24, 1869, April 1, 1870. The Ku Klux Klan disbanded itself in September, 1869. See Pulaski *Citizen*, September 17, 1869.

better and grow prosperous . . . in the proportion that they come immediately under the direction and control of Southern whites. . . . Slavery brought our negroes from a state of barbarism, and if freedom improves them, they will one day thank God for the mysterious providence which placed them in contact with the Southern people."[49]

The truth was otherwise, of course. The silence of the black communities after 1869 reflected grief and bitterness rather than contentment. The freedmen had come to understand intuitively that politics was their last, best hope for real power and thus absolute autonomy. They had taken great strides in educating themselves, to be sure, but by the end of the decade only a small proportion of black children were attending school and only one black family head out of five was even minimally literate. The path to independence by way of formal schooling was obviously a long one, laden with obstructions, perhaps impassable. Similarly, although the freedmen made great economic progress in the postwar years, as a class they remained poor and dependent. By 1870 only 6 percent of black families owned any land, as compared to 53 percent of whites. Furthermore, 88 percent held less than $300 worth of real and personal property—the median level for all Middle Tennessee families in 1870—while only 28 percent of whites held so little (see Table VII). Two-thirds of black families were propertyless. Blacks as a whole owned but 1 percent of the region's total wealth in 1870, though they made up 35 percent of the population. Only six black family heads out of one hundred in that year practiced skilled trades (see Table VIII), and even fewer had professional occupations or farmed their own land. The great majority of black workers in 1870, as in 1860, toiled in white people's fields, homes, and shops. Furthermore, although some frantic whites interpreted the gun-toting defiance of the freedmen as a bid for conquest, it was in truth only a defensive safeguard against white violence. Armed rebellion against the determined white majority would obviously have been hopeless. Politics was the only potential avenue to full independence, and that road was now almost completely blocked.[50]

49   Columbia *Herald*, May 13, 1870.

50   The lower limit of each wealth decile in Table VII is as follows: first decile, $6,200; second, $2,500; third, $1,250; fourth, $600; fifth, $300; sixth, $110; seventh through tenth, zero. See Lincoln County *News*, January 26, 1867, for evidence of how black hopes were related to Reconstruction politics. Although their political power was greatly diminished by the return of former rebels to the ballot boxes in 1869, relatively large numbers of Middle Tennessee blacks continued to vote throughout the 1870s and 1880s, attaining some access to local and state office in those decades. By 1890, however, black franchise and officeholding were greatly curtailed by legislative enactments.

Table VII. Race of Family Head by Wealth, 1870 (total population)

Wealth rank (deciles)	Percentage of families, by race of head	
	White	Black
1	15	0
2	16	1
3	14	0
4	14	4
5	13	7
6	7	10
7–10	21	78
	White	Black
N	784	416
Percentage of total families	65	35
Mean wealth ($)	4,763	113
Percentage of total wealth	99	1

Proportion of white families with zero property = 17 percent   C = .51408
Proportion of black families with zero property = 67 percent   N = 1,200
χ^2 = 431.0 with 6 d.f., signif. = .0

Table VIII. Race of Family Head by Occupation, 1870 (total population)

Occupation	Percentage of families, by race of head		N	Percentage of total families
	White	Black		
Professional	8	1	65	5
Landed farmer	40	2	321	27
Minor professional	3	1	27	2
Skilled worker	9	6	95	8
Unskilled laborer	4	20	115	10
Landless agricultural worker	30	58	473	39
None	7	12	103	9
	White	Black		
N	783	416		
Percentage of total families	65	35		

χ^2 = 316.1 with 6 d.f., signif. = .0   N = 1,199
C = .45679

Some blacks, resigned to political defeat and subordinate status, turned their hopes and their zeal inward. A black woman who lectured to a large audience of freedmen in Columbia in November, 1869, urged them, according to the *Herald*, to "become more virtuous than they had been in the past. She impressed upon them that poverty was nothing so long as they are virtuous and try to learn." Others saw no alternative but to leave the heartland. This was a drastic, wrenching decision, for the freedmen's roots ran deep. In this land they had come of age as individuals and as a people, and to tear themselves from it would be difficult and painful. Nevertheless, many did so. Within weeks after the 1869 election, hundreds of blacks in Maury County were preparing to emigrate to Florida or the Southwest. A newspaper later reported that during 1870 at least a thousand Rutherford County freedmen had moved on. Periodic black exoduses from the region continued through the 1870s.[51]

Most Middle Tennessee blacks remained, however, their dreams shattered. But their cause was not altogether lost. They had been repulsed from their farthest point of advance, to be sure, but not all the way back to their point of departure, for they had prepared a fallback position. They withdrew behind the battlements of the impregnable black fortress which they had constructed in the postemancipation years. This was a world unto itself, with its own self-sustaining and self-regulating families and communities and its own leaders, religious faith, moral standards, heroes and villains, myths and celebrations, and self-definition. Within the tragic context of their legal, political, economic, and social subjugation, the freedmen of the heartland seized and triumphantly held an enclave of autonomous black culture and ideology.

51 Columbia *Herald*, August 12, 20, November 19, 1869; Taylor, *Negro in Tennessee*, 108–24.

Chapter X

Reunion, Redemption, and Sanctification

White Society, 1865–1870

T HE MOOD of white Middle Tennesseans at the end of the Civil War was a curious amalgam of grief and joy, resignation and hope. There was sorrow for the Lost Cause and the passing of the old world: "I feel some times as if I was just merging into a new life," a Montgomery County woman wrote in July, 1865. "At first I felt as if I could not bear [defeat]. And it is hard enough now." But there was rejoicing for the end of slaughter and destruction: a war-weary Williamson County man declared with profound relief, "At length we have a partial peace, God be praised, and long, very long, may it continue. All wars are follies." There was widespread resignation to Northern victory and Federal supremacy: Andrew Johnson's son in Nashville noticed "a great many returned rebels in the City—as a general thing the mass are behaving themselves very well—but there are Some exceptions—especially when they get to drinking." But there was also abundant hope that the heartland's trial by fire had appeased a wrathful God and purified an accursed people: in November Brother Watson of the Wilson Creek Primitive Baptist Church of Williamson County preached consolingly to his congregation from the fortieth chapter of Isaiah: "Comfort ye, comfort ye my people, saith your God. Speak ye comfortably to Jerusalem, and cry unto her, that her warfare is accomplished, that her iniquity is pardoned: for she hath received of the Lord's hand double for all her sins."[1]

---

1 Lucy C. Bailey to her brother, July 7, 1865, in Lucy Catherine Bailey Papers, TSLA; John S. Claybrooke to Mrs. William C. Dawson, July 24, 1866, in Claybrooke and Overton

The mood of white society was also one of determination. Heartlanders were intent primarily on rapidly rebuilding their devastated land and restoring normality to their disrupted lives and livelihoods. The Clarksville *Chronicle* echoed that sentiment in July, 1865: "We want to see people resuming their former avocations," it announced; "we want to see business reviving and the channels of trade re-opened. We want to see discord superseded by peace, and demoralization corrected by honest industry. We want to see Judges superseding Commandants of Posts, and the soldier giving place to the citizen." Beyond that, however, two salient concerns aroused whites to resolute commitment. One was their impotence—their subjugation by outsiders and their loss of mastery over their own destiny. The other was their ravaged social edifice, demolished by the war and swallowed up by depravity, violence, and anomie.[2]

Among the causes of wartime chaos none had been more telling than the assault on the aristocracy. Exiled, impoverished, and humiliated by the avenging Northern army, the heartland's ruling class by 1865 lay prostrate amid the battered remains of Middle Tennessee society. But after the war the aristocracy regained its commanding position in white society.

Three facts explain the remarkable resurgence of patriarchal power and authority in postwar Middle Tennessee. First, the economic foundation of upper-class ascendancy endured. Aristocrats lost fortunes between 1862 and 1865 in slaves, crops, Confederate bonds, and other personal property, and most faced continued privation after Appomattox. A Fayetteville lawyer, for example, wrote in November, 1865, that he and his wife "find living pretty expensive—every thing is high and no prospect of cheapening. . . . I think I have done very well but Priscilla thinks it rather hard living as we do not have butter potatoes &c all the time." A Davidson County planter confided sadly to a friend in 1866, "The results of the war have been disastrous to me in all points of view. The loss of my three boys is of course irreparable but thinking that there may be yet a few years of work in me and having still some children left to educate and set out I should be very well pleased to spend a few years in the culture of cotton. . . . Unfortunately I have scarcely any thing to begin on." But land and acquired skills had not gone up in smoke or run away. Professional men retained their learning and talent, and (though some waited months for

<hr>

Papers; Robert Johnson to Andrew Johnson, May 31, 1865, in Johnson Papers; Wilson Creek Primitive Baptist Church, Williamson County, Minutes of Sermons, November, 1865. Public resignation to Federal supremacy is further documented in J. O. Shackleford to Andrew Johnson, May 28, 1865, and James L. Scudder to Johnson, July 7, 1865, in Johnson Papers; *House Reports*, 39th Cong., 1st Sess., No. 1273, p. 117.

2   Clarksville *Chronicle*, July 14, 1865.

seized plantations to be returned by Federal authorities) planters retained their expansive fields. Thus most elites were able to regain a good portion of their lost riches. The same lawyer who complained of high prices and scarcity, for example, simultaneously reported that "the practice of Law is very good. John [his partner] and myself are employed nearly all our time." The great patriarch William G. Harding likewise restored his fabled Belle Meade plantation to something approaching its old glory within a few years of the war's end. Though the Civil War annihilated much wealth in Middle Tennessee, it precipitated no fundamental redistribution of that which remained. The heartland's plutocracy in 1870, though considerably poorer in dollars, monopolized the region's wealth in about the same proportion as in 1860.[3]

Table IX documents the concentration of wealth and the relationship of wealth to occupation among whites in 1870. It should be compared with the 1860 data in Table III (Chapter III). The richest tenth of families actually increased its share of all white wealth over the decade from 65 to 68 percent. The poorer half of families retained its minuscule 2 percent. Although white society as a whole was considerably poorer in 1870 than in 1860 (average family wealth declined from $8,957 to $4,763, median wealth from $1,500 to $901), great economic distance still separated those in the top wealth rank from those in the lower ranks. Furthermore, in 1870 professionals and landed farmers together monopolized the upper wealth ranks to about the same extent as in 1860 (most notably the top rank, of which they constituted 92 percent in both years), although the economic predominance of the landed farmers slipped in favor of the professionals. Hurt more than any other group by the loss of slaves, landed farmers saw their share of wealth decline from 71 to 59 percent, while that of professionals rose from 19 to 26 percent. Nevertheless, the two groups together held a share of all wealth in 1870 nearly as great as in 1860. Both groups also saw sharp declines in their average wealth but remained substantially wealthier on the average than other occupational groups.[4]

3 James R. Bright to his brother, November 20, 1865, in Douglass-Maney Papers; George D. Crosthwait to Robert Caruthers, September 13, 1866, in Robert Looney Caruthers Papers, SHC; Herschel Gower, "Belle Meade: Queen of Tennessee Plantations," *THQ*, XXII (1963), 216–17. The efforts of planters to reclaim confiscated estates are documented in Campbell Brown to Mrs. R. S. Ewell, August 31, 1865, in Polk-Brown-Ewell Papers; R. W. Johnson to W. D. Whipple, May 28, 1865, in Letters Sent, 1864–65, No. 190, E3011, RCC; H. P. Van Cleve to H. C. Whittemore, June 17, 1865, in Letters Sent, 1863–65, no. 196, E3071, *ibid.*

4 The lower limit of each 1870 wealth decile (considering white families only) is as follows: first decile, $10,001; second, $4,501; third, $2,501; fourth, $1,501; fifth, $901; sixth, $501; seventh, $301; eighth, $101; ninth and tenth, zero.

Table IX. Wealth by Occupation of Family Head, 1870 (whites only)

Occupation	Percentage of families, ranked by wealth (deciles)									N	Percentage of total families	Percentage of total wealth	Mean wealth ($)
	1	2	3	4	5	6	7	8	9+ 10				
Professional	27	12	14	11	5	4	0	3	3	63	8	26	15,323
Landed farmer	65	77	73	74	59	36	11	4	1	311	40	59	7,081
Minor professional	0	4	3	4	3	3	4	4	3	23	3	1	1,942
Skilled worker	3	7	6	5	10	16	11	14	9	70	9	3	1,536
Unskilled laborer	0	0	0	2	1	1	4	12	9	31	4	0	329
Landless agricultural worker	0	0	1	1	20	37	64	60	56	232	30	2	332
None	5	0	4	4	3	4	6	4	19	53	7	9	6,177
	1	2	3	4	5	6	7	8	9+ 10				
Percentage of total wealth	68	15	7	5	3	1	1	0	0				

Sample mean = $4,763
Sample median = $901
Proportion of families with zero wealth = 17 percent

χ^2 = 533.0 with 48 d.f., signif. = .0000
C = .63639
N = 783

Not only did a wealthy elite continue to dominate Middle Tennessee economically after the war, but to a great extent that elite consisted of the same families who had ruled the heartland before the war. Land and professional skills remained for the most part in the possession of those who had always had them, as did poverty and ignorance. Thus few heartlanders moved very far up or down the economic ladder between 1860 and 1870. Table X documents the economic mobility of those Middle Tennessee families in the 1870 sample who could be located in the 1860 census returns for Tennessee. It shows that 71 percent of those who had been among the rich (top wealth decile) in 1860 remained in that rank in 1870— a far greater stability than any other rank experienced. Another 22 percent of the 1860 rich fell no lower than the second or third deciles, remaining at least well-to-do. Only seven rich antebellum families out of one hundred ended the decade in the middle or lower economic ranks. Considerable upward and downward mobility is evident in most ranks below the richest, but it is apparent that very few families that were below the third decile in 1860 managed to become rich by 1870 and that few above the fifth decile in 1860 declined into poverty (deciles nine and ten) over the decade. But although most of the 1860 poor remained in the bottom three wealth deciles in 1870, a substantial proportion (31 percent) rose into the middle class (deciles four through seven) and some even higher, into the ranks of the rich or well-to-do. Clearly, economic opportunity existed in postbellum Middle Tennessee, as it had in antebellum times: class lines were not impermeable. Fundamentally, however, the table depicts an entrenched economic elite.[5]

Aristocratic hegemony was not simply a matter of land and money and knowledge, however. It required also a justifying ideology. That ideology survived the war intact. No sooner did Yankee pillaging and punishment cease than the humbled patriarchs of the heartland rose to their feet, the exiled returned home, and the aristocracy reasserted its customary social authority. With the exception of slaveholding and officeholding, patricians soon restored all the tangible and intangible tokens of their antebellum predominance: their fine homes and gracious manners, their private academies and classical erudition, their genteel soirees and medieval tournaments. They continued above all to assume the right (and the duty) to command in a world of God-given inequality among men, to be imperious yet protective lords to their obedient white lieges, stern yet caring pater-

---

5 Appendix A has details on the tracing procedure employed. The inability to locate every family may skew this tabulation, so the table should be considered suggestive rather than conclusive. Here, as elsewhere, rounding sometimes brings column totals slightly above or below 100 percent.

Table X. Wealth Rank over Time, 1860–1870 (whites only)

Wealth rank in 1870 (deciles)	Percentage of families, ranked by 1860 wealth (deciles)									N	Percentage of total families
	1	2	3	4	5	6	7	8	9+10	N	
1	71	26	15	2	4	0	0	0	2	50	13
2	12	43	33	17	4	0	4	6	6	53	14
3	10	12	15	29	14	7	0	6	6	44	12
4	5	2	5	35	14	17	25	8	6	47	13
5	0	7	13	6	28	17	17	10	8	44	12
6	0	2	3	6	8	21	21	21	6	34	9
7	0	2	5	0	4	24	21	19	11	26	7
8	0	0	0	0	4	14	8	10	23	22	6
9+10	2	5	10	4	20	3	17	19	34	54	14
	1	2	3	4	5	6	7	8	9+10		
N	41	42	39	48	50	29	24	48	53		
Percentage of total	11	11	10	13	13	8	6	13	14		

N = 374

familias of the family of white society. They could maintain that assumption because, although poor and politically impotent by the standards of 1860, they reigned over an impoverished and emasculated society.[6]

Third and most important, the common people continued to sanction the traditional class structure, to accept patriarchal dominion and noblesse oblige, and to proffer their fealty in return. Unlike the blacks, whose accommodation to antebellum paternalism had been enforced by the whip and who had rejected that ethic as soon as the whip was snatched from their master's hand, the plain folk of Middle Tennessee had internalized paternalistic values and compliantly reconciled themselves to the hierarchical world supposedly decreed by nature. When the Civil War had offered the white masses the same revolutionary opportunity it had offered blacks, the whites declined to seize it. Despite the persistence of the uglier aspects of elitism—aristocratic hauteur and hostility to education for poor whites, for example—the white commoners of the heartland emerged from the Civil War in 1865 as firmly committed to their inveterate class ideology as they had been the day the rebel cannons opened fire on Fort Sumter.[7]

Few heartlanders below the rank of the highborn, however, had leisure in the postwar years to ponder weighty questions of class and ideology. Most were preoccupied with making a living in hard times. Even those of substantial means could not always rest easily. Walter Jennings of Maury County, for example, whose family had owned fifteen or twenty slaves and three hundred acres, returned from the Confederate army at the war's end and "went to work on what was left of my Father's farm, with a blind horse and crippled mule, the only live stock left by the Yankees. Rebuilt a flouring mill and cotton gin and did all kinds of honest work to get a new start

6   The persistence of aristocratic social practices is indicated in Jordan, "My Recollections"; Pulaski *Citizen*, October 18, November 15, 1867, April 3, 1868. Instances of aristocratic paternalism toward white common folk in the postbellum era are in James W. Hendricks and William A. Vardell files, Civil War Questionnaires (Confederate). The Washington Papers, 1865–70, give a good impression of the persistence of aristocratic culture and values.

7   Deference to the aristocracy is documented in report of George Judd, August 6, 1868, in Narrative Reports, FB Records; E. H. Truman to Samuel Hunt, June 28, 1866, in American Missionary Association, Tennessee Records. For evidence of aristocratic opposition to public education see report of N. G. Alexander, January 5, 1869, in Eaton, *First Report*, cl; Fayetteville *Observer*, December 17, 1868. Spokesmen for the "New South," who advocated remaking the Southern economy and society in the image of the industrializing, bourgeois North, were as vocal in Middle Tennessee as they were everywhere else in the postwar South. Their numbers were few, however, and their rhetoric did not persuade the mass of heartlanders, who remained loyal to their traditional agrarian ethic and aristocratic class structure. Examples of New South advocacy are in Clarksville *Chronicle*, January 29, 1869; Clarksville *Weekly Chronicle*, September 29, November 10, 1865; Pulaski *Citizen*, February 22, 1867.

in life." James P. Brownlow, a young Giles County soldier whose father had been a well-to-do land- and slaveowner, came home penniless in 1865. Borrowing some money, he attended an auction of surplus Federal army property, bought a few mules, horses, and wagons, took them back to Giles, and sold them for a profit. Subsequently he took over half his father's farm but had to move into a dilapidated log house because his sister occupied their old home. In 1867, still struggling, Brownlow sold part of the farm and started a store in a nearby village. Eventually he gave up and emigrated to Texas. Many other heartlanders likewise sweated to restore their once comfortable standard of living. Nimrod Porter, who had lost thousands of dollars in slaves and other valuable property during the war, labored unceasingly in the months after Appomattox, though he was seventy-three years old. "Faerwell to the year 1865," he wrote in his journal on New Year's Day, 1866. "We are in some better condition now than we were the 1st day of Jany last but realy We have nothing to brag of, hardly able to live."[8]

The tribulations of the poor, however, were the harshest and most relentless. Even in the best of times before the war, propertyless whites in town and country alike had partaken only meagerly of the heartland's prosperity. They had suffered grievously during the war, and now they faced the task of making their way in a devastated land that had little wealth to share and many new (black) claimants to that wealth. Some whites received Freedmen's Bureau aid along with blacks immediately after the war; in fact, the supervisor of the bureau in Tennessee asserted in late 1865 that his agents had distributed more free rations to needy whites than to blacks that year. But like the freedmen, poor whites ultimately had to rely on themselves. Their postwar travail is poignantly illustrated in a letter written by an impoverished Giles County man in 1870: "I had a hard time in the war I Sureved four years I come home without a doller and sick and had nothing at home mi farther and mother was both ded no won to help me nor pittey me. . . . I went to work as soon as I got able to work and work hard to try to make aliving without eney [of] thar help and by the help of God I have made aliving ever sence."[9]

The response of lower-class whites to the two central facts of the region's economy—poverty and emancipation—constituted one of the most mo-

8   Walter S. Jennings file, Civil War Questionnaires (Confederate); Brownlow Autobiography; Porter Journal, January 1, 1866.
9   Trowbridge, *Picture of the Desolated States*, 287; report of M. Walsh, October 22, 1866, in Reports of Outrages, FB Records; T. B. Williams to his sister, November 27, 1870, in T. B. Williams Letter, TSLA. See also Zachary T. Dyer file, Civil War Questionnaires (Confederate).

mentous developments within the white community of the postbellum heartland. As freedmen left the farms and poured into towns and villages seeking work at any wages, they took many jobs away from whites. (Urban whites in some numbers were already idle, moreover, because of the decline of industry.) That pressure, conjoined with the concomitant labor vacuum in the countryside, propelled white workers by the thousands to the farms, where they hired on as hands or contracted to work as tenants. Typical of these was John L. Young, a Nashville man who had worked at odd jobs in the city and "never plowed a day until after the war," when he returned from the army and took up cotton growing. Furthermore, large numbers of Southern white immigrants came to the heartland in 1865 and afterward (particularly East Tennesseans of secessionist sympathy, driven from their homes in that region's continuing civil war), and they too passed through the villages and towns crowded with blacks and proceeded to the farms, where they were welcomed by farmers desperate for labor.[10]

Signs of change appeared all around the region. A Lincoln County farm owner wrote in 1865 that "the Negroes we had . . . are all gone except 2 old men and one old woman, in their place we have a small white family, the Mother Son & daughter so we are still able to get along pretty comfortably." Early the next year he reported, "I have ingaged a [white] girl to assist Mary Winn and we get along better in house matters than when we had Harriet [a former slave] and all her crew. I have rented out my land hired two young men to make fences and repair the farm and get more done than I would with double that number of negroes." Nimrod Porter, who had customarily employed slave labor on his farm before the war, hired a white man for $10 a month in November, 1865, and three months afterward hired another "at $15 per month, he pays his own board lives in the office, has a verry young & pretty wife says he is a pretty good Blacksmith." A year later Porter noted in his journal, "There was 2 young [white] men here last night by the name of Bryant from Tuskaloosy [Alabama] they were hunting homes to live & crop it with some one." Late in 1868 he took in another man, who "came last night at dark asked to stay all night . . . he was a foot had no horse he was an Irish man 3 years from Island he was made welcome he is permitted to stay until other agreement is made." The next day Porter observed with satisfaction that "our little

10 Fayetteville *Observer*, February 27, 1868; John L. Young file, Civil War Questionnaires (Confederate). The movement of East Tennesseans to the heartland's farms is documented in Pulaski *Citizen*, March 17, 1866; Campbell Brown to Mrs. R. S. Ewell, September 3, 1865, and to R. S. Ewell, August 20, 1866, in Polk-Brown-Ewell Papers; Hiram Bogle to O. P. Temple, August 26, 1866, in O. P. Temple Papers, Special Collections, University of Tennessee Library, Knoxville.

Table XI. Residence by Occupation of Family Head, 1870 (whites only)

Occupation	Percentage of families, categorized by residence			N	Percentage of total families
	Town	Village	Farm		
Professional	29	16	2	63	8
Landed farmer	0	0	54	311	40
Minor professional	16	1	1	23	3
Skilled worker	29	28	2	70	9
Unskilled laborer	9	17	1	31	4
Landless agricultural worker	0	0	40	232	30
None	17	38	0	53	7
	Town	Village	Farm		
N	119	87	577		
Percentage of total families	15	11	74		

$\chi^2 = 730.4$ with 12 d.f., signif. = .0   N = 783
C = .69471

Irish man Garay is helping get wood feed &c seems like he is willing to do any thing he can."[11]

As migrating black and white families passed one another on the roads leading to and from the heartland's farms, white society was transfigured. (Compare Table XI with Table I, Chapter II.) In 1860, 21 percent of white families had lived in towns, 12 percent in villages, and 67 percent on farms. By 1870 only 15 percent remained in towns and 11 percent in villages, but 74 percent resided on farms.[12]

Moreover, the occupational structures of town, village, and countryside

11 Lucius Bright to Elizabeth Elliot, March 5, 1865, February 9, 1866, in Elliott Papers; Porter Journal, November 19, 1865, February 13, 14, 1866, March 23, 1867, November 10, 11, 1868. George A. Washington rented out numerous sections of his huge Robertson County plantation to various white tenants after the war, a practice he had seldom engaged in before the war. See Jane S. Washington to Joseph Washington, January 20, 1867, in Washington Papers; Legal Documents (contracts), *passim*, 1865–70, *ibid.*

12 It might be objected that the revised definition of a town (see Appendix A) accounts for this notable decline in the proportion of town families between 1860 and 1870. But even if the 1860 definition were used, white families in 1870 would still be only 17 percent urban—a sizable decrease in either event. Moreover, the 1860 and 1870 farm figures are completely comparable because they are based on occupation and farm operation, not district population, so the substantial increase in farm families which they reveal is unequivocal. The postwar agrarianization of whites is all the more striking in light of their impressive urbanization between 1850 and 1860, as noted in Chapter II.

underwent important changes. As black workers moved into villages and towns, whites decamped. The proportion of skilled workers declined over the decade from 31 to 28 percent of all white village family heads and from 35 to 29 percent of all white urban family heads. That of unskilled laborers, who faced even greater competition from blacks, declined even more precipitously: from 25 to 17 percent of all white village family heads and from 25 to 9 percent of all white urban heads. Since few blacks could compete for professional positions, however, white professionals saw no decreases; rather, their proportion rose from 8 to 16 percent in villages and from 19 to 29 percent in towns as white workers departed. Similarly, minor professionals increased as a percentage of white urban family heads, although they declined as a percentage of village heads. On the farms the proportion of landless agricultural workers rose sharply over the decade, from 29 to 40 percent, as white immigrants took up sharecropping; the proportion of landed farmers concurrently declined. In the population overall, despite the disappearance of overseers and the slight proportional decline of landed farmers, the proportion of family heads claiming agricultural occupations increased notably over the decade, from 62 to 70 percent.

Table XII traces the residential mobility of those white families in the 1870 sample who could be located in the 1860 Tennessee census returns. Like the economic mobility table discussed earlier (Table X), it cannot be considered statistically representative. But it does suggest the extent to which white town and village families took up farming after the Civil War in response to the black exodus from the countryside. One of five families (19 percent) living in a town in 1860 was engaged in farming by 1870. An even greater proportion (63 percent) of 1860 village families began farming by the end of the decade. Approximately the same proportion (62 percent) of 1860 nonfarm families (those who did not farm but who cannot be unequivocally assigned to one of the other two categories because data on their district population are lacking—see Appendix A) likewise took up agriculture. There was little movement in the other direction, because of declining opportunities for whites in the towns and villages now crowded with blacks. Only 5 percent of the 1860 townsfolk moved to villages, only 12 percent of villagers moved to towns, and only 11 percent of farm families gave up farming.

Table XIII similarly depicts the occupational mobility of white Middle Tennessee family heads and documents the shift from nonagricultural to agricultural work, especially among the laboring classes. Nearly half (44 percent) of the skilled workers of 1860 were farming their own or someone else's acres by 1870; only 39 percent continued to ply a trade. What is more, nearly two-thirds (64 percent) of the 1860 unskilled laborers took up

Table XII. Residence over Time, 1860–1870 (whites only)

Residence in 1870	Percentage of families, categorized by 1860 residence				N	Percentage of total families
	Town	Village	Nonfarm	Farm		
Town	77	12	24	4	56	13
Village	5	24	14	7	39	9
Farm	19	63	62	89	344	78
	Town	Village	Nonfarm	Farm		
N	43	41	21	334		
Percentage of total families	10	9	5	76		

N = 439

farming by 1870, the great majority of them (not surprisingly) as landless tenants or hired hands rather than landed farmers. Only about one unskilled worker in four (27 percent) continued in that work over the whole decade. Although in part this shift no doubt represents the natural tendency of young men to work their way up the occupational ladder as they mature, it also suggests the considerable effects of black emigration from the farms and into towns and villages during and after the war. Interestingly, numerous whites whose jobs were not threatened by the influx of freedmen took up agrarian pursuits. Of the 1860 professionals, 29 percent went into agriculture; of the minor professionals, 45 percent; of those without occupation, 53 percent. As with residential mobility, there was little movement in the opposite direction. Only 6 percent of the 1860 landed farmers took up a nonagricultural occupation (18 percent lost their land but did not give up farming). Only 15 percent of the 1860 landless agricultural workers likewise left the farm for other pursuits (32 percent worked their way up to landed farmer status). Overseers—who found themselves out of work after the war when the plantations were broken up into tenant farms—all stayed in agriculture.

The three preceding tables document the remarkable and important fact that in 1870 white Middle Tennesseans were notably more rural and less urbanized than they had been in 1860. This pronounced agrarianization of white society after the Civil War stands in striking contradistinction to the broad trend toward urbanization in nineteenth-century America—a trend often conceded the inexorability of historical law.

The postwar transformation of the heartland's social landscape strained the customarily harmonious relations between white propertied and propertyless classes. Some commentators expressed fears of class conflict be-

Table XIII. *Occupation of Family Heads over Time, 1860–1870 (whites only)*

	Percentage of family heads, categorized by 1860 occupation									
Occupation in 1870	*Professional*	*Landed farmer*	*Minor professional*	*Skilled worker*	*Overseer*	*Unskilled laborer*	*Landless agricultural worker*	*None*	*N*	*Percentage of total families*
Professional	56	2	9	10	0	0	4	0	40	9
Landed farmer	27	74	36	27	43	14	32	13	213	49
Minor professional	4	1	27	0	0	0	0	7	7	2
Skilled worker	4	2	0	39	0	9	6	13	37	8
Unskilled laborer	0	1	0	0	0	27	5	13	13	3
Landless agricultural worker	2	18	9	17	57	50	48	40	108	25
None	7	3	18	7	0	0	5	13	21	5
	Professional	*Landed farmer*	*Minor professional*	*Skilled worker*	*Overseer*	*Unskilled laborer*	*Landless agricultural worker*	*None*		
N	45	201	11	59	7	22	79	15		
Percentage of total families	10	46	3	13	2	5	18	3		

N = 439

tween labor and capital. No such outright warfare ensued, but the new relationship between poor yet proud white laborers—many of them unused to the drudgery of farm work—and middle- or upper-class white farm owners—most of them accustomed to bossing their field hands like slave drivers—generated great friction and sparked many an angry confrontation. Samuel Henderson, a Williamson County planter, bickered constantly with his employee R. M. Freeman in 1867 and 1868; during one altercation Henderson "frailed him well with my stick the first white man I ever struck in my life." Former slaveowner Joseph B. Killebrew of Montgomery County engaged several members of a poor-white family to sharecrop his plantation, but he soon grew disgusted with them and eventually dismissed them all. Not only were they shiftless and ignorant about tobacco cultivation, but, as the patrician Killebrew remarked disdainfully, "They were very stupid, the old man being a real halleluiah preacher without any education whatever." In April, 1866, only two months after hiring the new farmhand with the "young & pretty wife," Nimrod Porter complained in his journal that "Andrew Harris seems to be verry loving with his young wife they have not been in the habit of gitting up until after sun up then . . . it is 2 or 3 hours after sun up before they git out to work. I have called him up this morning & told him to go to work he obeyed ruluctantly he has to rise earlyer after this or we will not agree." Harris's work habits did not improve, however, and on July 5 Porter fired him, "made him settle up . . . made him give up my new axe he feloniously carried off . . . he said his wife took it she behaved like a bitch & he like a cowardly rogue."[13]

The new postwar economic forces of fission which thus threatened to split white classes apart were powerful, but there remained old social forces of fusion which were stronger yet and kept the classes stoutly joined. One was race. Slavery was gone, but racism lived on to unite all whites— farm owner and farmhand, aristocrat and plebeian—in the determination to keep their land the white man's domain and to slap down any "uppity" black who defied them. The other force was ruralism. The same country roads that brought poor whites from towns or villages or other regions and into conflict with rural landowners also brought them within the broad, unifying embrace and informal collectivism of the rural community, which had speedily revived after the suppression of wartime chaos. Tenant and landlord might wrangle day in and day out about oversleeping or pilfered

13   Henderson Diary, January 25, 1867, March 10, 16, 1868; Killebrew Autobiography, I, 172–73; Porter Journal, April 26, July 5, 1866. Comments on the potential conflict of labor and capital are in Fayetteville *Observer*, February 24, 1870; Pulaski *Citizen*, October 5, 1866.

tools, but they also worked side by side late into the night at hog-killing time, celebrated and drank together after the harvest, rode to town to fetch the doctor when the other fell ill, and joined hands in prayer and fellowship every Sunday. No less than its traditional dimension of hierarchy, which ranked each member according to his status, white society after the Civil War restored—and even extended—its traditional dimension of community, which linked rural folk of every rank in a partnership of faith and mutual dependence.[14]

Confident that white society was once again firmly reunited following its wartime disintegration, whites took up the task of redeeming that society from its bondage. They perceived the regime of the Radicals and their allies as an imperial rule by outsiders, a yoke of tyranny on the shoulders of a subject people. Their hatred of their oppressors was implacable, their denunciations of them bitter, their fear of them substantial. Nimrod Porter noted in the summer of 1865 "a verry greate feeling agt the authorities [whose] course is much regretted they are overbearing insulting & imposing to the citizens [who] are oblige to beare it I dare not even complain what will be the result god only knows." He further declared that the object of these despots seemed to be "to stay here . . . & live high & assoom authority & drink good liquer and dominion over the citizens generally (they are despised by all)." Porter also shared the belief of many whites that Radical rule was a conspiracy, a plot by a ruthless cabal that retained power by insidious means. "I have noticed a man (lawyer) staying about Town," he wrote in 1866; "I don't like his appearance he has nothing to say mutch to any body, he reads the papers verry much particularly the Radicle ones . . . just such a looking man as I would figer out to be a spy & reporter [*i.e.*, informer]." Two years later, when an itinerant book salesman visited Porter's home and gave him some religious tracts, Porter again grew suspicious: "I have no dout he was a reporter for the Radicles."[15]

White heartlanders struggled grimly to reclaim their native land from the outsiders. They fought them with ballots and with guns. The political battle was not easily or quickly won, but in the meantime whites did achieve a satisfying victory in another arena. Unable to drive the alien intruders from their land, white Middle Tennesseans banished them from their social world. They refused to fraternize or even shake hands with Radical politicians, activist Freedmen's Bureau agents, or Northern mis-

14 Jordan, "My Recollections," gives a good impression of the persistence of traditional rural life after the Civil War.
15 Porter Journal, July 9, 25, 1865, April 5, 1866, May 9, 1868. See also Cheatham County Republicans to William G. Brownlow, June 3, 1867, in Petitions, Governor Brownlow Papers.

sionaries and in some cases declined to rent them rooms or trade with them. In 1867, for example, the Pulaski bureau agent had to take up quarters in his office with his wife and children after local whites decided he was inciting the freedmen and agreed not to board him any longer. A Nashville missionary told a colleague in the North in late 1865, "From the *citizens* [here] the less you expect the lighter will be yr disappointment. . . . If you do Miss'y or educational work in this country yr teachers & preachers must come prepared . . . to depend on themselves for every means of living." [16]

Public revilement by white spokesmen served further to stigmatize the outsiders. The editor of the Pulaski *Citizen* abandoned his customary primness when he urged whites in 1867 to shun the Radicals: "We would," he wrote, "as soon invite the vilest, slimyest, nastiest, filthiest, most poisonous and treacherous reptile that crawls upon the earth to a place at our table." The Giles County deputy sheriff reached even greater heights (or depths) of vituperation. On leaving office in 1868 he addressed native Radicals directly in a newspaper advertisement, characterizing them as "filth, more disgusting than the putrifying carcass of a Yankee-Government horse, that has died with the glanders. A corroded harridan, after a prostitution of forty years, is a purer theme for moral contemplation than you, and a bastard tick at the root of a bull's tail presents a more beautiful aspect to the mental vision." The ultimate effect of such figurative branding and public ostracism was not only to isolate the outsiders socially but to reinforce the ideological unity of native whites by confirming their sense of legitimacy and common purpose. [17]

As it formed ranks to oppose the foe, the white community enlisted a few new recruits and cashiered some old veterans. Among the Northern newcomers were some whose political persuasion accorded with that of native whites, and they were made welcome. One former Union officer, for example, ran for office in 1867 as a Conservative candidate in Marshall County. Conversely, native whites who appeared overly friendly to the Radicals or freedmen were summarily drummed out of the corps. A Williamson County minister, for instance, was blackballed by fellow clergymen in 1866 for performing marriage services for blacks; and in 1867 white Maury countians boycotted a physician who had treated black patients. The white community was even more wrathful and unforgiving,

16 Report of M. Walsh, October 7, December 7, 1867, report of Joseph W. Gelray, October 1, 1868, in Narrative Reports, FB Records; Fayetteville *Observer*, May 2, 1867; Pulaski *Citizen*, September 13, 1867; Edward P. Smith to M. E. Strieby, October 11, 1865, in American Missionary Association, Tennessee Records.

17 Pulaski *Citizen*, August 30, 1867, January 31, 1868.

however, toward native unionists. Whether Radical or Conservative, heartlanders who had maintained their loyalty to the Union during the war were still pariahs after Appomattox. A Federal general reported in 1866 that white Middle Tennesseans "are more unfriendly to Union men, natives of the state of Tennessee, or of the south, who have been in the Union army, than they are to men of northern birth." A Bedford County unionist who had suffered cruel persecution by his neighbors during the war wrote angrily in 1867 that the "strong hostile feeling with rebels against the Union party is as strong now as at any other time . . . and were it posable for them to ever get in power again (which they cannot) they would have the same tyranical disposition that they did exhibit in 1861." [18]

As they battled resolutely for their society's redemption, white Middle Tennesseans also prayed earnestly for its sanctification. They were haunted by a deep-rooted conviction that their people were not only tyrannized by enemies without but enthralled by wickedness within. Though the communal and hierarchical corpus of society was rapidly healing its wounds, the war-wracked moral and spiritual essence of society remained, to the heartlanders' minds, sullied and depraved. The editor of the Pulaski *Citizen*, for instance, reported on a religious meeting at a nearby village in 1866 and expressed the hope that it would "widen and deepen until its influence reaches this sin-cursed town and community." Concerned elders of the First Presbyterian Church of Clarksville resolved in 1867 "that whereas . . . while a state of war existed in the country many things were done and many were omitted which at other times would not have been allowed . . . now a stricter and more consistent deportment should be demanded." Likewise perturbed, the fathers of Zion Presbyterian Church in Maury County proclaimed, "Whereas, During the terrible conflicts which have passed over the country . . . religion has been and still is, at a very low ebb, and the conduct of many professors has been such, as to justify the declaration, 'the Master has been wounded in the house of his friends. . . . ' Therefor resolved, that . . . we humble ourselves before God . . . [and observe] a day of fasting and prayer in consequence of the low State of religion in our midst. Peradventure, God may hear, and answer our prayers, and revive his work among us, and especially in our own hearts." [19]

18 Lincoln County *News*, May 11, 1867; report of Charles Johnson, June 1, 1866, report of M. Walsh, September 16, 1867, in Inspection Reports, FB Records; *House Reports*, 39th Cong., 1st Sess., No. 1273, p. 109; William Taylor to Enon Primitive Baptist Church, August 18, 1867, in Enon Primitive Baptist Church, Bedford County, Church Letters.

19 Pulaski *Citizen*, August 10, 1866; First Presbyterian Church, Clarksville, Session Minutes, Vol. II, April 17, 1867; Zion Presbyterian Church, Maury County, Session Minutes, August 22, 1865. See also Legislative Petitions, 1865, No. 12.

Considerable evidence was at hand to confirm the heartlanders' judgment that their society was morally decadent. Ruined churches with
empty pews offered mute but convincing testimony, at least to the devout.
But believer and skeptic alike were persuaded by an even more conspicuous symptom of degeneracy: crime. The wartime floodwaters of crime
had receded when order was restored in 1865, but they stubbornly remained beyond their antebellum confines, not far below the high-water
mark. "We hear of thefts in all parts of the country," the Gallatin *Examiner*
reported in the fall of 1865. Crime plagued town and countryside alike.
The Fayetteville public square, for example, became a dangerous place
after dark, when, as the *Observer*'s editor complained, "Riot seems to
reign." Meanwhile, in a village in Giles County agitated citizens held
a public meeting to deal with "the crime of horse stealing [which] has
become so common and of such frequent occurrence in our vicinity."
Nimrod Porter's journal entry for the last day of 1866 summed up his impression of the year: "stealing, robing, & taking every thing that can be got
hold of has been the order of the day & night."[20]

The persistence of crime in the postbellum heartland suggests that the
reconstitution of community in the countryside and of effective formal authority in the towns was less complete, or at least slower, than appeared on
the surface. In the rural areas wartime chaos had destroyed the traditional,
informal instruments of communal control over individual conduct and
had fostered a pervasive anomie that stripped antisocial behavior of its ille-
gitimacy. Despite the speedy restoration of relative safety and order in
1865, the rural community could not immediately reassert sovereignty
over every individual. In the woods and on the back roads there skulked a
few diehards who refused to return to the reopened churches, did not care
a damn what their neighbors said about them, and intended to continue
the thievery and mayhem to which they had grown accustomed since
1862. Wartime social degeneration manifested itself even in the towns,
where authority had perhaps been weakened but not destroyed, in the
form of an urban crime wave that continued after 1865.[21]

Moreover, even among the vast majority of heartlanders who came back
within the pale of community or government, one vestige of wartime

20 Gallatin *Examiner*, October 21, 1865; Fayetteville *Observer*, April 4, 1867, February 20, 27, 1868; Porter Journal, December 31, 1866. See also Pulaski *Citizen*, November 29,
December 20, 1867.

21 For an example of a larcenous band of rural social outcasts see Porter Journal,
May 23, June 30, 1867. Though its roots were to be found in wartime social disorganization,
the crime problem was aggravated by the postwar economic depression. See, for example,
Pulaski *Citizen*, December 13, 1867.

amorality remained: the sufferance of, and frequent resort to, personal violence. "Our late war made life cheap," the Columbia *Herald* remarked in 1870 in an editorial on recent killings. "Before the 'unpleasantness' between the States, a murder committed in our county sent a thrill of horror throughout its length and breadth. . . . But now, alas! what a change has come over the spirit of our dreams." Much of the heartland's postwar violence, as several observers noted, grew out of feuds and quarrels that in antebellum days had often been resolved peacefully by mutual agreement or community intervention. "Middle Tennessee is disturbed by personal animosities and hatreds," a Federal officer told a congressional committee investigating Reconstruction violence, "much more than it is by the disloyalty of persons towards the government." When an election day gathering in rural Maury County in 1869 erupted into a brawl among whites, the *Herald* explained that "the fuss did not have its origins in politics . . . but was caused entirely by too much busthead [whiskey] and by old family feuds." Though the shredded fabric of the heartland's white society was quickly rewoven and made whole again after the war, the persistence of crime and violence indicated that not every stray thread was in place.[22]

Many Middle Tennesseans were convinced, however, at least at first, that social explanations of postwar turpitude and lawlessness were beside the point. To them, the spiritual nature of such troubles seemed self-evident. They saw their land stained with impiety and iniquity and reckoned that it could be purged only by faith and rectitude. And they presumed furthermore that their sinfulness had provoked God's wrath and brought down upon them divine punishment in the form of poverty, pestilence, and blight. Within a few months of the war's end the believers sparked a religious movement that proceeded to sweep the region, "a general awakening among God's people, throughout the land," as one newspaper characterized it. The spirit waxed ardent as the months and years passed: "The people of God are becoming more prayerful and more engaged in his cause," another newspaper declared in 1868, "and more of the world are uneasy in their guilt." The burgeoning revivalism won the souls of Middle Tennesseans in numbers unmatched in previous decades (and it sometimes joined hands with the similarly flourishing temperance movement in the region, which aimed to purify the body while the churches purified the heart). The faithful of McKay Cumberland Presbyterian Church of Williamson County, for example, came together in the fall of 1867 for a revival that lasted a week and saved forty-three souls: "Preach-

22 Columbia *Herald*, August 12, 1869, January 7, 1870; *House Reports*, 39th Cong., 1st Sess., No. 1273, p. 109. Violent feuds are noted in Fayetteville *Observer*, October 8, 1868; Pulaski *Citizen*, February 21, 1868.

ing in the main," the church scribe recorded, "was characterized by a holy unction, the impress of which was soon apparent, both on the Church and world. . . . Husbands, wives, parents and children, were together crying for mercy. . . . This meeting was a decided victory, which diffused new life into the Church."[23]

The journal of Jeremiah W. Cullom, an itinerant Methodist preacher of Montgomery County, vividly captures the excitement and exultation that invariably seized such gatherings. On September 3, 1867, Cullom opened a revival and afterward reported that "the power came down on the Christians. Oh such a good meeting. This has been the best season for *me* that I have had on the circuit. I love *everybody*." The next day his work continued: "Oh such Divine Power! At prayer meeting this morning a melting influence came down on us. A number of the hardest sinners came to the altar. At night between thirty and forty mourners came forward, and numbers of others in the congregation were broken down. The people of God looked on in amazement. In fact we felt bewildered and scarcely knew what to do." "When will we ever forget this night," he wrote two days later; "I think I never saw the like before. We had some of the most clear and startling conversions I ever witnessed, and the whole community seems under the Divine influence." Rapturously Cullom described the experience of one mourner, "a man in the prime of life and of fine sense. . . . He was carried off from the church last night apparently deranged. His shrieks were heard afar as he was conducted home, and tonight he was in such a helpless condition he had to be brought to church and lifted bodily into the altar. . . . Quick as a lightning flash he was converted and shouted at the top of his voice 'Glory to God.' . . . Glory to God say I, and let all the people say amen!"[24]

While with one hand the churches strove to ignite the inner fire of Christian zeal in everyone across the land, with the other they purged and chastened their own sin-drenched flocks. With renewed energy and determination, elders scrutinized the behavior of church members for signs of irreligion or profligacy, which might offend God or threaten the purity

23 Murfreesboro *Monitor,* September 9, 1865; Shelbyville *American Union,* September 30, 1865; Shelbyville *Republican,* October 16, 1866; Pulaski *Citizen,* September 14, 1866, March 20, 1868; McKay Cumberland Presbyterian Church, Williamson County, Records, Session Minutes, n.d. (probably February 1868) (MS in TSLA). See also Columbia *Herald,* June 17, 1870; Fayetteville *Observer,* May 17, August 23, 1866, July 11, 1867, August 26, 1869; History of Presbyterian Church, Petersburg, Lincoln County, in Historical Records Survey, Tennessee, *Presbyterian Church Records, Tennessee* (Nashville, 1937–41), II, 2. The temperance movement and its relation to revivalism are noted in Fayetteville *Observer,* January 10, 1867; Pulaski *Citizen,* February 21, 1868.

24 Jeremiah W. Cullom Diary, September 3, 4, 5, 6, 12, 1867 (MS in TSLA).

and unity of the congregation, and they exhorted every worshiper to do likewise and to shun the ungodly. "Now I beseech you Brethren," wrote the clerk of Hannah's Gap Baptist Church of Lincoln County in 1868, "mark them which cause division and offences contrary to the doctrine which ye have lerned and avoid them for they that ar such serve not our Lord Jesus Crist but there own belly and by good words and fair speeches deceive the harts of the simple." In 1866 the fathers of McKay Cumberland Presbyterian Church affirmed that "members who indulge in dancing intoxication profane language & such irregularitys bring a reproach on religion therefore Resolved unanimously that such offences will be promptly investigated. . . . A motion prevailed making it the duty of each member of this Sesion to report at each meeting all things worthy of notice which had come to his ears."[25]

The repentant wrongdoer could usually expect no worse than a public admonishment, but for the obdurate or flagrant sinner the punishment was spiritual exile. When, for example, evidence proved that Sister Susan Walker of the Robertson Fork Church of Christ of Marshall County had been "keeping a disorderly house" as charged by the session in 1867, "the Brethren agreed to withdraw from her. She is therefore a member among us no longer." Of particular concern to the faithful was the intrusion of "worldliness" into the immaculate and insular sodality of the congregation, for the outside world was seen now as more godless and depraved than ever before. Thus, when Sister Ann Redman of Poplar Grove Cumberland Presbyterian Church in Williamson County confessed in 1867 that she doubted her faith and had "frequently engaged in dancing," the church elders were distressed equally by her unbelief and by "her devotion to the maxims and pleasures of the world," and they subsequently "excommunicated [her] from the fellowship of the . . . Church."[26]

Outside the churches, too, whites who fell from grace endured castigation and ostracism. At this point the two discrete crusades—one to sanctify white society, the other to redeem it—converged, for the defilement of

25   Hannah's Gap Baptist Church of Christ, Lincoln County, Records, Session Minutes, Vol. I, July, 1868 (Microfilm copy in TSLA); McKay Cumberland Presbyterian Church, Williamson County, Session Minutes, December 12, 1866.

26   Robertson Fork Church of Christ, Marshall County, Session Minutes, October, November, 1867; Poplar Grove Cumberland Presbyterian Church, College Grove, Williamson County, Records, Session Minutes, September 21, November 24, 1867 (MS in TSLA). Other examples of church discipline in this period are plentiful, particularly those in response to dancing and other "worldliness." See, for example, Union Baptist Church, Wilson County, Records, Session Minutes, November, 1867 (in 1896 record book) (MS in TSLA); Mount Lebanon Missionary Baptist Church, Marshall County, Records, Session Minutes, January, February, 1867 (MS in TSLA).

the community by unregenerate constituents and the oppression of it by despotic outsiders had come to be seen in white eyes as two sides of the same odious coin. The coalescence of sanctification and redemption in the white mind was most saliently manifested in the mayhem of the Ku Klux Klan. The same robed nightriders who threatened, whipped, and murdered Radical activists and defiant blacks likewise chastised morally delinquent native whites. In 1868, for example, hundreds of Klansmen appeared at the home of a disreputable Rutherford County white man, accused by neighbors of abusing his little daughter, and ordered him out of town. That same year another large band of Klansmen visited a Murfreesboro man who had allegedly deserted his wife for a black woman and forced him to return home. Masked men entered the house of a Pulaski white woman who had been "living in open and flagrant lewdness with negroes," according to the newspaper's report, shaved her head, tarred her, and whipped her bare back. Nimrod Porter went into Columbia one day in March, 1868, and "saw a [white] man in the market house dead he had been taken out of Jail last night & . . . hung until he was dead . . . this man killed a man near Francis 3 or 4 days ago and robed him."[27]

It would be a distortion to insist that the postwar Klansmen were merely the wartime guerrillas redivivus, but it is instructive to consider the strong points of similarity between the two groups. Both appeared in response to an unprecedented crisis which they believed imperiled the very existence of their society. Both were made up of men who lived in the community and were harbored by it, and both waged a covert but lethal war against their enemies. Both acted to defend the community not only against outside aggressors (whether Yankee soldiers or Radicals) but against those within who threatened communal integrity (whether collaborationists and runaway slaves or horse thieves and philandering husbands). And, ultimately, both degenerated from disciplined and obeisant (though brutal) instruments of white society's will into gangs of larcenous and ungovernable hooligans without social purpose or sanction.[28]

Unlike the guerrillas, however, the Klansmen saw at least one of their

27   Report of J. K. Nelson, May 15, 1868, in Reports of Outrages, FB Records; Pulaski *Citizen*, June 26, July 10, 1868; Porter Journal, March 4, 1868. Other examples are in Lincoln County *News*, September 26, 1868, which documents the murder of a man by the Klan because of his activities as a bandit during the war; Thomas B. Alexander, "Kukluxism in Tennessee, 1865–1869," *THQ*, VIII (1949), 211, which notes the lynching of a white horse thief in Pulaski; and Thomas F. Carrick file, Civil War Questionnaires (Confederate), which states that the Klan took note of whites who would not work and thereafter "made them work."

28   The eventual degeneration of the Klan and its loss of social legitimacy are evidenced in report of J. McMullen, August 1, 1868, in Narrative Reports, FB Records; Fayetteville *Observer*, November 24, December 22, 1870.

aims achieved, for the Conservative political triumph of 1869 freed white society from its captivity. Joyfully white heartlanders could proclaim the fulfillment of biblical prophecy, citing the Lord's promise to Jeremiah that He would restore the people of Israel after their subjugation: "And their nobles shall be of themselves, and their governor shall proceed from the midst of them." When Conservatives confirmed their supremacy the following year with the ratification of the new state constitution, they exulted in their victory and announced with self-satisfaction a new era of harmony: as the Columbia *Herald* declared, "The issues out of which grew animosities between the different peoples of our commonwealth are settled, and disposed of forever, never to be resuscitated. The disfranchised citizens are enfranchised, and 'the State is [at] peace.'" [29]

Thus, within a mere four years after Appomattox, white Middle Tennesseans had accomplished much that they had set out to do. They had rebuilt their ruined farms and villages and towns, reknit their unraveled society, rekindled their slackened piety, and recaptured their conquered homeland. Nevertheless, they remained a troubled people, for crime, poverty, and pestilence still afflicted them, and they feared that they were yet unpurified in the eyes of their Creator.

Those plagues were not lifted, but before the decade's end the white people of the heartland had moved decisively toward delivering themselves from the profound sense of guilt, corruption, and unworthiness which the plagues had aroused. The solution they found was not political, economic, or even religious. It was instead social and ideological, for it involved nothing less than a revolution in their conception of society.

Increasingly in 1865 and after, whites blamed all of their calamities on the freedmen. Were fields barren and the economy feeble? Then they were so, whites insisted, because of the indolence and self-indulgence of the freed blacks, who frolicked while white men and women toiled. Did deadly smallpox and cholera blight the towns? It was so because lazy blacks crowded into filthy urban tenements and shantytowns, where such diseases thrived. Was God angered by the murder, theft, and licentiousness that inundated the land? Blacks were the perpetrators; and such were the fruits of emancipation. [30]

---

29 Jer. 30: 21; Columbia *Herald*, April 1, 1870.

30 Evidence that whites blamed blacks for economic problems is in report of M. Walsh, November 4, 1867, in Narrative Reports, FB Records; Fayetteville *Observer*, October 24, 1867; Pulaski *Citizen*, November 22, 1867. Blacks are identified as the cause of the smallpox epidemic in Sumner County Court Minutes, June, 1865, Vol. 1858–66, p. 403. Crime and immorality are attributed to the freedmen in Pulaski *Citizen*, December 13, 1867; Columbia *Herald*, October 29, 1869, January 7, 1870; report of M. Walsh, February 29, 1868, in Narrative Reports, FB Records; A. R. Wynne to Andrew Johnson, September 8, 1865, in Johnson Papers.

That such imputations could assuage white guilt bespeaks the fundamentally different image of society which whites were gradually adopting in the postwar years. Before the war, the dominant social institutions of the heartland had been largely biracial. The churches, the rural communities, and the slaveholding families of both town and country embraced blacks as essential (though subordinate) constituents. Most blacks, for their part, acknowledged the authority of these institutions and accepted the privileges and responsibilities of membership. Of course, these institutions coexisted with important uniracial social institutions: nonslaveholding white families, slave and free black families, the black urban communities, the slave communities of the plantations. But in a fundamental sense antebellum whites and blacks lived in a biracial world.

Whites incorporated this basic social reality into their ideology. They viewed blacks as an integral component of society, a society they envisioned metaphorically as a household, which, like the literal household, bore responsibility for the actions of all its members. In such a household the guilt of one was the guilt of all. Blacks, however, subscribed to a different vision of society, and after emancipation they renounced the world they had known and withdrew to their own institutions. Helpless to prevent this social mitosis, which split the biracial family, church, and community into white and black ones, whites eventually responded by reading the intractable freedmen out of their ideological world: as one newspaper advised whites in 1867, "Do not harbor the enemy in your house."[31]

Thus, in the minds of whites the previously integrated household of society became an all-white household whose erstwhile black co-occupants had moved out to separate quarters. By attributing all their troubles to the freedmen's depravity, therefore, whites could banish the responsibility for such afflictions from their hearth and could again stand immaculate before their Judge. It is perhaps illustrative of this evolving sense of purgation that as the year 1870 ended and the new year began, Elder Fain of the Wilson Creek Primitive Baptist Church of Williamson County was inspired to preach to his white brethren from Romans 6:22: "Now being made free from sin, and become servants to God, ye have your fruit unto holiness, and the end everlasting life." In such convictions lay not only the moral origins of white self-complacency but perhaps the ideological seeds of Jim Crowism.[32]

31 Fayetteville *Observer*, August 15, 1867. By 1870 only 17 percent of white families in Middle Tennessee had a black living in their households. In 1860, 33 percent had had slaves in their households.

32 Wilson Creek Primitive Baptist Church, Williamson County, Minutes of Sermons, January, 1871 (on the desertion of this church by its black members after the war see Chapter IX).

By 1870 Middle Tennessee encompassed two societies, one black and one white, societies increasingly insular, increasingly distinct. Like brothers who had grown up together but then gone their separate ways, blacks and whites would never forget their kinship and shared experiences, but they would never again be intimate companions. Their lives, inextricably entwined in the days of their youth, took divergent paths in adulthood, and their contacts grew less frequent, more perfunctory. The black man continued to work with the white man, of course, but at sundown he returned to his own black family, perhaps in a black village or urban settlement, and on Sunday he hearkened to the words of a black preacher. When he did right he sought only the praise of his black peers, and when he did wrong he acknowledged only their rebuke. Likewise, the white man continued to oversee his black laborers, but he went home to a white family and prayed in a white church. And more and more he came to view the black people around him not as neighbors ready to share the labor and leisure of communal life, nor as fellow Christians seeking salvation, nor as innocent children in need of guidance, but as strangers—and surpassingly outlandish and troublesome strangers at that.

The white man deemed himself righteous, comfortable, and safe, for he had built a new social edifice on the ruins of the old. It was a patchwork affair, to be sure: he had used the old foundation stones that remained—race, hierarchy, and ruralism—but had to make do without those that had been destroyed—slavery and prosperity. It was furthermore a smaller structure than its predecessor, for it accommodated only one people now, not two; and it was old-fashioned and a little shabby, for it held fast to the archaic class ideology and traditional agrarian ethic of days gone by without retaining the national prominence and agricultural splendor of those days. Nevertheless, it was a sturdy edifice, buttressed by intensified white racial solidarity and by broadened rural communalism among whites. Its builder gazed upon it and was pleased; and to succeeding generations he proudly recounted how in the years after Appomattox he had redeemed it from its villainous expropriators and sanctified it in the eyes of the Lord.

Conclusion

T HE STORY of white and black Middle Tennesseans during their passage from the old world to the new is fraught with ironies. These ironies derive from the stark discrepancy between the inveterate convictions of whites and the newly revealed truths of the 1860s. White heartlanders stood optimistically at the threshold of the new decade in 1860, certain that the future would only enhance the luster of their prosperous and sublime society. The ensuing years brought instead not only the destruction of their prosperity but the virtual obliteration of their social edifice and its underpinnings of community, hierarchy, and slavery. The national preeminence of their land was likewise one of the war's many victims, and Middle Tennesseans found themselves after 1865 in the unfamiliar backwaters of American political and economic life.

The travail of their society begot further ironies. Convinced of their unchallengeable moral and physical mastery over their black slaves and of the slaves' docility and contentment in bondage, whites watched dumbfounded and helpless after 1862 as their bondsmen fled in droves. After Appomattox, stubbornly confident (despite the evidence of black assertiveness) that they could restore the harmonious household of society and keep the two races together under one communal roof, whites soon saw their house divided by the social and cultural exodus of the freedmen—a second self-emancipation following on the heels of the first. Thus did the supposedly passive black people of the heartland seize the moment and transform their world, while their no longer all-powerful former masters grudgingly conceded their own impotence.

A final irony is evident in the divergent paths that black and white society pursued after their parting. Freedmen by the thousands abandoned the farms and agrarian life to take up residence in the towns, which became the heart of the flourishing black culture of the postwar years. They renounced paternalism and servility, insisted on dealing with whites as employees and citizens rather than as subjects, and within their own society eschewed rigid class distinctions. While the heartland's blacks (whom whites deemed incapable of advancement) were thus moving toward modernity, whites themselves (by their own reckoning, the avatars of progress) took a step backward. Many left the towns to escape the black influx or to seek new jobs to replace those eliminated by the wartime devastation of the region's industry; they subsequently took up work on the farms, where they were needed, and surrendered themselves to the traditionalism of the rural communities. More than ever, the countryside in 1870 was the heart of white society. Furthermore, white patricians and plain folk alike preserved and reaffirmed their strict class identity and their archaic ethos of paternalism.

The heartland's postwar white society was an atavism, more rural, more agrarian, more hidebound than it had been a decade earlier. Historians seeking the origins of both the "New South" and the "Solid South" might ponder the implications of this fact. Clearly, in Middle Tennessee at least, the genesis of the progressive, bourgeois New South lies elsewhere than in the Civil War and Reconstruction. The Solid South of whites united across class lines, however, was fully inaugurated in the heartland before 1870; but it was not the product of any procrustean unity imposed on inherently antagonistic white classes by Reconstruction political conflicts, as some historians have claimed for the South as a whole. It was instead the consequence of two things: the whites' inveterate racist and paternalistic ideology, of course, but also their newly reinforced traditional ties. The widened embrace of rural communalism among whites and the withdrawal of blacks from the formerly biracial community drew whites together in work, faith, and mutual dependence even more firmly than before. And these powerful, intrinsic social and ideological adhesives continued to unite them long after their political victory.

The repeated collisions of reality and illusion failed to shake white Middle Tennesseans from their complacent certitude. As they entered the 1870s, they were as much as ever inclined to grant the freedmen nothing and themselves everything. If they were less sanguine about the future than they had been a decade earlier, they were no less convinced of the unworthiness of the blacks and the legitimacy of their own fossilized social system and stale ideology. The freedmen, for their part, gathered in their new homes and churches and communities, rejected the white world and its gospel of racial and class inequality, stoically endured their legal and economic subjugation, and prayed hopefully for brighter days ahead. The Civil War in Middle Tennessee—more precisely, black initiative unleashed by the war—had liberated black society and pointed it toward the future, only to immure white society and point it toward the past.

Appendix A. Sampling and Quantitative Analysis of the Manuscript Census Returns of 1860 and 1870

For this study I drew a random sample of 1,000 families from the 1860 free population census schedules for the thirteen Middle Tennessee heartland counties and another random sample of 1,200 families from the 1870 schedules. I then searched the 1860 and 1870 agriculture and 1860 slave schedules for information on these same families. For each I recorded information about occupation, wealth, district population, farm size, slaveholding, and other variables. I coded all these data onto 8,800 IBM cards, which I then submitted to the ministration of the computer, using the Statistical Package for the Social Sciences (SPSS) program. The information derived from this analysis is the source of all statistics in this study which are otherwise unattributed.[1]

I made both samples large so as to enhance their reliability (a random sample of 1,000 or more cases has an extremely high probability of matching the characteristics of the entire population) and to ensure that important subgroups of the population such as white families in 1870 and farm operators in 1860 and 1870 would have sufficient representation in the sample to permit their discrete analysis at the 95 percent "confidence level" demanded by statisticians. I chose the family rather than the individual as the unit of analysis both because the numbering and arrange-

---

1   The Middle Tennessee census schedules used for this study were Eighth Census, 1860, Manuscript Returns of Free Inhabitants, Slaves, and Productions of Agriculture, in NA; and Ninth Census, 1870, Manuscript Returns of Inhabitants and Productions of Agriculture, in NA. I used microfilm copies in the Main Library, University of Tennessee, Knoxville. The sampling method I employed, which involves assigning consecutive numbers to every element of the population and then drawing random numbers from a random number table, is the same one used and described in Randolph B. Campbell and Richard G. Lowe, *Wealth and Power in Antebellum Texas* (College Station, Tex., 1977). On SPSS see Norman H. Nie *et al.*, *SPSS: Statistical Package for the Social Sciences* (2nd ed.; New York, 1975).

ment of the population (which facilitate sampling) are by family in the census schedules and because in the historical context the family is the most meaningful element, the basic social unit. Of course, making the family the unit of study still permits the analysis of one important class of individuals—heads of families—since a random sample of families will perforce yield a random sample of heads of families. (Census takers always listed the head of the family first.)

Some aggregate population figures are available from published sources, and these can be compared with the sample figures to test the reliability of the sampling. The total number of individuals represented in the 1860 sample of 1,000 families is 5,507; thus the average size of each family in the sample is 5.51 persons. From the published 1860 census reports can be computed the true average family size for the entire free population of the Middle Tennessee heartland: it turns out to be 5.52—the sample average is off by less than 0.2 percent. The 1870 sample has an average family size of 5.53, only slightly larger than the 5.47 calculated from 1870 aggregate data for the entire population. The proportion of black individuals in the 1870 sample is 36.9 percent, in the entire 1870 population 37.1 percent. The 1860 aggregates indicate a ratio of 56.4 farms for every 100 families in Middle Tennessee. If the 1860 sample is accurate, it should include about 564 farms: the number in the sample is indeed 564—a perfect correlation between sample and "universe." The 1870 aggregates show 46.2 farms for every 100 families, which should yield 554 farms in the 1870 sample of 1,200 families: the number in the sample is 543, or only 2.0 percent below that expected.[2]

These close parallels between aspects of the sample and the population which can be compared impart confidence that the sample will match the population in all its characteristics. It is the discovery of the unknown characteristics of the population—that is, those for which only raw, unaggregated data exist—which is of most interest here and which is of course the purpose of the sampling. For all their assiduous fact-gathering, the census takers and compilers of 1860 and 1870 did not have our modern passion for statistics. Nor did they explicitly ask all the questions we would like them to have asked. Therefore I have manipulated the census data, using certain reasonable but admittedly arguable assumptions to

2 *Population, 1860*, 466–67; *Statistics of the United States, 1860*, 348; *Agriculture, 1860*, 215; *Statistics of the Population, 1870*, 61–62; *Statistics of Wealth, 1870*, 242, 246, 362. The total number of families in the heartland in 1870 (65,021) is from my tabulations of manuscript data, since it was not given in the published aggregates. The number of farms given here is that determined by the Census Bureau using its definition of a farm; I have used a different definition when analyzing farms in the text.

carry the data beyond their nineteenth-century limitations and make them useful to us.

Some of this manipulation is more or less unexceptionable. In a few cases, for instance, census takers (who were paid per farm recorded) listed separate farms for two members of the same family. Such farms were undoubtedly operated as one, and I have so treated them. Similarly, I have combined data on individual wealth and slaveholding where more than one member of a family was listed with such property. This accounts in part for the discrepancy between the number of slaveholders per 100 families in the heartland, taken from published aggregate sources and used for regional comparisons in Chapter I, and the smaller percentage of slaveholding families in the sample, given in Chapters II and III. But this discrepancy arises mainly because many "slaveholders" counted in the aggregates—taken from the slave schedules—were in fact estates, trusts, or institutions that do not appear in the population schedules and have not been counted as families in the sample. The figures for slaveholding based on the sample are therefore conservative: they do not include slaves owned by estates or trusts, slaves of which a family might have had current use and prospective ownership.[3]

More problematic is defining "rural" and "urban" Middle Tennesseans in 1860 and 1870. The distinction was recognized by contemporaries but did not preoccupy them as it does modern students of society. In all thirteen counties in the region in 1870, and all but three in 1860, the census takers did note the civil district in which each family lived and did compile separate civil district population totals (a county might encompass anywhere from eight to twenty-five districts). They did not specify towns, however, and since towns were almost never coterminous with districts, few town populations can be specifically calculated and in any given district the town and country families cannot be distinguished. There is, moreover, no general agreement on just what constituted a "town" in the nineteenth-century South.

The best that can be done therefore is to compare the published population totals of districts containing known "towns"—the county seats and any other places referred to in contemporary sources as towns—with

3 Census takers' instructions required counting hotels, boardinghouses, and similar institutions as one family, but only three such "families" appear in each of my samples and so no appreciable distortion results. My statistics on total family wealth and slaveholdings will be generally comparable to those in other studies which deal only with heads of families, because almost every family's property was listed under the head's name alone. A preliminary computer check showed that over 94 percent of all wealth in the 1860 sample, and over 93 percent of all slaves, were listed under the head of the family.

those of known rural districts and then designate an arbitrary minimum "urban" and maximum "rural" population. For 1860 a cutoff point of 1,500 defines as urban seventeen districts with known towns (total population 55,615) and only five districts that were probably just populous rural districts (total population 7,827). It defines as rural more than 180 districts (total population 173, 658), only four of which could be considered small towns (total population 4,892). After separating out those families in the sample who lived in rural districts as thus defined, or who lived in urban districts but operated a farm or were headed by a person with an agricultural occupation, the remainder is an approximate but usable list of "town" families.[4]

General population growth in Middle Tennessee brought many rural districts above the 1,500 level after 1860, so I have set the rural-urban cutoff point for the 1870 analysis at 2,000. This designates twenty-one urban districts encompassing nineteen known towns (population 82,018) and only two populous rural districts (population 4,295) and excludes eight districts with very small towns (population 13,172).[5]

Unavoidably, the arbitrariness of the definition means that some truly rural families in the sample are included in the "town" category as analyzed in Chapter II and elsewhere and a few small-town urbanites are included in the "village" category (which consists of families who lived in rural districts but did not list an agricultural occupation or operate a farm). But these are likely not enough to affect the analysis seriously. "Farm" families, on the other hand (the third residence category delineated), are unambiguously identifiable by occupation (farmer, overseer, farm laborer) or farm operation, and they include families in urban as well as rural districts.

Analyzing occupations, too, requires imposing modern constructions on historical data. Many historians have devised occupational categories for their nineteenth-century subjects, but most of these schemata complement urban studies—for which differentiating among types of professionals or artisans or laborers is useful—rather than the study of areas such as Middle Tennessee, where most people worked on farms. The best analytical approach to occupations in the rural nineteenth-century South

4   Families in the three counties not reporting district totals in 1860 have been left out of this count and out of all tables involving residence. This omission results in a smaller sample size for the 1860 residence tables and accounts for the very slight differences in the overall breakdown of occupation and slaveholding in Tables I and II (Chapter II) on one hand and Tables III, IV, and V (Chapter III) on the other.

5   District population figures for 1860 and 1870 are in *Statistics of Population, 1870,* 261–69.

is that of Frank J. Huffman, Jr., in his dissertation on Clarke County, Georgia. I have adopted *in toto* his eight-category breakdown (but not his nomenclature): professional, landed farmer, minor professional, skilled worker, overseer, unskilled laborer, landless agricultural worker, and no occupation.[6]

Nearly all occupations I found in the census manuscripts fit unambiguously into one or the other of these categories (the reader may consult Appendix B to judge this for himself). Many family heads, most of them women, had no occupation listed, or a nonremunerative domestic one. I have assigned them to the no-occupation category unless they had a farm, in which case they are designated landed farmers (if their families had any real property) or landless agricultural workers. Dual occupations (generally farmer and professional or farmer and artisan) are more troublesome; I have simply counted the occupation given first. I have not analyzed the occupations of female spouses because almost all were domestic and nonremunerative.

Farms, unlike slaves, were always listed under the name of a person (almost always the family head), who was also in the population schedules. If we count as one farm those few cases in which two members of the same family had separately listed farms, the random sample of families yields a (smaller) random sample of farms, since each farm in the agricultural schedules has an equal chance of being picked. This permits the separate analysis of Middle Tennessee farms presented in Chapters II and VIII. These sections discuss farm *operators* and their farms, not "farmers." Many persons not calling themselves farmers had farms, and some listed as farmers had no farms.

The data in the agricultural schedules are quantified and unequivocal: number of improved acres, value of livestock, bushels of corn produced, and so forth. But the Census Bureau's definition of a farm—requiring a minimum of three acres of land, whether improved or unimproved   was too generous. I have analyzed only farms with at least one acre of improved land, since no "farm" without improved land could have had any significant agricultural production. Farms thus dropped from analysis constitute about 6 percent of the sample of farms.

6   Frank J. Huffman, Jr., "Old South, New South: Continuity and Change in a Georgia County, 1850–1880" (Ph.D. dissertation, Yale University, 1974). Merchants had a distinctive economic role in the nineteenth century South, and they have been the subject of considerable scrutiny by historians. Some might therefore argue that the merchant class deserves a separate occupational category. In my sample, however, such a category would have so few cases as to render it meaningless for purposes of quantitative analysis, so I have included merchants with other professionals.

Until 1880 the Census Bureau did not require the specification of tenant farmers. In the 1860 and 1870 schedules farms were listed under the name of the "operator," whether owner or tenant. I have assumed, however, that a farm operator who owned no real estate (and whose family owned none) was a tenant. This method is not foolproof, of course, since a farmer might have rented a farm and yet owned real estate elsewhere. But the assumption can be tested because in a few districts the census taker exceeded instructions by marking tenant-operated farms in the agricultural schedules. Forty-six such farms appear in the 1860 sample, of which forty-four are identifiable as tenant farms using my assumption. Ninety-three tenant farms in the 1870 sample were marked, of which my assumption identifies eighty-nine. This represents an accuracy rate of 96 percent for both samples.

A more important question than the proper sampling and manipulation of the census data is the fundamental reliability of those data. How accurate are these facts and figures? Any careful researcher is immediately put on guard by the frequent appearance of round numbers in the age, wealth, and agricultural columns of the census manuscripts. (One Davidson County census taker's wry notation in the margin of the 1860 slave schedules drolly illustrates the frustrating inexactness of enumeration: next to the entry describing a 110-year-old slave he wrote, "Thinks he is much older, Indeed he thinks he recolects seeing the corn stalks deposited in the Trees by Noah's flood.") This is not really a cause for concern, however. Estimation is to be expected of a minimally educated, rural society unaccustomed to meticulous record-keeping. Errors resulting from such estimation or from inadvertent mistranscription by census takers should, in any event, average out in a large sample.[7]

More serious is the possibility that systematic errors might grossly bias the census reports. This has inspired several historians to evaluate rigorously the accuracy of the 1860 and 1870 censuses. They award generally high ratings to both, with two reservations: possible undercounting of the poor in both years and underreporting of property in 1870. (The Census Bureau in fact dropped the real and personal property questions after 1870 because of alleged widespread underreporting that year.)

Undercounting of the less wealthy (and thus less visible) populace may indeed have occurred in Nashville and other large towns in the heartland, where transients could elude the most diligent census taker. But the great majority of Middle Tennesseans lived on farms or in villages, where a man knew all his neighbors (one of whom was the census taker) and strangers

7   Eighth Census Slaves, Davidson County, District Twenty, p. 18.

were conspicuous. Few could have dodged the count in these localities. Those in the big towns who did could represent only a tiny fraction of the population, not enough to distort noticeably the overall enumeration.

Underreporting of property in 1870 was common in the South but seems to have been related to the fear of whites in certain regions that Radical Republican state governments would use the wealth data to assess higher taxes. Such a fear could not have troubled Middle Tennesseans in the summer of 1870 because their state had by then returned to Conservative control. There is no convincing reason, therefore, to challenge the overall reliability of the census data analyzed in this study.

The tables in the text, all derived from the 1860 and 1870 census samples, are cross-tabulations of two categorized variables. The numbers enclosed by lines in each table always refer to percentage of the particular category of the variable displayed across the top of the table, and thus they always total 100 (with allowances for rounding) when read *down* the columns. Outside the lines that enclose the cross-tabulation, that is, at the bottom and right peripheries of the table, I have given (when necessary) separate frequency distributions (in both absolute numbers and percentages) for each variable and in some cases discrete means for each category.

Each table gives also the total number of cases ("N") considered in that particular analysis. This number rarely equals the size of the entire sample because census takers did not always record every item of requested information for every family. I have omitted cases with such "missing values" for any variable from all tabulations of that variable.

Also provided with most of the tables is the X^2 statistic with its associated "degrees of freedom" and "significance." These are used to judge whether the observed relationship in the sample cross-tabulation mirrors a true relationship in the population or is merely the result of chance. As a general rule, statisticians reject as too likely to be random any sample correlation whose X^2 significance is greater than .05. For all the tables in this study it is considerably lower, and thus we may have confidence in the actual existence of the observed relationships.

The X^2 statistic tells us only the probability that a relationship exists; it tells us nothing about the strength of that relationship. For that we require a "measure of association." One of the most useful is Pearson's contingency coefficient (designated "C"). The minimum possible value of C is zero, indicating that there is no relationship between the variables. The maximum value (indicating a perfect relationship—all the cases in a given category of one variable are associated with one and only one category of the other variable) depends on the table size. For a table of two rows by two columns it is .707, but it approaches 1.0 as the table size increases. All the tables in this study have C values somewhere between these extremes, indicating a stronger or weaker relationship between the variables.

No X^2 or C statistics are provided for Tables X, XII, and XIII (Chapter X), which trace the economic, residential, and occupational mobility of individual white families over time. To compile these tables it was necessary to begin with the families from the 1870 sample and trace them back in time, rather than taking the 1860 sample and tracing forward. This is because the 1860 census of Tennessee has been indexed but the 1870 census has not. For several reasons, not every 1870 family could be located in the 1860 census. Some, of course, had immigrated to the state after 1860; a few others may have been missed by the antebellum census taker. Many have such common names that they cannot be distinguished from other families with the same name, especially if there are no children or boarders or spouse whose names and ages and places of birth could provide confirmation. Undoubtedly many others cannot be identified in the earlier census simply because their names were garbled by the census taker. In any event, only 439 of the 784 white families in the 1870 sample could be traced back to 1860. Since this group cannot be considered a true random sample that necessarily approximates the characteristics of the entire population, it is meaningless to apply the X^2 test to the tracing tables, and I have chosen to omit C as well.

Nevertheless, the tracing tables are included in Chapter X because they are, if not conclusive, at least highly suggestive of the experiences of individual families over time—experiences that can only be inferred, not proved, by comparing the two independent random samples of 1860 and 1870. In tracing the family head's occupation back to 1860 I used the following rule of thumb: if the 1870 family head was not a family head in 1860, but was instead a female spouse, or a child of any age living with his parents, or a minor boarder, I counted the occupation of the family head in determining 1860 occupation. But if the 1870 family head was a family head or an adult boarder in 1860, I counted his or her own occupation.

When tracing wealth rank I omitted from the cross-tabulation all the 1870 families whose heads had been children or minor boarders in 1860. A widow generally inherited her husband's estate upon his death, so it is not unreasonable to compare her family's wealth before the husband's death with that afterward. But most children, whatever their family's economic circumstances, set out in the world propertyless or nearly so, expecting to inherit the family's wealth only many years down the road. Therefore, to include in the wealth table children who started their own families after 1860 would be to weight the cross-tabulation unrealistically in favor of those whose family wealth declined over the decade. If the 1870 family head was an adult boarder in 1860, I did not count the entire family's wealth in determining 1860 wealth rank but only his and that of his immediate (nuclear) family.

Any reader interested in a more extensive quantitative analysis of the 1860 and 1870 Middle Tennessee census returns than this study offers should consult my dissertation, "Civil War, Black Freedom, and Social Change in the Upper South: Middle Tennessee, 1860–1870" (Ph.D. dissertation, University of Tennessee, Knoxville, 1983). It includes cross-tabulations not only of residence, occupation, slaveholding, wealth, and race, but of age, sex, family structure, place of birth, literacy, and a number of agricultural variables, as well as a separate analysis of black families in 1870.

Appendix B. Occupations of Family Heads in the 1860 and 1870 Census Samples

(Verbatim transcriptions from population schedules)

Professional

Agent for iron works
Attorney General
Banker
Baptist clergyman
Book merchant
Botanic doctor
Broker
Builder [*i.e.*, contractor]
Captain, steamboat
Chancery court clerk
Circuit Court clerk
Clergyman
Clergyman of Cumberland Pres-
    byterian Church
Confectionery store [owner?]
Corn merchant
Cumberland Presbyterian minister
Dentist
Doctor
Druggist
Dry goods merchant
Episcopal clergyman
Family grocery [operator]
Fancy goods dealer
Foundry [owner]
Grocer
Grocery keeper

Grocery merchant
Horse doctor
Hotel keeper
Indian doctor
Judge, Chancery Court, State
Justice of the Peace
Lawyer
Magistrate
Mail contractor
Marble manufacturer
Marketer
M.D.
Merchant
Methodist clergyman
Methodist minister
Methodist preacher
Methodist Episcopal clergyman
Minister
Minister, Old School Presbyterian
Missionary Baptist minister
Old School Presbyterian clergy
Physician
Preacher, Methodist
Principal, Fisk University
Professor in college
Professor of Languages in Cumberland
    University
Professor of Music
Public officer

Real estate agent
Retail grocer
Retail liquor [dealer]
Retail merchant
Retired merchant
Secretary, insurance company
Shoe merchant
Tobacco merchant
Tobacconist
Town register
Trader
Trader in real estate

Landed Farmer

Farm hand
Farm laborer
Farmer
Farming
Works on farm

Minor Professional

Assistant clothier
Bar keeper
Bartender
Boarding house keeper
Book agent
Bookkeeper
Clerk
Clerk at express office
Clerk at hotel
Clerk at woodyard
Clerk—dry goods
Clerk—railroad
Collector
Constable
Dry goods clerk
Freight agent
Huckster
Ice cream saloon [employee]
Keeper of poor
Keeping boarding house
Keeps news stand

Keeps stable
Landlord Kingston Springs
   [boardinghouse?]
Livery and sale stable keeper
Peddler
Postmaster
Railroad clerk
Railroad contractor [*i.e.*, agent]
Saloon keeper
Schoolteacher
Teacher
Teacher, common school
Teaches school
Tippling house keeper
U.S. gauger
Wood dealer

Skilled Worker

Barber
Bell hanger
Blacksmith
Boot and shoe maker
Bootmaker
Brass molder
Brick maker
Brickmason
Builder [*i.e.*, carpenter]
Butcher
Cabinet maker
Cabinet workman
Carpenter
Carriage maker
Carriage trimmer
Chair maker
Coach maker
Coach smith
Confectioner
Cooper
Daguerrotypist
Distilling
Engine builder
Engineer
Engineer (steamboat)

Foreman in sawmill
Foundry man
Gilder
Gunsmith
Hatter
House carpenter
Machinist
Master machinist
Master mason
Master plasterer
Matrass maker
Mechanic
Miller
Millwright
Moulder
Painter
Piano tuner
Plasterer
Printer
Railroad engineer
Retired blacksmith
River pilot
Rock mason
Saddler
Sawyer
Shoemaker
Spirits rectifier
Stiller [*i.e.*, distiller]
Stone cutter
Stone mason
Surgical instrument maker
Tailor
Tanner
Tinner
Wagon maker
Watchmaker
Wheelwright
Wood carver
Wood turner
Works at shoemaker's trade

Overseer

Overseeing
Overseer
Superintendent on farm

Unskilled Laborer

Attending sawmill
Boatman
Carder
Common laborer
Cook
Day laborer
Domestic servant
Domestic service
Dray driver
Drives hack
Driving team
Factory operator [*i.e.*, worker]
Gate keeper
Hackman
Hod carrier
Keeping toll gate
Laborer
Labors in wool machine
Nurse
Omnibus driver
Ore screener
Porter in railroad depot
Porter in store
Railroad hand
Railroad laborer
Runs express [*i.e.*, messenger]
Seamstress
Servant
Steamboat hand
Teamster
Toll gate keeper
Waggoner
Washer
Washerwoman
Washes and irons
Well digger
Whitewasher
Wood chopper
Wool carder
Working in carding factory
Working on timber
Works for carpenter
Works in blacksmith shop
Works in brickyard

Works in cotton mill
Works in ore bank
Works in sawmill

Landless Agricultural Worker

Farm hand
Farm laborer
Farmer
Farmer—rents
Farming
Hired farming
Laborer on farm
Retired farmer
Tenant
Works on farm

No Occupation

[Blank entry]
Gentleman
Keeping house
Lady
No occupation
Rents house
Sewing
Spinning
Spinster
Sportsman
Unknown
Weaving

Unclassifiable

Loose occupation
Prostitute

Bibliography of Primary Sources

MANUSCRIPT COLLECTIONS

Amistad Research Center, Dillard University, New Orleans

American Missionary Association, Tennessee Records.

Duke University

Ames, Electa. Papers.
Handy, Frank A. Diary.
Magee, John E. Diary.
Pope-Carter Family Papers.
Williamson, Alice. Diary.

Library of Congress, Washington, D.C.

Johnson, Andrew. Papers.

National Archives, Washington, D.C.

Eighth Census, 1860. Manuscript Returns of Free Inhabitants, Tennessee.
Eighth Census, 1860. Manuscript Returns of Productions of Agriculture, Tennessee.
Eighth Census, 1860. Manuscript Returns of Slaves, Tennessee.
Eighth Census, 1860. Manuscript Returns of Social Statistics, Tennessee.
Ninth Census, 1870. Manuscript Returns of Inhabitants, Tennessee.
Ninth Census, 1870. Manuscript Returns of Productions of Agriculture, Tennessee.
Ninth Census, 1870. Manuscript Returns of Social Statistics, Tennessee.
Records of the Bureau of Refugees, Freedmen, and Abandoned Land. Record Group 105. Records of the Assistant Commissioner for the State of Tennessee,

1865–69, and Records of the Superintendent of Education for the State of Tennessee, 1865–70.

Records of the Civil War Special Agencies of the Treasury. Record Group 366. Letters Received, First Special Agency.

Records of the Office of the Adjutant General. Record Group 94. Letters Received (Main Series), 1861–70. American Freedmen's Inquiry Commission, Preliminary and Final Reports.

Records of the Office of the Judge Advocate General. Record Group 153. Court Martial Case Files, 1809–1938.

Records of the U.S. Army Continental Commands, 1821–1920. Record Group 393, Part II.

Southern Historical Collection, University of North Carolina, Chapel Hill

Brady, Elias. Papers.
Carmack, Francis M. Diary.
Carney, Kate S. Diary.
Caruthers, Robert Looney. Papers.
Gale-Polk Papers.
Harding-Jackson Papers.
Killebrew, Joseph Buckner. Autobiography.
Kimberly, John. Papers.
Moore, Harriet Ellen. Diary.
Pise, David. Journal.
Polk-Brown-Ewell Papers.
Polk-Yeatman Papers.
Porter, Nimrod. Journal.
Ransdell, D. M. Diary.
Ready, C. Alice. Diary.
Shoffner, Michael. Papers.
Wilson, Thomas B. Reminiscences.

Special Collections, University of Tennessee Library, Knoxville

Temple, O. P. Papers.

Tennessee State Library and Archives, Nashville

Bailey, Lucy Catherine. Papers.
Barker, John Nick. Diary.
Brownlow, Governor William G. Papers.
Brownlow, James P. Autobiography.
Civil War Veterans Questionnaires.
Clarksville, Tennessee. Correspondence Concerning Civil War Guerrillas.
Claybrooke and Overton Papers.

Confederate Collection.
Cooper Family Papers.
Cox, Jesse. Diary.
Crockett, Andrew. Papers.
Cullom, Jeremiah W. Diary.
Douglass-Maney Family Papers.
Duling, John. Memoir.
Eaton, John. Correspondence.
Elliott, Collins D. Papers.
Faw, Walter Wagner. Papers.
Garrett, Jill K. Collection.
Gordon, George W., and William T. Avery. Papers.
Hamilton Letters.
Harwood, J. C. Diary.
Henderson, Samuel. Diary.
Jordan, John Leland. Recollections.
Kennedy, Sarah Ann (Bailey). Letters.
McEwen, Sallie F. Diary.
Matthews, James Washington. Journal.
Orr Family Diaries.
Paine Family Papers.
Patten, Zeboim Cartter. Diary.
Pope Papers.
Sailor's Rest Plantation, Montgomery County. Papers.
Shackleford, R. A. Letters.
Smith, Nancy B. Letters.
Talbot and Related Families Papers.
Tennessee Annual Conference of the Methodist Episcopal Church. Journal.
Tennessee Comptroller of the Treasury. 1857 Tax Aggregates.
Tennessee Legislative Petitions.
Washington Family Papers.
Washington, Jane S. Letter.
Whiteside Family Papers.
Williams, T. B. Letter.

CHURCH RECORDS

Tennessee State Library and Archives, Nashville

Bethlehem Baptist Church, Robertson County.
Cedar Lick Baptist Church, Wilson County.
Cool Springs Primitive Baptist Church, Peytonsville, Williamson County.
Enon Primitive Baptist Church, Unionville, Bedford County.
Fall Creek Baptist Church, Lebanon, Wilson County.
First Presbyterian Church, Clarksville, Montgomery County.
First Presbyterian Church, Gallatin, Sumner County.

First Presbyterian Church, Murfreesboro, Rutherford County.
Hannah's Gap Baptist Church of Christ, Lincoln County.
McCains Cumberland Presbyterian Church, McCains, Maury County.
McKay Cumberland Presbyterian Church, Williamson County.
Methodist Churches in Middle Tennessee District.
Mount Lebanon Missionary Baptist Church, Marshall County.
Mount Moriah Primitive Baptist Church, Fayetteville, Lincoln County.
Mt. Olivet Baptist Church, Mt. Juliet, Wilson County.
Mt. Olivet Primitive Baptist Church, Lincoln County.
New Hope Primitive Baptist Church, Fairfield, Bedford County.
Poplar Grove Cumberland Presbyterian Church, College Grove, Williamson County.
Presbyterian Church, Lewisburg, Marshall County.
Robertson Fork Church of Christ, Marshall County.
Silver Creek Society of the Cumberland Presbyterian Church, Maury County.
Trinity Episcopal Church, Clarksville, Montgomery County.
Union Baptist Church, Wilson County.
West Station Primitive Baptist Church, Sumner County.
Wilson Creek Primitive Baptist Church, Williamson County.
Zion Presbyterian Church, Columbia, Maury County.

COUNTY GOVERNMENT RECORDS

Tennessee State Library and Archives, Nashville

Bedford County, Circuit Court Clerk's Office. Minute Books, Vol. 1864–65.
Bedford County, Clerk and Master's Office. Minute Books, Bks. 1859–65, 1865–68.
Bedford County, County Court Clerk's Office. County Court Minutes, Vols. A, B.
Cheatham County, Chancery Court. Minutes, Vol. 1857–67.
Cheatham County, County Court Clerk's Office. Court Minute Books, Vols. A, B, C.
Davidson County, County Court Clerk's Office. County Court Minutes, Bks. H, I, J, K.
Davidson County, First Circuit Court. Minutes, Civil and Criminal, Vols. II, AA.
Giles County, Chancery Court. Minutes, Vols. IX, X.
Giles County, Circuit Court. Minutes, Civil and Criminal, Vol. 1865–66.
Giles County, County Court Clerk's Office. County Court Minutes, Vol. II.
Lincoln County, Chancery Court. Minutes, Vols. 1860–63, 1865–68.
Lincoln County, Circuit Court. Minutes, Civil and Criminal, Vols. 1859–63, 1865–67.
Lincoln County, County Court Clerk's Office. Minutes, Bks. 1856–60, 1860–63, Vols. A, B.
Marshall County, Chancery Court. Minutes, Vol. C.
Marshall County, Circuit Court. Minutes, Vol. D.

Marshall County, County Court Clerk. Minutes, County Court, Vols. J, L, M, N, O.

Maury County, Circuit Court Clerk's Office. Civil and Criminal Minutes, Vols. 1860–61, 1862–66.

Maury County, Clerk and Master's Office. Chancery Court Minute Books, Vols. VII, VIII.

Maury County, County Court Clerk's Office. Minute Books, Vols. XIII, XIV, XV, XVI.

Montgomery County, Clerk and Master's Office. Minute Books, Vols. IV, V.

Montgomery County, County Court Clerk's Office. County Court Minutes, Vols. XXVI, XXVII.

Robertson County, Circuit Court Clerk's Office. Minute Books, Vol. 1860–69.

Robertson County, Clerk and Master's Office. Minute Books, Vols. II, III.

Robertson County, County Court Clerk's Office. County Court Minutes, Vols. XIV, XV, XVI.

Rutherford County, Chancery Court Office. Minute Books, Bk. D.

Rutherford County, Circuit Court Clerk's Office. Civil and Criminal Minutes, Vols. 1849–67, 1867–71.

Rutherford County, County Court Clerk's Office. Minute Books, Bks. DD, EE, FF.

Sumner County, Circuit Court Clerk's Office. Minute Books, Vols. S, T.

Sumner County, Clerk and Master's Office. Minute Books, Vol. IV.

Sumner County, County Court Clerk's Office. County Court Minutes, Vols. 1858–66, 1866–69.

Williamson County, Chancery Court Office. Minutes, Vols. I, J.

Williamson County, Circuit Court Office. Civil and State Minutes, Vols. XV, XVI.

Williamson County, County Court Clerk's Office. Minutes, Vols. XVIII, XIX, XX.

Wilson County, Chancery Court Office. Minute Books, Vol. E.

Wilson County, Circuit Court Office. Circuit Court Minutes, Vols. 1860–71, 1861–67.

Wilson County, County Court Clerk's Office. County Court Minute Books, Vols. 1853–60, 1858–62, 1859–64, 1864–67, 1867–70, 1870–72.

PUBLISHED MATERIALS

Agriculture of the United States in 1860. . . . Washington, D.C., 1864.

Ambrose, Daniel Leib. *History of the Seventh Regiment Illinois Volunteer Infantry.* . . . Springfield, Ill., 1868.

Aptheker, Herbert, ed. *A Documentary History of the Negro People in the United States.* 3 vols. 1951; rpr. New York, 1969.

Beatty, John. *Memoirs of a Volunteer, 1861–1863.* Edited by Harvey S. Ford. New York, 1946.

Berlin, Ira *et al.*, eds. *The Black Military Experience.* Cambridge, England, 1982. Ser. II of Berlin *et al.*, eds., *Freedom: A Documentary History of Emancipation, 1861–1867.* 5 sers. projected.

————, eds. *The Destruction of Slavery*. Cambridge, England, 1985. Ser. I, Vol. I of Berlin *et al.*, eds., *Freedom: A Documentary History of Emancipation, 1861–1867*. 5 sers. projected.

Bickham, William D. *Rosecrans' Campaign with the Fourteenth Army Corps*. . . . Cincinnati, 1863.

Blegen, Theodore C., ed. *The Civil War Letters of Colonel Hans Christian Heg*. Northfield, Minn., 1936.

Burgess, John W. *Reminiscences of an American Scholar: The Beginnings of Columbia University*. New York, 1934.

Burton, Elijah P. *Diary of E. P. Burton, Surgeon, 7th Reg. Ill., 3rd Brig., 2nd Div., 16 A.C.* Des Moines, 1939.

Butler, Jay Caldwell. *Letters Home [by] Jay Caldwell Butler, Captain, 101st Ohio Volunteer Infantry*. Edited by H. Butler Watson. Binghamton, N.Y., 1930.

Chancellor, Sir Christopher, ed. *An Englishman in the American Civil War: The Diaries of Henry Yates Thompson, 1863*. New York, 1971.

"Diary of Jacob Adams, Private in Company F, 21st O.V.V.I." *Ohio Archaeological and Historical Society Publications*, XXXVIII (1929), 627–721.

"Documents: Civil War Diary of Jabez T. Cox." *Indiana Magazine of History*, XXVIII (1932), 40–54.

"Documents: The Shelly Papers." *Indiana Magazine of History*, XLIV (1948), 181–98.

Dodge, Mary Abigail [Gail Hamilton]. *Wool-gathering*. Boston, 1868.

Eaton, John, Jr. *First Report of the Superintendent of Public Instruction for the State of Tennessee*. . . . Nashville, 1869.

Eby, Henry H. *Observations of an Illinois Boy in Battle, Camp, and Prisons—1861 to 1865*. Mendota, Ill., 1910.

Fitch, John. *Annals of the Army of the Cumberland*. . . . Philadelphia, 1864.

Franklin, John Hope, ed. *The Diary of James T. Ayers, Civil War Recruiter*. Springfield, Ill., 1947.

Fremantle, Sir Arthur J. L. *Three Months in the Southern States: April–June, 1863*. New York, 1864.

Gammage, W. L. *The Camp, the Bivouac, and the Battle Field*. . . . 1864; rpr. Little Rock, 1958.

Graf, LeRoy P., and Ralph W. Haskins, eds. *The Papers of Andrew Johnson*. 6 vols. to date. Knoxville, 1967–.

The Great Panic: Being Incidents Connected with Two Weeks of the War in Tennessee. Nashville, 1862.

Hinkley, Julian Wisner. *A Narrative of Service with the Third Wisconsin Infantry*. Madison, 1912.

Hinman, Wilbur F. *The Story of the Sherman Brigade*. . . . Alliance, Ohio, 1897.

Historical Records Survey, Tennessee. *Civil War Records*. 4 vols. Nashville, 1939.

————*Cumberland Presbyterian Church Records*. 2 vols. Nashville, 1938–41.

————*Presbyterian Church Records, Tennessee*. 2 vols. Nashville, 1937–41.

————*Records and Histories of Certain Episcopal Churches in Tennessee*. Nashville, 1938.

House Reports, 39th Cong., 1st Sess., No. 1273.

Johnson, Adam R. *The Partisan Rangers of the Confederate States Army.* Louisville, 1904.

Johnson, Richard W. *A Soldier's Reminiscences in Peace and War.* Philadelphia, 1886.

"Major Connolly's Letters to His Wife, 1862–1865." *Transactions of the Illinois State Historical Society* (1928), 217–383.

Manufactures of the United States in 1860. . . . Washington, D.C., 1865.

Population of the United States in 1860. . . . Washington, D.C., 1864.

Rawick, George P., ed. *The American Slave: A Composite Autobiography.* 41 vols. to date. Westport, Conn., 1972–.

Report on Cotton Production in the United States. . . . Washington, D.C., 1884.

Scott, Samuel W., and Samuel P. Angel. *History of the Thirteenth Regiment Tennessee Volunteer Cavalry U.S.A.* Blountville, Tenn., 1903.

Senate Executive Documents. 38th Cong., 2nd Sess., No. 1209.

Skipper, Elvie Eagleton, and Ruth Gove, eds. "'Stray Thoughts': The Civil War Diary of Ethie M. Foute Eagleton." *East Tennessee Historical Society's Publications,* No. 40 (1968), 128–37, No. 41 (1969), 116–28.

Smith, David M., ed. "Documents: The Civil War Diary of Colonel John Henry Smith." *Iowa Journal of History,* XLVII (1949), 140–70.

The Statistics of the Population of the United States . . . (June 1, 1870). . . . Washington, D.C., 1872.

Statistics of the United States . . . in 1860. . . . Washington, D.C., 1866.

The Statistics of Wealth and Industry of the United States . . . (June 1, 1870). . . . Washington, D.C., 1872.

Swint, Henry Lee. "Reports from Educational Agents of the Freedmen's Bureau in Tennessee, 1865–1870." *Tennessee Historical Quarterly,* I (1942), 51–80, 152–70.

Tennessee. *Report of James T. Dunlap, Comptroller of the Treasury . . . 1861.* Nashville, 1861.

Tennessee General Assembly. *The Code of Tennessee, Enacted by the General Assembly of 1857–'8.* Nashville, 1858.

Trimble, Sarah Ridley, ed. "Behind the Lines in Middle Tennessee, 1863–1865: The Journal of Bettie Ridley Blackmore." *Tennessee Historical Quarterly,* XII (1953), 48–80.

Trowbridge, J. T. *A Picture of the Desolated States; and the Work of Restoration, 1865–1868.* Hartford, Conn., 1868.

Underwood, Betsy S. "War Seen Through a Teen-Ager's Eyes." *Tennessee Historical Quarterly,* XX (1961), 177–87.

Volwiler, A. T., ed. "Documents: Letters from a Civil War Officer." *Mississippi Valley Historical Review,* XIV (1928), 508–29.

The War of the Rebellion: A Compilation of the Official Records of the Union and Confederate Armies. 70 vols. in 128. Washington, D.C., 1880–1901.

Williams, Frederick D., ed. *The Wild Life of the Army: Civil War Letters of James A. Garfield.* East Lansing, Mich., 1964.

Williams, W. "A Reminiscence of Clarksville, Tennessee." *Confederate Veteran,* XXII (1914), 206–207.

NEWSPAPERS

Clarksville *Chronicle*, 1860–62, 1865, 1868–69.
Clarksville *Jeffersonian*, 1860–62.
Clarksville *Weekly Chronicle*, 1865–67.
Columbia *Herald*, 1865, 1869–70.
83rd Illinoisan (Clarksville), April 21, 1865.
Fayetteville *Observer*, 1860–62, 1865–70.
Fayetteville *Union Herald*, June 18, 1862.
Gallatin *Courier*, 1861.
Gallatin *Examiner*, October 21, November 11, 1865.
Lebanon *Record*, September 19, 26, 1868, July 3, 1869.
Lincoln County *News*, 1866–70.
Murfreesboro *Monitor*, September 9, 1865.
Murfreesboro *Union Volunteer*, May 20, 1862.
Nashville *Daily Gazette*, 1860.
Nashville *Daily Press*, 1863.
Nashville *Daily Times and True Union*, 1864–65.
Nashville *Dispatch*, 1862–64.
Nashville *Patriot*, 1860–61.
Pulaski *Citizen*, 1866–69.
Shelbyville *American Union*, 1865.
Shelbyville *Expositor*, October 11, 1861.
Shelbyville *Republican*, 1866, 1868.
Shelbyville *Reveille*, December 4, 1862.
Shelbyville *Tri-Weekly News*, June 19, 21, 1862.
Sumner County *Republican*, 1868.

Essay on Secondary Sources

CHAPTER I

The best physical descriptions of Middle Tennessee are in James M. Safford, *Geology of Tennessee* (Nashville, 1869), 81–84, 97–100; *Report on Cotton Production in the United States* . . . (Washington, D.C., 1884), 378–86, 398–401 (which includes a soil map); and Joseph B. Killebrew *et al.*, *Introduction to the Resources of Tennessee* (Nashville, 1874), 2–5, 286–96, 619–22. Sam Bowers Hilliard, *Atlas of Antebellum Southern Agriculture* (Baton Rouge, 1984), graphically depicts the geographical distinctiveness of the Middle Tennessee heartland.

Robert E. Corlew, *Tennessee: A Short History* (2nd ed.; Knoxville, 1981), is the standard history and conveys a good sense of the importance of regionalism in the state. An older but still useful general survey of economic, political, and social development up to the Civil War is Thomas P. Abernethy, *From Frontier to Plantation in Tennessee: A Study in Frontier Democracy* (Chapel Hill, 1932). The vibrant antebellum political scene in Middle Tennessee and the state as a whole is examined in Paul H. Bergeron, *Antebellum Politics in Tennessee* (Lexington, Ky., 1982).

CHAPTER II

Comparable statistics on farm size and the concentration of acreage and slaves in other Southern subregions lend support to the thesis that Middle Tennessee was a "third South," with larger and more prosperous farms than the highland South, yet smaller farms and a broader distribution of agricultural wealth than the plantation-dominated Deep South. See especially Fabian Linden, "Economic Democracy in the Slave South: An Appraisal of Some Recent Views," *Journal of Negro History*, XXXI (1946), 150, 168–74; Gavin Wright, "Economic Democracy and the Concentration of Agricultural Wealth," in William N. Parker (ed.), *The Structure of the Cotton Economy of the Antebellum South* (Washington, D.C., 1970), 72–83; Roger L. Ransom and Richard Sutch, *One Kind of Freedom: The Economic Consequences of Emancipation* (New York, 1977), 71; Randolph B. Campbell and Richard G. Lowe, *Wealth and Power in Antebellum Texas* (College Station, Tex., 1977), 70–78, 156–57, 160–69; Frank Owsley, *Plain Folk of the Old South* (Baton Rouge, 1949), 150–229; Steven Hahn, *The Roots of Southern Populism: Yeoman Farmers and the Transformation of the Georgia Upcountry, 1850–1890* (New York, 1983), 15–49, 295–304; and Orville Vernon Burton, *In My Father's House Are Many Mansions: Family and Community in Edgefield, South Carolina* (Chapel Hill, 1985), 40–44. For a more extensive analysis of Middle Tennessee agricultural statistics and a detailed comparison with those for other regions, see Stephen V. Ash, "Civil War, Black Freedom, and Social Change in the Upper South: Middle Tennessee, 1860–1870" (Ph.D. dissertation, University of Tennessee, Knoxville, 1983), 193–239.

The following sources discuss the agricultural development of the Middle Tennessee heartland up to the Civil War, emphasizing the region's corn and livestock economy, its fertile soil, and its role in an interregional trade network: Lewis C. Gray, *History of Agriculture in the Southern United States to 1860* (2 vols.; 1933; rpr. New York, 1949), II, 644–45, 651, 753–58, 774, 811–22, 837–54, 870–92; Blanche Henry Clark, *The Tennessee Yeomen, 1840–1860* (Nashville, 1942), 69–150; Sam B. Hilliard, *Hog Meat and Hoecake: Food Supply in the Old South, 1840–1860* (Carbondale, Ill., 1972), 193–95; Walter Martin, "Agricultural Commercialism in the Nashville Basin, 1850–1860" (Ph.D. dissertation, University of Tennessee, Knoxville, 1985).

The best description of antebellum Nashville is in F. Garvin Davenport, *Cultural Life in Nashville on the Eve of the Civil War, 1825–1860* (Chapel Hill, 1941). The general backwardness of Tennessee industry in this period is discussed in Constantine G. Belissary, "Industry and Industrial Philosophy in Tennessee, 1850–1860," ETHSP, No. 23 (1951), 46–57. But see also Susanna Delfino, "Many Souths: Changing Social Contexts and the Road to Industrialization in Antebellum Tennessee," *Southern Studies*, XXII (1983), 82–96, which points to considerable industrial progress in the state.

Information on local government in antebellum Tennessee is in Tennessee General Assembly, *The Code of Tennessee, Enacted by the General Assembly of 1857—'8* (Nashville, 1858), 139, 141, 223–24, 754–75; Ralph A. Wooster, *Politicians, Planters, and Plain Folk: Courthouse and Statehouse in the Upper South, 1850–1860* (Knoxville, 1975), 79–86, 91–92, 99, 100–106; and Roy Bell, "History of County Government in Tennessee, 1834–1860, and Its Failure in the 20th Century" (M.A. thesis, University of Tennessee, Knoxville, 1938), 34–57. On the binding out of apprentices see Durwood Dunn, "Apprenticeship and Indentured Servitude in Tennessee Before the Civil War," West Tennessee Historical Society *Papers*, XXXVI (1982), 25–40.

Two general surveys of public education in antebellum Tennessee both stress its inadequacy. See Robert H. White, *The Development of the Tennessee State Education Organization, 1796–1929* (Kingsport, Tenn., 1929), 39–77; and A. P. Whitaker, "The Public School System in Tennessee, 1834–1860," THM, II (1916), 1–30. Class distinctions in education are documented in Fred A. Bailey, "Caste and Classroom in Antebellum Tennessee," *Maryland Historian*, XIII (1982), 39–54. Bailey's work is the first thorough investigation of the voluminous Tennessee Civil War Veterans Questionnaires, a source comparable to the WPA slave narratives as a rich repository of rare, firsthand accounts by the common folk of the antebellum South.

The two best studies of antebellum Southern religion are Donald G. Mathews, *Religion in the Old South* (Chicago, 1977); and Albert J. Raboteau, *Slave Religion: The "Invisible Institution" in the Antebellum South* (New York, 1978). Both emphasize the importance of church discipline, the identification of the church community with the social community, and the role of evangelical religion in creating an ethos of self-esteem and liberty among the white and black masses. Useful studies of individual denominations are John L. Eighmy, *Churches in Cultural Captivity: A History of the Social Attitudes of Southern Baptists* (Knoxville, 1972); Herman A. Norton, *Tennessee Christians: A History of the Christian Church in Tennessee* (Nashville, 1971); and B. W. McDonnold, *History of the Cumberland Presbyterian Church* (Nashville, 1899).

CHAPTER III

The antebellum ideology of patriarchy and paternalism, which broadly defined the social roles of husbands, wives, and children, masters and servants, and aristocrats and plebeians, is discussed in Joel Williamson, *The Crucible of Race: Black-White Relations in the American South Since Emancipation* (New York, 1984), 24–35; and Michael P. Johnson, "Planters and Patriarchy: Charleston, 1800–1860," *JSH*, XLVI (1980), 45–47. In Middle Tennessee this ideology held sway in the white mind and, as I have tried to show in the narrative, it also manifested itself in actual practice at the level of family, church, and community, each of which embraced members of every class, race, and sex. Although blacks rejected the ideology, they participated in the day-to-day reality of these integrated institutions, and therefore I think it is fair to characterize antebellum Middle Tennessee as a "biracial" society.

My analysis of this society focuses on class, race, family, community, and ideology. I emphatically acknowledge the crucial importance of gender, but I must leave it for others to explore. The body of literature on nineteenth-century Southern women is small but growing, and it is broadening to include the common folk as well as aristocrats. Two of the most important recent studies are Catherine Clinton, *The Plantation Mistress: Woman's World in the Old South* (New York, 1982); and Deborah Gray White, *Ar'n't I a Woman? Female Slaves in the Plantation South* (New York, 1985).

Serious study of the Southern family was stimulated by Bertram Wyatt-Brown in an article more than a decade ago in which he described the South as a family-centered society. See Bertram Wyatt-Brown, "The Ideal Typology and Antebellum Southern History: A Testing of a New Approach," *Societas*, V (1975), 1–29. Historians have begun to take up the challenge, and two recent works in particular deal with the family in far greater detail than I am able to offer here. See Jane Turner Censer, *North Carolina Planters and Their Children, 1800–1860* (Baton Rouge, 1984); and Burton, *In My Father's House*.

Only the outlines of the vast body of literature on class relations in antebellum Southern white society can be sketched here. Historians in the first decades of this century stressed the economic—and by implication social—hegemony of the planter class. See Ulrich Bonnell Phillips, *Life and Labor in the Old South* (Boston, 1929); and Gray, *History of Agriculture*. In the 1940s a flurry of writing appeared in reaction, not so much to the sophisticated interpretations of the earlier historians, but to the simplistic popular image of Southern society as a tripartite hierarchy of planters, poor whites, and slaves. This revisionist movement, led by Frank Owsley and his students, recognized the existence of class distinctions in the South but denied any real class conflict. These scholars discerned a large, prosperous middle class of yeomen between rich and poor whites, documented close relations existing between planters and yeomen, and asserted that social mobility and broad popular participation in politics undermined class antagonisms. See, among many such examples, Owsley, *Plain Folk;* Clark, *Tennessee Yeomen;* Chase C. Mooney, *Slavery in Tennessee* (Bloomington, 1957); Fletcher M. Green, "Democracy in the Old South," *JSH,* XII (1946), 3–23; and W. J. Cash, *The Mind of the South* (New York, 1941). Their work has been supplemented more recently by Wooster, *Politicians, Planters, and Plain Folk,* whose structural analysis affirms the basically democratic nature of antebellum politics and government.

These studies were a useful corrective to distorted popular views, but they came immediately under attack for their interpretive inadequacies. Fabian Linden's critique of the Owsley school pointed out that the existence of a large yeoman class meant less than the relative shares of wealth and power held by planters and yeomen—which Linden found to be extremely unequal—and he insisted that the Owsleyites distorted the picture of Southern society by ignoring thousands of unprosperous nonagrarian folk. Roger W. Shugg found outright planter autocracy and class conflict in antebellum Louisiana. More recently Jonathan M. Wiener, Randolph B. Campbell, and Richard G. Lowe have demonstrated aristocratic domination of wealth and power in Alabama and Texas. Fred A. Bailey has used the Tennessee Civil War Veterans Questionnaires to document not only significant class distinctions but a notable degree of poor-white hostility toward the slaveholding elite. See Linden, "Economic Democracy," 140–89; Roger W. Shugg, *Origin of Class Struggle in Louisiana* . . . (1939; rpr. Baton Rouge, 1968); Jonathan M. Wiener, *Social Origins of the New South: Alabama, 1860–1885* (Baton Rouge, 1978), 3–34; Campbell and Lowe, *Wealth and Power in Antebellum Texas;* and Fred Arthur Bailey, *Class and Tennessee's Confederate Generation* (Chapel Hill, 1987).

Other historians have agreed with Owsley and company that white Southerners were not torn by class strife, but they have suggested that biracialism and slavery rather than democracy and prosperity were the reasons. See Ulrich B. Phillips, "The Central Theme of Southern History," *American Historical Review,* XXXIV (1928), 30–43; Paul H. Buck, "The Poor Whites of the Ante-bellum South," *American Historical Review,* XXXI (1925), 41–54; and George M. Fredrickson, *The Black Image in the White Mind: The Debate on Afro-American Character and Destiny, 1817–1914* (New York, 1971).

Several historians have turned from the hoary debate over aristocracy versus democracy to search for more subtle patterns in Southern society. Chief among these is Eugene D. Genovese, who has delineated a precapitalistic ideology of paternalism, which tied yeomen to planters on a personal basis despite the repression and exploitation of the yeomen as a class. David M. Potter has suggested that the intimate folk culture that permeated Southern society lubricated racial and class frictions.

Bertram Wyatt-Brown has discerned at the heart of white society an ethos of honor that shaped the role of the individual within family and community. Bruce Collins has depicted the shared ideals, rituals, and purposes that drew whites of all classes together into a society of consensus rather than conflict. See Eugene D. Genovese, *The Political Economy of Slavery* (New York, 1965), 3–36; Eugene D. Genovese, "Yeomen Farmers in a Slaveholders' Democracy," *Agricultural History*, XLIX (1975), 331–42; David M. Potter, *The South and the Sectional Conflict* (Baton Rouge, 1968), 3–16; Bertram Wyatt-Brown, *Southern Honor: Ethics and Behavior in the Old South* (New York, 1982); and Bruce Collins, *White Society in the Antebellum South* (London, 1985).

A number of historians (including Genovese) have acknowledged the coexistence of two social systems in the antebellum South, delimited by geography. Most recently, Steven Hahn has contrasted the yeoman-dominated society of the upcountry—characterized by family farms, agricultural self-sufficiency, broad distribution of wealth, and egalitarian communalism—with the planter-dominated society of the lowlands, where staple-producing plantations and an international market economy prevailed, wealth was concentrated in the hands of a few, and the power and paternalism of the aristocracy gave society a hierarchical rather than communal structure. See Hahn, *Roots of Southern Populism*, 15–85.

Hahn's argument is cogent, but like other historians he ignores the existence of a third South—and a third social system—in Middle Tennessee and perhaps other regions. In many respects a seemingly contradictory amalgam of the highland and plantation Souths, Middle Tennessee featured (as I have endeavored to show in Chapters I and II) a number of sizable plantations which participated in an interregional market. But these plantations generally eschewed cotton or tobacco cultivation in favor of corn and livestock; and they did not dominate their region's acreage and production as did the plantations of the Deep South, thus leaving room in the Middle Tennessee economy for a large, independent, and self-sufficient yeoman segment. Moreover, as I indicate in Chapter III, Middle Tennessee's agricultural riches and unequal distribution of wealth sustained a powerful elite who (with the aid of racism, paternalism, and a tradition of deference among the white masses) reigned over the region's society as did the planter aristocracy of the Deep South. At the same time, however, the prosperity and economic independence of the plain folk, along with the bonds of religious fellowship and the ethic of neighborliness, sustained a robust egalitarian communalism that existed side by side with social hierarchy, aristocratic ascendancy, and conspicuous class distinctions. This was a society of not just one dimension, but two.

Comparable statistics on property holding and wealth distribution in other regions and in the South as a whole, which point up Middle Tennessee's broad-based prosperity, may be found in Lee Soltow, *Men and Wealth in the United States, 1850–1870* (New Haven, 1975), 23–24, 36, 44, 65, 96, 99; Michael Wayne, *The Reshaping of Plantation Society: The Natchez District, 1860–1880* (Baton Rouge, 1983), 6–11; Shugg, *Origin of Class Struggle in Louisiana*, 321–23; Linden, "Economic Democracy," 148–51; Campbell and Lowe, *Wealth and Power in Antebellum Texas*, 30, 38, 44–46, 59–64, 93, 101, 141, 144; and Burton, *In My Father's House*, 40–46. A detailed comparative analysis is in Ash, "Civil War, Black Freedom, and Social Change," 122–45, 164–78.

The historiographical debate over the master-slave relationship in the Old South has in recent years focused on Eugene Genovese's *Roll, Jordan, Roll: The World the Slaves Made* (New York, 1976), which asserts that the premodern, paternalistic ethos of the planter class bound their slaves to them as it did the white yeomen. A more recent study of Southern slaveholders, however, emphasizes their acquisitive, bourgeois nature. See James Oakes, *The Ruling Race: A History of American Slaveholders* (New York, 1982).

The relative independence of urban slaves is discussed in Richard D. Wade, *Slavery in the Cities* (New York, 1964), 238–39. A different view—that urban slavery, and especially industrial slavery, was as repressive in its way as plantation slavery—is taken by Robert S. Starobin, *Industrial Slavery in the Old South* (New York, 1970), vii–viii, 9–10, 115.

The existence of a rich, slave subculture within the antebellum South is among the most striking revelations of the current generation of historical scholarship, and its exegesis has dominated writing on slavery for more than a decade. Among the most important works, all of which implicitly or explicitly argue against the older interpretation of slavery as a thoroughly dehumanizing institution, are John W. Blassingame, *The Slave Community: Plantation Life in the Antebellum South* (New York, 1972); Genovese, *Roll, Jordan, Roll;* Herbert G. Gutman, *The Black Family in Slavery and Freedom, 1750–1925* (New York, 1976); Lawrence W. Levine, *Black Culture and Black Consciousness: Afro-American Folk Thought from Slavery to Freedom* (New York, 1978); Leslie Howard Owens, *This Species of Property: Slave Life and Culture in the Old South* (New York, 1977); Raboteau, *Slave Religion;* and Thomas L. Webber, *Deep Like the Rivers: Education in the Slave Quarter Community, 1831–1865* (New York, 1978).

Peter Kolchin has suggested, however, in a very persuasive essay, that historians have gone too far in declaring the total cultural independence of the slave communities. See Kolchin, "Reevaluating the Antebellum Slave Community: A Comparative Perspective," *Journal of American History*, LXX (1983), 579–601. In Middle Tennessee, certainly, the biracial rural community and the master-slave relationship shaped the slave's life to a greater extent than did the black subcommunity, which until emancipation was repressed and closely circumscribed by whites.

CHAPTER IV

Political events in the state leading up to secession are detailed in Mary E. R. Campbell, *The Attitude of Tennesseans Toward the Union, 1847–1861* (New York, 1961); Marguerite B. Hamer, "The Presidential Campaign of 1860 in Tennessee," ETHSP, No. 3 (1931), 3–22; and J. Milton Henry, "The Revolution in Tennessee, February, 1861, to June, 1861," *THQ*, XVIII (1959), 99–119. The ideology of the Southern planter class, its role in secession, and the unity of society in the secession crisis are discussed in James L. Roark, *Masters Without Slaves: Southern Planters in the Civil War and Reconstruction* (New York, 1977), 1–32. On politics and government in Tennessee during the state's brief Confederate period see John H. DeBerry, "Confederate Tennessee" (Ph.D. dissertation, University of Kentucky, 1967); and William Frank Zornow, "State Aid for Indigent Soldiers and Their Families in Tennessee, 1861–1865," *THQ*, XIII (1954), 297–300.

CHAPTER V

There is no general history of Middle Tennesseans under Federal occupation, though there are studies of wartime Nashville and Sumner County and of the military campaigns in the region. See Peter Maslowski, *Treason Must Be Made Odious: Military Occupation and Wartime Reconstruction in Nashville, Tennessee* (Millwood, N.Y., 1978), which focuses on policies of the occupation authorities; Walter T. Durham, *Nashville, the Occupied City: The First Seventeen Months—February 16, 1862, to June 30, 1863* (Nashville, 1985), and Durham, *Rebellion Revisited: A History of Sumner County, Tennessee, from 1861 to 1870* (Gallatin, Tenn., 1982), which provide general surveys of civilian life and military and political events; and Thomas L. Connelly, *Army of the Heartland: The Army of Tennessee, 1861–1862* (Baton Rouge, 1967), and Connelly, *Autumn of Glory: The Army of Tennessee, 1862–1865* (Baton Rouge, 1971), which cover major military operations.

Andrew Johnson's military governorship, his policy toward civilians, and his efforts to restore state and local government are examined in Clifton R. Hall, *Andrew Johnson, Military Governor of Tennessee* (Princeton, 1916); Edwin T. Hardison, "In the Toils of War: Andrew Johnson and the Federal Occupation of Tennessee" (Ph.D. dissertation, University of Tennessee, Knoxville, 1981); and Peter Maslowski, "From Reconciliation to Reconstruction: Lincoln, Johnson, and Tennessee," *THQ*, XLII (1983), 281–98, 343–61.

Devastation in the wartime South has not been adequately analyzed from a social perspective. Most studies offer only a broad, impressionistic picture of devastation without accounting precisely for its causes, its nature, or its differential distribution within a given region; or (in the case of the economic historians) they offer only an analysis of economic consequences. See, for example, Paul Gates, *Agriculture and the Civil War* (New York, 1965), 73–126; Fred A. Shannon, *The Farmer's Last Frontier: Agriculture, 1860–1897* (New York, 1945), 77–79; Thomas B. Alexander, "Neither Peace nor War: Conditions in Tennessee in 1865," *ETHSP*, No. 21 (1949), 33–35; James L. Sellers, "The Economic Incidence of the Civil War in the South," *MVHR*, XIV (1927), 179–91; and Ransom and Sutch, *One Kind of Freedom*, 40–44, 324n.

Wartime privation in the rural and urban South has been more fully and satisfactorily analyzed than has devastation, undoubtedly because privation in some form affected people in every part of the South. The distinctive experience of Middle Tennessee and other occupied regions, however—especially in the rural areas—has received little attention. Standard studies focus for the most part on Confederates behind the lines, where rural suffering was often a function of relative wealth. See Bell I. Wiley, *Plain People of the Confederacy* (Baton Rouge, 1943), 36–69, 90; Charles W. Ramsdell, *Behind the Lines in the Southern Confederacy* (Baton Rouge, 1944), 18–34, 44–56; Mary E. Massey, *Ersatz in the Confederacy* (Columbia, S.C., 1952),

7–58; Allan Nevins, *The War for the Union* (4 vols.; New York, 1959–71), II, 291–98, III, 376–92; Emory M. Thomas, *The Confederate Nation: 1861–1865* (New York, 1979), 199–201. Even those studies which deal with Tennessee are guilty of understatement, overstatement, or misstatement as regards the heartland. Thomas B. Alexander, for example, asserts that "thousands" died of starvation in rural areas of the state. This is very doubtful even for Middle Tennessee, which was probably harder hit than either East or West Tennessee. The author of the standard volume on Tennessee history states that during the war "urban dwellers [in the state as a whole] suffered more than their rural neighbors," and furthermore that "the sufferings of the people [in the state as a whole] are not to be compared with those of South Carolina or northern Virginia." Both these generalizations are untrue if applied to Middle Tennessee. See Alexander, "Neither Peace nor War," 34; and Corlew, *Tennessee*, 323–26.

Extensive institutional disruption has been documented in regional studies of other occupied parts of the Confederacy. See especially Charles F. Bryan, Jr., "The Civil War in East Tennessee: A Social, Political, and Economic Study" (Ph.D. dissertation, University of Tennessee, Knoxville, 1978); and Edward H. Phillips, "The Lower Shenandoah Valley During the Civil War: The Impact of War upon the Civilian Population and upon Civil Institutions" (Ph.D. dissertation, University of North Carolina, Chapel Hill, 1958). Institutional surveys, however, tend to concentrate on the experience in unoccupied regions, where continuity was the rule. See, for example, Willard E. Wight, "Churches in the Confederacy" (Ph.D. dissertation, Emory University, 1957).

CHAPTER VI

A thorough account of the demise of slavery as a social and legal institution in Tennessee, as well as the wartime experience of the state's blacks and the various groups of whites with whom they interacted, is provided in John Cimprich, *Slavery's End in Tennessee, 1861–1865* (University, Ala., 1985). See also Bobby Lee Lovett, "The Negro in Tennessee, 1861–1866: A Socio-Military History of the Civil War Era" (Ph.D. dissertation, University of Arkansas, 1978), which deals extensively with blacks in the Union army.

The standard study of the evolution of Federal policy regarding slavery is Louis S. Gerteis, *From Contraband to Freedmen: Federal Policy Toward Southern Blacks, 1861–1865* (Westport, Conn., 1973). On specific policy toward Tennessee slaves see John Cimprich, "Military Governor Johnson and Tennessee Blacks, 1862–65," *THQ*, XXXIX (1980), 459–70; Hardison, "In the Toils of War," 269–92; and Maslowski, *Treason Must Be Made Odious*, 97–117.

Most recent students of the wartime black experience have moved away from the assumption of older historians that slaves on the whole remained docile and faithful, toward the understanding that the slaves desired to be free and took an active part in their own liberation whenever possible. This modern consensus is best exemplified in Leon F. Litwack, *Been in the Storm So Long: The Aftermath of Slavery* (New York, 1979). But the experience of Middle Tennessee, whose black inhabitants saw invasion and war at first hand from an early date, sets the region apart from most of the South and demands discrete analysis. This is ably provided in John Cimprich, "Slave Behavior During the Federal Occupation of Tennessee, 1862–1865," *Historian*, XLIV (1982), 335–46. Cimprich's analysis shows, as does my own study, that though the heartland's slaves in general wanted and worked for freedom, they displayed a broad range of attitudes and behavior, which defies simplistic generalization. He thus judges as too narrow (but does not contradict) both Eugene Genovese's thesis that slavery's paternalistic ethos bound slaves so closely to their masters as to hinder black self-liberation in wartime, and Edward Magdol's quite different assertion that the quasi-independent slave communities had fostered assertiveness and millennialism which broke out into open disloyalty during the war. As Cimprich shows, examples of slaves who fit each of these models can be found in Middle Tennessee, along with many other examples supporting Paul Escott's contention that slaves distrusted whites and rejected paternalism but held no millennial hopes and remained loyal in many cases out of pragmatic considerations. See Genovese, *Roll, Jordan, Roll*; Edward Magdol, *A Right to the Land: Essays on the Freedmen's Community* (Westport, Conn., 1977); and Paul D. Escott, *Slavery Remembered: A Record of Twentieth Century Slave Narratives* (Chapel Hill, 1979).

That slaveholders elsewhere in the Confederacy (unlike those of Middle Tennessee) tried to maintain slavery after the war's end and clung obstinately to their proslavery ideology is shown in Roark, *Masters Without Slaves*, 94–108; and Litwack, *Been in the Storm So Long*, 179–90.

CHAPTER VII

Civil War guerrillaism as a social phenomenon has not received adequate scholarly attention, but three studies are worthy of mention here for purposes of comparison. Richard Maxwell Brown, "The American Vigilante Tradition," in Hugh Davis Graham and Ted Robert Gurr (eds.), *Violence in America: Historical and Comparative Perspectives* (Beverly Hills, Calif., 1979), 153–85, shows that over its long history vigilantism in America has most often been an attempt to impose social order on a raw, frontier society lacking the usual instruments of social control, namely institutions and communalism. Brown stresses the local popular consensus in favor of vigilantes, and especially the support of vigilantism by local elites, who had the most to gain from social order. If rural Middle Tennessee after the invasion is viewed as a "frontier," its customary institutions in disarray, guerrillaism there can be seen as part of the history of American vigilantism as described by Brown. Don R. Bowen, "Guerrilla War in Western Missouri, 1862–1865: Historical Extensions of the Relative Deprivation Hypothesis," *Comparative Studies in Society and History*, XIX (1977), 30–51, focuses on a specific outbreak of pro-Southern guerrillaism, and especially on the question of who the guerrillas were. He finds that they were generally the sons of community leaders, who were mostly prosperous, secessionist slaveowners—a threatened local elite. Phillip Shaw Paludan, *Victims: A True Story of the Civil War* (Knoxville, 1981), 56–78, suggests that in the highlands of western North Carolina anti-Confederate guerrilla activity represented in many cases a class conflict, pitting lower-class, nonslaveholding rural folk against the slaveholding, secessionist elite of the towns. The Bowen and Paludan interpretations seem inapplicable to Middle Tennessee.

General Buell's policy toward civilians, Andrew Johnson's early affirmation and subsequent repudiation of that policy, and Johnson's personal war against the patriarchy are discussed in Hardison, "In the Toils of War," 82–134, 179–85; and Maslowski, *Treason Must Be Made Odious*, 53–57, 67–68, 74–89. Hardison argues that Johnson was satisfied with a symbolic victory over the aristocracy through the use of tough language, forced oaths, and brief jail terms, since he never carried out wholesale property confiscation or political executions.

Banditry akin to that in Middle Tennessee arose in other areas of the South hard hit by the war. See Charles P. Roland, *The Confederacy* (Chicago, 1960), 176; Thomas, *Confederate Nation*, 247–48; Ella Lonn, *Desertion During the Civil War* (New York, 1928), 62–76; John Knox Bettersworth, *Confederate Mississippi: The People and Policies of a Cotton State in Wartime* (Baton Rouge, 1943), 227–41; and Bryan, "Civil War in East Tennessee," 147–49.

On the democratization of white society in the Confederacy behind the lines (which clearly did not occur in Middle Tennessee) see William B. Hesseltine, *Confederate Leaders in the New South* (Baton Rouge, 1950), 4–5; and Emory Thomas, *The Confederacy as a Revolutionary Experience* (Englewood Cliffs, N.J., 1971), 105–13.

Hardship, resentment, and alienation among the Southern white masses, leading to class friction in many parts of the Confederacy (though not in Middle Tennessee, where aristocrats suffered too) are described in Georgia L. Tatum, *Disloyalty in the Confederacy* (Chapel Hill, 1934), 3–23; Charles H. Wesley, *The Collapse of the Confederacy* (Washington, D.C., 1937), vii, 82–93; Wiley, *Plain People of the Confederacy*, viii, 36–54, 64–69; Ramsdell, *Behind the Lines in the Southern Confederacy*, 14–56, 90–119; Clement Eaton, *A History of the Southern Confederacy* (New York, 1954), 86, 247–48; Nevins, *War for the Union*, III, 380–92; Roland, *Confederacy*, 148–65; Stephen E. Ambrose, "Yeoman Discontent in the Confederacy," *Civil War History*, VIII (1962), 259–68; Roark, *Masters Without Slaves*, 35–67; Paul D. Escott, *After Secession: Jefferson Davis and the Failure of Confederate Nationalism* (Baton Rouge, 1978), x–xi, 104–35; Thomas, *Confederate Nation*, 233–35; Hahn, *Roots of Southern Populism*, 121–33. Most of these authors imply (and Thomas and Roark state explicitly) that these class tensions did not break out into open antiaristocratic rebellion. But Paul D. Escott, *Many Excellent People: Power and Privilege in North Carolina, 1850–1900* (Chapel Hill, 1985), 32–84, shows that lower-class violence aimed deliberately at aristocrats was frequent in several North Carolina counties.

Moral and social degeneration in the collapsing Confederacy has been noted by a number of scholars. See Wesley, *Collapse of the Confederacy*, 55–74; Wiley, *Plain People of the Confederacy*, 62–63; Nevins, *War for the Union*, II, 291–98, IV, 233–47; Roland, *Confederacy*, 176. To my knowledge, however, no historian has documented complete social disintegration in any region such as I have found in Middle Tennessee. This does not mean that no other areas experienced such; indeed, the prevalence of banditry elsewhere (as noted above) suggests that social chaos might have been widespread in occupied or contested areas. It means only that more detailed analyses from a social perspective are needed.

CHAPTER VIII

The triumphs and failures of public education in postwar Tennessee are explained in White, *Development of Education*, 78–113; and Frank B. Williams, "John Eaton, Jr., Editor, Politician, and School Administrator, 1865–1870," *THQ*, X (1951), 291–319. State legislation defining black legal status after emancipation is discussed in Theodore B. Wilson, *The Black Codes of the South* (University, Ala., 1965), 111–13. There is no modern history of Tennessee politics in this period, but two older studies are still useful. See Thomas B. Alexander, *Political Reconstruction in Tennessee* (Nashville, 1950); and James W. Patton, *Unionism and Reconstruction in Tennessee, 1860–1869* (Chapel Hill, 1934). Both highlight the distinctiveness of the state's short-lived Reconstruction, which was dominated by native white Radicals and escaped the imposition of Federal military rule.

The South's postwar labor system has been the subject of considerable attention by historians in recent years. Most agree that the adoption of sharecropping represented a victory by the landless agrarian workers over the landlords, who had sought to reestablish as nearly as possible the antebellum system of closely supervised gang labor. These historians differ, however, in their identification of the source of the postbellum workers' power. Eric Foner, for example, offers a political explanation, arguing that Radical Reconstruction and black enfranchisement overthrew the planter hegemony that had been revived in most Southern states during presidential Reconstruction. Roger L. Ransom, Richard Sutch, and Ralph Shlomowitz point to the postwar economic environment, a seller's market in labor in which employers had to compete for workers. Jonathan Wiener's class analysis focuses on the ability of the newly liberated blacks to wring concessions from the planters through resistance and class struggle. See Eric Foner, *Nothing but Freedom: Emancipation and Its Legacy* (Baton Rouge, 1983), 39–73; Ransom and Sutch, *One Kind of Freedom*, 65–70; Ralph Shlomowitz, "'Bound' or 'Free'? Black Labor in Cotton and Sugarcane Farming, 1865–1880," *JSH*, L (1984), 569–96; and Jonathan M. Wiener, "Class Structure and Economic Development in the American South, 1865–1955," *American Historical Review*, LXXXIV (1979), 970–1006.

These interpretations are not mutually exclusive. They are in fact complementary, and all three factors—political, economic, and social—were at work in Middle Tennessee in the immediate postwar years. Black enfranchisement kept political power in Republican hands and held the planter class at bay, while the resistance of black and white workers to gang labor aggravated the rural labor shortage and forced employers to offer concessions such as sharecropping. The eventual political triumph of the Conservatives in Tennessee and across the South, however, enabled landlords to reassert control through coercive labor laws which severely restricted the bargaining power and independence of the landless rural workers. Foner, Ransom and Sutch, and especially Wiener all emphasize the repressiveness of these antienticement, vagrancy, and other statutes, a perspective shared by William Cohen, "Negro Involuntary Servitude in the South, 1865–1940: A Preliminary Analysis," *JSH*, XLII (1976), 31–60. Shlomowitz, however, minimizes the effect of these laws on the free labor market.

The postwar rise of tenantry in Middle Tennessee should not obscure the fact that the region's agriculture remained (at least through 1870) in an important sense much as it had been before the Civil War. That is, it continued to be dominated by owner-operated family farms of middling size. Though tenantry spread far and wide in the heartland after 1865, it was more important as a social than as an economic fact. Tenants represented one black farm family out of four and nearly three white farm families out of ten by 1870, but together those black and white tenants cultivated less than one acre of five in the region and their holdings generally were on the poorest land. For a detailed statistical analysis of the region's postwar agriculture see Ash, "Civil War, Black Freedom, and Social Change," 694–722.

CHAPTER IX

On postwar white racial thought in the South see Lawrence J. Friedman, *The White Savage: Racial Fantasies in the Postbellum South* (Englewood Cliffs, N.J., 1970), v–vii, 19–36, which underscores the determination of whites to keep blacks servile. Dan T. Carter, "The Anatomy of Fear: The Christmas Day Insurrection Scare of 1865," *JSH*, XLII (1976), 345–64, shows that this outbreak of mass hysteria (which swept Middle Tennessee as it did other parts of the South) followed a pattern identical to that of antebellum slave uprising scares. On the decline of paternalism and the rise of employer-employee relations between blacks and whites across the South see Roark, *Masters Without Slaves*, 111–55. On the use of the criminal justice system to control the freedmen see Edward L. Ayers, *Vengeance and Justice: Crime and Punishment in the 19th-Century American South* (New York, 1984). Two general studies suggest that as a rule Southern white churchmen did not object to the postwar withdrawal of blacks to their own churches and in many cases welcomed it. See H. Shelton Smith, *In His Image, But . . . : Racism in Southern Religion, 1780–1910* (Durham, N.C., 1972), 208–44; and Eighmy, *Churches in Captivity*, 31–33.

Allen Trelease, *White Terror: The Ku Klux Klan Conspiracy and Southern Reconstruction* (New York, 1971), is the standard work and contains much specific information on Middle Tennessee. See also Thomas B. Alexander, "Kukluxism in Tennessee, 1865–1869," *THQ*, VIII (1949), 195–219; and George C. Rable, *But There Was No Peace: The Role of Violence in the Politics of Reconstruction* (Athens, Ga., 1984), 69–70. For an excellent, brief analysis of how Southern blacks were subjugated after the Civil War not only by violence but by law, social custom, and economic pressures, see Pete Daniel, "The Metamorphosis of Slavery, 1865–1900," *Journal of American History*, LXVI (1979), 88–99.

There is no recent study of the Freedmen's Bureau in Tennessee, but see Weymouth T. Jordan, "The Freedmen's Bureau in Tennessee," *ETHSP*, No. 11 (1939), 47–61; and Paul D. Phillips, "A History of the Freedmen's Bureau in Tennessee" (Ph.D. dissertation, Vanderbilt University, 1964). The failure of the bureau in every state to achieve lasting legal or economic security for the freedmen is discussed in Donald G. Nieman, *To Set the Law in Motion: The Freedmen's Bureau and the Legal Rights of Blacks, 1865–1868* (Millwood, N.Y., 1979); Claude F. Oubre, *Forty*

Acres and a Mule: The Freedmen's Bureau and Black Land Ownership (Baton Rouge, 1978); and William S. McFeely, *Yankee Stepfather: General O. O. Howard and the Freedmen* (New York, 1970).

The active participation of the freedmen in the postwar struggle for their advancement is the theme of nearly all recent works on blacks in this period. These studies stand as a rebuke to the once-fashionable portrayal of blacks as passive characters in Reconstruction. See, for example, Magdol, *Right to the Land;* Peter Kolchin, *First Freedom: The Responses of Alabama's Blacks to Emancipation and Reconstruction* (Westport, Conn., 1972); and especially Leon F. Litwack's comprehensive and magisterial *Been in the Storm So Long*. Gutman, *Black Family in Slavery and Freedom*, 363–431, discusses the black family during Reconstruction and documents the strength of family and kinship ties. The freedmen's energetic pursuit of education is discussed in William Preston Vaughn, *Schools for All: The Blacks and Public Education in the South, 1865–1877* (Lexington, Ky., 1974). That blacks across the South associated the Pauline epistles with slavery while cherishing the Old Testament as the Scripture of liberation is shown in Levine, *Black Culture and Black Consciousness*, 43–44, 50–52.

Joel Williamson, *Crucible of Race*, 44–50, suggests that in the immediate postwar period blacks attempted to duplicate the white institutions—Victorian family, Christian church, and yeoman farm—that had long been held up to them as ideals, thereby moving toward "whiteness" even as they moved away from whites. The freedmen of Middle Tennessee certainly followed this pattern, but, as I have pointed out in the text, their postwar urbanization and egalitarianism marked a sharp divergence from white culture.

Black political activities are covered in Alexander, *Political Reconstruction in Tennessee*, 122–62; Alrutheus Taylor, *The Negro in Tennessee, 1865–1880* (Washington, D.C., 1941); and John Cimprich, "The Beginning of the Black Suffrage Movement in Tennessee, 1864–1865," *Journal of Negro History*, LXV (1980), 185–95. On the continuing oppression of the freedmen in the post-Reconstruction period, see Joseph H. Cartwright, *The Triumph of Jim Crow: Tennessee Race Relations in the 1880s* (Knoxville, 1976).

CHAPTER X

The postwar fate of the Old South's elite has provoked considerable debate. Among older historians, Roger W. Shugg emphasized the survival of the plantation and of planter domination in Louisiana, and William B. Hesseltine showed that high-ranking Confederates continued to play leading roles after the war. W. J. Cash conceded that many planters were ruined, but he believed nevertheless that the aristocratic ideal remained strong in Southern thought; and, furthermore, he insisted that even if a new, nonagrarian ruling class did emerge in the postwar South it was composed of the sons of the old planter aristocracy, and thus social continuity was maintained. On the other hand, Clement Eaton asserted that not only was the old aristocracy's esprit completely destroyed by the war, but its economic and political power as well. Most influential was C. Vann Woodward, who posited the rise of an urban, probusiness elite, which replaced the planters, won over the masses with racist rhetoric, and then proceeded to rule in its own interest.

More recent historians argue on the same terms, but their conclusions are not always so boldly unqualified. Jonathan M. Wiener documents the postwar persistence not only of wealth and power but of traditional ideology among Alabama's planter class; nevertheless, his analysis shows that the role of that elite changed after the war as it took over the functions of the merchant class. James L. Roark notes a loss of wealth and identity among the South's planters after 1865 but does not go so far as to say they were replaced by a new ruling class. Jay Mandle, Paul D. Escott, Harold D. Woodman, and Michael Wayne are more unequivocal but divide into opposing camps. Mandle argues that the plantation as an economic, social, and ideological institution survived the Civil War and thus perpetuated the power of the planter class. Escott shows how North Carolina's traditional ruling class (composed of professionals as well as planters) regained political power after the war and soundly defeated the democratic opposition. Woodman maintains, however, that even if Southern planters persisted they evolved into bourgeois employers as the South slowly became more modern and capitalistic. Wayne's study of the planters of the Natchez District endorses Woodman's thesis.

The evidence for Middle Tennessee suggests that perhaps both sides are correct in some ways. Clearly, the economic and political power of the heartland's antebellum elites (who were not all planters) was revived in the postwar period, as was their class esprit. But their old social relations survived only with respect to the white masses, who continued to share the aristocracy's premodern, paternalistic social ethos. The freedmen for their part rejected that ethos; and their relationship with the ruling class became an impersonal, capitalistic, employer-employee relation, such as Woodman describes.

See Shugg, *Origin of Class Struggle in Louisiana*, 235–76; Hesseltine, *Confederate Leaders in the New South;* Cash, *Mind of the South*, 110–15, 127–29; Clement Eaton, *The Waning of the Old South Civilization, 1860–1880's* (Athens, Ga., 1968), 139–40; C. Vann Woodward, *Origins of the New South, 1877–1913* (Baton Rouge, 1951); Wiener, *Social Origins of the New South;* Roark, *Masters Without Slaves*, 156–209; Jay Mandle, *The Roots of Black Poverty: The Southern Plantation Economy After the Civil War* (Durham, N.C., 1978); Escott, *Many Excellent People*, 85–112; Harold D. Woodman, "Sequel to Slavery: The New History Views the Postbellum South," *JSH*, XLIII (1977), 523–54; and Wayne, *Reshaping of Plantation Society*, 197–204.

Tennessee's vocal (but ultimately unsuccessful) proponents of the New South are discussed in Sarah M. Howell, "The Editorials of Arthur S. Colyar, Nashville Prophet of the New South," *THQ*, XXVII (1968), 262–76; Constantine G. Belissary, "The Rise of the Industrial Spirit in Tennessee, 1865–1885," *JSH*, XIX (1953), 193–215; and Samuel B. Smith, "Joseph Buckner Killebrew and the New South Movement in Tennessee," *ETHSP*, No. 37 (1965), 5–22.

On the unification of Southern whites by racism see Kenneth M. Stampp, *The Era of Reconstruction, 1865–1877* (New York, 1965), 163, 197–98; and Carl Degler,

Place over Time: The Continuity of Southern Distinctiveness (Baton Rouge, 1977). This view has been challenged by Armstead Robinson, who points to instances of biracial lower-class political movements that challenged aristocratic hegemony in the Reconstruction South. See Armstead Robinson, "Beyond the Realm of Social Consensus: New Meanings of Reconstruction for American History," *Journal of American History*, LXVIII (1981), 276–97. Manifestly, no such movements appeared in Middle Tennessee.

The Conservative campaign to overthrow Radical rule is detailed in Gary L. Kornell, "Reconstruction in Nashville, 1867–1869," *THQ*, XXX (1971), 277–87; James C. Parker, "Tennessee Gubernatorial Elections, I. 1869–The Victory of the Conservatives," *THQ*, XXXIII (1974), 34–61; Roger L. Hart, *Redeemers, Bourbons, and Populists: Tennessee, 1870–1896* (Baton Rouge, 1975), 1–12; and Alexander, *Political Reconstruction in Tennessee*, 199–225.

APPENDIX A

Of the many works on sampling techniques and quantitative analysis, I have found the following the most helpful: Charles M. Dollar and Richard J. Jensen, *Historian's Guide to Statistics: Quantitative Analysis and Historical Research* (New York, 1971); Hubert Blalock, *Social Statistics* (New York, 1972); R. Christian Johnson, "A Procedure for Sampling the Manuscript Census Schedules," *Journal of Interdisciplinary History*, VIII (1978), 515–30; Edward Shorter, *The Historian and the Computer: A Practical Guide* (New York, 1971); and Roderick Floud, *Introduction to Quantitative Methods for Historians* (Princeton, 1973).

Evaluations of the reliability of the 1860 and 1870 censuses are in Campbell and Lowe, *Wealth and Power in Antebellum Texas*, 22–24; Ransom and Sutch, *One Kind of Freedom*, 294–95, 371n.; and Wright, "Economic Democracy," 95–97.

Instructions to census takers are reprinted in Carroll D. Wright and William C. Hunt, *History and Growth of the United States Census . . .* (Washington, D.C., 1900), 148–62, 235–38; and Lee Soltow, *Patterns of Wealthholding in Wisconsin Since 1850* (Madison, 1971), 141–45. For the census index see Byron Sistler and Barbara Sistler (comps.), *1860 Census—Tennessee* (5 vols.; Nashville, 1981).

Index

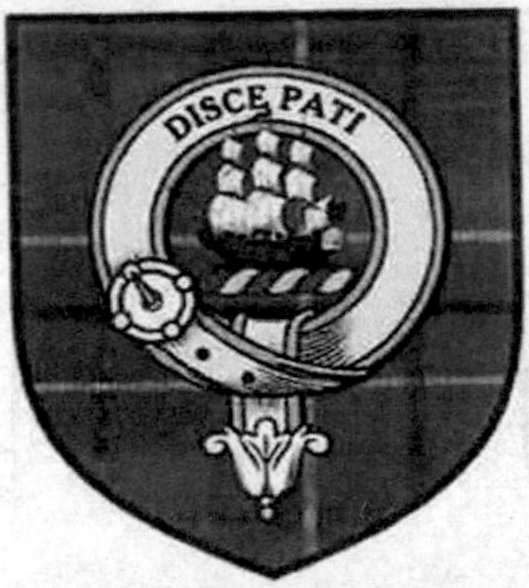
DISCE PATI